GREEN TEARS FOR HECUBA

An appreciative study
of the 'Trouble Times'
in Ireland

Dedicated to the Memory
Of the men who fought
And the people who endured

Green Tears for Hecuba

Ireland's Fight for Freedom

Patrick J. Twohig

TOWER BOOKS

1994

First published in 1994 by Tower Books, Ballincollig, Co. Cork

ISBN 0 902568 23 X

Some of the material contained herein has previously been issued in pamphlet form

Typeset by Tower Books, Ballincollig, Co. Cork
Photographic work: Janice O'Connell, N.D.A., I.P.P.A.,
4 Marlboro St., Cork
Printed in Ireland

OTHER WORKS BY THE AUTHOR:

The Dark Secret of Béalnabláth: In-depth study of the death of Michael Collins

Filí an tSuláin: A history of Gaelic Poetry

A Folk Register: Annotated verse-history of Ireland

Of Hope and Glory: Annotated verse-history of England

Of Dinosaurs and Double Eagles: Annotated verse-history of the U.S.A.

Rest the Poor Bones: Commemorating the late President Erskine Childers

Blood on the Flag: A translation from the Irish (due for publication)

Contents

LIST OF ILLUSTRATIONS

Prologue

Seán Keenan died on the Fourth of March, 1993, and was buried on the Sixth. Who was Seán Keenan? 'Veteran Republican', the paper said, 'and honorary Vice-President of Republican Sinn Féin, who was chairman of the Citizens' Defence Committee in Derry's "Bogside" in 1969-70'. I knew Seán Keenan. I made the acquaintance, but only slightly, of that aloof, brooding little man, ex-County Derry footballer, when, in some peculiar fashion now of little interest, I found myself A.D.C. and driver to Paddy Doherty, the 'King of the Bogside', with a reserved hot-line to the British military commander in the City, at Number-Ten Westland, throughout one hectic month in 1969 during and subsequent to the event known to a watching and waiting world as 'The Battle of the Bogside'. Seán Keenan said to me, more to himself — 'I want to be free for one hour before I die!'. Well, he wasn't, but nine months after his death a 'Joint Declaration' was signed (15 December, 1993) by the British Prime Minister and the Irish Taoiseach which seemed to indicate that he had died just a little too soon. He had spent sixteen years of his life in prison without trial. Now, in whatever afterlife he reposes, whatever Valhalla or Hades or theologically adjustable haven reserved for incorrigible patriots, it would be of great interest to note, on this the first day of the New Year, whether he nods his head in approval or shakes it in disbelief at the present indecisive maunderings of the two leading politicians concerned. One way or the other, in peace and reconciliation or in further futile strife, I am glad to have known a great Irishman named Seán Keenan. I hereby dedicate this work to his memory, as well as to the memory of the men who fought and the people who endured throughout the period covered in the text and usually referred to as 'the time of the Black and Tans'.

Patrick J. Twohig,
Churchtown,
Mallow.
1 January, 1994.

'What's Hecuba to him, or he to Hecuba,
That he should weep for her?'
(*Hamlet*, Act II, Sc. ii).

Introduction

Night has drifted down over the little hamlet beside the lazy, winding river. Stars glisten and scintillate through the frosty, translucent atmosphere of early Spring. It is a bright night, bright with the ethereal splendour of the trackless firmament, with a lightsomeness that is untouched by the deceptive magic of moonlight, yet sufficient to outline the chill reality of mountains, rocks and scraggy furze-brakes on the rising ground, while here and there a darker patch against the intermittent pattern of fences shows where the soil has been newly turned in preparation for an early potato crop. Oíche spéirghealaí, *a sky-bright night it is in the expressive idiom native to the Gaelic tongue of the sleeping village. Brighter glow the stars as the night wears on. Deeper and ever deeper grows the stillness. One by one the little squares of light from farmhouse windows on the far hillsides flicker a moment and die as the last stragglers from card tables and fireside parliaments turn their reluctant footsteps with guilty haste towards home; and in due time the minute hand of the big-faced clock high up on many a whitewashed kitchen wall climbs laboriously to keep a fleeting tryst at the hour of midnight, pauses an indecisive moment as if debating with the hour hand the futility of further effort and jerks precipitately into a new day. All is quiet now, not the live hush of expectancy because nothing unusual or startling could ever happen in this placid precinct of Heaven, but an all-pervading rest broken only by an occasional dog howling to the stars the deep sorrow of a lonely vigil or yelping violent resentment at an untimely intrusion on his solitude. Presently, when both animals and men have finally decided to call it a day, an entirely new sound makes the night air vibrant once more. Faint at first and gradually becoming more intense, to an acute ear it would be readily distinguishable from the sleepy mumbling of the river or the sudden little hustling gusts which, at that dead hour of night, could have been only the passing of a fairy troupe down the valley. To a knowing ear the easily recognizable hum of a motor car shows that for someone at least the preoccupation of the previous days has not yet ended. On and on it comes feeling its way cautiously round an interminable succession of bends and with headlights discreetly veiled it slips past the Church and Post Office, glides in among the few straggling houses and heads off into the open country. Behind it there is no shocking into convulsive wakefulness. The sleeping village sleeps on while the engine of the big, red 'BUICK' automobile began to labour a little as it accepted the challenge of a rising foothill. It eased itself over and along the top, ran fast and free down the incline and bounced over the hump-backed bridge where the billowing masses of ground fog obscured the Sullane river. Around the sharp bend by the shoulder of rock beyond the bridge the old Bardinchy schoolhouse loomed into silhouetted vagueness against the night sky and flickering starlight, standing alone amidst the furze and bracken and turf banks, a courageous little citadel maintaining the needful advance of learning into the badlands. Beside it appeared a little road branching to the left, leading apparently into the very heart of the mountains as they now welled up, large and forbidding, to the front and on all sides. The car following suit finally betrayed its destination as it eagerly picked up speed like a travel-weary horse sensing at last the intimate atmosphere of home. But not for long. A rough barricade of farm carts and general debris blocked the way while gun barrels, ranged along the fences on both sides, reflected dully but with sinister purpose the feeble rays of light from the stars. The 'headless coach' of local folklore had indeed come to Coomiclovane but could not pass the threshold. So it came and so it stayed. A form alighted, and another. Two more appeared and silently ranged themselves in line waiting for identification by the watchful eyes behind the glinting gun barrels. Jim Gray, the joking driver, emerged last of all and pleased to abandon himself to the almost doubting wonder of being home at last. He looked slowly all around him noting each familiar aspect. He looked at the distant hills and the near hills, at the nearer forms already materializing from behind barricades and fences, shadowy forms in the dim light, forms that whispered and then grew silent as if afraid of the tricks that might be played on the faculty of speech by the strange atmosphere which carried easily and magnified eerily the littlest murmur. Jim turned away from them to look back down the valley where the river fog could still be traced from its phosphorescent reflection, like a great serpent easing its many folds into the erratic bed gouged out of the earth for it while rivers ran. He let his gaze drift idly along the way and thought of the course the little river chose to follow to its very end where it joined the River Lee beyond Macroom and eventually lost itself and its virginal purity in the backing, sewer-fouled tidal waters of Cork City where unreality had only last evening been left behind, an occasion of wild daring and imminent death. He looked again at the men around him, now relaxed and chatting in the relief of an unique comradeship, uplifting and reciprocal, and from them to the barely defined opening in the hills where, he knew, lay a circular pocket, deep and solidly fortified by nature, fortified and secluded, that spelled reality for now. He took a deep breath of the crisp, reviving, bog-scented air, breathed out freely and strongly as if the same had been denied him for an age, and spoke — to everybody and to nobody, to himself, to the stars, to the night wind rustling on and off among the heather, to the heavens, to the friendly, big, black, beautiful, mysterious, ageless, kindly mountains: 'We're as safe here', he said, 'as if we were in God's pockets!'.*

1

Green Tears

'"I fought for my country", said he, grabbing his cap and making for the door!'. When I first heard this I was sitting in an easy chair at a Mission station in Africa. It was 1961, just thirty-three years ago. The late Father Brian Darcy (we knew him simply as 'B.D.'), of the Holy Ghost Order (who now, I believe, call themselves the 'Spiritans'), had just received the *Carlow Nationalist* newspaper from home. 'You're a Republican, Twohig', said B.D.; 'listen to this!'. It was from a report on the acrimonious doings of the Carlow County Council. Then I thought it was funny. Now I don't . . .

I fought for my country, he said. What country? Whose country? In this, the final decade of the Twentieth Century, warfare throughout the world would appear to be reverting to ancient inter-tribal animosity, even in presumably civilized regions. For Homeland, for Leader, for Christ, for Buddha, for Mohammed, for God, for Allah, seem to be giving way imperceptibly, as guiding emotions, to deeper and more remote impulses harking back to some 'Stone Age' when defence of one's new-found property was essential to permanence upon Earth. But for a certain type of man, Anglo-Saxon with some old Celtic affiliations, draped in a certain brand of uniform or a strange, surrealistic agglomeration of combat gear, with a powerful weapon in his hand to lend assurance, the motive cause, the driving force, the physical jerk amounting to an orgiastic impulse, is still seen to be 'for King and Country', or, rather, for Queen Elizabeth the Second and the last vestige of Empire and at a time when even English traditional royalty is seen to be disintegrating. For this Anglo-Saxon man (who has never heard of Rupert Brooke nor cares very much) a cold corner of a hot island offshore is destined to be 'forever England'. An independent observer, terrestrial rather than from latterly familiar outer space, would say that the Jewel wasn't worth the Crown, the Flame wasn't worth the Candle, the *force majeure* was nothing but an illusion . . .

I fought for my country! Back to Africa and inter-tribal animosity. Everyone said — When the Great Powers pulled out the natives would return to slaughtering one another as had apparently been their practice from time immemorial. Then came a man named Patrick, a black man. He had a dream. It was the ideal of a Republic culled from the simplistic writing of an heroic Irishman named Dan Breen (*My Fight For Irish Freedom*). As a consequence, Patrice Lumumba, the 'Mission Boy', inspired the Dark Continent for a moment of time, then vanished mysteriously, presumed murdered, leaving only a fading memory and a style in sun-glasses. That was likewise in 1961. We, the teachers, in a Mission school two and a half thousand miles across the Equator from the then Belgian Congo, had to endure the hostile and only partly understood remonstrances in class of the little black fellows who had never seen a snowball, who didn't know the Rock of Cashel from a baobab tree, but had been told that Irish 'servant girls' working across the water were 'the Jolas of England', from the traditional, dull-witted Jola slave-damsels of the Senegambia region of West Africa. Irish soldiers had recently landed on their sacred soil and despite the ridiculous fancy ('We fought everybody's battles but our own', my father said) of being there to protect the Africans from themselves, despite being there at the request of Premier Lumumba himself, despite being slaughtered for their pains at Niemba, they were the ENEMY. There were no black tears for Hecuba! Their memorial was not some corner of a foreign savannah that would be forever Ireland, but the expression 'Bloody Balubas' enshrined in the common language of the time. The dead Irish soldiers, like ourselves in the Mission compound far away, were merely 'Tubabs', evil-smelling Whites. We said missionary Ireland died that day in Africa. We were wrong. We 'Spiritans' had forgotten the Holy Ghost, not an easy thing to do . . .

I fought for my country! 'Look what we're fighting for!', said the mountainy man on the run along the rugged Cork-Kerry border in the Spring of 1921. 'It isn't worth wan clout of a fisht!', he said. Is it? Worth one clout of a fist, I mean? Is it worth fighting for? Is it worth dying for? Is it worth living for, that cynical 'alternative' cliché of 1961? Is it worth crying for, green tears or black? Who can say! . . .

During the military 'Terror' in the Summer of 1920 a squad of Black and Tans raided O'Connell's public house in the village of Kilnamartyra, Co. Cork, my home village. A bunch of local men were hustled out onto the roadway while a Tan officer shouted — 'Come on, you "Shinners", line up against that wall!'. 'I'm not a Sinn Féiner', ventured one little fellow. 'Well, I'll make a "Shun Foynah" out of you!', retorted the Britisher, giving him a swift kick in the backside. The toe-cap conversion is still very much with us. Seventy-two years later, in the town of Coalisland, Co. Tyrone, a squad of the grandsons, or possibly great-grandsons, of the said Black and Tans went on a rampage. Raging into a pub with cudgels flailing, they shouted — 'Come on out now, you bloody Shinners!'. Well, here we all are. We never went away. But the fear of us still seems to rankle in the Anglo-Saxon breast . . .

In 1939 an inspector visiting the Home Office stumbled across a tiny room containing a uniformed 'A' Division

constable, the morning newspaper, and tea-making equipment. Not unnaturally the inspector asked the constable what he was doing and was told that he was a protection officer. 'Protection?'. 'Yes, Sir, the Sinn Féiners'. As the I.R.A. had just launched another series of bomb attacks in the capital the inspector thought that the posting must be a recent innovation. However, the duty slate at Cannon Row Police Station revealed that the P.C. had been temporarily posted to the Home Office, not in 1939, but in 1921! For the past eighteen years the forgotten man had quietly drawn his pay every Wednesday and returned to his cubby-hole. Stranger things have happened in the army, of course — but only just.
(Extract from *London's Armed Police:* Gould and Waldren).

*   *   *

DIARMUID: We thought it a foolish thing for fourscore to go into battle against four thousand, or, maybe, forty thousand.

MACDARA: And so it is a foolish thing. Do you want us to be wise?

(From *The Singer*, by P.H.Pearse).

2

All For Hecuba

The image of the tragic Queen of Troy, wife of old Priam, seen running up and down barefoot, 'threatening the flames with bisson rheum', has long been accepted as a literary norm of political trauma with regard to the cosmic condition of womankind, her blinding tears for a doomed and historic city notwithstanding. 'And all for nothing! For Hecuba!'. For nothing? Revisionist historians, which in our day would appear to include not only some maverick professors, journalists on the make, but also a malleable general public, tend to imply the above with regard to our country's history and, as a consequence, make retroactive mockery of the lives and deaths of desperate people in the past — our people! The tragic Queen of Ireland had had her long ages of 'bisson rheum' for a burning country but never lacked for men and women prepared to quench the flames or burn in the effort. Greater love had no man — or woman! And we are now passing cynically through an era of such change that an imported Anglo-Saxon football hero can be seen to do more lasting harm to the spirit of the tragic Queen of Ireland than the Black and Tans ever imagined, if they had an imagination . . .

And here is where the story begins — with a statement

of fact with regard to that indeterminate period of our History as of the beginning of World War One, known then and later as 'The Great War', forward to Nineteen-Sixteen. That latter date means for everyone a brief insurrection in Dublin against the British occupation of our country. Only committed students of history will be aware that the same insurrection was almost country-wide and would have been but for a misunderstanding . . .

In August, 1914, Pierce Beazley (sic) started a Company of Volunteers in Ballingeary. It grew rapidly to a strength of about 100 men. John Shorten was the first Captain of the Company, but went to Cork after having been a short time in the position and was replaced by Eugene Moynihan. The Company was only a month or two in existence when the Split in the organisation generally took place. A full meeting of the Company was held in the Irish College (i.e. Coláiste na Mumhan, Béal Átha'n Ghaorthaigh) to decide what action would be taken. Father O'Callaghan (afterwards shot by Black and Tans in Liam de Róiste's house in Cork) was present at the meeting and spoke in favour of control by Redmond, although he had no official position in the Company. Seán O'Hegarty had given a statement, to be read at the meeting, to P. Ronan, but Ronan did not produce the statement and it was not read. A vote was taken. A minority voted against control by Redmond's nominees and withdrew from the meeting. The Company of National Volunteers, formed from the majority, lost vitality immediately and never afterwards functioned as an effective organisation. It dissolved completely in a short time. Some of its members subsequently joined the Irish Volunteers.

On a Sunday almost immediately after this meeting Tomás MacCurtain and Terence MacSwiney came to Ballingeary. Eugene Moynihan, Currahy, as Company Captain, had been notified of their intended visit. He did not tell anybody of it, with the result that there was no one to meet them. Pat Higgins, Seán Murphy and Paddy Corkery from Cork were with them that day. All wore uniform. Tadhg Twomey and Seán Lynch met them accidentally, but nothing was done that day. Very soon afterwards the men who had withdrawn from the Company met and formed a Company of Irish Volunteers. By November, 1914, their strength was about twenty, and that continued to be the strength of the Company up to Easter, 1916. The following officers were elected:- Captain: Seán Lynch; Adjutant: Tadhg Twomey; Treasurer: Dan Corcoran. There was no change in these officers up to Easter, 1916, and there were no other officers.

In November, 1914, the whole Company cycled to a meeting held in Kilgarvan (Co. Kerry) for the purpose of starting a Volunteer Company there. Terence MacSwiney spoke in Kilgarvan that day. Free Murphy was there also, and a Company was got going. We had no arms on this occasion but we had haversacks and bandoliers which had been the property of the original Company. Before the end of 1915 the whole Company cycled to Ballyvourney to a meeting held there to recruit Volunteers. Tomás MacCurtain and Terence MacSwiney cycled with us to Ballyvourney and spoke at the meeting. Paud O'Donoghue (Coachford) was there also. It was a terrible day of rain and storm. The only one to join the Volunteers in Ballyvourney that day was Dan Tade Sweeney, who afterwards paraded with the Kilnamartyra Company and went out with them on Easter Sunday, 1916.

The whole Company attended the Manchester Martyrs' Commemoration in Cork in November, 1915, all armed with shotguns. The whole Company also attended the St. Patrick's Day parade in Cork in 1916, similarly armed. Seán Lynch and Tadhg Twomey attended, each for a week, at the Training Course held in Cork in January, 1916. We got a single shot, large bore Snyder rifle from Jeremiah Twohig, school teacher, with about a dozen rounds of ammunition for it. We had a German Mauser rifle, which Terence MacSwiney got for the Company from the Cork Committee. We had enough shotguns to arm the remainder of the men. Bayonets were made for the shotguns but never put on. In 1915 and up to Easter, 1916, parades were held on one night each week and every Sunday. The normal training was close order drill, arms drill, extended order drill, target practice with a .22 rifle and route marches. Terence MacSwiney came out to us frequently. We paid 2d or 3d a week into a Company fund for the purchase of equipment. We got also some discarded equipment of the original Company and a part of that Company's funds. We had haversacks, bandoliers and belts. We bought caps for the St. Patrick's Day parade in Cork. We had no puttees.

The orders for Easter Sunday, 1916, came to us from Seán O'Hegarty a few days before. They were to the effect that the Company was to parade with all arms and equipment and a week's provisions at Ballingeary after first Mass on Easter Sunday and go to Kealkil to meet the Bantry Company there. This order was based on an instruction given to Seán O'Hegarty by Tomás MacCurtain and Terence MacSwiney when they visited him at Ballingeary on the Sunday before Easter Sunday. They had then informed him that his mission on Easter Sunday was to take charge of the Bantry and Ballingeary Companies at Kealkil, to take Kealkil Police Barracks and afterwards to block and hold the Pass of Keimeneigh. But, when he had assembled the two Companies at Kealkil, he was to take no offensive action until and unless word was sent to him to do so by the Brigade. Peadar O'Hourihan was to bring the word. Seán O'Hegarty was to wait until 4 o'clock for it. The Company paraded on Saturday night and all were instructed to assemble in Ballingeary after first Mass next day. No one, except Seán O'Hegarty, had any definite information that action was contemplated on Easter Sunday, but all understood that it was a possibility. The following officers and men paraded: Seán O'Hegarty (Cork), Seán Lynch (Derragh, Renaniree), Jeremiah O'Sullivan (Tuirinaneun, Ballingeary), Dan Leary (Gortaflodig), Tadhg Twomey (Tuirindubh), Liam Twomey (do.), Dan Corcoran (Ballingeary), Jeremiah O'Shea (do.), Tim Sweeney (Inchamore, Keimeneigh), Jack Sullivan (Inchabeg, Keimeneigh), Dan Sullivan (do.), Callaghan O'Callaghan (Inchamore, Keimeneigh), John Con Cronin (Carrig Lodge), John Patrick Cronin (Bawnatemple East), John J. Cronin (Gorteenacoille). When the Company was assembled in the village, and before it moved off to Kealkil, Peadar O'Hourihan arrived on a motor cycle and sidecar.

He brought a written message from Brigade Headquarters to Seán Lynch to the effect that the Company was to go to Kealkil, meet the Bantry Company there and await further orders. A policeman named Bennett came along while Lynch was reading the dispatch and did his best to have a look at it.

The arms which the Company had that day were: One long Lee Enfield rifle (Seán O'Hegarty's) and 50 rounds; One Mauser rifle with 20 rounds; One old Snyder rifle with 12 rounds; One .22 rifle with 100 rounds; Three .32 revolvers with about 80 rounds. Mícheál Ó Cuill (Irish teacher) had brought Seán O'Hegarty's rifle out from Cork some time previously, walking from Mullinroe to Tuirindubh. Some of the shotguns were the property of members of the Company and some were on loan from local farmers. None had been purchased. Between 100 and 300 cartridges had been loaded with slug. Four members of the Company walked to Kealkil; the remainder cycled. The cycling party arrived in Kealkil about one o'clock and the men on foot a short time before the arrival of the Bantry Company. The Bantry men carried no arms — visibly anyhow. Just after our arrival a policeman from Kealkil went off on a bicycle in the Bantry direction. Scouts were posted and some exercises carried out. Two men on outpost duty were held up by police who wanted to know if they had licences for their shotguns. No message came up to six o'clock. Although Seán O'Hegarty's instructions were to wait until 4 o'clock, he waited until 6 o'clock before dismissing the men.

All the police at Kealkil were at the Cross as we came through the village. They attempted to hold up some men and one Volunteer had been pulled off his bicycle. Seán O'Hegarty came up and asked the Sergeant if he was looking for trouble. The Sergeant said no, and it must have been clear to him from the attitude of the Volunteers that it would be inadvisable for him to provoke it. Seán O'Hegarty told Seán Lynch to take his men off, and the police did not interfere any further. All the men returned to Ballingeary and dispersed to their homes. On Monday, about twelve or one o'clock, Tomás MacCurtain and Terence MacSwiney and Bob Hales came to Tuirindubh in a car from the East. Mary and

Annie MacSwiney were staying there at the time. MacCurtain and MacSwiney walked to the house where Seán O'Hegarty was, some distance west of Tuirindubh. There they told him of the order cancelling the Easter exercises which they had received on Sunday. They had no information about the Rising which was then actually beginning in Dublin, and had no doubt but that it had been postponed. In the course of discussing the situation, it was clear that they accepted the message received on Sunday as representing the decision of all parties in Dublin, and their anxiety was to get to Dublin as soon as possible to discover what had gone wrong and to try and get things going again. They did not give Seán O'Hegarty any instructions. He walked east to Tuirindubh with them, and they left in the car, going towards Ballingeary, about 3 o'clock.

On Monday night late a car in which was Tadhg O'Leary, who worked in Suttons in Cork, and a driver, came to Tuirindubh. O'Leary was looking for MacCurtain and MacSwiney. They were not there. Mary MacSwiney went into Cork on Tuesday and Annie went on Thursday. To each of them Seán O'Hegarty gave a message for the Brigade Officers asking that instructions be sent to him. He received none. On Thursday or Friday Dan Twomey, who had been in Cork, came out. He had only unofficial information and brought no instructions. On Saturday Seán O'Hegarty sent Pat Sweeney to Cork with a further request for instructions. Sweeney reported back that he could not get near the Volunteer Hall.

Late on Wednesday night, or early on Thursday morning, Tadhg O'Shea came to Dooneens from the South. He sent word by Jack Sheehan to Seán O'Hegarty on Thursday to meet him there. Seán went to Dooneens and met him on Thursday. Tadhg brought a proposal from Tom Hales that the Ballinadee men would join forces with the Macroom and Ballingeary men and attack the R.I.C. post in Macroom. Seán O'Hegarty replied that he did not know the situation and the Brigade Officers in Cork did, and that he was sure they would do what was right. No orders came to the Company during Easter Week. On the Sunday after Easter Sunday Father O'Callaghan spoke during Mass in condemnation of the Rising. He said the hands of the clock had been put back for a long time by what had happened, and he advised that the arms should be surrendered. Mrs. O'Hegarty got up and walked out of the church. There were no arrests in the Company area. Most of the members of the Company were on the run for some time afterwards. No arms were surrendered and none captured in raids. In the second week after Easter, cavalry from Ballincollig raided as far west as Tuirindubh, subsequently retiring to Ballincollig. An I.R.B. circle of about five members, which had been organised by Seán O'Hegarty, existed in Ballingeary in 1916. There were no Fianna or Cumann-na-mBan organisations in the area at the time . . .

So ends the statement of fact. It was signed by Seán (Jack) Lynch, Tadhg Twomey and Jerh Shea of Ballingeary and Seán Hegarty of Cork City, now just names, and not even that to the present generation, but very real people when things of a vital historic nature were really happening in this country eighty years ago. The document is unique in that records of events leading up to the Insurrection of 1916 are practically non-existent with regard to military stirrings in the countryside. Moreover, every historian tends to plead that the Easter Rising was the essential catalyst for the subsequent War of Independence. Far from it. The above is indicative of real movement, imminent premonitions of political change in this country which took five, six or seven years to achieve. Just like that . . .

There was an old man I knew in Ballyvourney upwards of forty years ago whose one big regret in life was that he just missed the opportunity of 'blowing the head off Major Grant'. Connie Crowley (we knew him a bit less respectfully as 'Conneen Crowl') waited in his allotted position for seven days, twenty yards from the nearest bit of road. On the eighth day the major came. He made himself the spearhead of an attack and chose that particular section of ditch to climb over. The major carried two revolvers. Only Connie was not there to receive him. That morning he had been relieved by his commanding officer, and now somebody else was in his position. The major carried his two revolvers bravely. He was a British officer with a British officer's typical contempt for any 'rabble' of irregulars, particularly at the moment the rabble hidden away among the ivied rocks and furze screens confronting him, who prided in calling themselves the 'Army of the Republic of Ireland'. He showed great courage, so he did, but with a tendency towards the suicidal; or else he may have trusted too much in the metal vest which he was known to be wearing. A grave military error at any time to underestimate the potential of an enemy — and now he was extremely dead. Even if Connie had been left another day in the position he had come to regard as his very own he might quite possibly 'be afther blowing the head off Major Grant' with his old shotgun, or at least have blown him and his arrogance back off the fence. Stranger things had happened. Strange things were happening that day at Coolnacahera in the Spring of 1921, and things stranger still were destined to follow . . .

Seán South went North on New Year's Eve, 1956, to meet his doom. He went with hostile intent. From Limerick to Fermanagh, across the Border, was a 'garryowen' of no mean extent. He was a member of the Gaelic League, the Legion of Mary, the Pioneer Total Abstinence Association — not quite the embodiment of an Irish rebel, but close, a man who felt he had something to fight and die for. And so he did, at Brookeborough Barracks in the so-called 'Six Counties'. He probably saw himself as fighting for Ireland, this island which is as plain an entity geographically, physically, historically, socially, culturally and even religiously, as any place, any time. There were no 'Provos' then, in the Fifties, nor any other paramilitaries, just B-Specials and bloody-minded 'Orangemen' . . . blood oranges thriving in a cold climate! When the news broke in Ballyvourney, Mick O'Sullivan, engineer in Coláiste Íosagáin (author of *Where Mountainy Men Have Sown*), machine-gunner in his own

right in a previous generation, dare-devil if ever, jumped into his low-slung 'RILEY', raced down to the village of
Ballymakeera, a mile away, came to a screaming halt and,
to the consternation of the sedate villagers, yelled: 'She's
breeding 'em yet! She's breeding 'em yet!'. Mick's old
comrade-in-arms, Vice-Commandant Patrick ('Paddy
Donagh Owen') O'Sullivan, gentle and gentlemanly, said
to me half apologetically —'We, nayther, didn't fight for
fun!' . . .

> No more he shall hear the seabirds cry
> O'er the murmuring Shannon tide,
> For he fell beneath the northern sky,
> Brave O'Hanlon by his side;
> They have gone to join that gallant band
> Of Plunkett, Pearse and Tone —
> Another martyr for old Ireland,
> Seán South of Garryowen!

Who was I? A young priest with a degree in Celtic Studies
from Maynooth, chaplain by Government appointment to
the afore-mentioned Coláiste Íosagáin, the Irish speaking
Preparatory College for boy student-teachers, magnificent
in its day and in its setting, shrine of many fond memories,
now sadly crumbling in decay. I had been born within an
hour of the hanging execution by the British of young Kevin
Barry, medical student, in Mountjoy Gaol, Dublin, one Monday morning. His shocked spirit took my embryonic soul
by surprise. I have never lived it down . . .

3

RUMOURS OF WAR

In the natural order of offensive weapons bare fists came first. That is an elementary fact of experience which even the 'Ideal Sceptics' of long ago, if such there were who wished to free themselves from the bondage of external circumstances, might easily have been brought to see the force of with a punch on the nose (British), or a five in the eye (American), or a clout of a fisht (Irish). In the course of time some ancient pragmatists discovered the law of gravity and its practical applications, as well as the relative density of materials. They threw stones (The curious expression of my childhood, 'He furr a cruisht', seems to fit nicely into the Neanderthal context). Later on some caveman-scientist came to realize that by fixing a rock to a stick, or, if he happened to have artistic leanings, to a fallen enemy's thigh bone, he had a far more effective weapon 'than anything the world had ever seen before', as H.G. Wells might well say. And next a stone-age genius hit on an idea for disabling a man (wooden clubs, the cartoonists tell us, were reserved for women!) by chipping a flint to a sharp point and fitting a staff to it longer than the standard handle for stone axes of the period. He had a rudimentary spear, in fact, and it needed only the comparatively unimportant discovery of the qualities and the

18

process of working metals and the lance or spear had come to stay. It had come to stay so conclusively that in 1918, when more up-to-date weapons were in short supply, an 'Order of the Day' was issued from the headquarters of the First Cork Brigade in Cork City directing all battalion officers to set about organizing the manufacture of the type of weapon traditionally known in Ireland as the 'pike'. The pike had been proved obsolete, or at least inadequate for general use and eventual military success, in the Rebellion of Ninety-Eight, a hundred and twenty years before, and it had been proved in no uncertain manner. But such was the spirit of the current generation of insurgents, and such was the need felt among their leaders for giving them the comforting feeling 'of having something in their hands', as Captain Patrick ('Patsy Burrick') Lynch told me, that apparently the tragic lesson needed to be learned a second time.

So once again the pikes went into production and the anvils rang and double-timed tunefully to the vigorous whistling of 'The Rising of the Moon', the anthem of Ninety-Eight; and many a prowling police patrol went on its friendless way wondering at the flood of work that had lately inundated the local blacksmith which required his working on behind closed doors 'till all hours of the morning' as he emphasized with every blow of the hammer his determination that the pikes must be together at the rising of the moon. It was unlikely that any historical association could have given rise to a suspicion that there was something afoot. Still there always had been an edge to the glorification of the old pike and there always had been a clenching of fists and a sob for the memory of the dead in futile battle. Irish history especially is a tale of national resurgence coming from national martyrdom, life coming from death, new endeavours rising phoenix-like from the ashes of old disasters before they were yet grown cold. So, General Sir John Maxwell — 'Bloody Maxwell' they called him — might be regarded as the unwitting 'hero' of Easter Week, 1916, by shooting and lime-burning the leaders of the brief and rather insignificant Dublin City rebellion. No doubt he would have been surprised to hear it. But he had no time to wait. He had to hurry away to his wife's bed of confinement. A new human being had to be ushered into the world with all care and fatherly attention. He had to hurry. A few Irish poet-patriots were standing in the way. Could one of them possibly have written lines like:

> Lord, Thou art hard on mothers;
> We suffer in their coming and their going,
> And tho' I grudge them not, I weary, weary
> Of the long sorrow; and yet I had my joy —
> My sons were faithful, and they fought!.
>   (From *The Mother*, by P.H. Pearse).

*   *   *

There was great talk of Conscription in the Ireland of the Spring of 1918. In France the fighting men of Britain virtually had their backs to the wall, the sea wall north of the Somme, while their French allies were again reeling back to the Marne before the fearful onslaughts of General Erich von Ludendorff and his greatly despised 'Huns'. Powerful 'Big Bertha' had taken her stance for the pulverization of Paris. The American troops, who eventually proved the deciding factor in the war, were not yet properly in the field. John Redmond's 'National Volunteers' had whetted the appetite of the Imperial War Office for more material of the same kind. They, and the other 'loyalist' Irish regiments, had proved their mettle in Flanders, Gallipoli and other theatres. Being Irish they were expendable as cannon fodder, but as stop-gaps they were expeditious, and as storm troopers they had proved themselves almost unsurpassed. One of General Douglas MacArthur's proudest memories, after a lifetime of warfare, was the smashing of the Hindenburg Line in 1918. Of that achievement, at which he was present, he regarded as the most outstanding contributory cause the decisive breakthrough of the New York 'Fighting Sixty-Ninth', with the Canadians on their left and the Australians on their right, in all an approximate 90% Irish or Irish descent. But that was to be in the Autumn . In the Spring things were looking bad for the Allies. Men were needed — and prayers! Old Field Marshal Ferdinand Foch, French military tactical genius and Allied Commander-in-Chief, wrote to his sister who was Reverend Mother of a French convent in Riverside Drive, New York, beseeching her to get her schoolchildren to pray for him in his well-meaning efforts to make the world safe for 'democracy' or 'small nations' or something. He became the hero of the campaign. (*Note:* In February, 1921, when Catholic Ireland was at the height of its 'Terror' and fighting desperately for survival, Foch was an honoured guest with Lloyd George at *Chequers*. The world was safe for victorious old men!). The British Government relied more on manpower than on prayer. So talk and rumour became a reality with the passing of the Conscription Bill on April 16, 1918, applying compulsory military service to Ireland. Reaction was instantaneous. The Irish Parliamentary Party came home from Westminster to throw in their lot with their fellow countrymen in resisting it to the full. At a meeting representative of all parties in the Mansion House, Dublin, on April 18, the Anti-Conscription Pledge was drawn up expressing their determination to resist 'by the most effective means at our disposal'. The Bishops' Maynooth Manifesto appeared to add its timely voice of protest. 'The Irish People', it said, 'have a right to resist (Conscription) by every means that is consonant with the Law of God!'. Bishop O'Dwyer, of Limerick, had electrified the nation in 1916 by declaring publicly: 'Sinn Féin is, in my judgement, the true principle!'. Now the signs of the times were becoming unmistakable to all, to the superficial observers, to the small-minded 'shoneens' (i.e. Anglophiles in our midst), and even to the ageing survivors of a generation that had been weaned and reared in the Land League days and under the Home Rule persuasion . . .

And down in Cork the blacksmiths fell to hammering out a lively anvil chorus, to what end other than the end of a pike staff nobody seemed to know or care just yet. In the village of Ballymakeera Neily Creedon and Paddy Sullivan strove manfully at the task. Neily turned out a large supply of broad-bladed weapons. They were put in a safe hiding place. They may be there still if anybody could remember where. Paddy 'the Smith' managed a sort of bayonet which could be clamped to a handle, a shotgun or maybe, someday, a rifle barrel. *Chuir sé go maith chuige,* 'he put good to it', as they say in the Gaelic way. The work of both men was praised by Tomás MacCurtain, patriotic Lord Mayor of Cork, who, as O/C of the First Cork Brigade, made an inspection of the Seventh Battalion (Macroom) area just prior to Whit Sunday, 1918. So few specimens of the spearheads survived to 1950 (when this research programme was begun) that they must have been found useful, through the intervening years, for stirring pig swill or poking fires. When it came to handle-making the Coolea Company had a distinct advantage. Carpenter Jerry Dineen's steam-powered circular saw was the wonder of the age. A monstrous contraption (I was told), but it far outclassed the old style saw-pit and whip-saw combination still in use. A noted landmark, the mighty ash tree of Gurtyrahilly Cross, found itself a conspicuous target. It died for Ireland. In the course of a night it was cut down, cut up, cut round and shaped into pike handles. And the older generation, in the person of Ned McSweeney, had as usual its wry comment to make on this latest madness of the rising generation: 'I'm afraid, lads', he said, watching the ash tree tumble, 'I'm afraid ye're getting very wild!'. This primitive rearmament may have been a step in the right direction, but the exigencies of modern warfare demanded more than a fighting spirit and a just cause. The immediate concern of the Irish Republican Army was that if they were to have any hope of success they would need to be on an equal footing with the enemy, or very nearly so. His weapons would have to be their weapons. His weapons, therefore, would have to be taken out of his hands, and that same would require all the ingenuity and daring of which they were capable.

The Irish members in the House of Commons had warned the British Government that the imposing of Conscription would amount to a declaration of war against Ireland, and thenceforth three army corps would be needed to get one out of the country. The threat of Conscription swelled the ranks of the Volunteers beyond all bounds and expectations. Patrick Pearse had put into the mouth of one of his play characters the observation that 'men's lives get very precious to them when they have bought out their land' (with reference to the recent series of Land-Purchase Acts). But Pearse had been dead for two years and a display of aloofness, a 'conscientious objection' even in England itself, was now no guarantee of personal security from the hands which directed the destinies of vast armies of men. Otherwise, young Ireland had no liking to join the countless throngs of those whose earthly remains were fast mouldering into nothingness beneath faraway battlefields of Flanders and on the wooded slopes of the Ardennes plateau, in marked or unmarked graves from the banks of Marne to the marshes of St. Gond. The song writers beyond the Irish sea had been drawing inspiration from the wave of wistful nostalgia that had swept over the English nation for the menfolk who had marched away to war and were now reposing somewhere, in their remote and lonely graves, waiting to be remembered 'when the poppies bloom again' and the 'roses of Picardy' would once more spread their perfume over the chalk trenches 'in the hush of the silver dew'. Young Ireland felt not at all eager to subscribe to the sentiment. Consequently, many of them lived on to ruminate at leisure on the retrospective futility of war in general and 'war to end war' in particular. Moreover, poppies and roses droop and fade and die. Sentimental lyrics come and go and are forgotten. Newer graves and neater rows of little wooden crosses, in the wake of future wars, would yet draw the gaping attention of thoughtlessly irreverent tourists and sensation seekers while the inexplicable gymnastics of international politics mocked at the toils, devotion and supreme sacrifice of the men who died.

4

Point Counter Point

Aldous Huxley's clever novel, *Point Counter Point* (1928), satirizing the fun-loving Twenties, would need to be stretched beyond endurance to incorporate the Irish Troubles, which introduced that 'roaring' decade, even though the said Troubles acted not only as a political buffer between the Great War and the hedonistic Twenties induced by it, but made scapegoats of the Royal Irish Constabulary in a succession of quasi-comical though lethal overturns in a point-counterpoint situation. The satiristic old 'Peeler and the Goat' ballad of the Nineteenth Century never visualized the peeler becoming the sacrificial goat of the Twentieth!

* * *

The 'Troubles' came to Ballyvourney at Easter, 1918. After a big parade of Irish Volunteers in Macroom, at which local men were prominent, the British military arrived to raid for officers in the district. It was their first visit since Whit Sunday, 1916, when some of them had camped on the lawn of the 'Great House', at 'The Mills', and the remainder were billeted in Slievereagh schoolhouse just up the road towards Killarney. But now, at Easter, 1918, they were pleased to impose themselves on the villagers of Ballymakeera. They

25

belonged to the South Hampshire Regiment stationed currently in Macroom. The net result of the operation was the capture of the big drum and some band instruments from the Gaelic Hall. Marching instruments had become a symbol of disaffection. From now on raids by both police and military became frequent and regular, and with good reason too. The authentic 'Black-and-Tans' (*Concise Oxford Dictionary:* 'Armed Force recruited to fight Sinn Féin, 1921, wearing mixture of military and constabulary uniforms') were still unheard of. Ballyvourney had its first glimpse of them on a Saturday in March, 1920 (never mind the dictionary!), when they came to reinforce the police at the barracks beside 'The Mills'. The 'Auxiliaries', commonly but erroneously referred to as the 'Tans', arrived a few months later with their swagger, adapted 'Crossley tenders', and ever-ready 'Long-Webley' revolvers.

*   *   *

> Through bogs and mire and deep morass
> The Ballingeary police pass,
> Searching in the mountain caves
> For the Ballingeary braves;
> Out all night in frost and snow,
> Facing the wintry blasts that blow;
> Shivering, shaking, hungry, cold,
> Thoughts of country sold for gold;
> Nothing to reward his pains,
> Nothing to fill the prison chains;
> Farther than ever from his promotion,
> Still no strides for his devotion.
> Pity, my reader, if you can,
> The Ballingeary police man!

(Opportune doggerel from *The Southern Star* newspaper, 1918).

*   *   *

The Royal Irish police force were here, in mid-Cork, as everywhere else throughout the country, the mainstay of the

Law of the 'Sassanach'. Their barracks were the citadels that supported the symbol of his ascendancy, the 'Union Jack', flapping contempt for the subjugated people, though they were no longer actually 'hanging men and women for the wearing of Green'. The 'Tricolour' was fobidden by Law, but police baiting with the flag was becoming a favourite pastime. On Whit Sunday morning, 1918, the people of Ballyvourney, on their way to early Mass, were astounded to see the flag of Ireland waving proudly from the church steeple. Under cover of darkness Bob Hallissey, with the connivance of Fr. Carroll, C.C. had made the precarious ascent. The police duly arrived but it defied all their efforts to remove it. It seemed to be a battle won. A few days later another Volunteer, Dan Quill, shinned up a tall poplar beside the Behill river, three hundred yards from the police barracks. Swaying perilously far above the water he fixed the Tricolour to the very top where no 'peeler' would venture to follow. I was there when the mighty tree came toppling down during the big storm of St. Stephen's night, 1952, and found the wire which had secured the flag firmly embedded in the bark. It seemed even then a tangible but wistful link with a generation that was fast becoming absorbed into the intangible mass that is History.

*   *   *

'Isn't it a great pity without someone coming before them in the Glen in the evening!'. The speaker was Mrs. Jack Lynch. She was referring to the two peelers who had just gone by on a 'side-car' (the traditional jaunting-car) on their way to Ballyvourney northwards beyond the hills. (*Note:* Sir Robert Peel, as British Secretary for Ireland, had established the R.I.C. exactly one hundred years before. Surprisingly, Mrs. Lynch still lives with her daughter in Ballyvourney, having passed the century mark only last year!). The retarded trot of the horse against the steady pull of the rising ground, the absurd rigidity with which they sat their side-slung seats, would seem to make the preposterous suggestion a possibility and give a chance to snatch a point from the arrogant minions of the Law. But there were the rifles clasped firmly between their knees, the heavy revolvers very much in evidence. All in all it was enough to provoke anyone who knew that the policemen's intention was to protract a British insult to their own people by helping to outlaw an *aeraíocht*, a Gaelic festival of song, dance and story-telling in the open air. So the observation was not so startling as one might think from a young Irish woman on her way to Sunday Mass in Ballingeary, especially as her husband was the local captain of Volunteers and literally the 'man in the gap', living as he was beside the 'Mouth of the Glen' itself, at Béal a' Ghleanna. Captain Jack said nothing. After dinner he went down to the meadow to save the hay, the weather being blustery and tricky as July is wont to be. Trying to manage 'Italian' ryegrass single-handed in a stiff breeze was usually enough to keep a man busy and gave little time for other thoughts. Still the idea rankled in his mind. Two carbines and two revolvers — they would be a welcome addition to the four 'thirty-eights' given his company by Terence MacSwiney. The thirty-eights had cost twenty-eight shillings apiece. A lot of money. It would be satisfactory (he told me in 1952) to spread over the outlay by increasing the arsenal free but for the trouble of trying, and charge to the British Inspector-General. The more he thought about it the more he liked the idea. He leaned on his hay-fork and began to calculate. Six men, three on either side, could hide behind the protruding rocks midway in the narrow defile of Béal a' Ghleanna. After that everything would depend on timing, and the laxity of the policemen after a day's outing. Eager, but troubled at his responsibility, he contemplated a little longer looking down at the village of Ballingeary where it nestled beneath him in the valley of the Lee. So cosy and peaceful it looked, with Lough Allua extending away from it shimmering a dull marcasite from the overcast sky. He thought of Matt 'the Thresher' looking down fondly on Charles Kickham's Knocknagow ('The Homes of Tipperary'), his great, simple heart swelling with pride that he could do something, even the throw of a hammer, to help carry on the prestige of Gaeldom enshrined in those old mud walls and thatched roofs. 'For the credit of the little village!', quoted Captain Jack Lynch, heading his horse and half-loaded hay cart towards home. He sent to Ballingeary for Tadhg Twomey, his friend and confidant. Tadhg arrived game and sporting and ready to give it a try. They both knew where men could be found and Tadhg went away across the mountain on his bicycle to the *aeraíocht* in Coomiclovane. Late in the evening he returned with Liam, his brother, Dan Thady McSweeney of Ballyvourney, Jamie Moynihan and Neilus O'Reilly of Coolea . . .

Time was running out now. The police had failed in their objective and would be returning soon. Six men at the 'Pass' made their plans hurriedly but carefully, being mindful, as Jack said, of the Chinese saying: 'To guess is cheap, but to guess wrong is expensive!'. It would be broad daylight for some time to come, so they wore the half-face masks of 'banditti' but took the added precaution of blackening their faces inside the handkerchiefs. It was a wise move as things turned out. All six were well known to the police. Four carried revolvers. Jack Lynch had his double-barrelled shotgun, a crotchety old weapon with the lightest of hair-triggers. (*Note:* His own great-grand-uncle, another Jack Lynch, had been killed at Keimeneigh, in 1822, on the occasion of the famous battle, because of a too slow and awkward musket, commemorated by Gaelic poetess, Máire Bhuí Ní Laoire in her song, *Cath Céim an Fhia*). At the 'Mouth of the Glen' his standing order was — No shooting! If the need arose he himself would lead off with his D.B. For the purpose he had two home-made cartridges. The others had three shells apiece for the pistols. So they moved into position behind the rocky abutments while Jerh Shea, who had joined them, took his stand as a one-man flanking party on the heights above. A few minutes later the jaunting-car hove into sight lurching crazily as is generally expected of it, the driver perched high up in front, the two policemen sitting one on either side, Constable Bennett on the right and Constable Butler on the left. The horse slowed to a weary amble coming through the 'Pass'. On board the carbines (i.e. light Lee-Enfield .303 rifles for cycle or horseback use) had been laid aside. It was a fatal mistake. They never got a chance to use them. Butler, the younger man, seemed dazed when the order to halt broke the stillness of the glen. Even if there were any fight in him, after the day, he got no time to show it. A revolver exploded in his face and he toppled over onto the ground with a bullet through the neck. (*Note:* The evidence showed later that it had passed within one-sixteenth of an inch of the jugular vein. The man who fired it told me that he had never meant to do so — it was just the reflex action of a nervous hand). Constable Butler remained *hors de combat* for the duration.

But Bennett was tough, a lithe tiger of a man with the tenacity of a jungle cat in every sinew. Six feet of whip-cord, it was said that ne'er a man coming into Ballingeary village could stand before him. The odds were against him now. Two men stood before him, masked, armed and determined, but it was in keeping with the man's reputation that he never blanched and, instead of surrendering when called upon, made a wild grab for his rifle. At the same time Captain Jack, a powerful giant of a man himself, reached out and caught the policeman by the slack of his tunic, brought him, rifle and all, onto the road where he fell flat on his back. In the action Bennett slashed at his assailant's mask and tore it off, as well as a large sliver of skin from the bridge of Jack Lynch's nose. They were on top of him then, flailing, pounding, cursing, and all the while the infuriated policeman kept thumbing the swivel cut-off of the magazine (an obsolete feature of the Lee-Enfield and Lee-Metford). The others joined in the fray. They stamped on his wrist but failed to dislodge his grip on the gun while he fought them off with his free hand and savagely working legs. To the credit of the man he finally got to his feet in a bucking half-crouch, still holding his rifle. Meanwhile, Jamie Moynihan, who had been detailed to hold the horse, had severed the harness with a cobbler's knife from his pocket and released the rearing animal. Jamie came charging in carrying with him Captain Jack's gun which had fallen on the ground beyond the perimeter of the melée. Bennett was on his feet now. Jamie belted him on the head with the stock of the gun and the fight was over. For a gun that had the reputation of going off when touched it is truly amazing — both hammers were cocked — that it did not react to such violent treatment and cause irreparable damage.

The driver had run away. Help would be forthcoming. The policemen were left lying by the roadside, the side-car having been pitched over the precipice as a parting gesture. (*Note:* At the same spot, in my childhood, a large, luxurious motor-car lay down there for ages, the object of wonderment. It belonged to Musgraves, a business family in Cork City, but, so far as I remember, there had been no loss of life when it went down). Back at the Pass the raiders collected their precious arms and fled from the scene. In a short time it would be swarming with police and military. They had gone only a short distance when the captain noticed something amiss. Butler's rifle was not in the lot. Nobody could remember having seen it. They returned by a roundabout way and recovered it from the valley below where it had gone down with the side-car. Only ten minutes had elapsed, and it speaks for the toughness of Bennett and the sagacity of Butler that they were nowhere to be seen. On the following day Jack Lynch tried out his two cartridges on less offensive game. They were both duds. Some armaments to fight a battle with!

Here is in a constable to myself, the day after, and a bad
scowl on him. 'There now', says he, 'ye'll pay for it. It is the
law we'll have now — Curfew', says he. 'What kind of a law
would that be?', says I. 'I'll tell you', says he — 'A law that
any man won't be able to stick his head outside the door,
after nightfall, without having the nose knocked off him with
a bullet!'. 'It is the bad kind of law that is', says I.
(From the Irish of *Scéal Mo Bheatha*, the *Story of my Life*,
by Dónall Bán Ó Céilleachair, 'White' Daniel Kelleher of
Coolea).

(*Note:* The above account of the ambush at Béal a' Ghleanna is essentially as told to me by Jack Lynch, Jamie
Moynihan and Jerh Shea in 1952. M. O'Sullivan, in his book,
Where Mountainy Men Have Sown, gives it approximately
the same with slight variations, a feature that makes the study
of History more alluring than reprehensible. The ambush
happened on Sunday, July 7, 1918, and is commemorated
in an Irish poem by the well known Coolea poet, Pádraig
Mac Suibhne, 'An Suibhneach Meann'. In the interest of
authenticity, I need to emphasise once again that it was the
very first ambush in the War of Independence. Nevertheless,
the ambush at Soloheadbeg, Co. Tipperary, is still being
claimed, and celebrated, as the first, because Tipperary
stalwart, Dan Breen, said so in his book, *My Fight For Irish
Freedom* (1924). Solohead was not even a fight — just one
hidden volley and two dead policemen, but it did happen
on an historic occasion, the actual meeting of the first Dáil
Éireann, 21 January, 1919. There is a similar on-going problem about Béalnabláth, where Michael Collins met his death
on 22 August, 1922. It is still quite erroneously referred to
as 'The Mouth of the Flowers', and never questioned because
some newsman said so originally, whereas it means simply
'the crossing of the ravine', a fact borne out by the
topography).

*   *   *

The occasion was an *aeraíocht* in Coolea. The organizers were Dónall Bán Ó Céilleachair, Gaelic scholar and renowned, late-in-life author of a book of personal reminiscences as above, and Miss Katie McSweeney, national teacher, sister of 'An Suibhneach Meann', and energetic secretary of the regional branch of the Gaelic League. The venue was to be Páirc na Meaingilí, the 'Field of the Mangolds', just beside Dónall Bán's house, but two days before, on July 5, all meetings of whatever kind had been 'proclaimed' throughout Ireland. The prohibition included *aeraíochta* and *feiseanna*. (*Note*: A *Feis* differed from an *Aeraíocht* in that it was competitive and was usually held indoors). Word of the 'Proclamation' was passed on to the secretary on Saturday by Sergeant ('The Skipper') Flynn from Ballyvourney, but his warning was received with a bad grace and went unheeded. Incidentally, the *Eisteddfod* in Wales, a Gaelic festival on similar lines, was 'proclaimed' in Britain, by the new Norman conquerors, and for much the same reason, as far back as the twelfth century. So, the Coolea *aeraíocht* would be, in a manner of speaking, a test case. The Gaelic traditions were at stake. It would be put to the test. Anticipating trouble Dónall Bán took the precaution, on Saturday night, of hiding some pikes in a hay-field nearby and passed the word around where they could be found, if necessary. In case of a bayonet or baton charge he intended to make his stand with a pike in his hand because, as he explained to me rather sardonically in 1950, 'it was easier for me than to be running and I not able to run!'. The Field of the Mangolds sprouted a wondrous crop. Jason, the classical warrior, had apparently sown his dragon's teeth during the night. By early Mass time on Sunday it had become the Field of Ares full of armed and strange men ready to do battle for their king. But nobody wished to accomodate them. Fr. Carroll C.C., arrived on horseback among the loitering crowds and led them westwards into the quiet seclusion of Coomiclovane. The move disconcerted both soldiers and police who followed as far as 'the top of the height' near Bardinchy school, but failed to locate them. The *aeraíocht* proved a success in every sense and free from disturbance. A slight commotion occurred when a bizarre figure was seen striding down the hillside, a tall, strapping young man in kilts carrying a set of war-pipes over his shoulder. But he came as a friend and was made welcome, a true Gael among Gaels, and soon the little valley among the hills thrilled to the skirl of his pipes. Ian Graeme Baun Mackenzie-Kennedy, 'Scottie' to his many friends, had responded to the *dúchas* (nature) that was in him. (*Note:* This was the only item of entertainment that was still clear in the minds of many of the participants thirty years later).

About 'Scottie'. Last of the Stuart fighters, a man out of time and place, who espoused the collateral Irish cause, he was destined to perish far from Culloden Field while resisting the advance of hostile troops into Republican territory in Ireland's Civil War (cf. *The Dark Secret Of Béalnabláth,* by the author, *Vive Moi!,* autobiography of Seán Ó Faoláin, and Geraldine Neeson, Cork City musician and journalist, and friend of 'Scottie', in the *Cork Examiner,* in June 1979). A quest for the Irish language drew him to the West Muskerry (mid-Cork) *Gaeltacht* where he found, in Ballingeary and Gougane Barra, a veritable reproduction of the Lochaber country of the Scottish Kennedys (Clann Ulric) in Southern Invernesshire — rugged mountain and lake places around Loch Linnhe and Ben Nevis astride the Road to the Isles. The people of Ballingeary Ian Baun found equally to his liking and he settled down to munch his eternal *buachtarach* — a sort of muesli of oatmeal and treacle — as if he were still among the crofters of Skye. Young 'Scottie' adopted and was adopted. Only the Volunteers were chary at first. Appearances and more recent history were against him. It was known that his father was a major (Miss Neeson says a colonel) and his uncle had been a major-general, in the British Army. Moreover, the Mackenzie clan (Clann Choinnich), also one-time Jacobites, had acceded to the Crown after 'the Forty-Five' (battle of Culloden, 1745) and became the Seaforth Highlanders about the same time that the family alliance was formed when his great-great-grandfather, William Kennedy, M.D., married Mary Randoll Mackenzie-Scott. Ian Baun, however, leaned more towards the Kennedy side of the house, always wearing the family tartan plaid until it was replaced by the uniform of a republican soldier. (*Note:* Scottie's glengarry cap sported the Kennedy badge, a complex heraldic design of which he was infinitely proud. In the terminology of heraldry it had for crest a 'dolphin naiant proper' with the motto, *Avise la Fin*, for coat of arms, a 'chevron gules between three cross-crosslets fitchee sable, all within a double tressure, flory counter-flory fleur-de-lis of the second, and as supporters, two swans proper, beaked and membered gules').

The Scottish Kennedys were a tall people, stately rather than robust. Ian Baun was typical. In fact an extant photograph of him (cf. *The Dark Secret)* bears a striking resemblance to a well known portrait by Allan Ramsay of the Earl of Sutherland, one-time head of the Kennedy clan. Most historians agree that they came originally from Ireland, although some loyal English and Scottish historians have tried earnestly to discredit the Irish connection, giving the etymology of 'Kennedy' in various ways, as from the Scottish name 'Kenneth' (companion of St. Columba), or from the Scots Gaelic *Ceann a' Tighe* or even *Ceann Dubh*. One writer, more historian than logician, declared: 'How can we be expected to believe that the antecedents of so many highly respected Lowland and Highland gentry were Irish?' Yet, Donald, the Great Steward of Mar, a district associated with the Kennedy clan to the present day, had led a contingent to the aid of King Brian Boru at the Battle of Clontarf in 1014, and the great Brian was himself Mac Cennéidigh, son of Kennedy, chief of Thomond and hereditary ruler of North Munster (*Tuathmumhan*). The royal blood of the Bruces also flowed in the Kennedy veins. The Princess Mary, great-great-grand-daughter of Robert Bruce and sister of King James the First of England (James the Sixth of Scotland), married Sir James Kennedy of Dunure, a direct ancestor of Ian Baun. (*Note:* Scottie's vast family tree, painstakingly calligraphed by himself, is still in the possession of the Twomey family of Tureenduv, Ballingeary, with whom he lived). So, sedition was already hot in Scottie's veins when he joined the Ballingeary Company of the Volunteers. But otherwise there was little evidence of heat. In temper he was imperturbable. It was said that the only occasion on which his patience deserted him was when he was endeavouring, with the aid of young Dick Twomey, to roll a large stone to the mouth of a cave hide-out he had prepared against the troubled days that lay ahead. The rock proved intractable and, in sudden exasperation, Scottie blurted out: 'Oh, damn you, John Bull!'.

A stone monument in The Square, Macroom, commemorates, among other things, the fact that Ian MacCoinnich Ulric (Scottie's name in Scots Gaelic) was killed in action, in August, 1922, while fighting for Irish freedom. This latter statement would be disputed in many quarters, even angrily in our day (when it has become rather fashionable to be seen to be technically 'anti-Irish'), but the fact remains that, though foreign troops had been replaced by native troops, Scottie delivered up his life, his allotted twenty-three years, while still struggling for an intransigent ideal beside his comrades of the Seventh and Eighth Battalions. *Exegi monumentum aere perennius!* ('I have set up a monument more lasting than brass') from Horace would seem to meet the case. Otherwise, personal memories of Scottie have long grown dim in the land of his adoption. Memories of his fine character and singleness of purpose were still there in the Fifties. By strange contrast he was best remembered for the amusement he caused on so many occasions. As an enthusiastic Volunteer his efforts had the stamp of eccentricity even at a period when any initiative had to be novel in the extreme. 'Mackenzie-Kennedy' was a die-hard republican, but 'Scottie' was an overgrown child. His idea for a stovepipe cannon wound tightly with steel wire, to pulverize barrack-doors with, might or might not have worked. Nobody wished to try. The sail affixed to his bicycle was to a certain degree effective but a great deal more fun. His introduction to the Eighth Battalion of the formula for the manufacture of 'black powder' was helpful, but the very first experiment ruined his budding moustache. His playing of the bagpipes at the head of Dónall 'ac Taidhg McSweeney's funeral, at the old man's dying request, was certainly sounding a rare note in Ballingeary. Then there would be a droll sequel to the raid for arms which he conducted in the house of a gentleman acquaintance of his at Caherdaniel, Co. Kerry. The raid turned up only a pair of old swords and a humane-killer. When Tomás MacCurtain came to investigate the arms situation in 1918 Scottie stepped forward and in all seriousness announced: 'I have got a pigkiller!'. ('An extrovert, with a consuming curiosity about people and their motivations, he had a sharp, frequently-used wit and a clear, infectious laugh, and was excellent company' . . . Geraldine Neeson). Even his frequent trips across the hills to Killarney, carrying his pipes and his ration of *buachtarach*, had a touch of childish simplicity. His mother, frail, ageing, but queenly Victorian (there is a picture), had come to take him home, had failed, and instead settled in the Castle Hotel, Killarney, where he paid his respects at regular intervals. With his reversion to the ancient ideal one would say that his conversion to the ancient Faith was inevitable. It was so. Scottie found them integrated and harmonious, and the religious atmosphere of the home of St. Finbarr helped the change of heart. It was a big occasion for him. To mark it he carried with him to Rome an embroidered Tricolour, which he had worked himself, to be blessed by Pope Benedict the Fifteenth . . .

Friends who heard the tracer bullets slapping into Mackenzie-Kennedy's body as it lay in a dusty byway at Rochestown, near Passage by the Sea, have since wept for the big child innocently caught up in the ugly toils of inter-necine conflict that was none of his business. So he wanders onto the stage once more. For the moment we leave this blood relation of the Young Pretender, Bonnie Prince Charlie, tacking his sail-bike along on a south-west wind which might have carried his carefree singing back to Lochaber:

> Speed, bonny boat, like a bird on the wing;
> 'Onward', the sailors cry;
> Carry the lad that's born to be king
> Over the sea to Skye.

*   *   *

NOTICE OF APPLICATION to the County Court for Compensation for Criminal Injury to the Person.
Local Government (Ireland) Act, 1898, and the
Criminal Injuries (Ireland) Act, 1919.
County of Cork, West Riding, Division of Macroom.

WHEREAS some person or persons on the night of Sunday, the 7th July, 1918, about 8.30 p.m. o'clock, on the public road at Gortnabinna, in the parish of Kilnamartyra, and in the County District of Inchigeela, in said County, did maliciously attack and injure me in my person whilst in the execution of my duty and on account of my being acted and having acted as a Police Constable, one of them discharged a revolver or similar firearm, a bullet from which entered into and right through my neck and seriously injured the nerves thereof. AND WHEREAS I have sustained serious personal and permanent injuries and have sustained loss to the amount of one thousand five hundred pounds — shillings — pence. Notice is hereby given that an application, etc.
Applicant: James Butler,
No. 1 Company,
Royal Irish Constabulary.

*   *   *

Well, who did it? WHO DID IT? No answer! So the learned judge, King's Counsel, awarded £1,300 damages (a large sum in those days, as we invariably remark nowadays) to be levied from the Macroom Rural District Council and through them on the ratepayers at the additional and unheard of rate of five shillings and tenpence for four electoral divisions concerned, or at a proportionate rate on the baronies of East and West Muskerry, certain persons being exempted, after application, on the grounds of their 'evident loyalty to the Crown', and the impossibility, therefore, of their being cognizant of, and being in sympathy with, the aforesaid atrocity. On behalf of the respondents in the appeal the learned counsel remarked that 'such acts were sometimes prompted by the passion or heat in a particular locality where certain incidents on the part of the authorities, rightly or wrongly, engendered that state of feeling'. (From the *Cork Examiner)*. As it happened, the two police officers concerned, Constables James Butler and James Bennett, were made the scapegoats of the Force, being deprived of their weapons in a manner which set their authority at naught, the first of many — Soloheadbeg was still unthought of — to be similarly treated. For the distinction they were awarded £800 and £500 respectively being doubly lucky in escaping with their lives and in having their cases considered while judicial proceedings under the British regime had still some vestige of meaning. To what extent they in particular contributed to the 'passion or heat' in the locality has not been satisfactorily established. In effect they were just unfortunate, as they had simply being doing duty at the barracks in Ballyvourney while their colleagues were elsewhere (as already related) manufacturing the incidents. 'Rightly or wrongly' is the moot point for historians, not so easily settled in the context as the judge thought when, in summing up, he set out the premise, rather unconvincingly, that 'everybody seemed to admit that the police force was necessary in every country'. There were many who believed that the present incumbents in Ireland were dispensable to the extent of doing them grievous bodily harm. In point of fact, the R.I.C. day was done. Its members in future were simply cock-shots. The 'Mouth of the Glen' had set the mould.

* * *

The psychological disadvantage of never having been under fire before more than eliminates the physical advantage of darkness and numbers for those who find themselves in that unenviable position for the first time. That is exactly what happened to a bunch of Volunteers, under Section Leader Mick Dineen, at the chapel gates, Ballyvourney, on Sunday night, October 6, 1918. Sergeant ('The Skipper') Flynn and Constable Flanagan were on the beat. They carried guns which had now become more an invitation to violence than their usefulness in maintaining the Peace of the Realm would seem to warrant. When the charge came the sergeant found time to draw his revolver. He plugged the surrounding atmosphere generally with his full complement of slugs and the effort died in its tracks. It did not appear as if the Volunteers themselves were prepared to pay much attention to a particular directive from the Executive Council issued earlier in the year. G.H.Q. had in mind a probable Peace Conference at a possible end of the Great War later in the year. The directive said that all units should refrain from physical force for the present while maintaining resistance of a 'moral' nature. Posters were printed and hung up calling on the public to boycott the police. For a while this had the effect of making life miserable for them and their families. Just the same, 'incidents' continued to occur at regular intervals. The crossing of the 'energy barrier' was in sight. A horse-drawn mail car was held up outside the village of Ballymakeera and deprived of the R.I.C. correspondence while under fire from a military patrol which happened the way. The Mouth of the Glen affair had brought military authority to a great part of West Cork, and now these latest incidents produced more specific action in the Ballyvourney region. An area within a three-mile radius of the village was proclaimed as a 'special military area' under the Defence of the Realm Act ('DORA'). All meetings, including the cattle and pig fairs and the butter market, were banned and travellers had to procure a special permit to leave the district. This state of affairs continued right through to the end of hostilities. But the police had moved before DORA. No one had been recognized at the chapel gates, so four men were picked up at random and tried by a military court in Cork City. They were Jeremiah and John O'Riordan of 'The Rookery', Patrick Hegarty of Ballymakeera, and Cornelius O'Sullivan of Danganasillagh. They refused to make a statement or to recognize the court, a procedure which later became quite familiar and now has worldwide significance. Nevertheless, they were sentenced to six months' imprisonment apiece but were actually released in November. The futility of holding them or their likes, at this early stage in the conflict, was expressed by the Governor of Cork Gaol when he told the Chief Warder: 'Get those bastards out of here!'. Somehow they were held for two days beyond the appointed time. John 'the Rookery' was last in line for his pass at the gate. The joker in him would not let the occasion pass without comment. He said: 'Remember now, when I'm back in here again there's two days coming to me!'. The Chief Warder looked after them and said: 'They'll be back all right!'. One of them would not however. The 'Big 'Flu' was raging worldwide. Con O'Sullivan, brother of Vice-Commandant Patrick (Paddy Donagh Owen) O'Sullivan, of Danganasillagh, contracted it immediately and died a week later.

During the Winter months the country was fully occupied with the 'flu epidemic. It put a noticeable damper on the subversive activities of the Irish Volunteers. Many people succumbed, occasionally two from the one family being buried on the same day. The European Armistice passed almost unnoticed on November 11, but a sudden renewal of interest came with the dissolution of the English Parliament on the twenty-fifth. 'Sinn Féin' (prn. 'Shin Fane'), the political association of national endeavour advocating passive resistance to British rule (taking a line through the Hungarian model of 1848), which was founded in Dublin by Arthur Griffith in 1905, prepared to contest every constituency against southern Parliamentarian and northern Unionist alike, the aim being sovereign independence and an island republic. The result of the election came on November 4, 1918. It showed an overwhelming victory for Sinn Féin. 'We Ourselves', as the phrase implies in the Irish language, had now to find somewhere to go when the bonfires had died down and the victory parades had passed away. All parades had previously been 'proclaimed' but a sinister change of emphasis had now occurred. For the Volunteers footdrill continued twice weekly, as usual, and on one momentous occasion 'manoeuvres', including a sham battle, were staged at Clohiny under the direction of Captain Jack Lynch. There were no guns in evidence. The R.I.C. held a watching brief with the object of note-taking and making arrests later on. Clohiny ('the ivied rock'), between Ballyvourney and Ballingeary, was the dead centre of the area, and four companies, including Inchigeela and Kilnamartyra, participated. And so they marched and manoeuvred and trained in anticipation of a day that might or might not come, and an opportunity that might or might not present itself; and what was lacking in precision and finesse was amply made up for by enthusiasm and a knowledge that their playing at the 'art' of warfare was no mercenary obeisance to established tradition but the last ditch in an effort to maintain the tottering remnants of racial integrity that was life of their life and faith of their faith. It was inevitable that they received lessons in drill that never graced the approved textbooks. Jack Lynch led his men across a field in a snappy, four-deep formation. He was justly proud of his ability and the formation and concentrated on maintaining the quick-march. Suddenly the

fence loomed up and the unexpectedness robbed his mind
of the correct command in such a case. Inspiration was slow
in coming as his 'army' waited with the tense expectancy of
raw recruits for the order that never came. 'Let ye swing
round like a gate!', he yelled in desperation as the front ranks
were beginning to telescope. A company of seasoned regimen-
tal soldiers would have been equal to the situation, but it
was well for the prestige of fighting men everywhere that
the ensuing scramble to maintain ranks happened on a
moonlit field in West Cork rather than in Pall Mall or Pennsylvania Avenue in the full light of day . . . .

> Angrier than the sea the shout
> Of Erin's hosts in wrath combined,
> When Terror heads Oppression's rout
> And Freedom cheers behind.
>> (Sir Samuel Ferguson: 'Aideen's Grave').

5

'Mr. Shakespeare Is Ready'

But Mr. David Lloyd George, British Prime Minister and Liberal Party leader, 'The Welsh Wizard' to his enemies, 'L.G.' to his friends, lost his unenviable job through emulating Ethelred the Unready! The 'P.M.' died in his tracks in 1922 having threatened all-out war on the Irish and the Turks, or, if you prefer, the 'Shinners' and the 'Bashi-Bazooks'. Is it Peace or is it War?, the man said to the tormented Arthur Griffith and conscience-stricken Michael Collins, exactly three years on from where we are now, as he clinched the Treaty Negotiations in December, 1921, to his own satisfaction, while his courier, with the sensationally dramatic name, waited in the wings to deliver the prepared missive to its final destination in Belfast. *Is it Peace?*, the ex-P.M. wrote in 1923 in his review of the situation, indicating that War was probably far from his mind. They say he was bluffing. But who was to know! The dilemma cost us a very regrettable though brief Civil War and the death of Ireland's greatest revolutionary at Béalnabláth. So, three years before that we were tentatively preparing for hostilities against the great British Empire which had just concluded a major war in Europe, while America's President Woodrow (What a name!) Wilson, whose heart had bled for big nations at war, became coyly evasive with regard to a pathetically small nation whose hard-working people had helped build his mighty country. How does one enter the Lion's den, then?. On tiptoe, or roaring like a mouse? . . . .

Two years further back . . . .

'Bob Holland of Inchicore said that two drunks who marched up the quays with them to Richmond Barracks after their arrest ended up deported, as did a Russian national, Antli Makapaltis'. (From *Frongoch, University of Revolution* . . . Seán O'Mahony, FDR Teoranta, 1987). Mr. Robert Holland, of 6 Riverdale Terrace, Inchicore, Dublin, said much more than that, about the events and aftermath of 1916, and he was very incisive and extremely witty about it. However, his memories remained just in the form of private notes and never saw any form of publication. More's the pity! One extract from his Frongoch experience is worth throwing in here, not for continuity but for reasons that will become evident in the text. It came to me, many years ago, I know not how . . .

The Camp was surrounded with wire entanglements and, at intervals of about fifty yards, a 'crow's nest', or elevated sentry-box, with searchlight equipment. Lights-out at nine o'clock. Each sentry would call at half-hour intervals: 'All's well, Number One; All's well Number Two', and so on around the camp. The sentry personnel were all men of the Home Guard. They were drawn from every county in England, Scotland and Wales. All were over the forty-years mark. Some were friendly, others not so. My hut mates were all older than me. The Hut Leader was a man by the name of Crayton (*Note:* There was no 'Crayton' among the official list of inmates at Frongoch. The nearest was 'Craven'). A candle-maker by trade, he worked in Lalor's on the Quay (*Note:* It will be remembered that so did Cathal Brugha). County Galway was well represented, especially Loughrea, and Fermoy had quite a few. One man, who sat and slept in a corner all by himself, was poor John Cooper. He was well into his fifties, spoke very little, and, in debates in the

Hut, took no sides. In fact he was held in a kind of suspicion. I never knew why. No one had cause to suspect him. It was only his silence. He never spoke of home (*Note:* Seán O'Mahony gives his address as 33 Lennox Street, Dublin, and his denomination as 'ICA', for Irish Citizen Army), or anything about the Insurrection, and it was well known that I could get more out of him than anyone else. He received no letters or parcels from home, but, after long persuasion, accepted a small amount of gifts from me. He had no money, and he had no 'vices', neither smoked nor drank. The only subject he took an interest in was National Socialism. He had all the Pros and Cons off to a fine art. He had question and answer for all its benefits for mankind. I believe he had read any and every book or article written by any author on this subject. He was a non-Catholic, and, I believe, not even born of Catholic parents. In fact he never once spoke of religion to me or anyone either in the prison (in Dublin) or the internment camp (in Wales). He said some prayers every time we prayed, removed his hat and knelt down just like the rest of us, and I would say that it was his open confession of not being a Roman Catholic, while still participating in the Rosary every night, that made the men suspicious of him. He would not attend Mass, and would remain in the Hut while it was on. One of the Galway men once said to him — 'Why not see a clergyman of your religion?'. He did not answer him. His hero was James Connolly, and he had fought with him in the G.P.O. He was eventually released and nobody solved the problem.

I will leave the Interment Camp for a while as I had promised myself and the other members of the Hut, if I was released and back in Dublin, I would try to contact Cooper. I found him in 1926. He was bent and stooped of shoulder, wearing a discarded clergyman's three-quarter (size) coat, black trousers, black leggings, black boots held together only with black threads but polished to the last, black slouch hat, stiff and dirty collar, and a string for a tie. He was in Camden Street and had an old attaché-case. I asked him how he was doing and got the answer I expected — 'I am doing a little peddling in small wares and can make enough to pay my digs'. He talked of the Insurrection, and the Black and Tan War, and the ultimate finish. He did not agree with the Treaty and remarked that it was only a postponement of hostilities, that another generation was being born to be a thorn in the British Empire's side, that complete and total defeat of herself and her Empire was our only salvation. 'She is preaching Christianity', he said, 'with the Bible in one hand while, with the other, she is writing prescriptions for new tortures and villany on the unfortunate people under her heel. All this has been carried on down the centuries, always the same tale to tell the world. Another atrocity cannot be committed under a democratic Government such as we have today. When I was a little boy this was said after the Famine, and when old people of that time were children they heard the same tale. I have lived to see the cloak of Democracy off, a word she (i.e. Britain) should remove from her Dictionary and replace with Hypocrisy. Why did she hysterically rush the executions of our Leaders in Sixteen, and even tie poor James Connolly in a chair when already he was mortally wounded? Why did she hush-hush the murders and atrocities that were committed at that time? We were told later that such happenings could not or would not take place again, but we saw still worse in 1919 to 1921' — and here he cited the brutal murder of Dick McKee, Peadar Clancy and McKelvey (*Note:* Some mistake here — Joe McKelvey was a Free State execution), the men hanging by handcuffs from the centre rail of military lorries and shot under the excuse that they were trying to escape, of the murder of Father Griffin (*Note:* Fr. Michael Griffin, of Barna, Co. Galway, was shot in November, 1920, to prevent his attendance at an American Court of Inquiry to which he had been summoned), the sacking and burning of Balbriggan. Poor John Cooper had all our history, day and date, off by heart.

I pressed him to take what little money I had in my pocket. With reluctance he did. He would not give me his address or promise to meet me again. We parted. The next time we met was at Synge Street Christian Brothers' Schools during the Elections of 1932, when we had a long chat. Our next meeting was in the recreation grounds of the South Dublin Union. It was no surprise to me to see John a pauper, for other men who had participated in '16 had already died and were buried as such. Others only escaped a pauper's grave through a few friends subscribing to give them a funeral. Here to me was history repeating itself. I had attended the funeral of Fitzharris, or 'Skin the Goat' as he was better known by. (*Note:* The reference is to the Phoenix Park murders in 1882). When he died in the S.D.U. we took his remains out by the Pig-Town Lane entrance. I was a young boy and I thought it bad form of the men to let him die in this institution. Little did I think that, when I became a man, the same thing would happen, but it did and is happening up to this day, September 29, 1949, and will continue to happen until all who fought and made sacrifices are dead, for no legislation has ever been introduced to save them from the terrible stigma — Pauper! He (John Cooper) had been in the institution some time and told me that he was in the Protestant Section. He had received the 1916 medal, the 'Black and Tan' medal and a pension of six shillings per week under the 1934 Act. Under the Poor Law Regulations he had to agree to five shillings per week being stopped out of his award. He told me that he went outside the Institution once a month when he got the four shillings (i.e. the balance), and his complaint was: Could the old system of Poor Law be changed now that we had our own elected Government? Being referring back to the laws invoked by 'Our Gracious Majesty, the King or Queen', etc. etc. — that was his big bug. The second bug was, under the Act the men in the beds on either side of him, who had fought in His or Her Majesty's Forces in South Africa or France, were enjoying the full British pension awarded to them, and the local authorities could not take or interfere with it in any way. In fact, they had a British Legion Committee visiting them, and poor John Cooper was in a hot spot.

I was at this time one of the County representatives on the Board, but as the Law was, could only carry it out. He had sympathy, but that is as far as it went. Every one of the members used the 'National Spirit' dope when it was advantageous to themselves, but to do a thing to elevate an inmate, whose only crime was to serve his Country, that was asking them too much. I brought John's case, and many other cases, to the notice of the Authorities, but could make no impression, and it still is the same and likely to remain the same until all the generation who fought for the portion of freedom we enjoy are dead. On the Board I had one friend, and although we had differences of opinion he was an untiring worker on the problem. He was one whole man, and he tried time and time again. We got no results. I published, and he, being Chairman of the Board (Alderman P.S. Doyle, T.D., P.C.), gave me latitude on every occasion and allowed me to make speeches in the Board Room at every opportunity, so that the Press would have a report and that our comrades in the Institution might get special treatment. Our Legislators never found time to bring in a special Bill to cater for this. Time passed on and to our discredit many a man who sacrificed home and position, and many a boy who sacrificed his career, found his reward in a pauper's bed in the S.D.U., with only the happy recollection that the Institution was in 1916 the Headquarters of the Fourth Battalion and Commandant Eamonn Ceannt. Dr. O'Dwyer, the R.M.S., one day told me that he would recommend Cooper for light work, and in this way would be able to have his pension restored to him. Cooper's job was to flush the sinks at either end of the landing in the block of buildings where he was housed. It might seem strange that Peadar Doyle (*Note:* There were actually two Dubliners of that name in Frongoch) and myself, being on the Board, could still not do anything, for the Law prevented us. Any motion put forward had to be sanctioned by the Minister for Local Government, and if we committed ourselves we were open to a surcharge at our own expense. (*Note:* Surprisingly the Minister for Local Government at the time was Seán T. O'Kelly, but, in fairness, it must be said that he was working against a hostile Senate with regard to Local Government matters. cf. *De Valera*, by T.P. Coogan, 1993). My last time to see poor John Cooper was when I brought him to have a photograph taken of all the surviving members of the G.P.O.

garrison in Croke Park in 1941. He died in 1941, and so passed on one of Ireland's best sons to his eternal reward. . . .
('I fought for my country' said he, grabbing his soul and
making for Eternity!).

*   *   *

Now, onwards once again . . .

Once upon a time there lived upon an island a merry and
innocent people, mostly shepherds and tillers of the earth.
They were republicans, like all primitive and simple souls;
they talked over their affairs under a tree. The island was
caught in a swarm of pirates; and the shepherds had to turn
themselves into rude warriors. At first they were utterly
broken down in blood and shame, and then, after years of
horror and humiliation, they gained a little and began to conquer, because they did not mind defeat. (G.K.Chesterton).

*   *   *

On the River Lee, beside the road between Macroom and
Inchigeela, there was (until the new Hydro-Electric Scheme
of 1953) a notable and extensive marsh known as 'The
Gaeragh' (from 'gaorthadh', a wooded river-valley). It began
at Toon's Bridge, just beyond where the Toon river joined
the Lee, and appeared as the outcome of a none too friendly union of the two rivers, with a maze of waterways
meandering in labyrinthine confusion among the tree-covered
islets. Midway in this three and a half miles of picturesque
disorder Gaeragh Bridge ventured a precarious crossing, appearing as a succession of diminutive bridges undulating between and over a succession of equally diminutive rivulets.
Macloneigh Bridge concluded that unruly state of affairs
where the adjacent sandpit, crowned with an ivied ruin and
graveyard, stood like an esker and showed the impress of far
higher water levels in far distant times. Such was the Gaeragh,
famed happy-hunting ground of illicit 'poteen' makers for
generations, a present peril to the inured and unwary, and
a veritable *Nirvana* for sportsmen in search of diversion

among the wildfowl. In such congenial surroundings, and far removed and secure from prying eyes, the Macroom Seventh Battalion, First Cork Brigade of the Irish Volunteers, was accustomed to hold its council meetings and deliberations during the years of national resurgence after the disastrous insurrection of 1916. So here, like a latter-day Robin Hood, Commandant Dan Corkery, newly returned from internment in Frongoch prison camp in North Wales, and having learned no loyalist lessons therefrom, mustered his merry men under the greenwood tree . . .

One day a fine big country lad was put into our cell (i.e. in Kilmainham Gaol after the Insurrection). There were seven of us in it. Murphy said loud enough for him to hear — 'He won't sleep crossways in this kipp!'. Pulling down my shoulder he whispered in my ear: 'Paddy (Daly), that's done it, if by jabers he is a bloody country peeler. I would bet my last few bob on that'. This big fellow looked at Murphy a moment, and then in a temper said: 'I am Dan Corkery of the Cork Volunteers'. Little Murphy from under my arm stuck out his head and said, 'and I am Dan McGrew from Kinnegad!'. Corkery told us all about the Kent family from Mallow (Fermoy) when he got the chance. He was impressed by the way the people gave us the feeling that we were not all alone. I made myself known to him after a few days. He could never couple up little Murphy as being a fighting Dublin man. Murphy would always say: 'The bullet that comes out of a Lee-Enfield is a .303 and it does not matter. They are all the same size no matter who presses the trigger, let him be a little fellow like me or a big fellow like you, only there is more of you to shoot at than me, so that makes the bloody louser that shot me up a sharp shooter — I suppose a Liberty boy in the Dublin Fusiliers. However, God gave me strength to live it down and that some just German will give him his reward when he returns from his furlough. Amen. Ah, no matter! When you list you have got to soldier, and when you join the Navy you have got to go to sea, but when you fight to free poor old Ireland you have got to do every bloody thing that John Bull thinks of. Well, no matter,

> Murphy, you are a son of Erin, and as the Orangeman's Hail
> Mary says backwards: "God bless the Pope, the holy man,
> and to Hell with the King and his ass-load of bloody devils,
> may God forgive me, Amen!". . . .
>
>   (From Bob Holland . . . *Frongoch Statement*).

The west country, eventually the Eighth Battalion, was still
graded as a sub-battalion of the Seventh and had not yet
grown to the extent that it needed a separate formation, the
companies that had been set up in the outlying districts being completely dependent on the parent Seventh. Captain
Tadhg Twohig's Ballyvourney Company kept in contact
through its First Lieutenant and Adjutant, Jerh ('Con Joe')
Lucey. Jerh travelled by bicycle carrying with him the minutes
of company meetings and brought back instructions, orders
and other communications from the Brigade Council in Cork
City, which were always sent directly to Macroom H.Q. This
unsatisfactory state of affairs continued until the rapid
development of the Volunteer movement, due to the Conscription scare in the Spring of 1918, necessitated the formation of new battalions and brigades all over the country.
So to Ballyvourney came Tomás MacCurtain himself on Whit
Sunday, 1918. Tomás came and Ballyvourney was the better
for his coming. Tomás went away and left not a void but
a fullness of renewed endeavour, a transcendental fire of the
spirit that eventually pervaded all elements of the community
and burned on unabated and with a singleness of purpose
long after the last echoes of the Civil War had died away
among the hills. A few days previously he had arrived in
Macroom accompanied by Adjutant Paddy Higgins. To grace
the occasion the Seventh Battalion abandoned the Gaeragh
and repaired to the home of the O'Connors, of Mullinroe,
a couple of miles north of the town. His arrival coincided
with the funeral of Volunteer Denis Quinlan, of Inchigeela,
son of an R.I.C. sergeant already deceased. There had been
a training session at Sleaveen, above the town. Two men, on

their way home, found young Quinlan lying dead by the road-side, his revolver nearby. He had shot himself. On Thursday night he had been on an arms raid to Enniskeane with Jerh Twohig (an uncle of the present writer). They made the journey on bicycles and procured a silver-plated revolver from the home of a Protestant family named Shorten (*Note:* The Shortens of West Cork are even still half Protestant, half Catholic). They returned (my uncle said) leisurely and in good spirits to Ballyvourney. On the following morning they separated, Quinlan holding on to the gun, and the next time my uncle saw him he was lying in a pool of blood on top of Sleaveen hill within sight of the Gaeragh. A rather curious incident at his funeral gives an idea of some conflict of emotions at the time. As the Tricolour was being pinned down on the grave, a woman, presumably a relative, snap-ped: 'Take that rag away from there!'. His uncle quietly replied: 'It may be a rag but it is going to stay there anyway!'. Many people, even staunch Sinn Féiners, were still hostile to the Volunteers, regarding it as a foolish and misguided youth movement that could only prejudice the constitutional efforts of other more established political parties.

Later that same day found Lord Mayor MacCurtain in earnest colloquy with the men of the sub-battalion at their headquarters in Renaniree. On the far side of the hill was Ballyvourney — the 'Capital of Irish Ireland'. The title had been conferred when local competitors had carried off most of the prizes at the first *Oireachtas* of the Gaelic League in Dublin in 1898. To see the place and attend a *Feis* the London branch of the League had organized an excursion at the turn of the century. He too had to see it. He was himself a traditional fiddle player of renown . . .

It was Ballyvourney's day of days — Whit Sunday. Anywhere else in the world it was Pentecost, or just another Sunday, but here an immemorial custom never failed to muster a crowd that literally packed the single street of Ballymakeera village, overflowed into shops and alley-ways, sidled into every nook and cranny and oozed onto the converging roadways, perpetually drifting back again like foam drawn irresistibly towards the centre of a whirlpool; crowds of merrymakers, promenaders, tinkers, traders, crowds who came to see the crowds, crowds who came with the laudable intention of paying homage at the revered and time-hallowed shrine of St. Gobnait, and the few, comparatively few, who succeeded. For weeks before, mothers had scared their erring offspring by threatening that they would 'not be let to the Whitchen'; but came the day with all hatchets buried for the time being. And while thimble-riggers, wheel-of-fortune spinners, and loud-voiced sellers of assorted knick-knacks and confectionery claimed the attention of young, very young, not so young and the temporarily rejuvenated, the most noteworthy personage in all that huge gathering wended his way unheralded and unnoticed. He was a figure apart, his face that of a man going towards the mystic Jerusalem of no return. At Renaniree he had been heartened by the quality of the 'pikes' and the earnest faces of the young men who had awaited his coming. But the General Election was still far ahead and much was to happen in the meantime to bring about the big change in civic feeling which the result of that election indicated beyond all shadow of doubt.

At the moment 'civic feeling was a mixed bag', my father said. The new Volunteers were concentrated mostly around the villages. The organization had spread itself on a personal basis, and those who continued as active members were mainly those who had been at school together. As they said of the playing fields of Eton, the Irish 'Troubles' were fought on the playgrounds of the national schools. The teachers (my father was one of them), though paid by the British Government, were known to be particularly patriotic. Unlike the R.I.C. the national teachers were a dangerous legacy at seventy-eight pounds sterling per annum. They inculcated ideas of freedom with the history lessons, a situation much maligned nowadays. The primary school age extended to seventeen and the brightest trained as 'monitors'. During the coming struggle those who took part were mainly between the ages of seventeen and twenty-two. The older men were mainly apathetic, some even openly hostile for a time. A certain section of the community (e.g. shopkeepers, business people and better off farmers), denoted rather contemptuously as *Ceithernaigh* (i.e. 'Kerns'), were still in favour of English rule. Doubtless they had their reasons. The country was undergoing an era of prosperity. Prices were exceptionally good particularly with regard to farm produce and livestock, due to war conditions, and those who stood to benefit thereby had no desire for 'trouble', meaning a lesser state of prosperity as the outcome of any form of agitation. Then there was a large number of followers of the above, farm hands, family retainers and associates, who probably had no ideas about anything, my father said. So, were it not for the threat of conscription earlier in the year it is just possible that the Volunteer movement might to a great extent have fizzled out, and that in spite of the efforts over the years of Sinn Féin and its paper, *The United Irishman*, as well as the Gaelic League and other societies, to correct a great canker of the national spirit which had spread its malignant growth over the nineteenth century — the lurid fact that the people of the country as a whole had become so used to the heel of oppression that they had become almost immune to the shame of it to the extent of developing a kind of slavish liking for it.

By year's end Sinn Féin would appear to be in a strong bargaining position due to the overwhelming victory in the General Election, though they were denied the right to send an emissary to the Paris Peace Conference at Versailles. Seán T. O'Kelly, later President of the Republic, held a watching brief as representative of Dáil Éireann in Paris. Against this the British had a large number of unemployed and bothersome ex-service men from the Great War, as well as a lot of undesirables in their many gaols . . .

The end of the War brought civil disorder, another and un-warranted police strike, a resumption of Irish terrorism and an increasing use of motor cars and firearms by criminals. Nearly five years of wholesale slaughter on the Western Front had apparently cheapened the value of human life.

(From *London's Armed Police*. Gould and Waldren, 1986).

In Ireland the chips were down and the wheel was spinning merrily!

6

Nineteen-Nineteen

On January 7, 1919, the decision was taken to convene 'Dáil Éireann' (prn. 'Dawl Ay-ran'), as the new constituent assembly, and on January 21 it was put into effect. There had been none such since the execrative Act of Union in 1800. The newly elected members met in the Mansion House, Dublin, and formally inaugurated the Government of the Irish Republic. Eamon de Valera, unemployed mathematics teacher and erstwhile professor at St. Patrick's College, Maynooth, was chosen as *Príomh-Aire* i.e. Chief Executive or President. This Dev achieved *in absentia*, which in translation means in Lincoln Gaol in the English midlands, from where he escaped and came home taking office on April the First. (*Note:* The escape has been extensively recorded, especially with regard to the part taken in it by Michael Collins, and the bad language used by both when the substitute key broke in the lock. However, an unknown item might be of further interest. The late John Madigan, of Freemount, a friend of the present writer, made a fortune as a farm contractor in Lincolnshire in the early Thirties. One of his clients, a local farmer, told John a strange story. As Dev swung, solo and morose, down the old Roman *Fosse Way* to Nottingham, your man overtook him with a cart-load of sheep on his way to market. He hoisted the 'Long Fellow' in among the baa-baas, and thus the President of the Irish Republic was transported into the country of Robin Hood. Dev had an unique way of accepting philosophically any humiliation for the purpose of a lifetime. It was probably his country rearing. Incidentally another significant acquaintance of John Madigan was Mrs. Margaret, Lady Thatcher. As a little girl he frequently gave her a drive to school, usually finding her sitting on a wall reading, perpetually reading. It makes one wonder as to what History is really made of!). From now on the Dáil had perforce to meet in secret while its members proceeded with their new-found responsibility of organizing the country's affairs, keeping their fingers crossed in anticipation of the inevitable repercussion. For the moment the cat was out and the mouse was playing. The British had large problems with world affairs in Paris until the signing of the Treaty of Versailles in May. Sinn Féin had twisted the lion's tail in real earnest. The violence of his reaction might be fairly assessed from the severity of the shock. But the time was not yet. The whole political world, friendly, hostile or indifferent, seemed to hold its breath, watching and waiting, while the new-born Republic struggled to find its feet and having found them essayed the first few steps in the general direction of what is musingly referred to as 'self-determination'. And so 1919 was a momentous year, a year of transition, a transition that was no fortuitous grasping at volatile opportunities but a clearly defined, premeditated trend towards maturity. Necessity ordained that the primary instinct of self preservation should come early to the young republic, and so it was also a year of intense preparation, a feverish clearing of the decks with a view to the impending struggle for continued existence. The veterans, the men who fought, told me, with the understatement peculiar to their kind, that there was 'no activity worth mentioning' during that year. Each battalion area set to the task of preparing for action. The stock piling was elementary. The 'arms race' began almost from scratch. Locally it was confined, or rather extended, to collecting shotguns and bicycles. The bikes, though useful, could have been done without just yet but the guns were a necessity and, as might be expected, the manner of acquiring them varied according to the predispositions of the owners. Some people handed them over willingly enough. Others made a show of resistance in order to impress the 'Law' in case of an awkward investigation later on. One young Volunteer, named John Lucey, had a peculiarly demoralizing experience at 'The Mills', Ballyvourney. The lady of the house was 'of the Quality', strong in mind and body, and he was a mere 'workman'. When he presented himself she was standing at the kitchen 'range' cooking breakfast, with a laden frying-pan in her hand. She had her back to him and he foolishly held a revolver in his hand. Let's call her 'Mary Kate'. In one move 'Mary Kate' swung and let him have the pan and its contents full in the face. He was carried out by his companion who reported to his officer for further orders. Many a proud owner sorely resented having to part company with a treasured possession. One man, at least, might be excused his bitterness. During the Truce he said: 'I gave them (the ''boys'') me fine double-barrel shotgun with the twishted barrels for shooting Black and Tans and they never gave it back to me!'. However, the artistic value of damask ('twist') engraving on sleek twin barrels became a very superficial asset to the man behind the gun as the leading 'Whippet' of a convoy raced, belching Vickers fire, along a straight, or a laden Crossley tender nosed around a bend into an ambush position; and by the time the serious business of 'shooting Black and Tans' had been brought to a satisfactory conclusion the abrasive action of home-made slugs and buckshot had done irreparable damage to many a weapon designed for a somewhat more refined but considerably less hazardous form of life taking. If the loss of the gun was great in the owner's eyes it was, after all, only a negligible contribution compared to that of the man who was to test and prove its inadequacy against the steel flanks of a 'Lancia', or its futile range-finding against a three-nought-three!

At a staff meeting of the First Cork Brigade, in Cork City, early in 1919, it was decided that, for maximum efficiency in all quarters, it was necessary to have a separate battalion on the extreme western approaches to the county. The ensuing Eighth Battalion area was destined to become a microcosm of the overall War of Independence right to the end of hostilities and a vital issue even in the misguided Civil War to follow. The system of appointment of officers from H.Q. had not yet been adopted generally. Election by the men themselves was the way it had to be. They chose men whom they respected and trusted, whose judgement they were prepared to accept, and under whose leadership they would give of their best. (*Note:* Todd Andrews and Ernie O'Malley showed disappointment at the outcome, and Donagh McNelis was disdainful in practice). Patrick O'Sullivan of Kilnamartyra (later a doctor in Aghada and deceased only a couple of years) became the brilliant Commandant of the Eighth Battalion. Veteran Dan Thady McSweeney, of Ballyvourney, was Vice-Commandant but (for mental health reasons) found himself unable to fulfill his commitment and handed over to Paddy ('Donagh Owen') O'Sullivan, also of Ballyvourney, who held the position right through to the end. The battalion area fell naturally into five company districts comprising Kilnamartyra, Ballyvourney, Coolea, Ballingeary and Inchigeela, denoted as A, B, C, D and E Coys., respectively, and headquarters was established at the home of Mr. Jack Sheehan, of Renaniree, whose son, Neilus, was to prove himself an efficient and resourceful adjutant to the battalion. (*Note:* He died only last year at the age of ninety-three. The last of his memoirs run through these pages as well as *The Dark Secret*). Each company then elected its own officers, viz. Captain, First and Second Lieutenants, Adjutant, Quarter-Master and Section-Leaders, and so completed its incorporation into the Army of the Republic. They were destined to frustrate, if not wholly defeat, the military might of the British Empire. It was as if the gallant but somewhat ludicrous Home Guard, 'Dad's Army' even to themselves, had pushed the invading Germans back into the English Channel.

> The Great War not only served to give military experience to a large number of Irish freedom fighters, it shifted people's perception of what was possible and impossible. War weariness had set in . . . the southern Irish decided to step up their campaign for independence.
>
> From *Monty: The Making of a General.* Nigel Hamilton, 1981).

The Spring of 1919 saw events taking a serious turn throughout the country. The necessity for securing arms brought frequent attacks on police barracks, and retaliation by the R.I.C. often resulted in fatalities on both sides. The police being Irish, our 'Troubles' may be said to have begun and ended with a civil war. 'The situation in Ireland was rapidly approaching a state of war and it seemed that no hope of a peaceful settlement remained'. (Dorothy Macardle in *The Irish Republic*). In Cork a general order was circulated from Brigade H.Q. to proceed with the attacks. Plans were duly drawn up by the Eighth Battalion, but a countermanding order from H.Q. prevented their being put into effect. This was due mainly to the recommendation of Donagh McNelis (Donnchadh Mac Niallghuis) who happened to be in the locality at the time, had brief access to all battalion council meetings and took a poor view of their initial attempts at a plan of campaign. McNelis was a North of Ireland man (from Malinbeg, Glencolumbkille, Co. Donegal) who had found it necessary, because of his political activities while working in Belfast, to transfer to Cork City. He stayed at the home of Mr. Denis Kelleher (future father-in-law to my uncle, Jerh Twohig), 28 Leitrim Street, and in the meantime continued to be an active member of the Volunteers. In November, 1918, his lodgings were raided by the R.I.C. and in the ensuing scuffle he shot and wounded a Head-Constable. Both he and Mr. Kelleher were taken to Cork City Gaol where the latter served a sentence of six months' imprisonment. McNelis himself was rescued by men from the city area. Posing as visitors they overpowered those of the warders who were known to be unfriendly to the movement, tied up the Sub-Chief Warder at the gate and made good their escape. So, to Ballyvourney came 'the wee man from the North', and it fell to the lot of the local company to look to his welfare during his enforced stay. He proved a light burden because he trusted more to his own resources, fought shy of people and while 'on the run' in the vicinity of Coomlomnachta, in the townland of Fuhirees beyond Coolea, preferred to sleep in outhouses or in a tent on the hill facing Buckley's house, with his revolver always handy, rather than in normal dwellings. (*Note:* The site of his outdoor tent is still pointed out by Miss Katie Buckley in a declivity among the rocks four hundred yards from her back door) . . . .

Old Mike Buckley knew him well, remembered him well after all the years. Old Mike was proud to have known 'Donnachadh'. You could see it in the gleam in his eyes, the indulgent smile around at the 'Station' crowd, and small wonder too! The old man went on remembering aloud as he sat at the breakfast table after the early morning house-Mass. The curate sat dumb as usual but taking it all in. The Parish Priest, Fr. Thomas O'Brien (the noted 'Tom O' of an older generation) puffed at his pipe, listening abstractedly. On one occasion he could remember having been under fire from the Tans himself, as a young lad in faraway Ballycotton by the sea. Maybe he was remembering now. Who could say! Old Mike rambled on lucidly reminiscent, conjuring up a vision of handsome, regular features, crisp curly hair, and a hard-set mouth that somehow belied the shy softness of the inscrutable brown eyes. 'He was a nice, quiet sort of a fella', said Old Mike, — 'you'd never think that he'd shoot a man!' 'Some fellas had a nice, quiet sort of a way of doing it', dryly commented Father Tom, and the memories languished and died . . .

Rather surprisingly McNelis soon faded out of the picture completely, retracing his rebellious steps to carry on the fight in his native surroundings. He was not the one to give in or to give up while anything remained to be fought for, and wherever he was he was sure to be a rebel. I have often wondered how he went in the Civil War, if at all. (*Note:* Unwittingly his name became involved in the many spurious stories associated with the death of Michael Collins at Béalnabláth, 22 August 1922. 'McNelis shot him!', I was told during my search for *The Dark Secret* — 'He was seen in the vicinity that day!'). However, the final chapter of his story appeared in *The Irish Press*, 21 December 1954. It came under the caption, 'HERO OF 1918 GAOL RESCUE DIES IN SLIGO'. It said

Veteran I.R.A. officer Donnchadh Mac Niallghuis, Rosses Point, Co. Sligo, who has died, was a central figure in a sensational rescue from Cork Gaol on November 11th, 1918. A Donegal man, Mr. Mac Niallghuis was a member of the Cork City Battalion, Irish Volunteers, in 1916. On the morning of November 4th, 1918, five R.I.C. men, one of whom was armed with a .38 Webley revolver, raided his lodgings at Leitrim Street, Cork. In the struggle which followed Head-Constable Clarke was seriously wounded, and it was only when armed reinforcements, under a District Inspector, arrived that Mac Niallghuis was finally overpowered and taken to Cork Gaol. The Brigade Staff, knowing what his fate would be if Clarke died, decided to rescue Mac Niallghuis who was acquainted of the plan by his brother, Fr. P. Mac Niallghuis and Florrie O'Donoghue. The rescue was carried out without a shot being fired. Waiting outside the gaol during the operation was the late Fr. Dominic, O.F.M. Cap., Brigade chaplain.

(*Note:* The two famous Capuchin friars, Fr. Dominic O'Connor and Fr. Albert Biddy, adhered to the Republican cause from beginning to end, functioning in the Four Courts, Dublin, during the start of the Civil War. Later they were expelled from the country, died in the U.S.A., and their bodies were returned to Ireland amidst extraordinary scenes of emotion).

*   *   *

Necessity, as the acknowledged mother of invention, in time of war is known to be mightily prolific. But when necessity is dire, as in the Irish War of Independence, the inventiveness then becomes an improvisation and the need of the moment, while giving forth many normal offspring according to opportunity and fecundity, may produce some weird if not totally monstrous issue. Nowadays, taken out of their context, those efforts of a former generation would appear to be practically all abnormal and deranged. One needs to bear in mind that we are considering a war fought at almost every level of combat development, with ancient weapons ranging both side by side with and against the most modern. (*Note:* Extreme examples from history would be the use of British fieldguns against the Zulus in 1879 and the Dervishes in 1885, all spear-wielding fanatics from both ends of the African continent. British historians regard the Battle of Omdurman, in 1898, as the scene of the last cavalry charge of the British Army, seeming to ignore the charge of the Lancers, from Marlborough Barracks, down O'Connell Street, Dublin, in 1916). The wonder of it is that such a short period of hostilities as the Irish 'Troubles' evolved within itself an almost complete range of development. In 1922, during the Truce, the gunners of *H.M.S. Barrington*, lying close inshore in Kenmare Bay, were pinned down effectively by heavy machine-gun and rifle fire from a task force on shore, but in the Summer of 1919 a closed door still presented a serious obstacle. That it was a barrack-door meant that it was being

regarded with active hostility by republican eyes. Such a door
had slammed for the last time at Ballyvourney in February,
1918, on a number of Volunteers who were trying to gain
entry by trickery. Only the force of an explosive charge, or
some similar agency, could open it again. A cannon would
do of course. There were two fronting the castle in Macroom
having been placed there, in an ornamental capacity, by Lord
Bantry some time after the Crimean War. Ten feet long and
several tons in weight, they sported in bas-relief the traditional crown of St. Edward surmounting the monogram
'G.R.' of one of the Georges, which suggests that the terrible twins may even have roared defiance at Napoleon at the
battle of Waterloo. They had been last fired on Tuesday, 29
June 1887, by the loyalists of Macroom to mark the golden
jubilee of Queen ('We are not amused!') Victoria, and despite
the efforts of budding theorists of the resurgence, were destined to remain forever silent. Monster muzzle-loaders, they had
been used to good effect against the notoriously tough greatcoats of the Czarist cavalrymen in the Crimea. That was an
era of change from muzzle-loaders to breech-loaders and
from solid ball to explosive shell, but the British militarists
still favoured the muzzle-loader. Necessity decreed that in
1919 one of them could still be effective with the materials
to hand, viz. 'black' powder and twenty-eight ounce, iron
playing bowls, for reducing a police barracks. To offset the
windage — the cannon had a bore of six inches — the bowls
would need to be enclosed in a cylindrical cannister like the
murderous grapeshot of former years. (*Note:* Unknown to
the theorists, a local historian, old Mr. Jeremiah O'Leary,
of the hardware store in the North Square, long since
vanished, told me, there was a stock of suitable cannon-balls
stored under the organ in the drawing-room of the Castle
itself). The idea has a curious association with a favourite
tale of St. Gobnait, the patron of Ballyvourney, who lived
in the sixth or seventh century. With her bowl, or 'bulla',
a smooth sphere of agate still extant and an exact replica

of a cannon-ball, she is said to have reduced the castle of the *bodach* (tyrant), an oppressor of the people, simply by standing on a vantage point beside her abbey at Gortnatubrid and hefting the rebounding missile across a quarter of a mile of the picturesque little valley. The castle was sited on a rock, still named for it, close to the Ballyvourney barracks and directly behind the later Coláiste Íosagáin preparatory college. So, *cherchez la femme!* — it remained but to fetch the lady and folklore would have had a spectacular realization in history. The 'lady', however, proved unco-operative. For one that had trundled up from the coast to Balaclava behind a double file of six horses, one farm cob and a jennet, optimistically introduced into the Castle grounds by Ballyvourney Company under Paddy Donagh Owen (he told it to me with many a laugh), in the dead of night, were totally inadequate. For security the animals had to be stationed half-way down the Park while a section armed with poles advanced on the nearest gun. But ne'er a budge would she budge, and had to be left regretfully pointing her dead snout into darkness and ghostly battles of other days.

In the realm of ideas again, the mountain brought forth the mouse. Bob Hallissey remembered the light brass cannon on top of Ross Castle, Killarney, that had been used by the Confederate garrison against the Cromwellians in 1652, when the latter brought flat-bottomed boats overland for its reduction, and the Protestant landowner and Gaelic poet, Pierce Ferriter, was hanged for conducting its defence. Playing safe the 'boys' decided to go and investigate on the following Sunday. Came Saturday and the morning paper to the O'Sullivan household. Mrs. O'Sullivan glanced over the news headlines and her son, Paddy, the Vice-Commandant, listened in silent dismay while she told of marauders at Ross Castle who had come as thieves in the night to deprive it of its brazen ornaments. He had been forestalled and to add to his chagrin his mother, all unawares, made a caustic remark about the value of a little old brass gun as a weapon of offence in these our times. The culprit was Commandant (later General) Seán Moylan. Many years later Commandant-General Ernie O'Malley, itinerant organizer for G.H.Q. and trouble-shooter for Michael Collins, was to report on the outcome in his book, *On Another Man's Wound*. The gun selected blew up at the second practice attempt. When all the pieces had fallen to earth and the billowing smoke had blown away, '"It would have made a fine landmine", said Seán Moylan, when he had ceased to curse', and Mrs. O'Sullivan was never a woman to say, 'I told you so!' (*Note:* Another of the guns, which had proved successful in practice, failed in timing as it was moved in a carriage along the railway line for an attempt on Rathmore Barracks, as described by Manus Moynihan in *Statement*, and a more extensive account of the O'Malley incident, as above, appears in *Kiskeam Versus The Empire*, by Fr. John O'Riordan, C.Ss.R.).

About Macroom Castle. It was one of the oldest inhabited castles in Ireland and also one of the most magnificent structures of domestic architecture in these adjacent countries. Originally erected by the O'Flynn clan (on an earlier foundation by the Norman Carews), who held extensive territories at one time in Muskerry (i.e. mid-Cork, known as *Múscraí Uí Fhloinn*, or Muskerry of the O'Flynns), and in Carbery (i.e. West-Cork), it then passed into the possession of the still more powerful Dermot McCarthy More (i.e. the 'Great') whose family mansion it became, and in this capacity it was for hundreds of years a stronghold of Gaelic Ireland against the invading Saxon. In the name of Queen Elizabeth the First, the matriarch who learned to confuse contrariness with arbitrariness, Sir Charles Wilmot attacked and captured it in 1602 and put all the defenders to the sword. Twenty years later the McCarthys regained their property. In 1650 the Castle was occupied by Dr. Boetius McEgan, Titular Bishop of Ross (West-Cork), at the head of a large Irish army, but in a general action which took place in the

Park before the Castle he was defeated by a Parliamentarian army under Lord Broghill, son of the Earl of Cork, and was later executed in front of Carrigadrohid Castle, four miles to the east on the River Lee, for refusing to persuade its Irish garrison to surrender. Dr. R. R. Madden, historian of the United Irishmen, mourns the patriotic prelate in his poem: 'The Mitred Martyr of Macroom':

> He died on the scaffold in front of those walls,
> Where blackness of ruin is seen from afar;
> And the gloom of its desolate aspect recalls
> The blackest of Broghill's achievements in war.

The owner of Macroom Castle was Lady Ardilaun, widow of the first Baron Ardilaun (Mr. Arthur Guinness), and a woman of considerable charity and culture (So said Mr. Jeremiah O'Leary, who knew her in the distant past). She lived in Dublin since her husband's death in 1915 . . . 'My father', she proudly wrote to the Town Park Committee of Macroom, 'was a direct descendant of Cormac McCarthy *Láidir* (i.e. the 'Strong'). The Castle from the time of Cormac McCarthy, born in 1411, has always remained in the possession of families allied by blood, except during periods of confiscation, after which it always came back to its original owners'. Lady Ardilaun was formerly the Hon. Olivia Charlotte White, a daughter of the third Earl of Bantry and sister of the fourth Earl, at whose death, in 1891, the 'Bantry' title became extinct. During the early 'Troubles' the Castle was in fact unoccupied except for a caretaker, a Mrs. McNally, and her teenage daughter. These two valiant ladies remained on at their post during the occupation of the Castle by the Auxiliaries (1920-1921), and found them 'very nice boys indeed' (the daughter told me when I spoke to her in Macroom in 1954), except for an occasional incursion into the sealed up store of Lady Ardilaun's furniture. And the window inside of which William Penn, founder of Pennsylvania and son of Admiral Penn, one of Cromwell's officers,

fight was on. A plan had been made for knocking a hole in the gable end and setting the building on fire with cans of oil and wood shavings. Patsy Lynch and Neilus O'Reilly, of Ballyvourney, ran the gauntlet of fire but their crowbars failed to make an impression. (Late in life Patsy still marvelled at the solidity of the masonry). Meanwhile a drunk had appeared on the scene. He was an ex-soldier. (*Note:* This was the only type of real drunk I remember from my childhood, except an occasional farmer, on the occasion of the monthly fair-day, lying in his cart and being led home by the horse. It is a strange thought that school children are noted alchoholics at the present time, which makes it a moot point as to what extent our world has advanced in the meantime; and the very latest directive from the Department of Education is that all school children are to be trained equally with gift-enticement rather than any form of correction. All of which makes Dean Swift so exquisitely prophetic in *Gulliver's Travels,* with the horse-sense of the 'Houyhnhnms' as against the 'Yahoos'). At Inchigeela the 'plastered' ex-soldier minced his way down the middle of the road by the barracks, and was right in it before he noticed anything. At first he thought that the sergeant was having fun at his expense with the shots and 'Verey' lights. He began to rail at the sergeant. Then he noticed the attackers and his bemused mind slowly grasped the situation. Bullets were whining angrily about him but booze, and the proud memory of other days, made him oblivious to the danger. Standing in the midst of it all he held forth encouraging the 'boys' to 'fire away', abusing the sergeant, or just talking to himself congratulating himself on his ability to come safely through another terrible war.

There have been different accounts of how the fray at Inchigeela ended, and likewise different tellings of why it ended abruptly and on an inconclusive note. One heard references to a mysterious, false order to retreat at a crucial moment passed on by an unauthorized and nervous man, and by listening a little closer one occasionally caught the whisper of a name. (Patsy Lynch gave me the name of a business associate of my father, but I felt he was more chagrined than sure). However, the boys withdrew more or less in disarray, but the police kept up spasmodic rifle fire for some hours. The spirited Sergeant Maunsell was an elderly man due to retire shortly on pension. His wife and family were in the barracks at the time of the attack. When this became known it was decided to call off the operation. Constable Michael Moore was promoted immediately afterwards for his action in defence of the barracks. On the following March 7 Inchigeela was attacked for a second time, but now the building was protected with barbed wire, loopholes and steel-shuttered windows. The I.R.A. withdrew almost without firing a shot, even though they had a landmine ready to blow in the door and some officers had come from Cork City H.Q. to direct the operation. After yet another futile attempt the place was ignored until the police were withdrawn, late in the year, when their influence in these isolated country posts had become largely nominal. But fate dogged the sergeant. I was told that he had been approached several times to tender his resignation. In that case his pension would have been forfeit, and my father, who was a native of the place, said that Dan Maunsell was a very obstinate man. On a Saturday evening in August he was ambushed and shot dead. Unknown to his attackers he had handed in his resignation on the previous day, but I have heard this strongly denied. He had been in Corcoran's Hotel drinking. Two local Volunteers took up a position in Brophy's farmyard, at the eastern end of the village street, and opposite the church. They were Ted Quinlan, son of a deceased R.I.C. sergeant, and whose brother had shot himself at Macroom, and Mick ('Seán Rua') O'Sullivan (according to the late Garda Jerh Buckley of Kilbarry). As Maunsell left the hotel by a side door (which is still there) they fired and killed him.

On that Saturday night Sergeant Maunsell, of the R.I.C. post in Inchigeela, was shot dead, and on Sunday morning one lorry load of police, with the County Inspector, left Bandon for Inchigeela, passing Lissarda on the way. Their passing was noted and a hurried mobilisation of the attacking force was called in order to engage them on their return . . . The cart was pushed across the road by Willie Powell, later O/C 'G' Company, and the order 'Hands Up!' . . . The enemy suffered some wounded but the attackers lost one fine soldier in Michael Galvin, who was Q/M of 'H' Company, and was shot through the head while leading the attack . . .

(From *The Story Of The 7th*, by Charlie Browne).

Michael Galvin, father of two, was in fact brother to the future Bishop Ned Galvin, of the Maynooth Mission to China, and his death was to mark the more noted anniversary of Michael Collins, who was killed exactly two years later, 22 August, 1922.

Now, back to the scheme of things. The most outstanding sign of a subjugated people must surely be a police force recruited from among the people themselves and paid for their loyalty to the occupying power. (*Note:* In a recent film, *China Hand*, the British police superintendant, at a parade, says to the reluctant visitor: 'I wanted you to see us THERE! The Royal Hong Kong Police, the best there bloody well is, any place, any time. Down there', pointing with his cane to the parade-ground, 'is pride in the uniform and in the job!'. I wonder! What I saw was row after row of an actual police parade of little screwed-up oriental faces, many wearing glasses, little light-weight men carrying carbines with fixed bayonets, and a big, sword-wielding, hard-jawed British officer shouting orders in the van). Apart from the emotive issue of the Royal Ulster Constabulary of the present time, one remembers Major Quisling, the notorious Nazi collaborator of World War Two, who died in 1945 and whose name was already appearing symbolically in the *Oxford Dictionary* of 1951. The Royal Irish Constabulary was founded by Sir Robert Peel during his term of office as Secretary for Ireland, 1812-1818. Ever afterwards they were to be known

and despised as 'Peelers'. Peel's objective had been 'the protection of life and property', and thereafter his men were
armed with lethal weapons for the protection of their own
lives. The unfortunate peeler became a blundering 'Punch'
in the comedy of errors which was the Irish political scene
throughout the subsequent century. The butt of many a
scathing caricature and the subject of many a comic song
('The Peeler and the Goat', for example), he is represented
in books and plays as bustling and bristling his way indig-
nantly through it all (*Note:* Oddly enough P. G. Wodehouse
treated his British policeman in a similar manner); but he
protracted the work of subjugation as no other organization could have done. Originally the R.I.C. took over from
the military and volunteer yeomanry. A century later, almost
to the year, they had to hand back to the military and
volunteer 'Black and Tans', who in turn conceded place to
the people's volunteer police who succeeded, for a time, in
maintaining law and order within the system. Recruiting for
the R.I.C. had been suspended on the outbreak of the Great
War in 1914. So had resignations on pension. As many of
the younger members went off to war the force was no longer
at full strength. After the Easter Rising, 1916, 'old sweats'
were sent out to R.I.C. barracks or stationed in vacant houses
nearby. They were too old to go to France. A bunch of them
were installed in Mount Massey, Macroom, and kept guard
over the courthouse in the town. These were 'the military'
who used to raid in 1917-18. But when the war was over a
change came. The First Manchester Regiment arrived at the
military barracks, Ballincollig, in June of 1920. A platoon
was sent to Ballyvourney and established themselves in the
doctor's house, *The Chalet*, between Ballymakeera and The
Mills. The affair at Beál a' Ghleanna ('The Mouth of the
Glen') had brought the district into the picture for good or
ill. In Ballyvourney Sergeant ('The Skipper') Flynn was at
the helm. He was an elderly man of a highly-strung
disposition, with apparently very little tact or even practical

intelligence, who succeeded in making himself obnoxious to many. One member of his force, Constable Sadlier, from Limerick, managed to remain on good terms with everybody. (*Note:* His son, Canon Jim Sadlier, was a fellow student in Maynooth and died recently). Flynn was always ready, I was told, to pry into and investigate every little incident. Small boys, some of whom are still alive, used to throw stones at him from behind fences. Constable Roger Ryan, from Tipperary, was, if anything, more seriously disliked. As against the officiousness of Flynn, he was the inveterate bully. On March 9, 1920, Sergeant Flynn was attacked at Rath Hill, on the road to Renaniree, and deprived of his revolver, by Jamie Moynihan, Captain of C (Coolea) Company, and Dan Sullivan, First Lieutenant of B (Ballyvourney) Company. In the scuffle the sergeant was wounded in the leg. In the ensuing *Hue and Cry* Dan and his brother were arrested and taken to Cork Gaol. A few days later four members of B Company lay in wait at the same spot for four policemen who had gone on patrol. The peelers became suspicious, skipped their customary route and succeeded in reaching their home base across country. And so it went on.

'The Skipper' had been disabled and was honourably discharged from the force. He was replaced by Sergeant Phelan, who kept a low profile, hardly ever left the barracks and, as far as was known, never sent in an adverse report to the British authorities. Under his charge were two Black and Tans. This strange, quasi-historical breed of law-enforcement agent began to arrive in Ireland on March 25, 1920 (cf. Chapter Six), and were meant to bolster up the morale of the somewhat disorganized and greatly depleted police force. The R.I.C. were still needed to act in a guiding capacity for the British Army. With regard to the Black and Tans, Dorothy Macardle has this to say in *The Irish Republic:* 'The dispatch of this new force to Ireland helped to relieve England of a very dangerous type of unemployable'. The name of 'Old Nick' himself was never held in more odium and fear. (*Note:* Old Pats Casey, of Ballymakeera, was an inveterate card player even into my time, but a nervous night traveller. They said, as they did about so many, that he 'was afraid of the fairies'. Rambling home one night he was set upon and given a really bad fright by some play-actor, and he told his wife: 'Well, thanks be to God it was a fairy and not a Tan!'). However, the two specimens sent out to Ballyvourney, on Saturday, March 27, must have been cast-offs, certainly an insult to the proven initiative of the Eighth Battalion. A man of reasonable observation told me categorically that there were no Tans in Ballyvourney — definitely no Tans! Still, there they were, day after day (said my father, a man of keen observation), leaning against the wall by the barrack-gate, smoking poisonous *Woodbines*, looking very fed up, never venturing further and never doin' nothin'. ('Chokey was never loike this, mite!'). Then, of course, one of them died, as will be recorded later. Perhaps the other died also. (*Note:* In the Fifties 'The Skipper's' widow, son and daughter, came from afar to see the spot where 'Daddy' had been wounded in the long ago. Unfortunately they inquired of Jamie Moynihan, who was hay-making in a nearby field. He 'put the run on them', as he told me later that evening, with roars and maledictions, at which he was adept).

8

Trial by Experiment: April - June, 1920

'History is bunk!', said Henry Ford. 'The history of the world is but the biography of great men', said Thomas Carlyle. 'History is just the portrayal of crimes and misfortunes', said Voltaire. 'The history of England is the history of progress', said Lord Macaulay. 'Irish history never happened', say the reformers of our time. 'An Englishman never remembers history, an Irishman never forgets it, and an American never reads it', said somebody I forget, perhaps myself. Rephrasing this last, an Englishman cannot afford to be logical about history, an Irishman cannot help it, and an American just does not feel the need to be. There are other peoples involved in history besides ourselves, and other nations great and small. (*Note:* The black American writer, Alex Haley (*Roots*), went to Africa to look for his history. He landed in my African country, the Gambia, which has no history but British, and is a conglomerate of very interesting tribes, mainly Jollof, Jola, Mandingo, Serer, Serehuli and especially an outstanding group, which stretched across the continent, known as Fula or Fulani. He discovered that they had one thing in common, a 'national' hero named 'Kunta Kinte', which he naturally made his own direct ancestor and transported him to America, the land of black opportunity.

Unfortunately for historical accuracy, Kunta Kinte was a mythical hero practically identical in status with our own Cúchulainn, and I had often been regaled with stories of him in class by my black students). In this country we tend to overlook the history of other countries. (*Note:* In an effort to correct this tendency, at least to my own satisfaction, a quarter of a century ago, I began to compose a series of verse histories, beginning with Ireland, then America and England, intending to go on to France, Germany, Australia and the Church, until I noticed that people tended to regard the idea as rather silly). The lesson of History, as much as any other lesson set to tax the human intellect, whose *raison d'être* is precisely to be taxed by lessons, has its natural culmination also, conceding place only to the pressure of the fact that the super-eminent logic in any lesson is the remembering of it . . .

Throughout Ireland, the New Year of 1920 had been heralded in to unseasonal and unwonted sounds. A 'Reign of Terror' (that timeless phrase from the bloody and fratricidal 'French Revolution' of which the French seem even still to be inordinately proud) was getting under way. No rejoicing bells to ring in the new. They were conspicuously absent. If, here and there, one did ring out to shatter the ominous silence, it was either an alarm bell or a funeral bell — some victim as likely as not. No joy in the people anymore — a hunted people listening for the rumble of lorries or the distant clatter of shots. That is how they recalled it for me in the Fifties even beyond the traumatic experience of a second World War endured beyond endurance, and beyond belief, by the common people in the land of the 'old enemy'. But away back then there was to be no public demonstration of rejoicing again in this country until the removal of curfew at the Truce of 11 July 1921.

Has anyone heard of a Black and Tan dying a natural death? Surprisingly, on the night of 4 April 1920, in the police barracks at The Mills, Ballyvourney, one of the doleful pair showed that he at least was subject to some of the ills 'that flesh is heir to', and that British occupation of our country had come to a sorry pass. He had been there just over a week. They buried him, through force of circumstances, in the backyard. Shades of Sir John Moore!

> 'We buried him darkly at dead of night,
> The sods with our bayonets turning',
> For we could not go out with those 'diehards' about,
> And the Courthouse so brightly burning!

Brigade H.Q. had ordered the Courthouse destroyed. It was a potential fortress for incoming enemy personnel. A police barracks at one time, a courthouse more recently, it stood in the private demesne of the landlord's residence, the Great House, occupied by the hated Colthursts for two and a half centuries. Sometime in the past, probably during the 'Whiteboy' disturbances of the Eighteen-Twenties, it had been rendered impregnable to attack, its windows steel-shuttered and barred. It certainly looked formidable, even in its stillness and vacancy still breathing life and emotion, somehow enhancing, in spite of its history, that little neck of the woods in which it sheltered. Today one has only to stand beside its ruins to get that certain feeling, to sense that awesome, vibrant, preinhabited air. There is always something poignant and touching — and dangerous — in the passing of a giant; monsters of stone or metal or plant life, mammoths of prairie or jungle, monarchs of the prize-ring, mighty men of history or mythology . . . Cúchulainn, Achilles of the Celtic 'Ulster Cycle', hero of the 'Red Branch', in his death-throes tied to a pillar-stone, his enemies fearful to approach for the hero-light that came on him in battle was still shining above his head. The Courthouse, a stronghold of the Ascendancy class, in its passing, near tragedy. Four men, the Commandant, O'Sullivan, the Captain, Moynihan, the brothers Lucey. One hundred and twenty gallons of petrol were deemed necessary to reduce it to ashes. One can might have done. Someone who had still to hear of the volatile quality of petrol, the quick evaporation, the penetrating fumes, LIT HIS PIPE. The four were upstairs, trapped. The only way lay downwards. The captain spied an opening and the others followed somehow. Three weeks of agony at 'Ben's' with the soldiers looking for them and the 'Cumann na mBan' (the quasi-militant 'Organization of the Women') doing their level best. Then the North Infirmary (now defunct) in Cork City. The R.I.C., in their barracks just across the fence, had not dared to interfere. Their Verey-light signals, little shooting stars, had faded in the blaze of the midnight sun.

The Coffey family, from Kilgarvan, Co. Kerry, had been squatting in the building for some months previously, and had been left undisturbed. Late at night they heard a commotion on the doorstep. Mrs. Coffey took it philosophically and prepared to leave. Before doing so she rolled her baby (Mrs. Diarmuid Crowley in my time) onto one arm, reached up to the mantelpiece for the bottle of Holy Water and shook it liberally over the men who stood before her, shamefaced and apologetic for having to disturb her and her family at such an unreasonable hour. 'God bless ye, boys!', she murmured and went out into the open lawn. In a few minutes the four were human torches stumbling crazily across the hallway of the savagely burning building. The initial roar had been as of a blaze in a mighty chimney of the Cyclops, and ten stupefying seconds later the Courthouse — like a miniature castle it was and is — screamed and writhed in its death agony as it was engulfed in flames. Somewhere in its infernal maw were four human beings. Mesmerized the men around watched the fire-belching door posts, at the top of the stone steps, as if they expected Lucifer himself to appear in a cascade of acrid-smelling brimstone. Four veritable demons charged out, their cries demoniacal, their words despairing, piteous, like those of the eternally lost . . .

Beside the Courthouse, in fact attached to it, the Great House itself was shuddering to its foundations, but its magnificence gained it a temporary respite. The massive appearance, the imposing French and bay windows, the ornate hall-door, the white stucco ceilings, the oak panelling, the stock of beautiful period furniture, the Carrara marble fireplaces, all tore at the heart-strings and made far more difficult the decision to destroy it, to consign it to the one element it could not withstand, having sheltered people from the elements for so long. . . .

That team included a young County Cork baronet, Sir George Colthurst, whose marriage took place in the same month — August, 1881 — as Nathaniel Hone's death. The wedding, in Cork City, was a great event, for the bridegroom was very popular; he was not only a cricketing hero but active in many philanthropic enterprises, particularly those aimed at providing employment and relieving the agrarian distress. He was also a considerable land-owner in the county and heir, through his mother, to the celebrated Blarney Castle; while his bride, Miss Edith Morris, was the daughter of another prominent County Cork family. The day was perfect; there was a line of nearly two hundred carriages outside the newly-completed St. Fin Barre's Church of Ireland Cathedral. The guests included most of the peers and peeresses of County Cork: the Bandons, the Donerailes, the Carberys, the Fermoys . . . Later that evening, in the opposite corner of the county, some fifty of the tenants of Sir George's Ballyvourney estate together with their womenfolk and children celebrated his marriage with a bonfire and barrels of porter, with singing and dancing to a fiddler. The Ballyvourney lands, which were more than twenty miles away from the principal Colthurst estate, had caused Sir George a certain amount of trouble shortly before his wedding; there had been the usual demand for a reduction of rent, and though he had offered his tenants a reduction of 15%, only a few of them had been willing to accept this. The rest had combined to hold out for more, but he had broken the combination by taking legal proceedings against the ringleaders. The outdoor celebration on his wedding night might have seemed like a happy ending to the affair, but at eleven o'clock, when it was in full swing, the revellers were suddenly surrounded by armed men with blackened faces who opened fire on them, wounding several. Others were beaten up with heavy sticks by their assailants, who then proceeded to drink what remained of the porter. On hearing of the outrage, Sir George and Lady Colthurst interrupted their honeymoon to visit the people who were injured, taking a doctor with them to attend to their wounds. A newspaper reporter who accompanied them to Ballyvourney saw a woman bless the young baronet and his bride. He also noticed that Sir George was building a fine new house for one of his tenants . . .

(From *Twilight Of The Ascendancy*, by Mark Bence-Jones, 1987).

As always, it is the way one tells the story. There is an alternative and quite contradictory account of the Colthurst family in Ballyvourney to be gleaned from the author's *Filí An tSuláin*, a history of Gaelic poetry where the 'Hidden Ireland', the soul of the true Ireland, its suffering and deprivation, is laid bare. In fact, the Colthurst estate in Ballyvourney was grabbed from the O'Herlihy family, the ancient *airchinnigh*, hereditary stewards of the monastery of St. Gobnait, from the early centuries of Christianity. But one needs to know the language, and the history!

The controversy over the burning of the Great House raged on for awhile (the men were still arguing about it thirty years later!) until the final curt communication from H.Q. brought forth a compromise and a suspended sentence. The danger of its being occupied by the enemy was great. So, H.Q. said that if it were inspected it had to go. On 9 June 1920 some British Army officers came and looked it over. The watcher on duty reported, and that night the Great House blazed. The owner, Mr. Willie George Williams, did not have an opportunity (he told me) of salvaging anything, not even the beautiful 'Grandfather' clock which stood by the wide, white staircase in the spacious hallway. But the needs of the time called for swift and decisive action. The Glebe House, Inchigeela, had met the same fate just one week before. (*Note:* In 1885 the Williams family from Macroom, originally from Wales, bought the business premises at 'The Mills' which had been set up in the converted coach-house by a family from Scotland, named Chisholm. By that time the Colthursts had retired to their mansion beside Blarney Castle, where they still reside, and used the Great House at 'The Mills' merely as a hunting-lodge. In 1916 Willie George Williams bought the Great House, which by then had come into the possession of a man named Hyde from Mallow. Subsequent to the inauguration of the Irish Free State, in 1922, Willie George was fully compensated for his loss, but he still complained particularly with regard to the contents. However, I was told by the 'opposition' that if he had removed even one article, e.g. the 'Grandfather' clock, he would have lost all. Once again, it depends on who's telling the story!) The present incumbent is Mr. Dónal Scannell, ex-Cork county footballer, from Ballymakeera Village, who is in the process of trying to restore the Courthouse, known locally as the 'Castle'. The Great House has completely vanished . . .

The nemesis of these great and beautiful buildings and others still to share a similar fate and disintegrate in billowing smoke and searing flame was, strange to say, a little iron-roofed shack hidden away in an alcove behind the village of Ballymakeera. Who would have believed it! The corrugated roof red with rust, the crumbling walls enclosing two small rooms, one of which contained a rickety deal table, some chairs and an old-style 'settle', all, such as it was, glorying in the now historic name of 'Liberty Hall'. (*Note:* It was from Liberty Hall, Dublin, that the Irish Citizen Army, under James Connolly, set out in 1916 for their rendezvous at the G.P.O., leaving their proud banner, 'We Serve Neither King

Nor Kaiser But Ireland', to flutter above the doorway). Headquarters, clubhouse, meeting place, tea-rooms, rest-house,
according to the occasion and need, 'Liberty Hall',
Ballyvourney, vibrated and hummed with sedition
throughout its meagre few cubic feet of air-space. Its new
spirit had been taking shape within the ambit of the newest
meaning, since Cork's Lord Mayor, Terence MacSwiney (who
had succeeded Tomás MacCurtain, murdered by the R.I.C.
in his home, and in the presence of his family, on the morning of Saturday, 20 March 1920) had sat at its table and
presided at its deliberations, leaving a projection of his gallant
spirit when he went away to prove his personal dictum that
'not all the armies of all the empires on earth can crush the
spirit of one true man'. Poor Terry! His idealism became
transformed into a tentative realism when 'Liberty Hall' em-
barked on the manufacture of munitions of war. This activity comprised the preparation of canister bombs (paint
tins filled with gun-cotton, detonators and short fuses, all
packed in concrete), the running and moulding of lead into
slugs for the shotguns, and the filling of cartridges. Gun-
cotton being in short supply, the antiquated 'black powder',
which derived its name and colour from its charcoal content, was being widely substituted for it. Instructions had
been circulated on the manufacture of this kind of gun-
powder. As distinct from the 'smokeless' types, the 'black
powder' was a mechanical mixture of saltpetre, charcoal and
sulphur approximately in the proportion of 74-14-12. The
saltpetre and sulphur were obtained from friendly chemists
in the towns, the making of charcoal, an ancient art in
Ireland, being carried out in various locations by the I.R.A.
themselves, the nearest to Ballyvourney being at Fileadown,
Glenflesk, Co. Kerry. The material used there was black alder,
but the decomposition by heat was induced in large metal
pots (Glenflesk had a noted iron-works from the long ago)
rather than the ancient process of sealing off the wood with
viscous clay, in the form of a beehive, before igniting. The

subsequent experiments in compounding the ingredients were carried out in a cave (still to be seen) near the 'Robber's Den'. The black powder thus obtained proved more dangerous to handle than more modern and more powerful explosives. Cartridges were generally filled with it and sometimes a burst gun barrel was the outcome. Once in a while fingers or hands were blown off in the act of shaping a primitive bomb. In the initial test of the product a filled lemonade bottle, with detonator and fuse attached, was embedded in the surface of the road at Fileadown. It left a crater seven feet in diameter, said Mike Donoghue, Intelligence Officer to the Glenflesk (D) Company, No. 2 Battalion, East Kerry Brigade of the I.R.A. (cf. *The Dark Secret*). Eventually, rather effective landmines were constructed from sections of drainpipe filled with black powder, closed at both ends with iron plates and secured with a through bolt.

The manner of making slugs or buckshot has a quaint interest all its own. A simple tool, akin to a pliers, was used. It was easily produced at iron foundries throughout the country, Horgan's, of Firville near Macroom, doing the job for the mid-Cork region. The jaws of the implement were two concave and complementary semi-spheres so that when closed in the molten lead and opened again a round pellet dropped into the cooling water. (*Note:* The regular 'sieve' process used by shot manufacturers either was impracticable or did not occur to them). Each pellet had a wee tail, like a tadpole, where the surplus lead had been squeezed through a special groove in the pliers. The removal of these caudal appendages was regular fatigue duty for the rank and file of the Volunteers. So it came about that to have three fingers of the left hand (or right, if one happened to be a 'kitogue') worn from filing was a tell-tale mark of a Republican, said Captain Patsy Lynch. 'If the opposition only knew', he said, 'they could have had us all!' But, then, Patsy was an inveterate joker with a permanent twinkle in his eye.

*   *   *

Half a Company of the 17th Lancers moved out to Liscarroll (from Buttevant) and took up quarters under canvas within the shelter of the old ruins of the Castle, which had been lying derelict since the wars of 1640-1650. This garrison immediately set to work to fortify their post by means of sandbags and barbed wire, with the result that, within a few weeks, they had the place made into an impregnable fortress. Remember the armament of the Volunteers, at this time, was not sufficient even to attack an ordinary cottage. Each company would have about 150 rounds of buckshot-loaded cartridges for the shotguns, and perhaps about six rounds for each revolver. It is difficult now to realise the mentality of the youth of that time, who were prepared, even with this poor armament to face undaunted the might of the British Empire.

(*Official Statement:* Commandant Paddy O'Brien, Liscarroll).

9

Trial by Endeavour:
July - September, 1920

So, 'Liberty Hall' watched and waited. Its name was borrowed, its history likewise, until it should have made its own. However, the contribution to date was little more than policy planning for Sinn Féin, and, as noted, the manufacture of munitions of war for the I.R.A. From first to last it had maintained its position of legal anonimity, never raided, never even getting the eye of suspicion from police or military. The policy emanating from its bedraggled *ambiance* was exclusive, very much within the meaning of the term 'Sinn Féin'. The avowed objective was a renewal of racial pride and self-confidence in an ancient people among whom these intangibles had become largely decadent for generations. The Liberty Halls throughout the country had set themselves to squeeze the last significant drop out of the expression 'Sinn Féin'. (*Note:* The expression was introduced by Arthur Griffith in 1905 when he propounded his new policy of passive resistance to English rule in Ireland by means of a national assembly in Dublin which would set up its own tribunals in place of the foreign courts of Law. The expression has had varied interpretations. It is the plural of 'mé féin', meaning 'I self', so, literally it is 'We self'. It is usually stated to mean 'we ourselves', but is also rendered, e.g. by *simpatico* British historian, Robert Kee, in his history of Ireland which he named *The Green Flag*, as 'Ourselves Alone'. In the long ago my father heard a Gaelic speaker trying to explain it, but when English words failed him he blurted out: 'Sinn Féin — Sinn Féin!' Its political philosophy was so insidious that British diplomacy always identified it with the physical force element in the rebellion, and is still doing so to the present day, while American public opinion, at last bestirring itself to reality, is labelling this as hypocrisy 'even as we speak'. Towards the policy of self-respect, stage-Irishry was discountenanced in any and every form. The play, *Handy Andy*, performed by a Dublin travelling company, caused a near riot in the town of Macroom. (*Note:* It is always a source of amazement to me to think that the 'stage-Irishman' image was created even before the Famine. I have failed to imagine the rollicking, hard-drinking, devil-may-care, song-and-dance Irishman, in a comic outfit, living in this country in 1840. But such was the idea of two famous writers, contemporaries and fellow workers, whose very names sound as if they were a line from a ballad of the *genre*. They were Lover and Lever, if you'll pardon the pun, to wit, Samuel Lover and Charles Lever. Lover's songs, e.g. 'Molly Bawn', 'The Low-backed Car', and many others, as well as his stage-craft, were emulated to a pardonable extent by Percy French, and Lever's novels fixed the 'Irishman' image world-wide, despite the starkness of the history and social conditions. All three were Protestant. Sinn Féin wasn't having any!). The song, 'Tipperary', famous foot-slog of the British Expeditionary Force in Europe during the Great War, found itself an abomination. Temperance was given a high priority to the extent that for a Volunteer to be seen entering a licensed premises came to be a slur on the organization. (*Note:* Fr. Mathew would have liked Sinn Féin!). Indeed, the phrase, 'Belonging to the Hall', had taken on a new and passionate meaning since the ambivalent, or ambiguous, days of the Ancient Order of Hibernians, revived by 'Wee Joey'

1a. Macroom Castle *circa* 1890.

Macroom Castle housed a company of British Auxiliaries
1920

1b. Macroom Castle, 1920–1921.

I naoí gcuimne

Tomás Ceannt   Risteard Ceannt

A fuair bás ar son poblacht na h-Éireann.
beal taine
1916.

bán árd

2. In memory of the gallant and tragic Kent family of
Bawnard, Castlelyons, Co. Cork.

3a. Mrs. Jack Lynch at a
hundred and two (1993). She
sparked off a Revolution.

3b. Mrs. Mick O'Sullivan,
'*Máire, my Girl*' (1994).

3c. Dan J. Quill, C Company,
in New York, *circa* 1924.

3d. Donagh McNelis.

4. C Company, 2nd Battalion, Royal Munster Fusiliers (based in Kilworth, Co. Cork), at Aldershot, England, 1913.

5a. The Master, and wife, Molly, on honeymoon, Easter, 1918.

5b. Jim Gray and his Ballyvourney bride, Miss May
McCarthy, N.T.

6. Captain Patsy Lynch, B Company, Eighth Battalion,
First Cork Brigade.

7. Vice-Commandant Paddy O'Sullivan, Eighth Battalion, in New York *circa* 1924.

8a. Truce-time picture of Commandant Patrick O'Sullivan, his brother, Mick (with Lewis-gun), and Drill Master Séan Murray, late Irish Guards.

8b. Ballyvourney Cumann na mBan, with Section-Leader Bill Hegarty.

Devlin in Belfast in 1905, who had invented the ready-mix formula for Politics and Religion. Otherwise, there was good cause for concern. On Whit Sunday, 23 May 1920, a rather spontaneous and random attempt on Ballingeary barracks, manned by R.I.C. and Black and Tans, had proved entirely abortive (cf. M. O'Sullivan: *Where Mountainy Men Have Sown*). June had slipped away with buildings crumbling in flames and regular soldiers making dusty country roads their front line in an all-out war. Came July to the roar of heavy transport vehicles establishing and maintaining uneasy lines of communication between isolated military posts. To the ordinary Volunteer it seemed that Brigade H.Q. were going to extremes on the burning theme. They kept sending for reports on all unoccupied buildings in spite of a certain apathy towards the policy of destruction which continued to prevail. In Ballyvourney the need became apparent too late and sentiment proved an expensive commodity in the times that were. In June the enemy stole a march and occupied the temporarily vacant doctor's residence, thus establishing a vital salient right in the home ground. 'Liberty Hall' found itself at grips with an urgent problem. The newcomers comprised half a rifle company of the First Battalion, the Manchester Regiment, a number of whom were of Irish extraction. (*Note:* The arrival of the Manchester Regiment in Ballincollig, 10 July 1920, its activities and personnel, are covered rather extensively by Tim Sheehan in *Lady Hostage*, 1990, having been culled from authentic British military sources). They came on the twelfth of July. There was a captain in charge, which was strange because a captain's command was usually a full company — about one hundred and ten men — but this particular officer was left only for a short while in doubt about the implication if he thought that 'his lines had fallen on pleasant sites', as the Bible said. The MANCHESTERS were brazen, but no more than they needed to be in order to maintain morale in such a precarious position. They started to put on a show right away, calling themselves the 'Men from Hell', and painted a skull and cross-bones on the wall by the front entrance. Otherwise they mixed freely enough among the people and generally acted in a friendly manner. The captain and lieutenant maintained a certain reserve but soon gained for themselves a reputation for gentlemanly behaviour. The local fowl runs suffered somewhat from the proximity of the army as chickens and ducks disappeared under the coats of predatory privates, but when a complaint was made the captain paid up without question having apologized for the conduct of his men. Likewise raids for arms were disciplined affairs usually conducted by the second-in-command, Lieutenant Sharman, and under his charge households were put to as little inconvenience as was consistent with the requirements of his job. Harrington's, of Coolavokig, had been a hotbed of sedition for years. Both sons, Danny and John, were active members of the Eighth Battalion. One night, when the family had retired to bed, the lieutenant arrived with a squad of men. As the house was being ransacked the girls of the family sat in a corner shivering. After a while one of them asked the officer if they might go back to bed. (My informant was Danny) . 'Certainly, Madam!', the lieutenant exclaimed, 'you should not have bothered!' His rejoiner placed all womenfolk outside the sphere of a commonplace military operation. And his politeness was not reserved merely for the ladies. As the soldiers turned their attention to the outhouses, someone — who must have been city reared — threw open the gate of the pigsty. A concerted charge and the snorting denizens were scattered to the four winds. Sharman rushed his men to the various danger points in the ramparts and regardless of his shining yellow leather boots and gaiters ploughed through the 'moonlagh' of the farmyard until every squealing porker had been safely returned to its place. By and by at the doctor's house ('The Chalet') the tension of the times began to tell on the soldiers' nerves. On several occasions they opened fire into the darkness for no better cause than a swinging lantern on a horse 'crib' headed for Macroom fair in the early morning, or old Patsy Lucey's donkey, a notorious wanderer, ruminating by the front gate. One of the soldiers appeared to have been an Irishman born, said to be a native of Wexford. For some reason he came under suspicion of collaboration with the I.R.A. A couple of his fellows decided to test him as he was on sentry-go one night. Pretending to be civilians they approached him from the main road and refused to halt when challenged. He proved his fealty, at least as custodian of the gate, by shooting one of them dead. Despite all of this, Lieutenant Sharman, a Catholic, went openly to Mass on Sunday mornings with only an orderly in attendance.

*   *   *

Summer, 1920. Trouble went on apace. After every Republican move, a flurry of reaction and counteraction from the enemy, a wave of repression with a salting of provocation, sometimes an understandable sublimation of stressful feelings into a form of 'good clean fun' . . . It is Sunday morning in Ballingeary village. After the final dismissal and blessing of the Mass, the mumbled *De Profundis*, a supplication for heretics and infidels, three 'Hail Marys' in memory of the Famine victims (as was the way before Vatican Two), and the people stream out from the village church into the early Summer sunshine to be confronted with a cordon of British military. There is an appreciable sprinkling of the dreaded two-tone uniforms which had now become for the Tans a deliberate dress plan rather than haphazard as before. Men hurriedly jostle back to the wall and keep their hands hoisted as ordered. At the end of the line a little man cowers in terror against his neighbour. His turn comes. After the search the question: 'Wot's yer noime?' Plaintively, like a muted scream, it rattles out: 'I'm Jerh Lucey's boy from Kilmore without a father or a mother!' The dumbfounded Tan asks him to repeat the oracle. He repeats. The Tan beckons to some comrades and they gather round. Sheer delight shows on their faces as they take turns at asking the question and receiving the answer. A pleasant time is had by all — except, that is, Jerh Lucey's boy from Kilmore. (*Note:* Jerh Lucey's of Kilmore now stands desolate, the old farmhouse just a crumbling outhouse for the later bungalow built by his son, Seán, which in turn now stands empty and disconsolate looking, with no vibration of times past to be detected around the overgrown yard. And Jerh Lucey's 'boy', a member of a large family, who lived in a neighbouring cottage, and were just 'boys' and 'girls' for neighbouring landowners, but honest and simple-minded, have gone beyond recall, as, of course, their brief tormentors who disturbed them in an unaccoutable manner and were known as the 'Black and Tans'). To the simple British soldier, differing from his victims only in a manner of speech, those strange people in a strange and distant land (the nearest point is all of fourteen miles!) were a continual source of wonder. (*Note:* An English journalist recently — 1992 — caused uproar when he referred in print to Ireland, with some sociological justification, I think, as a small country peopled only by 'peasants, pixies and priests'). Not only did they see the Irish as not conducive to British rule, but some of their customs were decidedly barbarous. A soldier back from a foray in Inchigeela hurried over to a pal. 'Want to know something?', he said. 'I saw a man eat horse-corn meal with sour cream!' 'And did he die?', naïvely asked the other. 'Did he die!', he exclaimed — 'He would kill both me and you!'. A favourite dish of the time was 'pinhead' oatmeal, milled in Macroom, and eaten with 'thick' i.e. sour, milk. This was one of my father's favourite stories, and he was from Inchigeela. Some stories from the period lack the ring of authenticity but might easily be true. Here is one which was told to me in Africa by the late Bishop Michael Moloney, C.S.Sp., thirty-five years ago, but the good bishop could 'lie like a "Second Nocturn"', as they say in France. An orderly, reporting to his commanding officer as to the location of a train which had stopped at Oola, Co. Limerick, said: 'Sir, this place, it's got a ho an' a ho an' a hell an' a ha!'. For the literally fastidious the name in Gaelic means simply 'Apples'.

As in all theatres of war, the principle held in mid-Cork that an army is as strong as its communication system, in practice, the ability of its transport to get through, a fact which was not lost on the restive spirits through whose territory it had to pass. To attack a military lorry, however, would be a new departure, a perilous novelty. It had never been done in Ireland. For the enemy it would be a rare, in fact unique, experience. It happened three miles from Ballymakeera village, 17 July 1920. The 'ambush' strictly so-called, kingpin of the War of Independence, had emerged from the crucible. The men who now set to forging it into the only adequate weapon of foot soldiers against a rampant mechanization were B (Ballyvourney), assisted by some members of A (Kilnamartyra) and C (Coolea) Companies of the Eighth Battalion. They fought on the eastern fringes of their battalion area at a place called Geata Bawn, the 'White Gate', gateway to the West, a formidable barrier of rocks astride the main road at the top of a steep incline. From the circumstances and drift of the battle it might be fairly termed hilarious, with due respect, for decency sake, to a matter of life and death between human beings. 'For', according to G. K. Chesterton, a kindly Englishman,

> The great Gaels of Ireland
> Are the men that God made mad,
> For all their wars are merry,
> And all their songs are sad!

And he meant to be kind about it. He saw himself like that . . .

Behind an upended flagstone, on a hump overlooking the roadway at Geata Bawn, reclined the gangling figure of Patey Twomey ('Peátí Taidhg Pheig') of Coolea, noted traditional-style singer of Gaelic songs both sad and saucy. Having fixed the stone in position he surveyed it sceptically for a moment, then apostrophized it with a wry smirk crinkling the corners of his humorous mouth (just like when he told me about it forty years ago): *'Dar Fia, a licín, ach is fuar fánach é mo bhrath ort-sa go mbeidh an lá so thart!'* (*Anglice:* 'By Jove, my little flagstone, I doubt if you'll be of much help to me before the end of this day!'). Beside him his partner, Lieutenant Dan O'Sullivan, was anything but amused. He looked glum and worried. On a ledge below, Jerry ('The Scholar') Lynch managed an uneasy smile. Still in his teens, he was the youngest lad present and the nearest to the expected enemy. (*Note:* 'The Scholar', as everybody knew him, had been removed from St. Colman's College, Fermoy, the diocesan seminary, following on the unveiling of a statue in the town to a local celebrity, when the noble head was found crowned with a chamber-pot, known in the College as a 'Charlie'. Apparently, in the small hours, Jerry had slipped over the wall, and so made it to Geata Bawn to become a fearless freedom-fighter. I hope it is true. I never liked St. Colman's!). All in all these three men had a difficult assignment involving a moral issue still compromised by the quick mental adjustments necessary for men leading a dual existence like they were, as soldiers mowing human life and as farmers mowing hay all in the course of a Summer's day. They had to introduce the killing. They had been appointed executioner to the driver of the first lorry which appeared unattended. Two had already gone by. While still miles away they had been signalled by the scouts as a pair. One pair or one single made little odds. The word was given. The men got ready. But only one truck appeared. Heavily laden and surmounted by soldiers it toiled its way upwards, gained the top and travelled on unmolested. What had delayed the other no one could say, but it made all the difference as it swung into view fully two hundred yards to the rear. In this situation an attack on one would have brought the men in the other into action in a manner of their own choosing, and rifles would have had an immense advantage over shotguns. So they had been allowed to pass. That was two hours ago. Evidently some of the boys thought that hostilities for the day were at an end. Coolavokig schoolhouse was just a quarter of a mile away. The schoolmaster, John Twohig (my father), was an old acquaintance. Some of them rambled down to review the situation in more academic surroundings, and a mystery was solved. They learned that the second lorry had delayed a few minutes by the school, the men curiously watching the schoolmaster teach his class in the open air as he was accustomed to do on fine days. It saved them. The boys returned to their positions and 'The Master' wandered off homewards on his bicycle. At the 'Half-Way House' he met the vehicle of doom. Kismet active or passive he would have liked to know.

John ('Jackie Stephen') Lucey saw it first. Scouting at the back of the school he spied it on the Carrigaphooka straight, a mile and a half away towards Macroom. It was now late afternoon. (*Note:* The Master, I remember, kept his school going until around five o'clock. He was indefatigable. In the evenings he took special students who were either good and were being primed for higher things or illiterate and were hoping to get to America). On and on came the British truck, straining up a long incline, disappearing from view, reappearing, until at long last it came slowly up the steep pull to the ambush position, while the eyes of the watchers blinked away the strain of heavy watching, hearts beat faster, stocks settled more comfortably into stiffened shoulders and fingers began to tighten on triggers. If there were reason or need for killing to be done anywhere in the world, to right a serious wrong, this surely was it. But a strange coincidence was already in the making. A motor car sounded from the west coming quickly into the trap and placed to meet the oncoming lorry right in the middle of the ambush position. (*Note:* It was a hackney car driven by a man named Randles, from

Kilgarvan, Co. Kerry, and was rushing a patient to hospital in Cork City. Tom Randles, with his brother Con, ran a garage in Kilgarvan and possessed the only car in the region. On this particular day, a local Protestant lady, Mrs. Dora Maybury had broken her arm, having been pushed by a drunken workman, and was being rushed to the Victoria Hospital, in Cork. She was accompanied by Mrs. Kate McCarthy, to whose daughter, Sr. Philomena, St. Clare's Convent, Kenmare, I am grateful for the particulars. Tom Randles heard the shots just as they passed the military lorry, knew what it was, told the startled ladies that it was the lorry backfiring, and raced off to Cork out of danger. The same motor-car figured later in the Civil War, when Con Randles crashed it rather than allow the Free State Army to use it for transport. His son, Fr. Tom, is now a priest in the Diocese of Kerry). The unexpected car created a first class dilemma for Commandant Patrick O'Sullivan. Two men (Section-Leader Mick Dineen and another) were stationed with a horse-cart in the mouth of a laneway to the west. Their job was to obstruct the lorry. They let the car through. The Commandant jumped down from his command post, on the blind side, in an effort to stop the car, but the driver failed to notice his pointed revolver. It was just as well as the occupants stood a serious chance of being killed in the next few moments. The British lorry and Irish motor car passed each other dead on the marked line with both parties blissfully unaware. The men detailed to put the lorry driver out of action were stunned by the incidence of a motor car in the line of fire. They held their fire. Jamie Moynihan shouted: 'They're getting away!'. Con Kelleher ('Con Seán Jerh'), an old poacher, jumped to his feet, swore a mighty oath (Jamie said), and let fly with both barrels, his shots just ahead of the barrage that now broke from the rocks all around. Standing high up in the body of the truck, the better to view the scenery, a figure in a blue naval uniform had been noted while they were still out of range. A temporary radio operator, as it transpired, he had been having his first view of the hills. But the hills became resentful and suddenly began to belch fire back at him. His disappearance among the troops (the 'Scholar' gleefully remembered) would have put a scalded cat to shame.

It was ironical that the driver, marked down for special attention, should become the hero of the day. Just beyond the second curve of the S-bend the lorry careered wildly across the road, hitting the bank on the northern side. As it rebounded the driver's left arm was seen to be hanging limp by his side while he frantically fought to control the vehicle with the other. Like a wild thing it charged back again and mounted the fence on the opposite side. A local farmer, Jeremiah Twomey, was making hay in the little field twenty feet below. He ran and crouched in the shelter of the high 'quay' wall and saw death looming large as the front half of the lorry swayed above him for a few petrifying seconds. Then a grinding of gears and it was back on the road again continuing for fifty yards with its left wheels running on the fence. The spare wheel, a door and a loaf of bread fell off on the ground. Just as it reached a telegraph pole set in the fence the driver, in spite of his disability, got the thing righted and they were away; but the buckshot had scattered wide with devastating effect. At the ambush site everybody was on his feet running and firing, firing and running. There were two rifles in action, one the light police carbine captured at the Mouth of the Glen in 1918, the other a service rifle purchased from G.H.Q. in Dublin. This latter was still to play a memorable part in the hands of Quarter-Master Danny Harrington. Picking his difficult target carefully at long range he fired at the tank and a stream of petrol spewed out onto the roadway, and that was that . . .

A long sinewy fellow unwound himself from a cramped position on a hump above the road, surveyed the fragments of his shattered flagstone, declined to comment for once, laughed a merry laugh at the memory of a blue-clad figure diving headlong among the khaki and set off with the others in hot pursuit. For all I know it may have been half true for Chesterton about those merry wars and what-not. A quarter of a mile from Ballymakeera village they found an abandoned lorry. It had run out of petrol. The soldiers had apparently walked on to the military post carrying their wounded with them. A dead man lay in the cab. On his shoulder straps gleamed the triple rosettes of a captain of infantry. The papers on the following day announced that Captain Airey, stationed currently in Fermoy military barracks, had been killed in an attack by Irregulars near Macroom. He had only recently been introduced into Ireland from Palestine. The reason was quite clear. He was described as 'an experienced guerrilla fighter'. He took his final lesson at Geata Bawn. What business he had there on that fatal day was rather shrouded in mystery. A story was current at the time that he had incurred the displeasure of the townspeople, in his short stay in Fermoy, because of an indiscretion with regard to a young girl, and that the military authorities, fearing a reprisal, had sent him on an enforced holiday for the time being. At any rate, when his death was reported it was assumed in military circles that word of his whereabouts had been passed on from Fermoy to the First Cork Brigade. Soldiers of his regiment ran amok in the town and sacked it for the second time in a twelve-month. (*Note*: Fermoy is a curious town in that it originated in a British military barracks. A report of a military survey in the Kilmainham Papers, in the National Library, and dated 12 September, 1760, indicates that a site on the hill north of the River Blackwater was the most suitable. Nothing happened for thirty years until an enterprising Scotsman, named John Anderson, came and began to build a town. In 1797 he let the present square as a temporary barracks. The East Barracks, a fine structure on the hill overlooking the river to the north, was opened in 1806. It had accomodation for about fifteen hundred infantry and two hundred cavalry.

Three years later the West Barracks was opened with accommodation for twice the number of troops. Fermoy had arrived. Mainistir Fhearmuí, the monastery of Fermoy, with its last remaining foundation blocks and headstones, disappeared into the new military buildings in the square and surroundings, and the ancient *Feara-muighe-Féine*, the men of the plain of the army, were back in style. Before the building of the new barracks, only John Anderson's mansion stood to the north of the river. All else was on the southern bank of the river Blackwater, giving rise to the expression still frequently heard: 'All to one side like the town of Fermoy!'. The soldiers trained there were used mostly in foreign wars, in America, South Africa, Egypt and India. The only Irish operations of an historic nature, before the War of Independence, were against the Young Irelanders in 1848, the Fenian Peter O'Neill Crowley in 1867, and the Kents of Bawnard in 1916. By that time the triangle of north Cork, defined by the towns of Fermoy, Mitchelstown and Buttevant, contained fifteen thousand British troops. At the start of the Civil War General Liam Lynch took over the military barracks in Fermoy and burned them down, of military necessity, six months later, on 11 August 1922).

> A small job and a failure, one would say? True in one sense; quite otherwise in the long view. It was a fine example of local initiative and enterprise, a courageous attempt with poor arms to acquire the essential things i.e. serviceable weapons, and a valuable prelude to the completely successful actions at Tureenduv and Keimeneigh a week later, and at the Slippery Rock on the eighteenth of the following month.
>
> (From *The Geata Bawn Ambush*, official statement by Captain Patsy Lynch).

Strange as it may seem, the schoolhouse at Coolavokig was never once visited by the military authorities in their investigation into the Geata Bawn affair. It is possible that they failed to identify the exact location. A couple of days later the schoolmaster happened to be engaged in surveying plots of ground at Poulnabro, a mile from Ballymakeera village. (*Note*: He lived in a local rented house where I was born three months later). The survey was with a view to getting a reduction of rent from the Macroom Board of Guardians. A party of British soldiers, in double file, led by 'a tall young officer' (presumably Sharman), swung into view at a bend in the main road a hundred yards away. The 'Master', ever resourceful, raised his hands, the 'client' and his aged father following suit. The soldiers marched down the by-road towards them. The situation was explained to the officer who did not seem greatly perturbed. He just asked the teacher to identify the other young man, and it was with difficulty that he recalled the name. He had heard it only the day before. The man was Michael O'Riordan, but everybody knew him simply as 'Mike Musger'. Then the officer asked Mike where he had been on the previous Tuesday. 'In the bog', he replied. The officer wanted to know where 'the bog' was. 'Four miles to the south'. 'Did you see or hear of any men around the place that day?'. 'No!'. (Mike was asked for his name once again during the round-up after the Coolnacahera battle in the following February. He replied: 'Michael O'Riordan — an' shure ye won't know me then ayther!'). Turning to the teacher the officer touched his pockets with his cane. The teacher said — 'No need!'. The officer smiled his agreement, gave an order to his men and marched off. Many of them, the 'Master' remarked, were quite young and appeared frightened. He himself was coming up thirty. This incident leads one to believe that the British thought the scene of the attack was two miles nearer to the village than it actually was. The surveyors resumed their work. Shortly afterwards another platoon, led by an N.C.O., came round the bend. On seeing the three men they appeared to hesitate. The 'Master' waved them on — and they went! (*Note*: I remember him saying something cynical about the effect of authority on the 'trained mind'. Something good — I forget what. As an old-style teacher, and a family man, he was a hard trainer himself!). After this the surveyors decided to abandon the profuse rocks of Poulnabro to their normal quiet. A few weeks later they would have got short shrift from the 'Auxiliaries'. With them it would have been a case of shooting first and asking questions at the inquest, or even, for convenience sake, letting somebody else do the asking . . .

So the long, long story dragged on. The First Manchester Regiment, according to military usage and necessity, maintained its own supply system and provisioned its various outposts by means of a weekly or twice-weekly supply lorry. It was one of these that had come to grief at Geata Bawn, and the MANCHESTERS duly took notice. Right away the number was increased to two vehicles together, and sometimes three. The system was simple. A telegraphed message would arrive at the Post Office at Ballymakeera for delivery to the captain at 'The Chalet', giving the approximate time of arrival of the convoy and the road it would follow. The main road by Geata Bawn was the usual one but once in a while, as a precautionary measure, the Clondrohid road to the north was chosen. Then the little military operation began. The platoon marched out from the post, scouted and patrolled the rocks for a distance of a few miles eastwards of the village to ensure the safe passage of the convoy on its outward and return journeys. The captain and the lieutenant took alternate days in charge of the job. Then on Friday, 12 August, bicycles arrived, but they were destined to serve their specific purpose only for a brief period. On Monday, 15 August (Feast of the Assumption), the patrol proudly rode out on their new machines along the road to Coolavokig, took up their positions, saw the lorries pass and re-pass and returned confidently to barracks. That very night their fate was sealed. The sight of the bicycles, with the rifles neatly clipped to them, proved too much for the members of B Company. They ached to possess. So the officers met come nightfall and discussed ways and means of persuading the cycle patrol to part company with their goods and chattels anon. During the discussion the bloodless coup of unarmed Midleton men against the Cameron Highlanders, two months previously, was cited as a precedent, and they finally decided to adopt the plan, with a couple of modifications. The village itself was chosen as the ambush location. It possessed a full and active group of Volunteers under the command of Section-Leader Bill Hegarty who was enthusiastic about the home site and quite confident of success. The position seemed suited to a rushed job as contemplated. There were a number of vacant houses, alley-ways and passages where men might take cover until the rush was ordered. The road rose gradually from about the middle of the street and disappeared round a bend at the eastern end. The situation looked good for the attackers. Two potential difficulties had to be allowed for. The officer in charge of the patrol would be carrying a revolver. He had to be held up quickly before he had time to draw his gun. Two men similarly armed were detailed to deal with him while two others carrying shotguns were given a roving commission in case any soldier managed to break away from the scrimmage and thought to use his rifle. That was the plan. On Tuesday night, 16 August, the whole company was mobilized, the plan was explained to them in detail and each man was allotted his position. The convoy was expected again on the following day, so it was now or never. But the plan had one outstanding drawback. They were proposing to wage war at home, quite literally for some of them on their very own doorsteps. The womenfolk especially could not be expected to like it. In fact they became so nervous and excited, when the positions were occupied on the following morning, that it was feared they would alert the soldiers to the fact that something was amiss. Reluctantly the company withdrew and occupied a new site about a mile to the east of the village, at Poulnabro . . .

At Poulnabro the hills stoop —
Vestal virgins pouring water;
And far away on thrones the mountains sit —
Mitred abbots, face serene and still.

Lightly the road leaps over the river's back,
And Sullane frightened by the sudden darkness
Rounds once skirt-stone,
And tig plays with the bank again
In brightness and in laughter.

A wagtail garland loops across the river,
And on his stand-stone nods to his seas applauding,
And all around are bubbles of lovely bursting birdsong
In Poulnabro.

So ran the imagination of a contemporary-minded poet, in 1950, as he leaned on the quay-wall, gazing around him reflectively and beneath at the singing river, while remote from his mind were thoughts of violence and sinister doings just as the events themselves were remote from him in time . . .

In spite of previous arrangements the sum total of firearms among them was one revolver. Jamie Moynihan, who was to have brought along his 'Bulldog' revolver to make a pair, was delayed and did not arrive until later, and John Harrington found himself in possession of the only gun in the group, as well as the lone and responsible role of restraining, wounding or otherwise putting the officer out of action. Against him he knew would be a Long Webley and Scott .455, a powerful, reasonably accurate but rather ungainly weapon, but his confidence in his own gun was unbounded. His brother, Fr. Michael, had sent it baked in a cake from Barhead, Scotland, during the period in which he had ministered there. Through the same channel he had also sent a breech-bolt for the company's .22 target rifle to replace one that had been lost. The Post Office officials who handled the products must have thought funny thoughts about the cakes baked in Barhead. The handgun was an American .32 revolver, with an unusually long barrel, and was so powerful and accurate that John (as he told me) considered he could do better with it at forty yards than with a rifle although he was an expert shot with both. (*Note:* As a point of technical interest, the gun would have been a Smith and Wesson, as that was the only company who ever manufactured a long-barrelled revolver. They did so around 1880 and then discontinued, less than a thousand having been produced in all. The model is now extremely rare and valuable. Wyatt Earp is depicted as using one at the O.K. Corral. Likewise a stock could be fitted to the butt [as with the German Mauser automatic, the famous 'Peter the Painter'] when it was referred to as a revolving rifle. A consignment was actually intercepted on the way into Dublin just before 1916 which indicates, I think, much more deliberation and foresight than is usually attributed to the leaders of the Insurrection. On the other hand, the 'Bulldog' revolver, a common enough weapon in the countryside before this period, was now regarded as practically harmless and little better than an encumbrance, though there was no doubt that it could do serious damage at short range. And Jamie Moynihan was wont to look down at it with disgust as his huge fist almost enclosed it. The target rifle was a curious adaptation. A common practice at the time was to insert a specially designed tube, called a 'Morris Tube', into the barrel of a regulation calibre rifle so as to accommodate a .22 shell for target practice). So, John Harrington, the boy from Coolavokig, composed himself to try conclusions with the Englishman. Then Fate once more took a hand. The scouts reported how they saw the pedalling soldiers approach the vital crossroads outside the village, unhesitatingly follow their leader onto the by-road northwards to Clondrohid, out of present danger and into the realms of History. The opportunity for an unarmed *coup de main* had passed and the order to make it into a flaming war had already been assented to in every man's mind. They raced over the mile or so of rough countryside, so typical of the locality, to the nearest section of the northern by-road. The shotguns were fetched from the house where they were stored. The 'shtuff', as they referred to the ammunition, created a problem. The cartridge cases had become swollen with damp and inadequate storage and each one had to be 'peeled' before it could be injected. They lay down in a cornfield but the corn was still young — the oats came in late in the mountain districts of the South and West — and Paddy Donagh Owen, the Vice-Commandant, looking over the scanty cover, decided that many of his men might stay where they lay on this field of pique and panicles. He withdrew the whole company to the 'Slippery Rock', at Béal a'Ghearra (lit. 'the mouth of the cleft'), and the stage was set for one of the most amazing and successful ambushes of the whole period.

By this time the convoy of two lorries had passed westwards to 'The Chalet', and repassed after an hour or so, all unsuspectingly. The cycle patrol saw it safely as far as the parish boundary beyond Danganasillagh ('the fort of the willows'), and were returning at their leisure. They freewheeled airily down the last incline, pedalled in loose formation along the level and began to close ranks again as they cycled slowly up the hill to Ullanes cross, passed the crossroads and gathered speed as they rounded the sharp bend at a smooth shoulder of rock (which gave its name to the spot), dipped quickly and unhesitatingly into the trap that had been so hastily laid for them. At the last moment Lieutenant Sharman must have noticed something, or been warned by a sixth sense, or it may be that he had developed an aversion to that particular spot as the most deadly trap on their beat. Nobody will ever know. The position was then in the nature of a mild, curving defile (now obliterated by a modern road in the interests of equally lethal weapons in the hands of equally amateurish but far more dangerous lunatics!). It was definitely the sort of place that any officer, with the responsibility for men's lives on his hands, would be anxious to get out of as quickly as possible. From the bend of the road already mentioned to the bend at the western end of the defile was a distance of one hundred and twenty yards, with a dip in and a pull out. Convenient sized rocks commanded both the entrance and the exit, and the southern flank, while at the opposite verge of the roadway, about the centre of the position, stood a solitary natural 'pill-box', solidly occupied on this occasion by an intrepid little band under Captain Patsy Lynch. Here, in their isolated redoubt, the trappers were trapped. Officer Sharman had to be dead before he reached them — and he was. Vice-Commandant Paddy O'Sullivan shouted to the patrol to halt and surrender. His voice reverberated like a bomb-burst on the lazy air of that August afternoon. Lieutenant Sharman, following his initial impulse, was standing on his bicycle pedals in an effort to race out of the place. He shouted to his men to follow him. The N.C.O. at the end of the file yelled a response. Again they were called on to halt but they kept going, every yard an agony for watchers and watched alike. Then the Vice-Commandant did a peculiar thing. Still conscience-locked about giving the fatal order he leaped out on his rocky eminence recklessy exposing himself in an effort to persuade the soldiers for their own good to submit reasonably and quietly. In the excitement of the moment he waved a revolver agitatedly in his right hand, and in his left a toy mascot he had received by post only that morning. But whether they were still unclear as to what their immediate good consisted of or, as trained soldiers, were blindly following their commander, or had an inborn contempt for the hostile intentions of irregulars, the 'tommies' failed to react and the crash of gunfire came simultaneously with the order to fire. Lieutenant Sharman was almost at point-blank range from the rock on which Patsy Lynch and his three companions lay in waiting. With the first volley Sharman on his bicycle slanted in towards the fence on the opposite side and lay quite still in the ditch, directly on a level with their stronghold. He 'must have been dead before he hit the ground' was Patsy's comment. Even had he got safely past this point, about fifty yards further on, and facing him directly due to the sweep of the road, were the deadly eye and quick hand of Mick O'Sullivan, of Kilnamartyra, controlling one of the two rifles in the lot. Beside him was an ex-soldier hardened in the ways of war.

The patrol dismounted rapidly. Some were wounded. Others thought to make a fight of it and were unslinging their rifles. A couple of volleys and there were five or six khaki-clad figures lying on the ground with bicycles and rifles strewn about everywhere. For a few minutes there was some desultory firing, the range varying from a few feet to fifty yards. Then the firing ceased. A soldier was seen running through a cornfield on the northern side, poor fellow!, and it was over. Sharpshooter John Harrington and medical student Frank Creedon held the furthest eastern position, a boulder topped with heather beside the 'Slippery Rock' itself and about twenty feet from the road. Frank (he was known as 'Francy') now wielded the long-barrelled thirty-two. John had Dr. Lynch's D.B. shotgun and when the firing started he wounded his two opposite numbers, 'aiming for the shoulder', he told me. They lay quite still on the road. Then the ejector of his gun jammed because the shells were too tight. He called back to Jerh Casey (who was humorously known as 'Strock') for his jack-knife. There was no answer. So he made his way back in the midst of the firing, retrieved his property and removed the shells. The battle was practically over as he returned to his position, but he found a private skirmish in full blast around the boulder. Left alone by his rock Frank had tried to get an occasional shot at some soldiers who were releasing rapid fire from prone positions on the roadway. Now the firing had died down and he could see groups of men moving in on all sides to take the surrender. He stood up to follow suit and the muzzle of a rifle appeared around the corner of the fence beneath him. He dropped to the ground just as the shot came and for a moment thought the rock had splintered at the impact. The soldier was lying in the drain on the near side of the road. One of the last men in the line, he was just outside the limit of the ambush position and as he lay he could not be hit from either side. He meant to use his advantage. Both of them had excellent cover though Frank's pistol was more easily manoeuvrable, long and all as it was, in those cramped conditions than the soldier's Lee-Enfield. Every time he stuck out his right eye around the corner Frank fired at him, with the result that they were both firing practically together most of the time. In this wise they had exchanged eight or nine shots when the soldier suddenly dropped his rifle at an order from someone on the road. John Harrington was standing over him, shotgun at the ready.

The brave, handsome Lieutenant Sharman lay prostrate in death at the head of his vanquished patrol, and groaning and moaning soldiers lay about on the roadway and in the dykes as the I.R.A. closed in from their positions and began to take charge of the situation. The badly wounded were hastily attended to as far as could be done without 'First-Aid' equipment. Patsy Lynch stooped over a prostrate form and asked: 'Are you hurt, you poor devil, or are you dead?'. The young soldier, probably having just received his baptism of fire, had only one idea. 'You are very cruel!', he said. The young republican, blunt but reasonable, could understand for him. 'Sure we wouldn't hurt a hair of ye'r heads', he replied, 'if ye only gave us the guns!'. One of the uninjured 'tommies' was given a bicycle and sent off to the village for priest and doctor. One of his not so fortunate comrades asked for a cigarette. Mick O'Sullivan made a thorough but unavailing effort to find one for him. Only gunsmoke was on the menu at the 'Slippery Rock'. The friendly overtures of the 'boys' met with some success until the 'tommies' realized that there was to be no more killing. Then they roundly

abused the attackers for their savagery and for what they regarded as an unlawful and uncalled-for attack. The others disputed
the point and for a while there was some heated arguing and
bickering. The lone warrior of the rock was a tall, redheaded,
plucky lad. His magazine was almost empty when he was taken.
(*Note*: A Lee-Enfield rifle magazine carried ten bullets). A
notebook in his pocket had the name — 'Private Hitchen'. He
made a wry remark about 'the hill tribes' (he pronounced it
'ill'), which apparently was the worst thing he could think of,
in his experience, to compare them to, and at such short notice.
He was asked: 'What brought ye over to this country, so?',
but could not think of an answer. The issue was not at all
clear to the ordinary soldier; doubtful if it still is in a country
with such an age-long habit of active soldiering abroad. The
cycle-messenger returned to the scene with more than he had
been sent for. He brought along his captain and twenty riflemen
with fixed bayonets. The attackers had gone off southwards
but a quick survey of Knockanure hill failed to locate them.
They were, in fact, at that moment a few hundred yards due
north having completed a nice little encircling manoeuvre. They
watched from an advantageous position and wondered whether
to resume the attack, but chivalry at this early stage was still
a consideration and though well armed now they decided to
desist. The booty consisted of ten bicycles, ten rifles and a
revolver, a thousand rounds or so of ammunition, and various
pieces of accoutrement with which the British soldier was equipped (and which Mick O'Sullivan and Julius Caesar so felicitous-
ly refer to as *impedimenta*). With all of this, except the bikes
which had been 'dumped', they moved higher up into the hills
and called it a day. There were now more hopeful visions of
other days to come. Here are two statements on the action,
one, laconic from the simple fighting man, the other, more
dramatic and elaborate from the writer:

The patrol had gone to the east on the Clondrohid road. It
would return to Ballyvourney on the same route when the

task of protecting the lorries was completed. It could be taken on the return journey. Michael O'Sullivan and Mick O'Connell (he was known as 'Mickeen the Soldier') of the Kilnamartyra Company, and Jamie Moynihan and Dan O'Sullivan from Coolea, had joined Paddy Donagh Owen and the Ballyvourney men under their captain, Patsy Lynch. It was decided to collect some shotguns, move across country to the Clondrohid road and select a position there. And so to the vicinity of the 'Slippery Rock'.

(Patsy Lynch in *Official Statement* to the Military History Society).

I came to the man whom we had last fired at. He lay in exactly the same position, his left hand stretched in the firing position and his right down on the road near the small of the butt. The rifle lay with a cartridge half thrust forward into the breech. His face was on the ground. I caught him by the shoulder and called 'Hallo'. No reply. I thought him dead. My left hand grasping his right shoulder I rolled him back. A fresh smiling face looked up at me with humorous eyes. 'You are not dead', I said. 'No', he replied lazily. 'You are wounded or you ought to be'. 'I don't think so', was the reply. I opened his tunic, button by button. Not a scratch. 'I am very glad indeed', I said. 'Thanks', was his smiling reply.

(M. O'Sullivan in *Where Mountainy Men Have Sown*) . . .

'HIC IACET' . . . Both Lieutenant Sharman and Captain Airey lie buried in the military cemetery at Pope's Road, Cork. Sadly their quiet graves are marked no longer. They would have expected and no doubt deserved at least that much. Vandalism, dogs, courting couples, playing children from the grubby locality, and the mindless general public have obliterated the face of that old and heroic graveyard, and the remaining headstones, mostly undecipherable, lean incongruously against a still standing wall. Ironically enough, Dr. Frank Creedon's home for many years back, until his death, stood just outside the wall of the cemetery, high up and overlooking the soul-less, unfeeling, every-day bustle of a city. Here, in an atmosphere of peaceful and abiding neighbourliness, and far removed from the rugged fastnesses and bitter animosities of their earlier fatal encounters, the spirits of the dead never deigned to disturb the transient but needful activities of the living . . .

The 'round-up' was inevitable. It came on the following day, Thursday. The British military authorities poured a large force of troops into the area. They camped at several points and swept the whole district which had become an ever deepening thorn in their sides and a continuing loss of soldierly prestige. No army likes to be humiliated, not so much through loss of personnel — which is an expendable commodity — as through being outmanoeuvred by an irregular force aspiring to military achievement. On their first evening out they camped at Geata Bawn and made a night raid on Ballymakeera village. They captured Jerh ('Con Joe') Lucey, the company adjutant. A jury had already been summoned to appear at the inquest on Lieutenant Sharman. For those who failed to turn up there was a threatened fine of £10. But nobody attended. In Jerh Lucey's pocket there was found a letter in Irish about this matter, which the soldiers tried unsuccessfully to decipher. He was taken to the police barracks for identification, and the R.I.C. obliged. As a result his home in the village was thoroughly searched and a notice put on the door as the prisoner was being taken past. That night he was kept at Geata Bawn, then on to Mount Massey, in Macroom, and to Cork Gaol. Vice-Commandant Paddy O'Sullivan and Captain Patsy Lynch, inseparable as ever, flitted about on the explosive fringe of the round-up, keeping an eye on things. They had prepared a trench for the military transport at Shea's Cross on the Danganasillagh road to Clondrohid. That was Saturday night. On Sunday morning it claimed its first victim. The Vice-Commandant himself, cycling to Mass, hailed someone on the further by-road to Liscarrigane and fell into it. The soldiers arrived that evening, knocked a gap in the fence and drove around it, but they did not omit to give their full attention to the locality it had marked down for them. On Monday the two men were following from a distance the course of events. Towards evening they became bolder and moved closer to their homes as the search began to slacken. They called to Patsy's home for news and had each a hand on the fence of the backyard when they were startled at the sight of a steel helmet on the other side. At the time one simply ran. They ran. The sentry must have been dozing in the sun because he never made a move. Fields fell behind them in heroic succession. A big double-ditch presented itself. They 'doubled' it and were still in mid-air when a sudden exclamation came from right beneath them. Old Mrs. Desmond (the family is still there) was sitting in the lee of the fence sunning herself. 'A Mhuire! What ails ye?', she exclaimed, 'or is it mad ye are?'. But they were still travelling as they hit the ground, while behind them, no doubt, the thoughts and dreams of placid old age rolled on along their well worn tracks untouched by the seemingly crazy and meaningless goings-on of youth.

The soldiers made a complete sweep of the mountains as far as Carriganimma village, on the Millstreet road, but without success. They plundered a bit as they went, collecting eggs, cream and other foodstuffs and actually threw away their 'bully-beef' and 'dog-biscuits'. A few men were taken prisoner but were released after interrogation. A 'tommie' with a sense of humour collected a man named Cronin and told him: 'As sure's your name is Cronin you'll be groanin' in the mornin' '. But he wasn't. The officer released him. A young farm worker, named Michael Murphy, was not so fortunate. His arresting officer smashed the barrel of a revolver against Murphy's teeth and jabbed it deep into his mouth. 'Where are they?', he grated. The gun rotated in the lad's mouth until roof and tongue were severely lacerated. Still no answer. They took him along with them, then, as they marched away towards Clondrohid. The officer had brought along a shotgun for alternative sport on the way. A rabbit popped out of a drain and bolted across the road. The officer dropped him with the smooth flourish of the practised hand. He turned to Murphy who marched beside him. 'I could shoot you just like that!', he said. The lad looked as if he believed he would but his spirit was undaunted. 'Small bother to you', he replied — 'I am somewhat bigger than a rabbit!'. They let him go then. Before the military departed they cut three deep crosses on the grass margin of the road near the 'Slippery Rock', a poignant gesture to the memory of fallen comrades, because it surely indicated, though not reported at the time, that two other soldiers besides Sharman had succumbed to their wounds. A week later Jerh Lucey was released from prison by mistake and arrived in Ballyvourney just in time for Bill Hegarty's funeral. On the same day the mails were raided by the I.R.A. in Bandon. They contained information that Lucey was to be picked up again. A warrant had been issued for his arrest. Word was sent by dispatch riders and Jerh went off 'on the run' to Midleton.

Section-Leader Bill Hegarty was shot dead on Sunday, September 5, 1920, just after 'dinner-time' i.e. about two o'clock in the afternoon. The shooting was generally regarded as a tragic sequel to the 'Slippery Rock' affair, a reprisal probably. (*Note*: A few months later Montgomery, as Brigade-Major and therefore responsible for military conduct in Cork, issued an order that unofficial reprisals were 'strictly prohibited' to troops and police alike). On the previous Friday night Bill Hegarty, Frank Creedon and John Stephen Lucey had slept at Healy's, Fileadown, under the 'Robber's Den', near Glenflesk, Co. Kerry. On Saturday they decided to cycle home to see how things were going. They arrived in the village that evening and, as it was dangerous to hang around, after tea they went 'back the road' (as Frank Creedon said), having in mind to spend the night in a farmhouse owned by Danny Arthur O'Leary of the 'Hibernian Hotel', Ballymakeera. In passing the church Bill suddenly said that he was 'going to Confession'. Frank 'wasn't in the mood', so he went on alone across the 'inch' to the Sullane river, crossed over on the stepping-stones and went on up the opposite hill to the house at Shanacloon. Bill arrived later. (*Note*: The curate who heard his Confession was Fr. Joe Shinnick. His brother, Fr. Ned, was stationed at the time in Coachford and had conscience problems about hearing republican Confessions. He was accustomed to tell the boys to 'go to Ballyvourney to my brother. He'll hear you!'. Fr. Ned, who somewhat favoured the Ascendancy, became *persona non grata* with the Republican movement and became dangerously involved later with the Dripsey ambush and the execution of Mrs. Lindsay). In the morning they went to early Mass and were in the village about midday when a convoy of military lorries, two open and one covered, with some armoured cars, passed through just as the people were returning from late Mass. The convoy apparently went as far as 'The Mills', remained there for about an hour and then returned, travelling quite slowly but never stopping. By this time Jerh Lucey and John Creedon had joined the other two at the village cross. After a while they got their bikes ready and were just about to head off again into the friendly retreats of Kerry when somebody came along and told them that one of the lorries, the covered one, had broken down on the road half a mile to the east, near the home of 'Master' O'Brien, teacher and noted Gaelic scholar (one of the group known as 'The Ballyvourney Four Masters'). A group of soldiers had pushed the lorry back and forth a few times, then put some rocks to the wheels and drove away with the others. Bill and Frank decided to go along and have a look at it before leaving. They cycled on up along the byroad towards the 'Slippery Rock'. Watching the lorry from a distance they could see no sign of life about it. A number of children began to gather round. A few days before this an armoured car had broken down in Co. Longford. Civilians who approached it were fired on and one or two were killed. They thought that a similar outrage was about to happen here. They cycled back to the crossroads and turned down the main road towards the lorry shouting at the children to get off home. As they passed they could clearly see the armour plating in the back with three loopholes cut in it. A sheet of canvas was draped over the top and came partly down the sides. The lorry was a type in common use at the time with steel plates all around the sides and a roof of wire netting on top to keep bombs from dropping into the body. (*Note*: The type was known as a 'Lancia', and was produced in Italy by the Italian racing driver and car manufacturer, Vincenzo Lancia, and was being used world-wide for troop transportation). The two men proceeded onwards to Toonlane Cross, on the road to Macroom, but when they looked back they saw to their horror that the children were still there and had been joined by a few others, including some adults. They expected to hear shooting at any moment and hurried back, but nothing happened. Then they decided to collect some men and fire at it from a distance. Another member of the I.R.A., Danny Healy, walked over, jumped on the tail-board and raised the left-hand corner of the canvas. A voice from inside yelled 'Get off!', and at the same moment the muzzle of a Lewis-gun was seen coming through the centre loophole in the back. Frank shouted 'Run!', dropped his bicycle and took a flying leap at the northern fence. One foot tripped on a heap of hand-broken road stones and he went sprawling over the low, grassy bank into the drain inside. The tumble saved his life. The jarring splutter of a machine-gun came while he was still actually in the air. On the road there was pandemonium. Frank made his way as quickly as he could on hands and knees while sods fell on him from the top of the bank as it was being sprayed with bullets. He peered over the fence and saw the children running wildly down the middle of the road. The gunner could not have fired on them because he would not have missed. He was evidently following with vicious intent the course of the man making his way to safety inside the fence. No doubt Frank had been recognized from the 'Slippery Rock' fight. Comparative safety he had but ultimate safety was still far away. A section of the fence jutted out into the field and his line of retreat was fully visible from the lorry. He crouched in the corner while bullets ripped into the fence right along to the point of the angle. Suddenly there was a lull in the firing and he crawled safely round the danger point. The gunner must have been putting on a fresh pan of ammunition because he opened up in fine style right away. At the crossroads there was an old ruined dwelling house, roofless, with ivy-covered crumbling walls. (*Note*: It was a landmark, named for a previous inhabitant, which I now forget). Frank crawled into it scared stiff and covered with dirt, but he had enough strength left in him, and concern for his comrades, to climb the wall and look back down the road. The lorry was still there. Bill was there too, lying in a peculiar slump on the road beside the bicycles. The shooting had stopped and a strange stillness had spread itself over the scene. As he wondered in vain if he could do anything for poor Bill, to his amazement he saw him get off the ground and, with both hands pressing against his side, stagger across and over the fence on the far side. The thought occurred to him that if Bill could keep his head sufficiently to stay under cover he might still succeed in crawling away to safety. Apparently he did so because he was lost to sight for about a minute. Then, twenty yards from the lorry, he reappeared still holding on to his side while running and staggering out across the field toward some rocks. He had got a further twenty yards when there was a single rifle shot and he fell. He got up again but now he turned right around and headed directly towards the lorry. He tumbled in close to the fence and almost on a level with it. That was the last time Frank saw him alive. A figure in a dark uniform got out of the lorry, pointed a

rifle in over the fence and fired two bullets into the wounded lad's head.

In the meantime John Creedon had managed to get safely over the fence on the southern side and crawled along in
the friendly shelter of it. He glanced back after a while and
saw Bill try to follow him, wander aimlessly about the field
and return to his death. He made the best of his way along
and as he was about to pass Master O'Brien's gate a volley
of bullets struck the pillar. He changed direction, got over
another fence and again met Jerh Lucey in safety. A couple
of hundred yards further on the road to Macroom, Michael
Lynch lived with his parents. His brother, Jeremiah, had lately
resigned from the R.I.C. Hearing the firing he went to the
little garden gate opening on to the road. As he turned back
he took a fatal bullet in the left side, through the pocket of
his jacket, the clean puncture showing that he had been fired
at directly. A girl who was passing by was asked to fetch the
curate, Fr. Shinnick. She did so. (*Note*: She later suffered
a nervous breakdown, as a result of her experience, and died
in a mental hospital). The priest came along promptly and
attended to Michael and on his way back showed sublime
courage and presence of mind by rapping on the lorry to
inquire if there were any others wounded. He got no reply.
Then he found tracks of blood and following them discovered
Bill Hegarty dead inside the fence. By this time Frank
Creedon had gone along the 'Top Road', crossed down to
the village and passed through John ('Maura Connie')
Twomey's grocery shop to the street. As he passed Hegarty's, old Mrs. Hegarty was sitting at the door as she was
accustomed to do, with her 'bad leg' resting on a box with
a cushion. She asked, 'Where is my boy, Bill?', the soft calm
of her voice betraying no disquietude above its usual slightly querulous intonation. Frank made no reply. Just then Fr.
Shinnick arrived in the village on his return journey to the
scene of the tragedy. With peculiar and rather macabre
foresight he took with him a donkey and cart which were

reposing in front of 'The Store', and later brought back the body in it. The lorry was still in position as he completed his errand of mercy and before returning he roundly abused the concealed killers and called down the wrath of God on them. Later it was learned that the remainder of the convoy had turned right at the 'Half-Way House', gone on to Kilnamartyra and from a vantage point on top of the chimney of an old ruin (still visible on the skyline) some officers had trained field-glasses on the lorry to watch the outcome. An examination of the terrain shows that this is quite feasible. It must have been a military operation of some category, possibly 'Operation Death-trap'. After the departure of the priest the 'broken down' lorry drove away, and the same trick was tried later that day at Carrigadrohid, beyond Macroom, but without result. Bill Hegarty was given an I.R.A. military funeral to the family burial ground in Kilgarvan, in Kerry. His comrades-in-arms mounted a guard of honour all during the wake. A huge crowd travelled to Kilgarvan to the funeral but no interference came from R.I.C. or military. Sergeant Phelan, who had replaced 'The Skipper' at the barracks, called on Mrs. Hegarty to sympathize with her, which she graciously accepted. (*Note*: The details of this account, from the 'Slippery Rock' ambush to the killing, were hand-written for me by Dr. Frank Creedon forty years ago. He added verbally that Bill Hegarty was a rather low-sized, agile young man, about twenty-seven years old at the time of his death, was a republican idealist of the type of Terence MacSwiney, had wit and humour galore and sang the songs of Ireland in a fine tenor voice).

*   *   *

The 'Auxiliaries', who also came to be popularly known all over Ireland as the 'Tans', did not occupy Macroom Castle until the early part of September, actually the day following the funeral of Bill Hegarty. 'Auxiliaries' was short for 'Auxiliary Police', which was their role in fact, or more precisely, the 'Auxiliary Division of the R.I.C.'. On their shoulders they wore the letters 'T.C.', for 'Temporary Cadet'. Dorothy Macardle (*The Irish Republic*) said they wore black. Tim Sheehan (*Lady Hostage*) said they wore blue, but he goes on to confuse them with the regular Manchester Regiment stationed in Ballincollig . . . 'Composed mainly of ex-officers of the Army, Navy and Air Force, most of these men had seen service in the recent European War . . . Eight companies of the force, each about one hundred strong, were eventually recruited under the command of Brigadier-General Crozier . . . Later one company was stationed in a commandeered house, Mount Leader, near Millstreet' (Florrie Donoghue — *No Other Law*). Ernie O'Malley (*On Another Man's Wound*) said that there were fifteen companies of them, of about one hundred each, and that they wore 'officers' khaki tunics'. Their headquarters was at Woodstock House, Inistiogue, Co. Kilkenny. They had begun to arrive in Ireland in July. A platoon of C Company was stationed in Macroom Castle, while the military still occupied Mount Massey to the north of the town. On the arrival of the 'Auxies' in September there was an immediate change for the worse in the Macroom region. On the very next day after their arrival they paid a visit to Ballyvourney. They appeared to wield the medieval power of 'the High, the Middle and the Low'. In Ballyvourney they called to the barracks, returned and raided the eastern side of the village. They just had a meaningful look around and said nothing, but their quietness was ominous as people subsequently had reason to know. Some of the boys who were in John Creedon's shoemaker shop, waiting for the press account of Bill Hegarty's funeral, had just time to make themselves scarce. In seven or eight little runabout trucks known as 'Crossley tenders' (there is a comprehensive note in *The Dark Secret*), the Macroom Auxiliaries roamed the countryside, but kept usually to the main roads. They were difficult to ambush as they changed their routes continually and moved very swiftly. In

October the police barracks and military posts in the Macroom region were mostly vacated and henceforth an area within a ten to fifteen mile radius of the Castle was left to the tender mercies of the Auxies. Every Friday night — pay night — without fail, up to the date of the Kilmichael ambush (28 November, 1920), when some sections of this particular company were cut to pieces so dramatically, they drove to Ballyvourney firing spasmodically on the way out and back. On one of these raids, when they were in a particularly nasty mood, they shot James Lehane dead.

*   *   *

The late Fr. Neil Kevin, of St. Patrick's College, Maynooth, in his gentlemanly mellifluous remembering of the 'Karrigeen' of his youth, mentioned in passing that — 'The war with England went on. The people called it the "Trouble". England had the old police force, the new police force known as the "Black and Tans", the military, and a force known as "Auxiliaries" who seemed to be freed from the restrictions of being either policemen or soldiers'. (From *I Remember Karrigeen*, sequel to *I Remember Maynooth*).

*   *   *

But they were fearless fighters, those Auxiliaries, skilful and able. And trained! An astounded Mick O'Sullivan (*Where Mountainy Men Have Sown*) saw a platoon of them, on a raid at Kilnamartyra, vault, one after the other and in full war kit, over a high garden wall. Carrying about with them an aura of awe and dread it is no wonder, while they were still around, that they had begun to chisel for themselves a niche in the folklore of the region. A story which gained much currency was 'the one about' the rear lorry of Auxiliaries at the ambush of Rathcoole, between Millstreet and Banteer, 16 June, 1921. It was blown sky-high by a land-mine. As it returned to earth the occupants, who had lost their rifles on the way up, drew their Webley revolvers and opened fire on the prone figures of the I.R.A. now visible to them behind the fences of the road. Believe it or not! On the Friday night raids in Ballyvourney their usual manoeuvre was to surround the village first, in the sense of encompass. It was like a challenge to a duel to anyone who might think to take them on. It would appear to be very reckless and daring and prodigal even of their own safety; but they had had much experience of this during the war when night patrols, on both sides, were a feature of the action, and served for taking prisoners or spying out the land, and death was a constant companion. Having controlled the village street and converging by-roads, some of them went from house to house asking for the head of the household. They lined everybody up on the roadway and gave the order: 'Paddy's Company, 'Shun!'. Then the householders were warned in the hearing of all that if there were any trouble in the district their houses would be burned down or they would be shot, according to the nature and extent of the 'offence'. At a prearranged time, so it seemed, a whistle was blown and they left. This ritual was peculiar to the Auxiliaries, and most of the raids were now left in their hands. The houses are still there, in spite of much trouble in the district, but the ritualists have gone. On one occasion Volunteer Mick Dineen's father was slow in falling into line. He was an old man. He got a shout — 'Come on, Dad, pick 'em up!'. The order was not unkindly but when an Auxie gave an order young and old reacted immediately. The guns seemed to be permanently in their hands and there was no telling when one might go off. Hence, in the continual ebb and flow of initiative between the opposing forces, when the Auxies became the hunted rather than the hunters, they were invariably dealt with ruthlessly.

*   *   *

For some time now that most extraordinary phenomenon of the resistance movement, the 'Shadow Administration', had been functioning successfully. It was, practically

speaking, a civic and legal secession under the aegis of Sinn
Féin. The moral pressure which it brought to bear proved
very heartening to the exponents of physical force. Now it
could be said that the Movement had reached the fullness
of its being with the two components of authority working
hand in glove and showing a compatibility that had to be
seen in action to be believed. The 'Department of Home Affairs', Dáil Éireann, had made the decree on June 29, 1920,
and Austin Stack, Minister for Justice, established his
'Courts'. As well as the 'Supreme Court', there were 'District'
and 'Parish Courts'. Strange to say, it worked, and attempts
at suppression gradually became futile. With the resulting
ignoration the long established courts of the British Administration fell by and large into disuse. (*Note*: These Irish
'Arbitration Courts', as they were called, were finally suppressed only on July 31, 1922, at the height of the Civil War,
and the resulting outrage against the 'Provisional Goverment'
brought about the resignation, on a matter of principle, of
two of the six signatories of the divisive Treaty, Robert Bar-
ton and George Gavan Duffy). In these 'Republican Courts'
the amateur judges endeavoured to give a good and fair decision, which may not always have been according to the letter of the Law so much as according to the conscience and
private knowledge of the judges themselves. (*Note*: The procedure in practice was somewhat reminiscent of the Brehon
Laws in the Ireland of long ago. The word 'Brehon' is an
anglicized corruption of *breitheamh* — Gen. Sing,
breitheamhan, now obsolete, meaning 'judge'. The facts of
a case were determined by laymen before submission to a
'Brehon'. They dealt with the actual realities of life rather
than the letter of the Law, while the official 'Brehon' was
an arbitrator, umpire and expounder of the legal system that
obtained, rather than a 'judge' in the modern sense whose
basis is Roman Law and alternative social systems). The
Republican judges were, as a rule, picked from among the
members of the local Sinn Féin Club (in fact the ancient

Brehon Laws were more properly known as *Féinechus*), sometimes from the ranks of the Volunteers who, having only one real aim at the time and practically no prospects — many of them later emigrated to America and some to Australia — could be depended on to be almost devoid of vested interests, or overmuch sentiment in regard to purely civil and personal matters. Others of the Volunteers inevitably had the unpleasant duty of putting the decrees of the courts into effect, serving summonses on defendants and 'sub poenas' on witnesses — their own neighbours and friends. Still, they carried out their duty with or without the aid of the newly formed 'Republican Police'. In some cases resentment ran high and the sting lived on afterwards, but generally the need of the times was recognized and displeasure was either non-existent or carefully subdued.

However, a recorded fine of five shillings (ten pounds in today's values) on a certain bright citizen in Ballyvourney (Michael 'Sonny' McSweeney of Gortnascorty — 'Sonny Mac' was still 'bright' in my time) for failing to appear as a witness shows that some people were already looking ahead and had a presentiment of unpleasantness to follow. All details were laboriously inscribed in a weighty court register (still extant), the last column but one (which was reserved for the signature of the judge) carrying the tentative question: 'Was order carried out?' (without the question-mark incidentally!), which query betrayed the weak link on which the entire chain depended. There had to be a last resort, of course. It took the form of a grandiose and rather startling 'Warrant of Execution'. The only one still extant from the doings of the Ballyvourney Parish Court complains that a particular defendant not only failed to pay his 'Rates' but contumaciously refused to comply with a decree of the court for twelve shillings rates and three shillings and sixpence ('three-and-six') costs. Halcyon days of litigation! And the ubiquitous joker who served the 'Warrant of Execution' (Jerh 'Strock' Casey, in charge of police) let him frizzle for a highly illegal length of time with the fancy that one might, under the new order, be shot for twelve bob!

The first law case to go on the books in Ballyvourney concerned a recalcitrant swarm of bees. (*Note*: The book, I fancy, may still be in the home of John P. Twomey who showed it to me in 1953). In fact the Commandant of the Eighth Battalion (Dr. Paddy O'Sullivan) summoned the court specially to deal with the troublesome matter, and the court found itself established as of that date. The panel of judges consisted of Jack Hegarty, Dr. O'Brien and Dónall 'Bawn' Kelleher, renowned Gaelic scholar from Coolea. The two litigants were farmers, next-door neighbours, and cousins, who suffered from the usual ills of living in close proximity. The plaintiff was a 'Sinn Féiner', the other had so far kept an open mind. The 'usual ills' part was resolved in favour of the open-minded one, but the bees, true to nature, proved difficult. They were accused of trespass, a point of law with which bees are not notably conversant. In this case they had made a habit of alighting across the fence on a Sinn Féin whitethorn bush. While the case rested and the judges fidgetted, John P. Twomey, Court Registrar, out-solomoned Solomon by suggesting that the bees be moved. The order was duly made and the court solemnly rose, but not before the open-minded one shattered its dignity by shouting — 'Up Sinn Féin!'. 'John P.', as the Secretary-Registrar to the Sinn Féin court in Ballyvourney, was well known to one and all, and had a slight, though insignificant, association with the 'Slippery Rock' affair. A feisty little man, with big ideas and a sublime dignity all his own, he had hoisted the heavy registers under his arm on the morning in question and stepped out in lively fashion, from his home in 'Flatts', Ballymakeera, to attend a session of the court due to be held that day in the 'Gaelic Hall' at the back of O'Leary's Hibernian Hotel. His mind occupied with current matters of litigation, he was about to enter the village when he stopped abruptly, looked, wondered and scratched his shaggy head.

(He actually did it for me as he told me the story). His son, Pat, a 'Fianna Éireann' scout of fifteen years, had no business that he was aware of to be leaning his shoulder against the Post Office wall at that hour of the day. In the throes of cogitation and puzzlement John P. looked around, and then he discerned the cycle patrol of soldiers, in double file, approaching from the west. All things being now clear to him he looked around hastily, but by this time Pat was running helter-skelter down the village street to where Adjutant Jerh Lucey stood with a bicycle. John P. hurried on into the 'courthouse' and announced to the judge, Mr. Paud O'Donoghue of Coachford, that, as a result of his observations, he had deduced that an attack on the military was about to take place. The court was adjourned *sine die*.

* * *

Early in August, 1920, the local military O.C. in Liscarroll, a Lieutenant Honeywood, sent a message to me to call to the Military Post. I called up (i.e. to the Castle) and remained at the outer gate and asked the sentry to notify the officer i/c that I was there if he wanted to come out. He came out and, following discussion on some general topics, he informed me that he would hold me personally responsible in the event of any attempt being made on the R.I.C. I immediately enquired of him whether he had service in the Great War. He stated that he had. I then asked what their normal procedure was in dealing with spies. He replied 'Shoot them!'. I then politely informed him that we intended to follow similar action with the R.I.C.

(Commdt. P. O'Brien: *Official Statement*).

10

Trial by Ordeal: October-December, 1920

'The Law' in Ballyvourney, as elsewhere throughout the country, gave up the ghost in the middle of October, 1920. The R.I.C. left the barracks and the Military abandoned the doctor's house, 'The Chalet', on October 16. All British forces were now being concentrated in the towns, or, at least, in stronger positions, obviously with a view to shortening the front. The fight was getting hot and the Republican forces opposing them were quickly becoming stronger and apparently highly organized. At midday on October 20 the I.R.A. assembled to burn down the abandoned police barracks. While preparations were being made for the burning two sentries, John C. Creedon of Coomaguire and Peter Dineen of Coomnaclohy, were posted to cover the western and eastern approaches respectively. John C. saw them first. They came at him from the Coolea side. (*Note*: The Irish expression for coming on someone unexpectedly is rather quaint. It is *aniar aduaidh*, literally 'from west-north-west'. Latterly the expression has been abandoned in favour of more 'logical' forms!). The Auxies seemed to have the instinct of the old Danes for coming unawares on people. It was part of their act. This time they were 'coming round the mountain', two lorry loads of them, driving madly as was their

bar-leaners. They were in a bad mood. Tadhg Dineen, national teacher and Gaelic poet from Slievereagh, heard one of them mutter something like — 'We want blood!', or 'We'll have blood!'. Soon afterwards the mistaken identity tragedy took place, a little way down the by-road, that was still in the Fifties so touchingly remembered as 'the shooting of Jim Lehane'. In Tadhg Dineen's pockets they found a novel by Charles Garvice, a popular British author of the time (now forgotten), and a communication from the British Board of Education headed: 'On His Majesty's Service'. With an expression of surprise the searcher asked — 'What are you?', and, without waiting for an answer, he left taking the document with him to consult with a superior officer. Tadhg lost no time in slipping out the back way, though, as an inveterate reader, he much regretted the loss of the Garvice (prn. 'Jerviss', I seem to remember) book. The Auxie was already on his way in, stepped aside to let Tadhg pass and just murmured 'Cheerio!' to him. Relating the incident in Irish to my father, years afterwards, the ever lighthearted and happy-go-lucky Tadhg rounded off by saying — '"Cheerio!, imbaiste", arsa mise'. (trs. '"Cheerio, by golly", said I'). Before the search reached Jerh Lucey the searchers came to Mike O'Leary, V.C., who, as Sergeant Mike O'Leary, had been an international figure since his capture single-handed of a German machine-gun nest at La Bassée, near Lille, in Flanders. (*Note*: A native of Kilbarry, between Macroom and Inchigeela, Lance-Corporal O'Leary, orderly to a Lieutenant Innes of the Irish Guards, won his Victoria Cross on February 1, 1915, at the recovery of some front-line trenches that had previously been lost to the Germans by the Coldstream Guards. In a solitary escapade, O'Leary raced along a high railway embankment, assaulted two barricades, killed eight Germans and captured five more, thus eliminating the immediate threat to his No. 1 Company. For this achievement he received the Victoria Cross, which is mentioned in the official British history of the Great War, as the first V.C. of

1915. He was immediately promoted to sergeant and later to lieutenant, and was used by the British for recruitment purposes. The resentment to this activity was inopportune as the Volunteer movement was still far from being developed. During the Trouble he was well received by the Republicans, as I remember. I met him only once. He was married to a Ballyvourney girl, O'Hegarty from the 'Farm Yard'. Bernard Shaw is said to have based his play, *O'Flaherty, V.C.,* on his exploit. When I met him I was surprised at his slight build, average height and unassuming manner). Now the great Mike was having a drink with his brother-in-law, Bill Hegarty. One of the Auxies snapped — 'You haven't got your hands up!'. O'Leary, who was not in uniform, turned out the lapel of his coat and flashed the green ribbon of the Victoria Cross, the highest insignia for gallantry in the British Army. They immediately saluted. It was required military etiquette at the time. He let it sink in. Then in his best barrack-room manner he grated: 'These boys are all friends of mine. Now, get out, you scum!'. They went, and that ended the searching for the night. But they did not forget him, as will appear later.

Tragedy was still very near. Wanted men were everywhere. Tadhg Dineen went into John Creedon's cobbler's shop in the back laneway, thinking that by pretending to have his boots repaired he had a passable excuse for being around that night. He found Dan O'Leary there before him. 'Danny Arthur', as he was known to one and all, in aftertimes a Free State senator, was a 'wanted' man just then . He had been elected a Sinn Féin member of the Cork County Council. Next door, in a little unoccupied apartment, Captain Patsy Lynch had taken temporary refuge at the first warning of danger. Too late he found that there was no way of escape, either out the back or onto the roof, and already the Auxies were moving up and down the laneway outside. He turned at bay and put his back to the wall facing the closed door. The big, heavy Smith and Wesson revolver in his hip pocket felt bigger and heavier than ever. He eased it a little and waited. Unknown to him a young boy, John Healy (later De La Salle Brother Natalis, whose own brother, Dan, was a Volunteer and associated with the shooting of Bill Hegarty), who had slipped in just before him, crouched in a corner, unseen and fearful, and watched him prepare to meet the inevitable. No panic. No involuntary twitch of a muscle to betray an inward fear. Just dourly waiting to go out where he had come in, when the time was there, with a blazing gun clearing a precarious passage. But there was no sudden rush inwards. No challenge. Nobody came.

In O'Leary's hotel bar, Dr. O'Brien, a Midleton man doing duty locally, had awaited his turn to be searched. Temporarily a member of the Arbitration Court bench, he had in his pocket a telegram which said: 'Get two Sinn Féin magistrates to sign the order'. It happened to be an answer to a query of his made to a neighbouring doctor, Dr. Goold of Raleigh House near Macroom, as to what steps he should take to have a patient (actually the girl messenger at the shooting of Mike Lynch and Bill Hegarty) committed to the mental hospital. On being questioned about it the doctor's answers were not very civil and he was marched out to one of the waiting lorries. His confrère's house at Raleigh (*Note*: This word is not pronounced as in 'Walter — '. It is from the Irish, Ráth Laoi, meaning the fort of the Lee) was raided that same night and turned practically upside-down in the hope of securing some evidence about those 'Sinn Féin magistrates'. (*Note*: Dr. Pat Goold lived in the house originally occupied by Art O'Leary who was killed at Carriganimma, in 1733, by a rival, Abraham Morris, High Sheriff of Cork. His wife, Eibhlín Dubh Ní Chonaill, the dark Ellen O'Connell, aunt of Daniel O'Connell, the Liberator, composed a beautiful lament for him in Irish. Dr. Goold was a personal friend of Jeremiah O'Donovan Rossa, journalist and Fenian, whose Phoenix Society, in Skibbereen, was the original hard core of the I.R.B. The family still hold an original letter from Rossa to the good doctor, and surprisingly believe their friendship to have been the cause of the ransacking of the house by the Tans. Dr. Goold was one of the many mighty presences who brooded over my far too impressionable youth!). Now back to Ballymakeera where things were happening elsewhere that night. So much energy force had to produce an explosion. It came soon enough. Con Creedon, blacksmith, who had his forge just off the by-road which left the street at right-angles and went away southwards, came to the door of his house to see what he could see. He saw an Auxie listening at the window of the house next door. He retired immediately but the soldier followed him and called out a lad of sixteen who was in the house. He happened to be an orphan from an industrial school who was apprenticed to the trade. Paddy O'Sullivan, Con's son-in-law, went out to explain that they were responsible to the school authorities for the boy's conduct and welfare. Fancy trying that one on a Tan! He had a child in his arms and was told to take the child inside. He did so but took the precaution of closing and locking the door behind him. Shortly afterwards they heard some footsteps and Mrs. O'Sullivan peeped out. She saw two men go down the road towards the Sullane bridge. One was a civilian. The other was in uniform. As they passed the bar of light from the window she had no difficulty in recognizing their recent acquaintance, the Auxiliary with the motor-cyclist's helmet and the broken nose. The other was James Lehane. Jim was a middle-aged, easy going man, big and harmless. All this, and one thing and another, kept him from taking an active part in the events of the time. It was ironic, therefore, that fate should single him out as a victim to be sacrificed on the altar of a people's agony, and that his violent death should always be remembered as one of the most poignant tragedies of the period. On this particular evening he happened to be in a house in the village — his own home was at the East End — when an Auxie walked in. When questioned he gave his name as James Lehane. The name must have meant something to the soldier who was obviously the worse for drink. (Another Jim Lehane, known as 'Spatter' Lehane, from Gortyrahilly southwards of the village, was in the hue-and-cry at the time). He was ordered out of the house and directed down the by-road where, about fifty yards from the village cross, the Auxie emptied his revolver into him. Other Auxies ran towards the spot but immediately the usual whistle blew for 'All Aboard' and they made for the lorries at the double. Some of the villagers went down and found Jim Lehane slumped against the fence with his feet towards the road. His pipe was still in his hand and his tobacco pouch lay on the roadway beside him as if he had been taken completely unawares. There was no question about the killing. That day was done. All inquests had been abolished since the third of September.

*   *   *

'Hundreds of Protestants fled the area,and the repercussions in the North were frightful. But P (Pete Kearney) amd T (Tom Barry) were not finished creating repercussions, for some time later they were both in action again, and this time their target was not poor unfortunate Cork Protestants: this time it was a Cork Catholic. His name was Michael Collins'. (Kevin Myers — *An Irishman's Diary* in *The Irish Times*, December, 1989). The anglophiles ('shoneens') and Protestant-orientated (university professors) among us are still fighting dead battles and killing dead people with platoons of snipers, out of sight and out of mind — a very safe and comfortable position, but how else does one get notice in a dead alley for the recreation of History! And how well the old scholastic *Petitio Principii*, the fallacy of begging the question, has matured in our day!

*   *   *

Do ghaibh rabhta fíoch ár bhfear thar chlaí,
Do steall, do scaoil fé'n 'Auxies';
An mór-sheisear déag díobh fann do shín

142   CHAPTER TEN

Ar an ród san i Sean-Chaiseal.
Do ghaisce maoidheam, a Chill Mhichíl —
Choinnis brat na Saoirse a' mannar,
Is chun Chorcaigh Thiar thugais ceannas síor,
Is an Chraobh do Dhíorma an Bharraigh.

Date: November 28, 1920.
Occasion: The Kilmichael Ambush.
Poet: Patrick McSweeney (Pádraig Mac Suibhne, 'An Suibhneach Meann'), national teacher and doyen of 'Dámhscoil Mhúscraí Uí Fhloinn', the bardic school of Muskerry-Flynn, reformed in Coolea by the late Daniel Keohane (Dónall Ó Ceocháin), and the only one of its kind now functioning in Munster or, for that matter, in the whole of Ireland. (cf. *Filí an tSuláin,* by the author). The above might be roughly rendered: 'Our men made a raging charge over the fence, attacked and shot the Auxies, all seventeen of whom they laid low on that roadway at Shanacashel. Your valour I extol, O Kilmichael — you kept the flag of Freedom flying and to West Cork you brought eternal glory, and victory to Barry's Column'.

*   *   *

C Company of the Auxiliaries, stationed in Mount Leader, Millstreet, and particularly their platoon in Macroom Castle, were a confirmed thorn in the side. Third Brigade H.Q. had its baleful eye on them. H.Q. was contemplating something big and decisive. At such times H.Q. liked to be impressive and to impress, which was only right and proper. Sweeping orders usually resulted. So while H.Q. was considering suitable treatment for C Company all hostilities ceased by order. Eventually some officers came from Cork City and inspected possible ambush sites in the Ballyvourney region. This took a few days — from Wednesday to Sunday, in fact. Sunday was 28 November, 1920. The officers had completed their report for H.Q. and left Farmer Harrington's (Knocksaharn) late to prepare for their return journey to the city. It was dark, being Winter time. Paddy Donagh Owen noticed a peculiar glow in the sky to the southeast. They wondered about it. But it was a time when startling occurences had become commonplace, and the commonplace was no longer worthy of note. So curiosity marked time until the morning paper. What they learned then was that Commandant Tom Barry, with his Third Brigade 'Flying Column', had forestalled them. By the time he had finished with the arrogant C Company (or, rather, a section of them) they were so badly cut up that they were withdrawn altogether from the Castle. The glow in the sky had been from the British lorries burning at Kilmichael. So the ambush idea for Ballyvourney was shelved. Instead the police barracks was burned down during the following week, this time successfully, and, it would seem, needlessly. (*Note*: Tom Barry was prone to exaggeration. In his book, *Guerilla Days In Ireland,* he says :'One hundred and fifty of this new force of Auxiliaries arrived in Macroom in August, 1920, and commandeered Macroom Castle as their barracks'. Possibly one-third of that number, or even less, settled in the Castle. For more reliable information, from alternative sources, cf. Chapter Nine *supra*). The late Brendan Behan, the internationally renowned but unfortunately decrepit Dublin playwright and author, penned his own ditty (for his play, *The Hostage*) on the topic of the Kilmichael Ambush, probably the most famous ambush ever. More a partial re-writing than a parody, Behan's version was along the lines of the stately ballad, 'The Boys Of Kilmichael' (St. Michael features largely in the locality in holy wells and old churches). In contrast to the austere phraseology of the Coolea Bardic School, Behan's lines are predictably high in obscenity and pub heroics:

> On the Eighteenth day of November,
> Just outside the town of Macroom,
> The Tans in their big Crossley tenders

> Came roaring along to their doom;
> But the boys of the Column were waiting,
> With hand-grenades primed on the spot,
> And the Irish Republican Army
> Made s--t of the whole mucking lot!

A multifarious freedom nowadays permits one to fill in the blank letters, re-arrange the transferred epithets (except the wrong date!), and publish with impunity. Still, the record of the memorial service for the dead soldiers, conducted in Macroom Church of Ireland parish church by the rector, the Reverend A. J. Brady, gives them a certain posthumous dignity and places them among the human race with details of their home addresses. Of the seventeen killed the record book shows sixteen, and it states:

> 16 members of the R.I.C., 11 of whom were churchmen (C. of I.), were killed in Kilmichael Ambush on Sunday, November 28th., 1920. Bodies all brought to England. Memorial Service in Macroom on December 1, 1920. The following is the official list of the casualties:
>
> Colonel F.W. Craik, M.C., (late Bedford Regiment), 57 Stanton Street, Newcastle-on-Tyne.
> Captain P.N. Graham (late Northumberland Fusiliers), 14 Wootton Road, Abington, Berks.
> Major F. Hugo, O.B.E., M.C., (late Indian Army), Grove House, Southgate, N.
> Captain W. Pallester (late R.A.F.), care of Mrs. Brooke, 71 Primrose Avenue, Shire Green, Sheffield.
> Captain C. Wainwright (late Royal Dublin Fusiliers), 13 Brunswick Road, Gravesend.
> Cadet W. T. Barnes, D.F.C. (late R.A.F.), 47 Glebe Road, Sutton, Surrey.
> Cadet L.D. Bradshaw (late R.A.F.), 34 Larkhill Terrace, Blackburn.
> Cadet J.C. Cleave (late R.A.F.), Crowdale, Canterbury.
> Cadet A.G. Jones (late Suffolk Regiment), 56 Swindon Road, Wroughton, Wilts.
> Cadet W. Hooper-Jones (late Northumberland Fusiliers),

Mount Pleasant, Hawkstone, Tottington, Bury, Lancs.

Cadet E.W.H. Lucas (late Sussex Regiment), Terringes, West
Tarring, Worthing.

Cadet H.O. Pearson (Yorkshire Regiment), 22 St. Paul's
Square, York.

Cadet F. Taylor (late R.A.F.), 21 Seaview Road, Gillingham,
Kent.

Cadet B. Webster (late 8th Black Watch), 300 Langside Road,
Crosshill, Glasgow.

Temporary Cadet C.D.W. Bayley (late R.A.F.), 24 Reynard
Road, Chorlton-cum-Hardy, Manchester.

Temporary Constable A.F. Poole (late Royal West Kent Regiment), 35 Rodney Street, Pentonville, N.

*   *   *

The one who ran away did not live to fight another day. He
was captured near the 'Cross-of-four-roads' (now submerged
by the Gaeragh Reservoir), Annahala, on his way into
Macroom, and was shot of necessity, and buried in Annahala
bog. His name was Lieutenant Cecil Guthrie. His story is
worth recording. For the purpose I think I may quote
extensively from *Memories of Dromleigh, A Country
School, 1840-1990,* and under the article title, 'The Fearful
Aftermath':

Mary O'Mahony (Mrs. Hourihan), Dromleigh, and the late
Kate Murphy, Cooldorrihy (Mrs. McSweeney, Ballabuidhe),
retained vivid memories of Kilmichael Ambush and its effects on the locality. They both remembered the lorry loads
of Auxiliaries passing by on the road to Dunmanway on that
cold Sunday afternoon in November, 1920.

Mary recalls being outdoors playing with her younger
brother and wondering how the drivers would escape in an
emergency, as they were at a lower level than the body of
the lorry, on which the troops sat unprotected from the
weather.

The children always played a game connected with the in-
frequent motorised traffic, as to which could hear the sound

of the engines longest. On this occasion their rumble ceased abruptly, and in the ensuing silence they heard gunfire. They thought Fr. Gould, the local curate, was out shooting rabbits. The reports continued, and shortly they saw columns of smoke rising in the distance. Their father went to Coughlan's pub and very soon news of the ambush filtered through, with reports of the deaths of all the Auxiliaries and three of Barry's men, Pat Deasy, Michael McCarthy and Jim O'Sullivan.

Kate Murphy was staying with her sister, Mrs. Cronin, at Kilmichael Bar at the Cross. When news of the ambush came through they closed down, fearing reprisals. During that wild wet night she remembered hearing footsteps on the road and seeing a solitary soldier making his way towards Macroom. She thought it was Guthrie, an Auxiliary survivor, who got no further than Annahala.

Mary O'Mahony is one of the eight children marked present in Dromleigh's Roll Book on November 29th, 1920 . . . The master, Patrick O'Riordan, supervised them in a tense, fearful atmosphere until they heard three lorries pass by on the main road at midday. He then dismissed them. The locals saw one lorry return almost immediately carrying a wounded Auxiliary who had spent that terrible night among the dead at the road-side. Later they watched as the two lorries bearing the dead came slowly along, with the soldiers walking behind. They had burned two houses near the site of the ambush, O'Donoghue's and Kelly's. Now they took Jim Coughlan, the Postmaster, with them. As a Government Official, he should have reported the ambush to the authorities. He was an elderly man but was forced to walk behind the lorries. As the macabre procession approached Horgan's corner gunfire was heard and it was thought that Jim Coughlan had been shot. But the soldiers had fired at Jim O'Mahony and Jer Horgan who hid in bushes and had a narrow escape. Jim Coughlan spent three months in Cork Gaol . . .

Many of the locals left home and went to stay with friends and relations as they knew the Auxiliaries would be back . . .

That Tuesday the troops returned to comb the area. There was nobody in O'Mahony's and they set fire to the house but it was not seriously damaged. The fire went up part of the walls and Mrs. Hourihan still has the picture of the Sacred Heart which was partly scorched but not consumed by the flames.

Denny Sullivan, who worked on Cronin's farm in Toames, had come by horse and cart to John Cronin's Kilmichael Bar for provisions. He was the only man on the premises when the soldiers arrived. They were not satisfied with his identification and he was taken out and shot . . .

Fr. Long, the Parish Priest, went to Macroom Castle and persuaded the authorities that no Kilmichael person had been involved in the ambush. Nevertheless, the men of the parish remained on the run until other events took the spotlight off Kilmichael.

Tom Barry (*Guerilla Days*) claimed that all of the Auxiliaries were dead before the departure of the I.R.A. Unfortunately he was in error. One soldier remained alive until next day, when he was picked up by the relief column. Lieutenant Guthrie was wounded, and may have played dead. He certainly was in the second lorry which had stopped about two hundred yards from the Command Post, and also would have been one of those who re-opened fire with revolvers on the three unsuspecting Volunteers who were killed. After the Column had departed he got to his feet and headed for Macroom. The only way he knew was the bog road from Dromcarra Bar towards Annahala. At that point there was a road across the Gaeragh, at about its mid-point (submerged in the E.S.B. flooding of 1953), and was really a series of little bridges crossing the many rivulets between the wooded islets of that time. Guthrie obviously was retracing his steps, as it were . . .

'The fight over, we proceeded to collect the arms left by the enemy, seventeen rifles and revolvers, together with ammunition and equipment. The two tenders were then set on fire, and the Volunteers prepared to withdraw as soon as they had laid out the dead Auxiliaries by the roadside'. (Liam

Deasy in *Towards Ireland Free*). And that is where Deasy erred. On the morning of Monday, 29 November, the relief convoy from Macroom was met on the battle site by an intelligence officer from Dunmanway. He was Lieutenant E. Fleming, D.I.3, representing Major Percival who was in charge of intelligence for West Cork. Lieutenant Fleming made a detailed survey of the scene and drew up a sketch-map indicating exactly where each body lay. (cf. Illustration). Nine bodies were laid out in the corner of a field immediately facing Barry's Command post. Lucas, the driver of the first lorry, lay on the road beside his burnt out vehicle. The remaining six, from the second lorry, lay singly and in various lone positions from one hundred to two hundred yards away towards the second lorry position. Two of them, Pallester and Taylor, had made a suicidal assault on a central strong point and died in the attempt. Two others, Pearson and Ford, attempted to join forces with the first lorry, failed and lay where they fell in a central position. The remaining three fought near the second lorry position, shouted 'We Surrender' and then killed the three Volunteers who stepped down to them, just before Barry's mobile assault party from below came at the double to finish them off. They were Jones, Barnes and Guthrie, the latter not appearing on the Intelligence Officer's sketch, as he had long gone. The official list of those killed appeared in the *Cork Examiner* and in a quite faulty manner. Colonel Craik, the Commanding Officer in Macroom Castle, was given as 'Captain Crake'. Cadet Cleave appeared as 'Cadet Glease'. But strangest of all, 'Ford' on the sketch-map does not appear on the list. (See Appendix B for explanation). The tough (or cowardly) Lieutenant Cecil Guthrie, probably a Scotsman, headed for the town of Macroom, through the Winter darkness, rain and cold, alone, wounded and despairing. The local Toames Company, under Captain Nicholas (known as 'Louis') Dromey, could not let him be. Word was passed on that he had called to Twohig's, of Cooldaniel, and asked to be driven into

Macroom. They pleaded that the horse was indisposed. He moved on past Dromcarra Bar (where the Dromeys have been for over a hundred years) and down the bog road towards the Gaeragh. He was trailed first by the O'Mahony brothers, John and Jerry, who were then joined by Danny and Mikey O'Shea. A message was sent to Louis Dromey, the captain. At the 'cross-of-four-roads' they lost him in the darkness. They headed for the wilderness crossing and passed him sitting in a bush. He said — 'Good evening!'. They walked on a little and then returned. He said — 'If I had ammunition for this, you fellows wouldn't take me!'. He threw out his now useless revolver. Louis Dromey arrived and a council of war was held. There were no alternatives. He was taken into a section of Annahala bog, shot and buried. His grave was kept a secret by those who knew, until finally one of them revealed it to some of his relations who came to search for him in the early Thirties. His remains were removed and buried in the Protestant section of Inchigeela old cemetery, where, under a massive slab, he awaits the Resurrection.

*   *   *

Forty years back, I said to my good friend, Captain Patsy Lynch — 'Patsy, did they ever identify that Auxiliary who shot Jim Lehane?'. 'Oh, sure', said the imperturbable Patsy — 'He was a fella named Guthrie!'. Poetic justice?

*   *   *

The Kilmichael Ambush had a marked effect on the district west of Macroom, which had lately been accustomed to receive special attention from the Auxiliaries. The 'nuisance-raids' (World War Two expression) ceased completely. (*Note*: It is hard to see how Tom Barry could imagine that because he killed a handful out of one hundred and fifty it should have had such remarkable results. He fought outside his own territory, but nobody grudged him that). After that memorable day one inhabitant at least, on his own fervent admission, breathed more easily. The Master of Coolavokig school lived within sight of that hazardous main road to Ballyvourney. Morning and evening, for five days a week, he ran the gauntlet of shuttlecock raiders and travelled that road in order to keep his school open, or walked 'to school through the fields' and still faced the open road at the end. But he considered that if 'law courts' and other legal colligations were to be an integral part of the programme in the rehabilitation of a nation, so much the more should be the education of youth. So, Coolavokig school remained open, and many another throughout the country perched similarly on the brink of a troubled volcano, while, compared to nimble-footed Irregulars at home in their native element, the intrepid school teacher, always an object of suspicion, was a sitting duck for trigger-happy and vengeful Auxiliaries. It is no surprise that some teachers mixed things a bit in the course of duty. The story was told of an inspector of schools who arrived at a school in the Rathmore area to find a stolid local farmer in charge. After the obvious question, in which the words 'you' and 'here' were prominent, he inquired where he might find the teacher and was told, 'at an ambush taking place down the road a piece'. He did not pursue the matter.

R.I.C. powers were now completely in the hands of the military authorities. Macroom had been the headquarters of the West Muskerry district, including Millstreet. A District Inspector of the R.I.C. lived in the town. The police garrison at the barracks comprised a Head Constable, some sergeants, and about nine or ten constables, all under the D.I.'s control, as were the remaining garrisons in the various subdistricts surrounding. But by late 1920 very few of the old R.I.C. would seem to have been left in the town. At the same time the 'Flying Column' was coming into its own. Conceived in Tipperary, born in Limerick, it was being nurtured to its full stature in Cork. Kilmichael was a case in point. The hectic little skirmishes at company or battalion level were no more because now the enemy travelled in larger convoys, or prepared for instant battle as the Auxiliaries obviously were. A stronger, more versatile and wider-ranging striking force was needed. The result was the Brigade Column or Active Service Unit ('A.S.U.'). While British General Sir Nevil Macready, Commander-in-Chief, was fulminating in Dublin against 'the Macroom affair' — 'every law of civilized warfare was thrown to the winds', he wrote — rebel Commandant Tom Barry, a Great War veteran himself, was re-forming and preparing to strike again at widely scattered points within his Brigade area. (*Note*: It is extraordinary how the British, who had fought so much all over the world, always seemed to do so vociferously and with a deluge of words. At Kilmichael the Auxies fought cursing and shouting while the I.R.A. were tight-lipped, silent and tense). Abstracting from a mentality which could regard any form of warfare as 'civilized' — and American Civil War General William T. Sherman, in an university lecture, said that war is all hell — one can already see the birth of the 'Commando' idea which worked its erratic course through a part of World War Two, from 'Cockle-shell Heroes' to 'Hazardous Offensive Operations' ('H.O.O.'). (*Note*: For some reason I have never quite figured out, the daring Commandos were treated rather ignominiously by Evelyn Waugh in his *Sword Of Honour* trilogy . . . 'When the exotic name, "Commando", was at length made free to the press it rapidly extended its meaning to include curates on motor bicycles'). The British Commandos, and their American counterpart, the Rangers, specialized in the swoop tactics of guerrillas to harass strongly established regular army units. The idea was not new even in the days of the now famous 'Flying Columns'. The Boers had used it, the Russians previously, the American Indians from time immemorial, not forgetting two staunch Irish exponents of the long ago, Art McMurrough Kavanagh (Fourteenth Century) and Fiach MacHugh O'Byrne (Sixteenth Century). Jenghiz Khan, the Mongolian 'Perfect Warrior', by way of answer to the conventional shock tactics of the steel-clad cavalry of the Middle Ages, formed his little roving bands and swept all before him, so proving that mobility is the true basis of strategy. From classical times comes the classic example of the Roman General, Q. Fabius Maximus, called *Cunctator* i.e. the delayer, whose 'fabian tactics' in the war against Hannibal (218 B.C.) are still a synonym for guerrilla-type fighting. (*Note*: In fact Q. Fabius was the one who invented the phrase which became so vital in our own country at a crucial moment of history, the final stage in the Treaty Negotiations, in December, 1921. Lloyd George said to Arthur Griffith and Michael Collins: 'Is it Peace or is it War?', as he held up the vital letters. Fabius said to the Carthaginians in 218 B.C.: 'Is it Peace or is it War?'. The Carthaginians said they didn't give a damn, so he dropped a fold of his toga and said: 'Then take war!'. Perhaps Collins knew. He was a great reader). The Roman general defeated the invader by always choosing his own battle-ground. And Nevil Macready expected the beleaguered and part-time Irish Republican Army to fight 'according to the accepted rules of warfare'. But then he was more a policeman than a soldier . . . 'The (Police) Commissioner's head rolled and a new incumbent, General Sir Nevil Macready, son of a famous Victorian actor, took office on 3 September 1918. Macready cannot have relished his task, especially after the Armistice on 11 November 1918. The end of the war brought civil disorder, another and unwarranted police strike, a resumption of Irish terrorism and an increasing use of motor cars and firearms by criminals . . . On 14 April 1920, General Macready relinquished his appointment as Commissioner in order to take command of the British troops in Ireland'. (From *London's Armed Police*). The primary aim of war, morality apart, is to win. Whether you lie in wait for the enemy or jump him under cover of darkness or scrub or outcrops of rock is quite immaterial. Before the end, the Black and Tans themselves saw the advisability of forming their own flying columns to meet strategy with strategy. Groups of them were dropped by transport vehicles, did a rapid wheel through a trouble spot and were picked up later at a pre-arranged assembly point. The natural development which came to both Commandos and I.R.A. Flying Columns, the ability to dig in, if necessary, and fight a pitched battle for at least a day, produced some of the most famous episodes both in our own War of Independence and in World War Two . . .

> From having pursued a policy largely aimed at the local police constabulary, the I.R.A. had responded to Martial Law by turning their attacks upon the military. Organizing themselves on similar lines (and uniforms) as the British Army, the I.R.A. had invented a new form of guerrilla tactics: the use of Flying Columns that could move in specially-trained units across large areas, calling upon local units to help in ambushes, concealment, re-supply and Intelligence. This was to become a model for guerrilla warfare the world over.
> (From *Monty: The Making Of A General*, by Nigel Hamilton, 1981).

Hugh Montgomery, first cousin to the future Field Marshal, a Lieutenant-Colonel in charge of Intelligence, was shot in Dublin on 'Bloody Sunday', 21 November, 1920, but it is difficult to say whether Monty was out for revenge when he accepted the position of Brigade-Major of the Kerry Infantry Battalion stationed in Buttevant, North Cork, on 6 December 1920. However, the burning of Cork by the Black and Tans on 11 December changed his destiny. He was re-appointed to the Cork Infantry Brigade, in Victoria (now Collins) Barracks, and his meticulous attention to military order and duty probably altered his career and changed the course of Irish History. However, he gives the Irish 'Troubles' only the scantiest of cover in his scantily written memoirs, merely remarking that it was in some ways worse than the

Great War, bad for both officers and men from a correct military point of view and that he was glad when it was over. Before that happened, he was to become seriously involved in a number of quite notable operations, though he did admit in the end that the logic of history showed that there was no place in Ireland for a British army.

11

A Matter of Life or Death

Is life so dear or peace so sweet as to be purchased at the price of chains and slavery? Forbid it, Almighty God! I know not what course others may take; but as for me, give me Liberty, or give me Death!

(Patrick Henry, March, 1775).

What was the young Virginian 'frontier lawyer' so concerned about when he made this declaration in a speech to the Virginia House of Burgesses? What was he scared of? Red Indians? Mexican banditti? Pirates of the Spanish Main? Not at all! Just a few thousand Englishmen in red coats, peaked or tricorn hats, white suede trousers and high boots, holed up in forts scattered about his vast continent, three to four thousand miles away from England. (*Lingua Franca*: You gotta hand it to the Brits. They somehow had the ability to scare the hell out of people anywhere by just being preposterous). A month after his famous speech the shot was fired which was 'heard around the world'. It happened at the other end of the Colony line, at Concord, and already the Massachusetts 'Patriots' were being dubbed by British propaganda as 'an army of wild Irish asses!'.

*   *   *

Soon after Kilmichael the remnants of C Company of the
Auxiliary Division were removed from Macroom Castle and
replaced by some units of J Company, who were said to have
been by no means as offensive as the original mob, or else
they may have had an alternative drill imposed on them by
authority and/or the hard lesson of Kilmichael. One way
or the other, they showed comparatively little activity during their stay at the Castle, and only once did they carry out
a night raid, within the meaning, in the Eighth Battalion
domain. It was January the Third, 1921. Some men were in
the roadside farmhouse of Casey's of Derryfinneen, just west
of Renaniree village, on the road to Ballingeary. They had
with them some ammunition and bomb making material
which they were preparing for removal to a place of safety.
The Auxies came driving up the narrow, winding, rising
mountain road, having crossed Lynch's Bridge over the River
Sullane, at Coolavokig, where, at the age of two months,
I had just taken up residence. The men in Casey's rushed
out the front door and headed up a laneway towards the
rocks, but it was too late. They were spotted and fire was
opened on them. The men were Jerh Healy and Neilus Murphy, and seventeen-year-old Jeremiah Casey, a member of
the household. They brought the ammunition with them.
One of the men stumbled and young Jerh Casey turned back
to help him. He was shot in the process, but urged the others
to keep on going. He was brought down and died shortly
in the room next the roadway. His bronze monument leans
against the outside wall of that room. So far as it can be
read, in its badly neglected condition, it says that the boy
was a member of A Company, and that 'he died in defence
of the Republic', which is a fair statement, and he had the
consolation of knowing, before he died, that his two companions managed to escape with the ammunition. His
brother, Dan, was arrested and taken to Macroom Castle,
but was released soon afterwards for want of evidence. Dan's
widow, Mrs. Margaret Casey, who lives quite close to the

now derelict old farmhouse, says that his release was contrived by 'a friendly gaoler'. (*Note*: If this were so it would have to be a man known as 'Paddy Carroll', an enigmatic Auxiliary who appears later in this story, and was either a clever spy or a soft-hearted Irishman).

*   *   *

With my rifle on my shoulder, sure there's no one could
  be bolder;
I'm leaving dear old Cork where I was born,
For I've lately got an order to cross the Kerry border,
And I'm off to Ballyvourney in the morn.
(To the air of 'Off To Philadelphia', if you're in the mood).

*   *   *

The great possibilities of the west country for guerrilla warfare had long been recognized by the H.Q. Staff of the First Cork Brigade in Cork City. Early in January, 1921, they took to the hills leaving only a skeletal organization to carry on among the laneways, wharfs, warehouses, that are the proper milieu of a resistance movement in an occupied city, where only the city-born could survive for any length of time. Brigadier Seán O'Hegarty, O/C, led out his staff by strange and devious ways. Night, an unlighted red 'Buick' open-tourer (commandeered for military purposes and destined to become a notable feature of guerrilla activity until the end of the Civil War), and ebullient but expert driver Jim Gray added up for the Staff officers to the marvel of an uneventful passage to Ballyvourney. At Patsy Lynch's, Ullanes, the Brigadier set up his temporary Field H.Q., and the 'Column' was formed. Within the Army fabric the Active Service Unit (its original name) was a strange phenomenon, a syncretized, special-duty group comprising the pick of the whole Brigade and its available armament, existing in, through and concurrently with the Brigade unit itself. (*Note*: Mick O'Sullivan said that 'the Flying Column was the Army'). It had its own Commander who was absolute in his own right, the Brigade O/C himself taking his place *per modum actus* simply as an active member, while retaining his status under the prevailing Army system. For two weeks they imposed themselves on the decent country people, who were going through financial hard times because of the decline in farm prices since the cessation of hostilities on the Continent. It was two weeks of intensive training, army style. Seán Murray, Drill Master and ex-Irish Guardsman, saw to that, while Seán O'Hegarty ruled the roost with an iron hand. (*Note*: Seán was a native of Carrignavar, near Cork City, and was brother of the somewhat more notable historian and bookman, P. S. O'Hegarty). The Brigadier was a caution. His austerity was a byword, his fastidiousness something you forgot only once. And he was tough. Though roughly ten years their senior (he was thirtyone), the route marches he directed tried the stamina of the fittest among them. The country lads were slower to catch on to his discipline, less alert than the city fellows (who knew him somewhat ironically as 'The Joker') in responding to orders, and less familiar with his character. Patsy Lynch, who loved a funny story, told me of the solitary outpost guard who reported in from his lonely night-watch on Carrigmore (the 'Big Rock') and was startled by a bark — 'Take that pipe out of your mouth and stand to attention while you are speaking to me!'. There followed a comically opened mouth and a pipe clattering on a flagstone. (*Note*: Both Seán O'Hegarty and his brother, P. S., were long standing members of the I.R.B., the successor of the Fenian Movement of the previous century, which, in a secret capacity, determined greatly the course of Irish History from 1916 through the Civil War when Seán opted for neutrality and P. S. 'went with Michael Collins').

*   *   *

It was Bernard Montgomery's misfortune to be cast into the Irish fray at the very worst moment, when insurrection, far from being contained by the massive increase of British troops stationed in the country, had escalated to the point of war. Although the intellectual and political centre of the revolt was Dublin, it was in the southern counties of the country that the British were hardest put to keep order. The countryside was poor in roads, and telephone and postal communications were in the pocket of the Irish Republican Army . . . He arrived at Cork on 5 January, 1921.

(From: *Monty: The Making Of A General*).

*   *   *

The first Flying Column commander to be appointed for the First Cork Brigade was always best remembered by his confrères (and even still by his gracious wife), without prejudice to the dignity and seriousness of his position, as 'Sandow'. Dan O'Donovan, heretofore Commandant of the First (City) Battalion, was of no more than medium height, but his fine physique, athletic ability, as well as the fiery, determined and energetic disposition for which he was noted, marked him down as a leader among men. The jet-black hair and sallow features rounded off a likeness which earned him the well-meaning label. (*Note*: Frenchman Eugene Sandow, 'the world's strongest man', appeared in a variety show at the Palace Theatre, Cork, at the turn of the century. He visited Murphy's Brewery and performed the feat of lifting a Clydesdale dray-horse off the ground with one hand, a tableau retained for many years as the company's trademark). . . .

The Column Commander reviewed his troops in the chill, quavering light of an early morning in late Winter (21 January, 1921). He found them drawn up on the narrow, sloping little field behind Burrick's house, facing the rugged brow of Brohill's Rock. The brittle wind whistled lightly among the boulders and furze bushes and through the chinks in the dry-stone wall to their back, and moaned a little at the corner of the old house to the side. A *sruthán* (stream) gurgled away in the *glaise* (gully) below. You could feel in your bones the cold of the unseen water. Rigid and silent they stood, four sections of fifteen riflemen each. They were, he thought, the best. What guerrilla leader ever thought otherwise! Here, on this misplaced parade-ground, he felt proud, optimistic, which was second nature to him, but disconsolate. The material was fine, the purpose assured, but the 'stuff' for maintaining same was precarious to say the least. Fifty rounds per rifle and a few pans for the two Lewis machine-guns were possibly sufficient for a short-lived and lively encounter, or, with care, a rather longer ambush or siege. On the success would depend the supply for the next effort. The failure . . .

The accomodation to date was nothing short of primitive, rudimentary, without the benefit of the ease and warm sunshine always associated with peoples and nations who let the world go by through the ages without the botheration of effort, and who are now, as the mis-named 'Third World', paying a terrible price in a hard, wholesale money-market era. But here, in rainy, cold, mid-west Cork, was just an abandoned old dwelling-house on the bare, windswept hillside, that had been doing duty as a cowshed. A matting of straw on the floor of the room off the 'kitchen'. The sleeping men ranged around the walls, feet towards the centre, backwoods style, complaining in their sleep from the cold, queasy stomachs breaking wind loudly and malodorously in the confined atmosphere, a racking cough somewhere in the darkness. Another lot similarly cooped up in a barn-loft a few fields away. The daily 'Mess' justified its vulgar connotation and survival impersonally contemned alike the discerning palate and weak digestion. After the morning's work-out, a row of mugs on the long deal tables. For lunch (they called it 'dinner'), a bleating sheep from the mountain, dispatched, skinned, cleaned and bundled into the pot, 'and she nearly warm enough at that', said Patsy Lynch. Quartermaster Seán Lucey and Orderlies Michael Dineen and Paddy Casey, of the local B Company, doing their valiant best notwithstanding. Mugs parading again for supper. It was only the beginning. Hereafter, and to the end, the staple diet — when they could get it — would be tea, 'loaf' bread and eggs, until it almost came out of their ears through nausea. Health often taxed beyond recovery, time has gleaned what the Tans failed to reap — a harvest of early deaths, shattered nerves, rheumatoid and crippled bodies. The constant companions of the creatures of the wilds, wanderers of the wastelands, they were to know abject poverty and destitution as well. The 'Arms Levy' might produce some feed for the guns, the 'Shirts and Socks Campaign' might bring an occasional change of clothes, but neither, ever, a clink in the pocket. A certain well-known citizen of Glenflesk, Co. Kerry (Mike Donoghue told me), who got no return from two companions for his round of drinks at Morley's Bridge public house, complained ruefully that 'one of them was an I.R.A. man and the other hadn't any money either!'. Pathos can sometimes mimic humour's titter, or, as poet Jamesy Kelleher put it in one of his Gaelic epics, *bíonn greann ag gigilt trí ghruain an domhain*, fun does be smirking out of the world's distress . . .

> That night I met the bold O/C;
> 'Remember this', he said to me —
> 'You'll get no clothing, food or pay,
> But just the honour in the I.R.A.'

Meanwhile the erudite 'nigger in the woodpile', the logomachist at home, could spin his periods and concoct his contrary arguments (as he still does in 1994, when to be seen to be un-Irish has become so fashionable) in that pleasant, post-prandial recess when the world rests and thinks, or just rests, and a favourite chair means such a lot and is so far removed, physically and philosophically, from a bundle of oaten straw in a draughty outhouse in the dead of Winter, with the wind telling, through spectres of Morpheus, of an enemy well-housed, well-fed, relentless, searching, ever searching; and the 'most unkindest cut of all' (because he was an honest priest) from the cruder protagonist, with the

clerically inhibited point of view, proclaiming from the altar:
'I.R.A. . . . I Rob All . . . I Ruin All . . . and, I Run Away'.
Et tu, Brute! . . .

The Column Commander was speaking. Honour in the
I.R.A. was his theme. His voice sounded thin and hollow,
unreal. The bitter wind played tricks with it, the high heavens
drew from its substance. He was sparing with his words, a
man of action rather than speeches. They were silent, listening, all impatient to go in where the smoke billowed out and
the mugs rattled. After dinner was for speeches. But this was
an order of the day, the field commander saying his say while
he had them together, because they were leaving tonight. Five
p.m. sharp. They would be in Coomroe, the 'red recess',
where the River Lee rose in the hills above Gougane Barra,
when they stopped marching. The interval was eighteen miles.
(*Note*: O'Sullivan's *Where Mountainy Men Have Sown* has
an alternative version to the Ballyvourney one in my time
. . . 'With the Lewis-gun section I travelled in one', i.e. of
two motor cars carrying the bedding and necessary equipment. 'The Column moved off across the hills while we, taking advantage of the twilight to drive without lights, went
by quiet roads around the feet of the hills. Our destination
was Carrig Bán, a deep secluded glen in Ballingeary'. Carrig Bán, the 'white rock' is in a neighbouring valley, and
sits beside a mountain thoroughfare traversed by Major Percival, a few months later, in the Big Round-up. I wonder
who was right! At least it is fun to speculate). Then another
two weeks of training. Then action. The night-watchers from
the high points were in, their oil-soaked torches no longer
needed. The day watchers were gone out, but at nightfall
they would come bringing their equipment — the telescope
from Rahoona Rock (the rock of 'Una's fort') that could
plainly discern the crossroads at Raleigh, near Macroom,
and the big binoculars from Carrigvore that could barely
detect the movement of lorries in the Square before the Castle
in Macroom, ten miles away. The Commander was asking

for questions. None came. The idea was clear. They went in to breakfast.

After training in Ballingeary, the final base camp for action was at Clountycarty, in a vacant house on a farm owned by the Harrington family of Coolavokig. It is even still a lonely, isolated place just south of Renaniree, overlooking the Toon valley, with the ridge of Cleanrath (the 'leaning fort') and Derrineanig (*Doire an Aonaigh*, the 'wood of the fair') rising steeply on the southern side. Here the men of the Column drilled, exercised and played football (my father said, being a good footballer himself) in full view of the inhabitants and in complete accord with them. From this camp they prepared several ambushes, but without success. Strong forces of the enemy still passed hurriedly along the roads westwards but at random. The occasional convoys were bigger now. Flying raids were rare. Some of the Brigade officers went to inspect the lie of the land at Keimcarrige (the 'rocky defile'), an obvious location three miles out of Millstreet towards Macroom. It was too far away. They decided to cancel it. On four mornings they went to the already historic 'Mouth of the Glen', near Ballingeary, and waited fruitlessly until night. Anxious to contact the enemy, they were having no success . . .

What he (Montgomery) did not bargain for was the sheer size of the Brigade he (as Brigade-Major) was meant to run — comprising no less than seven battalions! The 17th (Cork) Infantry Brigade was in fact the largest Brigade in Ireland, commanded by Brigadier-General H.W. Higginson, DSO . . . in the ensuing months its complement would rise to some nine battalions . . . By February, 1921, he (i.e. Major-General Sir Peter Strickland, the Divisional Commander in the South) was offering the GOC-in-C in Ireland, Sir Nevil Macready, his resignation, so weary and pessimistic did he feel . . . Bernard, as Brigade-Major, became responsible for a number of large-scale manoeuvres or 'drives' in which several brigades cooperated in traversing the countryside and flushing out rebels. Meticulously planned and executed, these drives nevertheless failed to locate, let alone destroy, the I.R.A. guerrilla columns; and were eventually discontinued.

(From: *Monty: The Making Of A General*) . . .

So, acting on the principle that all things come to those who wait, the Column officers decided to hold a continuous position on the main road near Ballyvourney for as long as was necessary or endurable. A stretch of road at Coolnacahera, about two miles from the village of Ballymakeera, was selected as the most likely spot. They were to begin on February 11, but it was St. Gobnait's Day, a local holiday, with a likelihood of many people passing during the day to the 'Rounds' at the revered shrine at Gortnatubrid (the 'field of the holy well'); so they called off the ambush and went instead to the 'Mouth of the Glen'. On the same day the Tans from Millstreet came down the little Cabaragh by-road and went on towards Clondrohid. The bridge over the Foherish river was down before them. Exasperated they shot a young man named O'Mahony, returned and went on to Macroom by the main road. Obviously they were developing a sense of anticipation . . .

The following is an extract from a letter to the author from Mr. Michael Kelliher, Lactify, Clondrohid, 27/2/1980:

As regards young O'Mahony, who was shot in Clondrohid, on February 11, 1921, the following are the facts. Daniel O'Mahony (16 years) was in his place of employment (Clondrohid Tavern) on the date in question. Also present — Daniel Kelliher (publican), Jack Seán Kelliher and Jim Seán Kelliher (both of Clashmaguire). Jack Seán's wife was expecting a child and they had come to the village to meet the midwife from Macroom, to escort her across the bridge. The roar of the lorries coming from Ballyvourney (direction) caused them to panic. All four ran from the public house. O'Mahony and Jack Seán went in one direction whilst the other two took a different route. Jack Seán's pipe fell as he was going over a fence, and, as he stooped to pick it up, he felt the bullet passing over him. He afterwards said that his pipe saved his life. O'Mahony was shot dead in the field back of Clondrohid Tavern. Daniel Kelliher made his way to the back of the A.O.H. hall, but the Tans surrounded him. He later said that they would have shot him were it not for the fact that the P.P., Fr. Dwyer (who was reading his Office in the vicinity) came to his assistance. Jack and Jim Seán got a buffeting from the Tans and they were taking Jack as a hostage but Jim volunteered to go in his stead. I have heard people refer to the Tans' conduct on that evening, as similar to Mad Dogs. There were two lorry loads of Tans, and it appears that they were very drunk as they had been drinking in Ballymakeera. During the Second World War a programme on the Radio, known as 'Germany Calling', could be heard regularly. The announcer was known as 'Lord Haw-Haw'. On the 11th of February (I can't recall the year) he announced that Daniel O'Mahony was murdered in Clondrohid by British Crown Forces on this date.

(*Note*: 'Lord Haw-Haw' was the pseudonym for adventurer William Joyce, of Galway, who was hanged by the British after the war 'for treason', on the technicality that his Irish passport still had the British crown on it, proving that he was a British citizen — a strange case of political revenge. Actually the British people rather enjoyed his broadcasts, as did the world over. He had strange tricks, like informing the people in a certain town that their town clock was running late. He took a peculiar fancy to the people of High Street, in Bristol. I lived there just after the war. He used to say: 'You people over there in High Street, Bristol, had better get to your shelters now. We'll be with you shortly'. Which they did gratefully, and returned to their homes, and a good night's sleep, as soon as the bombers had passed. Joyce's remains were finally brought to Galway in 1976 and interred in the New Cemetery. Fr. Paddy Lee, of St. Patrick's Parish, now a retired archdeacon, presided at the obsequies. At the request of Joyce's daughter, Mrs. Heather Ron

Iandolo, the Mass in the Catholic oratory of the cemetery was celebrated in Latin by permission of Bishop Michael John Browne. As I stood by the graveside I was gratified to watch the B.B.C. give the burial the full treatment to the extent of erecting an alternative scaffold to film the coffin as it descended into the ground. Heather, married to a London Italian, stood demurely in black and read feelingly from her thoughtful book of religious verse, *Prelude to Heaven*. It was a beautiful day. A few of his classmates from St. Ignatius' Jesuit College days were present. Women with baby-carts wheeled in and stepped over to sympathize with Mrs. Iandolo for her illustrious American-born Galway father. Thirty years on 'Lord Haw-Haw' had the last laugh!).

For the next few days the Column was shuttling back and forth between Coolnacahera and the 'Mouth of the Glen'. Finally they decided to settle in at Coolnacahera and wait. Somewhat cynically, and with hindsight, Patsy Lynch and Paddy Donagh Owen O'Sullivan told me in the Fifties that the local 'gomeen section', as they said, was always sent in advance . . . 'Into the valley of death', as it were. At eight o'clock in the morning of February 23, 1921, the main body marched from the camp while others repaired from their homes. It had become well known that they were there. Passers-by to and from Macroom could not help but notice them. It was now a challenge to the enemy. The twenty-third of the month was traditionally Ballyvourney fair day. All assemblies, including fairs, had been proscribed by the military authorities. Fairs were forbidden within two miles of Ballymakeera village and Macroom town. Such a restriction was not new in History. Fairs had been curtailed for a similar reason by the Statute of Kilkenny in 1367. (N.B. Reminds one of Juvenal's classic — *Quis custodiet ipsos custodes*?, Who shall guard the guards themselves? — as do so many forms of legal and civic restrictions in the chaotic world of today!). Thus it happened that the Ballyvourney fair, on this occasion, was held just outside the two-mile limit at Coolnacahera, in a field owned by Michael M. Twomey ('Mike Mhicil'), Sinn Féin County Councillor and member of the Macroom Board of Guardians. It was a largely attended fair as none had been held in the Macroom region for quite some time due to the prohibition. There were farmers from a wide area and 'jobbers' from far away. People said afterwards (according to my father) that it was the last of the 'good' fairs. A decided slump in the price of cattle, and farm produce generally, and land too (as my father was to learn to his cost — he had just paid a borrowed thousand pounds for a farm of fifty acres of land and two acres of rock, and got the same thousand back for it fifteen years later!), took place soon after this and 'war prices' came to an end rather abruptly. Nothing like a good old war to keep some people happy! Here, in this muddy and dung-garnished temple, they worshipped before the altar of Quick Profits. A couple of hundred yards away was the making of another war, but it was doubtful as yet if the ingredients would mix to the consistency of profit for all or any concerned. Business had begun in the early morning. Full daylight showed some of the boys roosting on their comfortless positions, plainly visible to any who cared to look in that direction. The carelessness was understandable for those brought up in the farming tradition, and many a glance was cast in the direction of the steady lowing of cattle and the other familiar sounds of the fair-field as a man here and there, with a wry, mordant recapitulation of History, struggled to make overtures to the unfriendly furze bushes and outcrops of stone. For many at the fair it was the first intimation they had of a 'flying column' in the district, or of their camp a few short miles away across the hills. Two days later the Tans came.

*   *   *

These were my arguments. Up until the Union of 1707, Scots law was founded not on the supremacy of Parliament, but on the Sovereignty of the people. If a law was oppressive, or against public policy, or even if it was obtuse and un-workable, it could be disobeyed and would fall into desuetude and be forgotten. In the last resort the real power of the Kingdom was not the parliament which passed the law, but the law courts and the people who took it upon their conscience to ignore a law which they considered to be un-workable. I lived, however, in a time when the Anglo-Teutonic doctrine of the supremacy of the central government had usurped the Scottish doctrine of the supremacy of the people. My academic arguments may have been good Scots law, but they would not have been accepted at the Old Bailey.

(From *The Taking Of The Stone Of Destiny*, by Ian Hamilton, Q.C.).

12

The Battle of Coolnacahera

The Master was preparing for school. It was Friday once again and he was looking forward to the week-end. He now lived in a long, low farmhouse by the Sullane river at Coolavokig (the 'retreat of the giant'), having left Capnahilla (the 'little corner plot'), an amateur farmer as ever was, having been raised in a cobbler's cottage near Inchigeela. Ten or fifteen minutes away across the fields Coolavokig schoolhouse was visible high up beside the Ballyvourney road where it wound its way carefully among a tumbling abundance of bare rocks. Things had been exceptionally quiet on the main road of late, but one never knew when they might appear again, and there was always the fear of what the consequences might be. The Master was no coward, but even for brave men the silence itself was ominous. The sullen roar of approaching Lancias, the snarl of Crossley tenders, and the sudden, startling appearance of the little 'Whippet' armoured cars with their smooth-working Rolls-Royce engines had seared a track on his subconscious mind that would not be erased for many a long day. Sitting by the turf fire in the quiet of a Winter's evening, many years later, or taking a walk in a country place in the still of a frosty night, he would suddenly hold up his hand with a hiss of warning and stay for a long moment listening — listening for something that a younger generation could not visualize, something that was only a belated echo from the vibrant pulse of another day. So, musing on his chances of rounding off the last school-day of the week without untoward incident, he prepared to resume the monotonous round of duty. Then it happened. His wife, Molly, rushed in breathless to the kitchen. 'The Tans are going up!', she gasped. 'Up' meant the quay-wall below the schoolhouse where passing traffic would be visible. There was no mistaking it. The dreaded trucks were going up, several of them, judging by the persistent rumble on the light air of that exceptionally fine morning in that exceptionally fine Spring of that exceptionally fine year. Already he knew the time, but an instinctive impulse made him glance once again at the big kitchen clock on the wall. Twenty to nine. That left him with a good margin to be at his job by nine-thirty if nothing happened. He ran out to the backyard and from a vantage point beside the old barn he was able to count seven Crossleys or Lancias (he just said 'lorries') going round the school bend. How many more had gone by, if any, he had no idea. He waited a few minutes and then the crackle of machine-gun fire pierced the air. It was his first experience of this and it formed an impression on his mind of a boy drawing a stick firmly across a sheet of corrugated iron. He stayed on to watch, and soon afterwards he heard the sound of a lorry rushing back down the road and on the kaleidoscopic quay-wall appeared what he took to be a tender making for Macroom at a terrific speed. The firing was now continuous, so he decided that it would be foolhardy to go to school at all that day. In any case he knew that no children would attend as none of them would have left home when the trouble started, and the road would soon become a busy scene of military activity. He was to pay for that decision.

*   *   *

On Thursday evening, before breaking positions, an order from the Column Commander had been passed from rock to rock. The weary round of waiting would be resumed once again on the following morning. Usually there were a few who had permission to spend the night in their homes and, inevitably, these failed to arrive on time with the marching Column. On location the first section, who were mainly drawn from the local company, held the eastern flank. Their job was to cover the road-block on the by-road which slanted north-west, forming an acute angle and hemming them in. They were also expected to provide enfilading fire when the trap had been sprung. V. Comdt. Paddy O'Sullivan did not remain with them, however, but lay further back on a razor-backed rock directly overlooking the ambush 'line' (a pre-arranged but imaginary spot on the road). His men were strung out between at various points of vantage and disadvantage. Quite near were the men of No. 2 Section with their Lewis-gun. Eugie O'Sullivan, with Mick O'Sullivan, his assistant, looked after their light machine-gun with tender loving care ('T.L.C.', as the American hospital system used to refer to it in my time), sweeping the whole stretch right along to the bend of the road. Eugie (everybody knew him as 'Foxeen', from his rust-coloured hair and sly ways) had the responsibility of firing the opening shot when all the cars in the convoy, if any chanced the way, were plainly visible to him on that plainly visible length of roadway beneath his lofty perch. (*Note*: According to M. O'Sullivan, he himself had 'laid the gun ready for action', as Eugie was late and slid into the position just in time to fire the opening burst, and O'Sullivan continues: 'On my left front I could see Corney O'Sullivan, Jim Gray, Seán Murray, Patsy Lynch, my brother Pat, Sandow and Jack Culhane'). At Eugie's back, he told me, was No. 3 Section, under Mick Murphy of Cork City (later to be Column Commander), while, down close to ground level, was a strong force of shotguns, interspersed with an occasional rifle, the close-work men, just inside the fence of the road (including two local stalwarts, Dan J. Quill and Dan Lynch, and the ever-dependable Second Lieutenant Mick Leahy of Renaniree), ready to give a hot reception to any who might run the gauntlet of a chance breakthrough. Away on the right across the road, and stretching almost at right-angles to it, a scraggy hump of a ridge insinuated itself from out the surrounding marshland. It was comforting to know that this solid natural emplacement was determinedly held by the men from Macroom, No. 4 Section, led by Comdt. Dan ('Colder') Corkery — 'the best fighters of them all', Paddy Donagh Owen said generously. Here they were admirably placed to wither up the resistance when the enemy would have jumped for cover behind the fence on their side of the road, which would be the only course open to him when the attack began. (*Note*: 'While waiting at our post, which was just across the road from the Command Post, we had received word that the Auxiliaries at Macroom had acquired two armour-plated lorries with sloped roofs of close mesh wire netting to prevent grenades from landing within . . . The fact that the force had left Macroom at 7 a.m. and took over an hour to reach our position, seven miles away, showed the amount of caution they exercised'. Charlie Browne: *The Story Of The 7th*). On the left of the Lewis-gun the small group already mentioned by M. O'Sullivan also included Brigadier Seán O'Hegarty, and was, in fact, the Command Post.

Patsy Lynch and his companions flattened themselves on a rock that was quite bare (he remembered) except for some odd clumps of Winter heather which only served to obscure their view on the left, the direction they were most likely to expect trouble from. And so they kept their eyes glued to the bit of road directly in front of them and waited. 'Sandow', the Column Commander, moved out and took up a lone position low down almost at road level, by a little rock that was no more than sufficient to measure his length on, where a hand-grenade might easily have reached him from the road. With a detachment of cavalry in the lee of Cemetery Ridge at Gettysburg, or on the Vorontsov Heights at Balaclava — if you do not know of those places, please do not read any further! — he would have been well placed for a decisive charge at the right moment. But the remark of French General Bosquet after the Charge of the Light Brigade — 'It is magnificent, but it is not war!' — applied still more to the essential profit and loss of guerrilla warfare. The Column Commander, always an impetuous fighter, was not in a position to command, to say the least, still less to command according to the trend of the impending battle, which, as things turned out, was not even visible from there.

*   *   *

The night of February 24, 1921, and the morning of the twenty-fifth, came very wet. Rain poured steadily from nightfall and continued on into the morning. The men at Clountycarty dozed fitfully on their bundles of straw or listened to the drumming of the rain on roof and windows, waiting in sleepless depression for the day. The prospect of lying on chilly, rain-soaked ground was enough to damp the ardour of the stoutest hearts among them. By morning the rain had eased off and spirits began to rise again. Hot tea and a lively march did the rest, and if one or two had surreptitiously slipped a drop of the 'craythur' (poteen whiskey) into their cups, when the Brigadier wasn't looking (he hated alcohol!), who could blame them! It was hard for anyone — barring an Auxie, of course — to feel full of fight at that hour of the morning after a night of rain. Those who had managed to shave by candle-light felt reasonably clean (N.B. I was told this, but it seemed to me like the futility of effort if one were to end up dead before the end of the day), and everybody felt reasonably cheered when at last they arrived to survey the state of their positions. The surveyal was short-lived. (*Note*: 'Their route was the same as that of the previous mornings . . . upwards through Clohina of the stunted oak and holly groves, down Capnahilla, along a boreen, past a disused farmhouse' — where, in fact the present writer was born just four months before — 'across the Sullane by Tom Murray's steps'. O'Sullivan: *Where Mountainy Men Have Sown*). They had barely settled in when the ominous rumble of approaching lorries began to be picked up and magnified by the surrounding rocks until they seemed to be almost everywhere, and the urgent whisper passed along the ranks, 'They're here!', the tensity of it seeming to pierce the noise and soar upwards in a screaming crescendo through the suddenly chilled atmosphere. Hands sweated and trembled on gun barrels that had first gone cold and then hot. Eyes pained with the strain of looking against the fear of what they might see and blood pounded in the ear-drums. All the training and preparation had been for this moment, and for those agile, apparently fearless, dark-clothed Britishers, with glengarries askew, who sat in their lorries and carried their rifles as if they were all moulded in one piece, who sprang to life with explosive, seemingly diabolical energy, who in and through and even after Kilmichael had still seemed indestructible — and now they were HERE! Their arrival closed a long chapter of waiting, and opened a new and strange one of resentment swelling into anger, anger giving place to a surging fury at their obnoxious and unjustifiable presence. As the first tentative volley showed several of them sprawling wounded and helpless like cowering dogs before the charge of buckshot, others bolting for cover in panicky confusion from the vengeful lead, the whole attacking force surged with the one desire and one spirit, bred of centuries of bitter chagrin, an overpowering urge to destroy . . .

The Tans were on the alert from Dan 'the Yank's'. They came slowly, sweeping the rocks around and ahead of them with their field-glasses. There were nine lorries with a small FORD car at the head. Four hostages were in one of the leading lorries. Carrying hostages had come to be a matter of course with them. The obvious advantages of an ambushing party, and the many disasters of late, had begun to tell on nerves that had to be always taut and waiting, expecting at every bend the searing crash of gunfire. The hostages were their answer to it, a means of hurling defiance at the hidden menace peering from behind rocks and fences. Major James Seafield-Grant, the Commanding Officer, was rather towards the middle of the convoy. His features refined and youthful looking (from a Press photograph), even to boyishness, for all of his twenty-nine years, he had only just lately been assigned to command the Auxiliary Post in Macroom Castle, following on the death of Colonel Craik. He had been decorated for gallantry in France (Military Cross) during the Great War, had been married in Dublin four weeks previously and had left for the South shortly afterwards. Fate led Jimmy Grant along strange ways to die by the side of a lonely, rock-bound road in West Muskerry. (*Note*: His only son visited the scene in the Summer of 1967).

Ex-soldier Eugie O'Sullivan crouched beside his machine-gun holding the sights steady on the bend beside the outcrop of rock where the road was lost to sight. Around and behind him the men were keeping well down. They had heard the rumble of the lorries some time before the frantic warning reached them. Around the bend came one hostage walking the middle alone, hands in the air and shouting. Just behind him came a small motor car moving along at a walking pace. A lorry followed, and another. Remembering his instructions Eugie fixed his foresight on the leading car and started to shift slowly with it. Almost immediately, it seemed, a shot went off far away on the eastern flank and a volume of firing shattered the already ruffled atmosphere. The walking hostage took a flying leap over the fence . . .

'Get out again', said an Auxie, presenting a revolver. The Auxie fell dead. 'Come over here', said another Auxie. 'Lie down there', he said, 'don't go out. We'll get those fellows after a while. They have got only revolvers'. The Lewis-gun spoke again. 'By God', said the Auxie, 'the bastards have got the quick-firing so-and-so's'.

(From *Where Mountainy Men Have Sown*) . . .

The car pulled up close in by the side of the road and was hastily abandoned, while the two lorries reversed almost out of sight. When the Lewis-gun began to splutter the men around raised their heads to see what was bothering the gunner. They were amazed to see a car and a lorry already abandoned, with the erstwhile occupants safely entrenched, for the time being at any rate, on the healthy side of the dry-stone wall. Steam spouted up from the radiator of the motor car to show that the engine was still running. Because of that vital bend the Auxies were partly safe from the attentions of Section 4 — the Macroom men south of the road. They established themselves temporarily and set to returning the fire of the Lewis-gun. I.R.A. rifles joined in and the battle began to rage. But for a slight chance the lorry at the end of the line would now have been just about where the leading FORD car stood spouting like a stranded whale. Most of the British were quickly drawn into and around the two cottages (still there) where they assumed a state of siege. A Hotchkiss machine-gun, hastily set up in the backyard of the near cottage, began to answer the Lewis-gun, its distinctive report, combined with the echo from the rocks, giving the impression to the opposing gunners of being fired close at hand.

The preparedness of the British had filched from the ambushers their trump card, the element of surprise. Coming into the head of the ambuscade they noticed something amiss, something they had quite obviously been looking for and expecting . . .

One of our men from the northern side of the road had, in defiance of his orders, left his post and crossed the road to one of the cottages, a little while before the enemy came. He was unseen in the dim pre-dawn light. When he heard the approach of the tenders he panicked and crossed the road to get back to his position. He was seen by the enemy.

(From *The Story Of The 7th*) . . .

The major immediately called a halt and all began to dismount, the hostages doing likewise. A single trooper set out on a lone course of inspection. He went in over the fence and began to climb up the little *cumar* (ravine). All around concealed were armed men. Over his head to the right was a machine-gun. Watchful eyes followed his every movement as the tension soared to breaking point. A shotgun in his path swung round level with him and, as the distance between them closed, a finger squeezed on the trigger, the gun roared a protest and the fight was on. (*Note*: M. O'Sullivan says that it was John Riordan, known as Jack 'the Rookery', who fired the first shot). Auxies, police and hostages raced helter-skelter for the shelter of the two cottages on the roadside. Some of them dropped wounded as firing broke out all along the line. Others took positions behind the lorries and began to reply as best they could to the fire directed on them from all of a semi-circular span. In this predicament Major Seafield-Grant alone thought of advance. A petrol tank beside him got pierced and was spilling its contents all over the road. 'Plug the tank, boys!', he said to those beside him, 'we'll need the petrol!', and went on over the fence into a hail of bullets. Immediately he was shot down. He got up again, turned as if to go back, and dropped dead with a bullet through the heart.

The Column Commander was in a serious predicament. Almost on a level with the Auxies who were still inside the opposite fence he was pinned down by their fire and could not easily reply to it, nor could he rejoin his comrades with any degree of safety. Something had to be done about it, and already the fight was changing location and character from a scattered skirmish to a consolidated resistance in and around the cottages. Helped by the Lewis-gun, Paddy Donagh Owen and Eugene Crowley laid on a burst of rapid fire just long enough to allow Sandow to roll out of his position and sprint for the cover of the higher rocks. He immediately took command of the situation. A quick survey showed him Section 4 already on the move south of the road, slipping from one hillock to another, sprinting across short, open spaces, taking advantage of slight hollows and furzy outcrops with consummate skill. A hasty order was sent to Sections 2 and 3 to break positions and swing around in a semi-circle to complete the pincers movement from the north as Section 1, the Ballyvourney group, now warming gallantly to the work, kept the enemy busy from directly in front of the little houses. Sections 2 and 3 packed up and moved off northwards, keeping to a little ravine that was no more than a rift in the rocks and led away towards the higher ground. They were already on their way when somebody remembered the machine-gunner. In the fuss of the quick readjustment he had been overlooked. Paddy Donagh Owen was sent back to collect him. He found Eugie, he said, still engaged at long range with some remnants of the Auxiliaries, contentedly pop-popping away with the tricky double-shot of the expert, the Hotchkiss now steadily answering in kind. Eugie gathered up his gun and bolted across to the nearest bit of cover, Mick O'Sullivan carrying a load of ammunition at the same time. Then Mick coolly doubled back under fire, collected the remainder of the pans and they were on their way. Behind them the song of the Hotchkiss went '*me-me-me, Doh..Doh..Doh*!.'

What of the other Lewis-gun dominating a salient in the Section 1 area? Completely controlling the whole existing front, even to the end lorry in the line, it remained silent after the first pan of ammunition. Forty-seven bullets (a full pan) went aimlessly into the ground and immediately afterwards the gunner, saying the gun had jammed, abandoned his position and retired completely out of the fight. Going up on the rocks he chanced to meet Brigadier Seán Hegarty on the way down. 'I wiped out a lorry load with the first burst', he announced blithely to the unspoken question. His

'Number Two' (assistant), in a bad mood, snapped back: 'I declare to my God, you put your head down and fired into the ditch!'. (*Note*: Charlie Browne — 'The eastern machine-gun, well placed for this field of fire, jammed after one short burst and remained inactive for the rest of the engagement' . . . M. O'Sullivan — 'The frailty of a member of the Column did far more that day to weaken our blows and at the same time strengthen the enemy. I am now referring to the unspeakable 'X'. He was responsible, a few weeks later, for the horrible murder of six of his comrades at Clogheen'). Whatever the explanation, the whole issue was seriously affected thereby. The original plan had not allowed nor bargained for any vehicles escaping and carrying word for reinforcements. The eastern flanking party had been placed in position primarily for the purpose of seeing to that, and they were considered sufficient. Some of the local battalion officers, more versed in country fighting conditions than the city men, had wanted to place a party with shotguns and a moveable barricade at Geata Bawn, half a mile away, but they were overruled. Instead an irresponsible youth from the city had been given a machine-gun and told to do the needful. Did his officers really have such confidence in him? Why had he joined at all? Why had he come out to the west country to carry on the fight under difficult conditions in the heart of the mountains? Why? Why? Why? (*Note*; On the way out to Ballyvourney from Cork City the young machine-gunner had boasted that he meant to earn the 'Croix de Guerre', the French supreme military honour, which had been so frequently in the news during the War years. His comrades just as airily corrupted his inept French and hung on him the label 'Crux na Gurra', and so he stayed. According to Charlie Browne he was an ex-British soldier named O'Connor from Cork City. Afterwards the country lads, with the tolerance inborn in them, still half-amusedly referred to him as 'Crux' while his own comrades stamped him with the name of 'Traitor'. In the confusion after Coolnacahera he was captured by the British while making his way alone back to the city. Shortly afterwards a number of young men from his battalion were surprised in a house in the suburb of Clogheen. Some of them were nailed to doors and had their tongues cut out and all were mercilessly slaughtered. It was established by the Brigade Council — at least to their own satisfaction — that 'Crux' had betrayed them either under torture or as an actual payee of the British. As the *Periurus Sinon* he fled the country, was overtaken and shot while boarding a streetcar in New York City and died a year later in hospital naming his executioners and carrying his secret with him to the end). So, at Coolnacahera the machine-gun detailed to close the open end of the ambuscade jammed at the crucial moment, or, alternatively, ceased firing. In proper hands it could have redeemed the situation because every vehicle in the line was standing still well within the orbit of its great fire power. It was no longer in action and, consequently, the occupants of the last transport vehicle, assailed only by shot guns, had little difficulty in performing that negligible feat of endurance and courage which, during the following days, inspired the wonder of the press reporters. The driver turned the vehicle and drove off frantically for reinforcements, his ears probably ringing from the noisy banging of twelve-bores in the rear. On his arrival at Macroom Castle an urgent message was wirelessed to Ballincollig and several hundred troops, as well as an aeroplane pilot, prepared to answer the call for help.

The battle for the cottages raged on, both sides realizing quite well that it was a race with time, the assorted bunch of Auxiliaries, Black and Tans and R.I.C. striving desperately to stave off the determined attack until help should come, the I.R.A. fighting just as desperately to round off their victory before radioed messages to the various strongholds at Bandon, Kenmare, Tralee and Ballincollig, brought troops from all points of the compass to envelop them. Comdt. Dan Corkery had his men ranged along a fence on the southern fringe of the battlefield from where they poured a heavy hail of lead into every visible opening in the two buildings and raked the rough ground, rocks, bushes and odd patches of cover where the surplus troops had been compelled to take refuge. The daring of the Macroom men, combined now with the steady firing from the rocks and hill on the northern side, made it a matter of time before the British would be forced to lay down their arms. Many of them were already wounded, some seriously. In the eastern cottage Lieutenant Soady, commanding the post, had got shot in the mouth and was in a bad way. Constable Cane was weakening fast from an ugly stomach wound. Already they were considering hoisting the flag of surrender. The end was inevitable. The casualties would be increasing. Then the reinforcements arrived. They made it just in time and victory abruptly changed hands. Around the bend at Geata Bawn came the long, impressive string of lorries, heavy ones, jammed with soldiers. They came slowly enough endeavouring to figure out the rival positions and the best manner of approach to the front line. Uncertain of the extent of the fighting, and of the location of the two forces, they halted in the hollow where the road began to rise up into the line of fire, and all dismounted. Officers hastily took up a stance at points of vantage and focussed their binoculars. The I.R.A. watched them with misgiving and began to open fire on them. The besieged force burst into new life at the thought of rescue and poured a heavy fire into the attackers' positions, but they went unheeded now for the new peril just beginning to advance along the road and inside the fences. The British did not fan out as the positions were not sufficiently clear, but to the I.R.A. it became obvious that the situation was no longer tenable. The arms they had hoped to collect were no longer within their reach. Their ammunition was practically exhausted after the vicious three-hour battle. There was no other course open to them but to withdraw. Section 3 went first. High up on the hillside they had little difficulty in slipping over the brow

and getting away among the rocks. Sections 1 and 2 fought
a desultory rearguard action and began to retire towards the
higher ground, carefully noting the enemy movements and
being carefully watched in turn. A small group still held out
behind the barricade on the by-road until their ammunition
was spent. Danny ('Right') Healy of Ballymakeera and Jerh
('Strock') Casey of Coolea crouched behind the boulders
and estimated their chances of getting away in safety. Both
well liked for their perennial gaiety (*Note*: It was a time when
'gay' was still hilarious!) and happy-go-lucky fighting
qualities, they were inseparable companions and had brought
fun and pointed wit to the struggle. 'There's nothing for it
now, boys', said Jerh despondently, 'only to say an Act of
Contrition!'. He began — 'O my God, I am heartily sorry
for . . . *thanam 'on diabhal*! ('the devil take you!'), did you
see that!'. A bullet had carried away a sizeable chunk of his
rough fortification and completely dissipated the fervour of
his atonement — but he lived to tell the tale!

Meanwhile the Macroom men south of the road were bat-
tling on vaguely aware that something had gone wrong . . .

> Time passed and then we became alert to the fact that we
> had not heard any firing from the northern side of the road,
> where our main body was positioned, and I was sent by our
> Battn. O/C to investigate. After a search there I found one
> of our 7th Battn. men — Paddy Mac O'Sullivan — who had
> been searching for us with a message directing us to retreat
> to the north. This he had received thirty minutes earlier . . .
> we discovered that we had left a pair of field glasses in our
> original position and in order to retrieve them, I was sent
> to the south with Jerh Cotter, O/C of 'D' Company , while
> the little column of about sixteen men waited in a tiny glen
> through which flowed a small stream.
>
> (Charlie Browne — *The Story Of The 7th*).

From their position very little of the northern front was visible. They noted the renewed efforts of the besieged soldiers,

the gradual lessening of the fire from the north, and, as a new sound of approaching lorries rose about the din of battle, the truth at last began to dawn on them. Word had already, as noted, been sent to them to abandon their position. It failed to arrive. They battled on a little longer. Then Comdt. Corkery, getting uneasy for the safety of his men, sent his adjutant to investigate. He returned soon with his story. So they packed up and retraced their steps to their original position on the scraggy ridge. Instead of dropping down the valley to the Sullane river bank and crossing over on the stepping-stones, as the Ballingeary men, under Lieutenant Connie Cronin of Gougane had already done, they surprisingly turned northwards again and, still within sight of the enemy, the intrepid Dan Corkery (father of three) led his men across the road under fire to follow in the general direction of the main body to the northeast. He himself had a narrow escape in the process. A burst from the Hotchkiss ripped the surface of the road just where he stepped. The Coolnacahera — or, as some say, Ballyvourney, and, even, Coolavokig — ambush was over and was quickly taking on the semblance of a rout, and worse was to follow. Still, it has gone down in History as one of the major engagements in the War of Independence.

*   *   *

From the outbreak of the Great War, in 1914, Crossley Motors Ltd., of Gorton, Manchester, made over their complete output of 20 h.p. chassis to the British and Russian Governments for the purpose of staff touring cars or aircraft tender bodies. THE AUTOCAR of November 6, 1915, has this to say about the famous little lorries:

The great success of this vehicle as a tender for units of the Royal Flying Corps (later the R.A.F.) may be attributed to several causes, foremost of which is the fact that the size of the engine and its power are particularly well suited to the work required of the vehicle. The 20 — 25 h.p. Crossley standard chassis has a four-cylinder engine, 4in. bore x 5½in. stroke, that is, 102 x 140 mm. A Smith four-jet carburetter is used, and the cooling is thermo-syphon assisted by a fan. A leather-faced cone clutch conveys the drive to the four-speed gear box, the final drive passing through a totally enclosed propeller-shaft to bevel gearing in the live axle. Semi-elliptic springs are fitted in front with three-quarter elliptic at the back. It may be mentioned that the 20 h.p. chassis weighs 27 cwt., with the tender body 34 cwt., and the touring body 37 cwt. The work which falls to the lot of the R.F.C. Crossley tenders is, to say the least of it, strenuous.

After the signing of the Anglo-Irish Treaty, 6 December, 1921, when British military equipment changed hands, it did not enhance the reputation of Michael Collins among southern Republicans to have inherited the hated little lorries, and their associations, from the old enemy.

13

Intermission

Consternation reigned in the village of Ballymakeera, Co. Cork, throughout the morning and forenoon of February 25, 1921, as the sound of heavy gunfire was wafted in from the east, and the people gathered an idea of the size of the engagement which was taking place. Hearts beat fearfully and speculation was rife as everybody expected that at last their village would surely be burned to the ground. Young and old prepared to evacuate *en masse*. Belongings were hastily got together and they started to move out. Adjutant Jerh Lucey (Jerh Con Joe) and Lieutenant John Sheehan, who were still in the village for the purpose of organization, attacked the telephone cables as a contribution to the war effort. They had no wire cutters and no time to look for same. They picked up a couple of rocks. Holding the wires down on one rock they pounded with the other. Jeremiah Lynch (Jerry Mike More), ex-R.I.C., happened to be passing by. He lent a hand and they succeeded in bursting through the cables. They moved on towards where the battle was taking place. Other men were doing the same from other directions. Jerh Lucey remembered a taunt from some of the village folk a couple of days previously — 'Where will ye be when the Tans come?' — the old grievance of residents in the vicinity of an

ambush who had to remain in their homes and endure the
capricious fury of the Black and Tans while the mobile and
evanescent Flying Column enjoyed comparative safety amid
the mist-shrouded hills and trackless boglands. So back to
the village went Jerh Con Joe . . .

The Auxiliaries and military had noted the complete
withdrawal of the Republican forces on the northern slopes.
They proceeded to surround and thoroughly sweep the area . . .

> From our position in the south we could plainly discern khaki
> figures on the northern slopes which told us that rein-
> forcements had arrived and were enveloping the entire posi-
> tion. In actual fact reinforcements had arrived forty-five
> minutes earlier and already wasted that much time in com-
> ing to grips with us . . . When we reached the crest of the
> rise, about half a mile to the north, we could see that the
> entire position which our forces had occupied was now
> covered with the enemy, while overhead an aeroplane was
> apparently directing operations.
>
> (Charlie Browne - *The Story Of The 7th*) . . .

The lorries rolled along the straight where they should by
now have been a mass of charred wreckage. The Auxies were
on their mettle. The newly arrived military were business-
like and matter-of-fact. It was the Auxies who had been attacked and the soldiers did not like the Auxies.

> There was little co-ordination between the Irish police, the
> 'Black and Tan' auxiliary forces, and the uniformed British
> Army. As a result Intelligence was feeble, counter-productive
> hostility was induced by the lack of control over the 'Black
> and Tans', and the military was torn between those who
> thought it best to ride out the storm, letting politicians
> negotiate a settlement, and those who advocated sterner
> measures designed to stamp out the I.R.A. completely.
>
> (From *Monty: The Making Of A General*).

A large, tawny donkey ambled up the road to meet them.
He was the property of Dan Kelleher whose son, Paddy

(everybody knew him as 'The Tearing Man'), had taken part in the battle and whose house was close by. The donkey mosied along the middle, unable to make up his feeble mind as to which side was the more suitable for grazing, both sides being free by kind permission of His Majesty of England, for which solicitude for large, tawny donkeys he was, or should have been, suitably grateful. Now if His Majesty had been more explicit and instructed him to keep to one side or the other it would have been easier on a donkey's mental cerebrations and final end. Musing thus he proceeded up the road and encountered the Auxies proceeding down. 'He's a dispatch rider's mount', they said, and all proceeding ceased. Not being so eloquent as the famous Bansha (Co. Tipperary) goat the donkey's intentions were gravely misunderstood. So they stuck bayonets in the ass's belly and he died roaring fit to be heard in Westminster. (*Note*: A curious phenomenon this, from a country of animal lovers, but it had become a crazy feature of the 'Terror'. A few days previously, after the tragic fight at Clonmult, East Cork, when a large number of unarmed prisoners were mercilessly slaughtered, the Auxiliaries visited the home of Comdt. Peter Hegarty at Ladysbridge, rounded up all the farm animals in the farmyard and bayoneted them to death. Hegarty's brother had been one of those killed at Clonmult. The women of the house were lined up and made to watch the slaughter). Thus far the Auxiliary Police showed themselves more thorough than the common or garden Royal Irish who were notoriously against cruelty to animals. After all, the Bansha 'peeler' in the ballad only arrested his goat for violating the 'Curfew'. Old Dan Kelleher mourned his loss for many a long day. At night time, when men gathered around the blazing hob and talk turned to the times and happenings of the ambush, the reputed deeds of bravery, the number of casualties real or imaginary, and the good fortune of the boys in effecting their escape, he would sit staring into the leaping flames only half listening, pulling at his pipe, sadly reminiscent, and every now and again, like the chorus in a Greek tragedy of old, punctuated the discourse with — 'Well, he was a damn fine donkey!'.

Old Mrs. Dan Kelleher pulled her shawl about her head and shoulders and went out onto the rocks to collect any property the boys might have left behind before the Tans should find it. The Tans on the roadway below saw the strange figure moving about from one position to another and promptly opened fire. The old woman did not understand the danger. Enveloped in her all-protective mantle she kept on her way. Providence guided her through the influence of some tutelary saint or guardian angel, for she returned in safety after securing some odd articles and establishing herself in folklore. People who had witnessed it from afar were convinced that St. Gobnait herself (I was told both versions) had passed over the scene of battle, impervious to the bullets of the enemy as she had been, long ago, to the assaults of other hostile marauders. Shortly afterwards some British officers arrived in the Kelleher home on their tour of inspection. They were polite to the old people and told them not to be afraid. They asked if there were any 'Shinners' in the house and took the truthful denial just as it was given. Then somebody found a teacup among the rocks. It matched up with some ware in the house and presuming correctly that the Kellehers had been supplying the men in ambush with refreshments they really turned the place upside-down. When they left finally Mrs. Kelleher again went out onto the rocks and found a pair of French 'field-and-marine' binoculars mislaid by one of them. She returned in triumph with her prize. Later on in the evening our old acquaintance from Poulnabro, Mike 'Musger' O'Riordan, slipped in and was shown the glasses to see if he could identify what they were. He said he was sure it was some strange kind of bomb, and the thing middleways was the 'pin' they talk about and that if you pulled it out it would blow the whole place to blazes. Ah, dear me! (*Note*: In the Fifties the glasses were still in the possession of Jerry O'Riordan's family, in Ballymakeera village, but lately I have failed to locate them).

* * *

Jerh Lucey was still in the village when the military arrived. Most of the men had gone but some of the women had decided to stay in their homes and brazen out the terror. Every man found would be a potential victim. Also there were some sick and helpless in homes which were sure to be marked down for destruction. Lieutenant John Sheehan's sister, Hannie, was very ill with 'Consumption' (*Note*: Ballyvourney was riddled with pulmonary tuberculosis before the advent of streptomycin), and had to be carefully moved to safer quarters. Artie O'Leary, son of hotelier Danny Arthur, was laid up with pnuemonia. His father's place was regarded as the principal target. They found him a secure retreat in the home of Mr. Patrick Collins, N.T. (*Note*: Pat Collins' three sons were to become quite notable later on. The eldest, whose name I forget and who taught in St. Colman's College, Fermoy, became editor of the famous humorous magazine, the *Dublin Opinion*. The second son, known, strange to say, as 'A - T - AT', was widely regarded for the development of a serum for arthritis, and Jack, the youngest, the Republican soldier and famous fist fighter, was to become a renowned trades union leader in the U.S.A.). Jerh Lucey, having lent a hand at moving various items of property about, began to think of heading in the general direction of 'the tall timber', or a few bushes at a reasonable distance would do just as well, but, as he passed through the village, a woman called to him for help to bury a box of valuables in her backyard. It proved his undoing. He was on the stairs to the attic when the lorries roared past and the village was surrounded. Too late he started to run. He was across the yard and half-way over the field heading for the wood before they spotted him. They raced to head him off, firing all the time. He reached the fence of the laneway higher up unscathed but as he rolled over it he was hit in the hand. He felt the sting of the bullet and the peculiar numbing sensation. He sped on in the shelter of the fence. More soldiers were ahead of him on the 'Top Road', covering the village from the back. The wood and comparative safety lay the width of a small field away on his left. He turned towards it and sprinted across the open. It was useless to zig-zag because the fire was now taking him cross-wise. A bullet ripped into his left foot, but the instinct of self-preservation prevailed and he never slackened speed. His pursuers realized his objective and some locals who were watching the chase from a secure position on the hump of 'The Curragh', south of the Sullane river, saw the ground churn around him as he covered the last few yards into the shelter of the trees. For the moment he was safe from the zipping bullets. He dodged through the scrub, got out of it again, raced along the road and up the adjoining 'boreen' (little road) towards Lynch's of Killeen, heading for the hills. He had gained a little ground because the soldiers could now follow him only by the trail of blood that ran out through his boot. Beyond Lynch's the *Bóthar Leathan* (broad road) straightened out to the top of a little hill. A fevered thought crossed his mind that if he could reach the brow and the gap in the high fence he would be safe. He was just there (he told me) when a bullet hit him in the right knee and he fell. A strange interlude in one man's life had come to an end. The soldiers crowded round him uttering threats of a homicidal nature. He was glad to see that they were the regular military, the MANCHESTERS, and not the Auxies as he feared. The threats stood far less chance of being put into effect. He was brought down to a truck on the 'Top Road' and driven into the village where the C/O from Ballincollig, Lieut. Col. F. H. Dorling, promptly recognized him (cf. Chapter 9) and said – 'You won't get away from us so easily this time!'. With nothing to lose Jerh Lucey replied, remembering Patrick Henry from his schooldays — 'If this be treason, make the most of it!'.

The British forces found the village of Ballymakeera devoid of menfolk. It was a hamlet peopled apparently by women whom the Auxies at least took scant notice of in their vengeful drive to pay off the blood-eric of Coolnacahera. Men were wanting but courage was not. Courage coupled with resignation, the suffering kind, the sort that endures through all, is a quality of womankind. They found it in Ballymakeera, staring sullenly at them out of windows, stubbornly barring doorways, answering questions misleadingly or not at all, or passing through their midst with a candour and obvious contempt that could cause armed men, used to the conditions of war, to squirm inwardly. Maude Collins, the teacher's daughter, had listened with the others to the distant rattle of musketry from the east as it ebbed and flowed with the changing battle scene, intensifying as the morning moved on and gradually dwindling off to spasmodic bursts and ragged, ever weakening fire. Her brother, Jack, had gone out there too that morning. But Maude knew no fear, and she refused to be upset by what the cessation of hostilities might portend. Not even when the disastrous news of the retreat came through and her father hastily evacuated the children from his school did she betray the least emotion not even at the sight of her mother praying incessantly and making frequent trips to the window with eyes full of the fear of what she might behold. Maude kept on calmly preparing tea for the children. Presently the crash of a rifle butt reverberated through the house. Instantly she was at the door and threw it wide open. Britain's 'greatest ambassador' stood there on the doorstep — 'Tommy Atkins' himself in battle regalia, complete with 'tin' helmet, rifle and fixed bayonet, in fact all the accoutrements of his much-vaunted ambassadorship. She looked at him scathingly, her long, thin, sensitive nose pulsating the while. (*Note*: This is exactly as my father told it, and he was a life-long family friend). 'What do YOU want?', she exclaimed, with the haughty, deliberate emphasis that was second nature to her.

'Any Shinners in there?', he asked lamely. 'There are a few children', she retorted; 'If you want to come in you may!'. Completely abashed he said he did not and went off, doubtless to report to his superior officer for further instructions with regard to a situation that was out of the ordinary for just a plain soldier.

By this time the village street was crammed from end to end with military vehicles. One moment it appeared almost deserted, the next, it looked ridiculously overcrowded. Any belated efforts at evacuating buildings, or transferring property, had to be hastily abandoned. At any rate much of it was plainly unnecessary, a partly hysterical urge to externate and relieve the pent-up emotions. An old 'character' of a woman (name withheld!) hurried across the street. For the moment she had it to herself and gloried in the knowledge. Under each arm she held a whole side of bacon which she was evidently transferring from a business premises (Twomey's grocery shop) in the north side to a non-business ditto in the south side, for what reason nobody, not even herself, could surmise. Just then the leading lorries zoomed around the corner into the village street. 'Jesus Christ!', she gasped, 'the bastards are here already!', dropped the bacon and fled.

In Con Lucey's shop a brave little woman felt the ground tremble as the lorries rolled past. Nurse Singleton (later Mrs. Creedon, who helped bring myself into the world at the height of the previous Winter's 'Terror') had been out at her job all morning. As the invasion struck she realized with dismay that she had two men on her hands, probably the only pair in the vicinity at the moment. Con 'the Shop' (as he was known) and Jerry O'Riordan had somehow failed to react to the general masculine stampede. She hurried them out the back way and saw them reach the end wall of the little garden just as the front door was flung open and a soldier marched in unceremoniously. He eyed her with suspicion. 'What's in there?', he demanded, indicating a large cupboard in a corner of the kitchen. 'I have no idea', she countered. 'It's locked', she added, hoping to hold his attention for a few vital seconds longer.

'Where's the key?'.

'I don't know!'.

Then a machine-gun opened up terrifyingly from the direction the two men had taken in their frantic flight. 'Jesus, Mary and Joseph', she prayed, 'take them safe!', and thought to herself - How can I ever again face their people after sending them out into it! For a moment she had a vision of two figures lying out in the field, a big man (Jerry) in a new, light-grey suit (strange thirty-year memory that!) stretched on his back and a little man (Con) in shirt sleeves crumpled grotesquely beside him, both lying dreadfully still with the stillness and peculiar flatness of the recently deceased. She went out onto the street feeling sick with apprehension, her unwelcome visitor having moved elsewhere. Kattie Hegarty (the late Liam Hegarty's sister) joined her there. Others ventured out. The firing continued on away to the back of the village. They did not know it then but all the fire was being directed at one man, a lone, pathetic figure making a desperate race for life and freedom, who just failed to make it to the brow above Killeen. From the street it sounded like a minor engagement. The soldiers who were not immediately concerned did not seem to care a great deal. Now they were chatty almost to friendliness. They seemed anxious to air their personal views on the current noises off-stage as anybody's or nobody's business according to how one's personal notion developed in the course of a chance conversation. For the most part they showed that peculiar misapprehension of the rank and file for the issues at stake. The officers understood, of course, but even the Army officers held rather aloof from Coolnacahera. Stray scraps of conversation revealed that lorry loads of reinforcements from Bandon had sat comfortably astride Rahoona hill to the south overlooking the Douglas river, within sight and sound of the battlefield, waiting to pick up possible stragglers, while the Auxies battled on in desperation and in imminent danger of being wiped out. (*Note:* I seem to remember that Stalin did the same to Warsaw in World War Two, sitting idle with his army across the Vistula while the city was being devastated by the Germans). Bandon would have got the message early. They had a naval radio section whose photograph is quite familiar. So the Bandon contingent would have made the journey to Rath Hill, via Macroom, the 'Half-Way House' and Renaniree, a distance of about twenty-three miles, in less than an hour. Rahoona Hill is just a mile across the valley of the Sullane and the battle would have been plainly in view for a further two hours. Intriguing attitude! And they even missed the Ballingeary men at the end of it all, as they crossed on the stepping stones and headed for Kerry via Coolea and Ballyfinnane bridge. Obviously there was no love lost between the Auxiliaries and the military. The soldier did his duty. The Auxie bore a personal grudge. Each despised the other for as much and carried his illogical point of view to any desirable extent without infiltrating the boundaries of compromise . . .

Danny Arthur's bar, in the 'Hibernian Hotel', was a place of primary interest to the soldiery. The proprietor, however, was not at home. Probably the most marked man in the district, though not a combatant, he had left in a hurry some time before. So, today, O' Leary's kept open house of necessity, and just about now O'Leary himself, with three companions, had negotiated the 'Top of Coom', a mountain pass eight miles away on the Kerry border beyond Coolea, and was going strong for Kilgarvan. With coat collars turned up, hats pulled down over their eyes, the little group had all the appearance of fugitives. (*Note:* Danny Arthur still thought it amusing thirty years later, though I rather failed to see the point. By that time he had become a somewhat gloomy and discontented man. The fact that he had been a Free State senator did not seem to affect his business interests in such a bastion of Republicanism. His hotel was always a centre of contention on the occasions when the village changed hands during the Civil War. He was a rather fine looking and personable man. In his political capacity he managed to help quite a number of Ballyvourney people and his place in Blessington, Co. Wicklow, was almost a home from home. My father liked him well, but, then, my father liked everybody). The fugitives turned quickly into the little 'Top of Coom' public house, just over the border. Dan Creedon could stand behind his diminutive bar and justly claim to have a more elevated, though necessarily intermittent, view of life's inexorable cavalcade, as it presented itself on the rectangular diorama outlined by his front door posts, on a segment of remote mountain road, backed by an expanding sweep of open moorland, than any other innkeeper in Ireland. Putting that simply, the 'Top of Coom' was the highest pub in Ireland. (*Note:* World traveller, writer and wood-cut artist, Robert Gibbings, brought eventual fame to the little tavern in his book, *Sweet Cork Of Thee*. One of my great memories was to see that massive, bearded and good-natured son of a Protestant clergyman, ex-Munster Fusiliers, fill that doorway as he gazed around him in amused delight and thoughtfulness, and I wished I could someday write as nicely as he did). But today Dan Creedon, likewise, was not at home to his unexpected visitors. He would be home soon, his old mother said. With his horse and 'side-car' (jaunting car) he had driven a section of Ballingeary men, under Lieutenant Connie Cronin, retreating from Coolnacahera, to Gort Luachra south of Kilgarvan, their very own destination, from where a vast expanse of mountain stretched southwards to Borlin and the secret fastness of Bonane. The kindly old woman advised them to be on the road before Dan and face him and his transport around once again. They could take the short cut across the 'ray', she said, and be well on the road to meet him. Out on the open 'ray' was still more dangerous. They listened acutely for any sound of danger pursuing that might be borne to them on the rarified atmosphere of that rugged frontier of the 'Kingdom of Kerry'. Presently they did hear a sound, a weird, disconcerting kind of atmospheric disturbance. They stood aghast, he said. Danny Arthur could a tale unfold. Around the bend of the little mountain road came light-hearted Dan Creedon, leisurely hupping his ambling nag and alternately startling the wild life and all within earshot with his lusty rendering of a popular patriotic ballad of the time as if the whole of the British Army had just lately been dispatched to defend a 'Union Jack' planted on top of contentious Rockall in the north Atlantic or a newly discovered ice-floe in the Antartic:

> 'Irishmen will never yield', he roared,
> While they're on the battle field,
> With gun, sword or bayonet or a sprig of sweet blackthorn!
> Show to me an Irishman
> Who does not love his native land!
> Oh, boys, I am proud I'm an Irishman born!'

Like Cortez, when he 'stared at the Pacific, and all his men looked at each other with a wild surmise', Danny Arthur O'Leary and his companions stared unbelievingly for a moment and looked at one another before making the surrounding hills re-echo to their howls of laughter. In such a situation not even iron-willed Hernando could have remained for long silent upon his peak in Darien.

Meanwhile, back in O'Leary's the soldiers were treating themselves well but not wisely. Whiskey and gin were doled out in 'tumbler' glasses. Many were young and not yet versed in the social ways and pretentious rituals of the 'hard likker' fraternity. After an interval of stupified dizziness they began to drop to the ground one by one until the purlieus of the hotel looked like the aftermath of a battle. (*Note:* This may sound naïve, but I have it in notes from serious-minded local women of forty years ago!). Clips of rifle ammunition slipped from pouches and lay unheeded until recovered later by enterprising members of 'Cumann na mBan' (the para-militant 'Organization of the Women'. See photograph). From the earlier firing the women felt sure that there must have been quite a lot of Republican casualties. They search-ed everywhere, but there was no evidence. They questioned officers and men, but without result. All the *clampar* (han-dy local Irish word for commotion) and gunsmoke meant so little after all. Presently Jerh Lucey was brought in look-ing wretched and spent, but uncowed. (*Note:* He was to lose the injured right leg and went to the end of his days a spright-ly and ubiquitous character on wooden crutches, who could easily outstrip any able walker at his best. In the Fifties he was an essential part of the Ballyvourney scene. Some thought his leg had begun to grow again. Others wondered what would become of the severed member on the Day of Judgement. At any rate, a British Army surgeon, with Great War experience, sawed it off, but they did give him a pen-sion for life, which option was taken up by Michael Collins at the change-over. It is no wonder that he voted for the Trea-ty!). When Jerh was brought down to the village the women fussed about, procured some pillows and made him reasonably comfortable. The soldiers grumbled. The officers sneered. Then the whistles blew and with a good deal of bus-tle, barking of dogs, revving of engines, the long cortège of twenty-three trucks and motor cars began to roll along the street, disappeared around the bend, reappeared as it slow-ly crawled up the hill beyond to surmount the top and drag itself away, constricting, expanding, undulating, like a nightmare caterpillar. The onlookers, highly relieved, kept their fingers crossed in case anything might happen to break the spell and the whole lot might turn round and come back again. The clear blue sky was still visible, sporting only stray wisps of sunflecked cloud where by now they had expected to see a thick pall of smoke hanging heavy above the fum-ing ruins of their village homes.

John O'Riordan drifted into the village. He was captured by Nurse Singleton. She had an idea that there might be some wounded lying above on the hill. A good deal of firing had come from that direction. They went on up. As they passed by, Lena Lucey, Jerh's sister, and Cumann na mBan member, filled John's pockets with handfuls of ammunition. They went on over the stream and faced the scrub by the wood. The going was rough and the drag on his pockets became irksome. He called a halt and laid his load carefully aside, pausing a moment to take a closer look at the bullets. Very few even of the fighting men had handled the stuff in such quantities, some not at all. Even out of their element like this they looked deadly, those multi-pointed clips of concentrated power and viciousness. The Nurse felt a shudder run through her at the sight, and covered them up hastily. They turned away and went up among the trees. There were no dead or wounded, but there was something else. There were soldiers on the 'Top Road', they realized with a start. Too late they spotted the four stationary lorries. 'Halt!' There was nothing surprised or irresolute about the authoritative snap of it. They halted. The Nurse felt her heart give a sickening jump. Her mind raced to frame a plausible explanation for their presence there, especially the man. My God! The bullets!, she thought. What an escape! An officer came down to them. What were their names? They told him. Their business? The Nurse, with tongue in cheek and a silent prayer for courage, began to state their 'business'. She was the official midwife for this locality, she said. She had received an urgent call and needed some help. This was the only man she could find willing to lend her a helping hand. The officer pondered a moment. Finally he ordered them up on the roadway, had them searched and allowed them to go on their way. There was no military trick involved. The soldiers were *bona fide* travellers on the 'Top Road'. An urgent message had come through to Tralee barracks at about 10 a.m. It appeared that some troops had run into trouble down the line towards Macroom forty miles away. A contingent set out half-heartedly, their minds already made up as to the part they intended to take in the scuffle. Assuming that the ambushers would retreat generally westwards – England was East – they selected a point of vantage. Taking the Coolea road from 'The Mills', they veered off at Muirnebeg Cross by the bog road for Togher, swung round in the wide arc the difficult by-road afforded and found themselves atop the heights of the 'Bóna Bán' (site of the landlord's 'whitewashed cattle pound' of earlier times), with a magnificent vista, incorporating St. Gobnait's historic home and shrine, spread out before them. But they were not on a sight-seeing tour. They were examining the hills northwards through binoculars, for already there were men on the hills, many of them, men with guns who were moving ceaselessly westwards apparently in the general direction of the more extensive mountains of Claedagh and beyond. As they watched, some scattered groups appeared around the shoulder of Carrigavadaroo ('the rock of the fox'), above Kippagh, and quickly dipped into the shelter of Coomaguire glen. Others emerged from the depths of Glen Dav ('the valley of the ox'), further to the north, and crossing the 'Mountain Road' took to the higher slopes of Mullaghanish. The movement was resolutely due west. Even at a distance they presented a bedraggled and disorganized appearance. It should be rather easy for four lorry-loads of well-armed, fresh troops to mop them up effectively. The engines roared into life and the column moved off. A rapid glide down the steep incline, past St. Gobnait's church and graveyard, through the narrow, bent Colthurst bridge (*Droichead an Ridire*) over the Sullane river, and they were on the main road again speeding the half-mile to 'The Mills', then turned quickly northwards, through the oak and alder grove of a previous encounter, to hurl their own battle challenge recklessly in among the sullen hills and hidden valleys. But the hills played a trick on those intrepid warriors and led them along false ways to mock at their aggressiveness and cool the ardour of their onslaught. ('Why skip ye so, ye high hills!'). For at close range the high places were deceptive. Kippagh loomed up large and craggy while the great Mullaghanish (innocent of its modern television mast) was remote and barely visible. They took the first branch line to the right and presently found themselves cruising along the 'Top Road' at the back of Ballymakeera village with no one in sight. After the brief interlude by 'The Wood', already related, they returned on their tracks, for they were still hell-bent and contumacious. The I.R.A. would now be well to the west of them where the mountains appeared to close in and form a kind of cul-de-sac (referred to locally as a 'cuddly-sock'), a dangerous trap to be caught in, but the spirit of adventure, or something akin to it, won the day and another battle was already in the making. They turned west.

*   *   *

To revert once again to the soldiers of the Republic, it was with a deep sense of frustration that they turned their backs on Coolnacahera and its battlefield, that historic day in February, 1921. They had set out that morning to do battle with the traditional enemies of their country. It was as simple as that. (*Note:* Nowadays, the philosophy of the movement seems to elude completely those whose business it is, or those who merely choose, to talk about the basic political aspirations of our nation. It would seem as if none of this had ever happened, or, if it had, it had best be forgotten. I suspect self-delusion which is a common condition, the conviction of ignorance which is a common fallacy, or a new willingness to turn one's back on one's enemy which is a common danger. None of this has ever produced, or could ever produce, the common good required). The battle to be fought at Coolnacahera was of a peculiar type in that it was not exactly one in which either side could hope to win, or fear to lose, any ground from the point of view of strategy or field tactics. The ground was there for either party to

traverse at will until such time as the other presented an effective obstacle to freedom of movement. Each had his own
point of view with regard to his line of action. The British
soldier was there because he had received orders to be there.
It might just as easily have been Hong Kong or Kuala Lum-
pur or the Canal Zone. It happened to be Mid-Cork in
Ireland. If, in the process of carrying out his orders, he contrived to make himself absurd it was in so far as he showed
a tendency to nurse a personal grudge against whoever it was
stood in front of him — Zulu spearman or Boer farmer or
Irish Sinn Féiner. For the rank and file, at least, the system
made no allowance for, nor in any way postulated the need
for, an elaborate thought process. 'Theirs not to reason why,
theirs but to do and die!', often without knowing why.
Anyway — 'Gallant six-hundred!'. He died bravely, or craven-
ly, or got maimed for whatever it was. On the other hand,
the I.R.A. man's fight was laced with sentiment, a deep-
seated feeling that he might not be able to translate effectively into words. When he talked, he talked of injustice. He
could become inarticulate with emotion. When he thought,
he thought of his hurt pride, pride in his nation, pride in
his neighbours, pride in himself, the shame of being walked
on. His blood boiled in exasperation. He fought readily and
hotly when he got the chance. He died bravely because the
heat of his anger eclipsed the fear of it, and when it came
he knew why it had come to him, why he had come to it,
and it was something to die for, not like dying with a ship
in a raging storm, screaming with terror, or wasting with
disease and grudging the Will of God. He sometimes thought
that he was also fighting for his Faith as well as his
Fatherland. The dreadful 'Penal Laws' left that mark on his
inherited temperament . But he knew of names like Tone,
Emmet, Davis, Mitchel, Butt, Parnell, names that struck a
spark of comradeship over the years intervening. They
thought like he did about Fatherland, but differently about
Faith. He was content to leave the problem chasing its tail

of complications and vague facts about those who thought contradictory thoughts about Patriotism and Nationhood and spoke authoritatively about his Faith. If his likes in the past had died bewildered it was because they thought they were right and found themselves judged wrong. Some of the boys knew of Michael Doheny, from Fethard, Co. Tipperary, one of the founders of the Fenian Brotherhood in the U.S.A., and that poem he had written while on the run, after the failed Young Ireland insurrection in 1848. A touching little bit went:

> 'Thy faith was tried, alas, and those
> Who'd peril all for thee
> Were cursed and branded as thy foes,
> A chuisle gheal mo chroí' (i. e. bright pulse of my heart).

All nice and catchy in the throat. *Taidhiúir*, that's what they would call it in Coolea, meaning 'sweetly sad', sweet and sad, like 'Caitlín Ní hUalltacháin', Cathleen, the daughter of Houlihan – poetic symbol of Ireland – gazing wistfully on her perennial champions. But death was neither, not sweet or sad, just cold and final, no joke for those who were face to face with it. But what else could a man do for what he believed in. Father John Murphy did it in Wexford in 1798 because they burned down his church. Who burned his church? Irish Protestant yeomen in an English army, that was who. Then there was Bishop O'Dwyer in Limerick in 1916 saying that Sinn Féin, in his opinion, was the true principle. Then Bishop Fogarty of Clare taking his stand, and nearly shot for it. That lieutenant killed at the 'Slippery Rock' was a Catholic too. A fine fellow was Sharman, they all said; tall, well-built, a perfect gentleman. At Mass and Holy Communion back at the chapel on Sundays. He should not have been killed. He went on patrol because his captain had a cold. Paddy Donagh Owen said that Mike Buckley, that brat of an ex-soldier from Kilnamartyra, who had been drummed out of the British Army for indiscipline and whom they knew as 'Mickeen the Soldier', treated Sharman like a dog, robbed him and kicked him in the ribs as he lay dead in the ditch. Who could say! The priest received his remains respectfully at the chapel. The boys really only wanted his gun and the guns of the others. A pity they had to hurt them. Paddy and Patsy were very upset at what Mickeen did. They tried to recover the lieutenant's effects to return them. They got a promise. Later they got the watch from the O'Sullivans. Still the British took revenge on Bill Hegarty. Poor Bill paid for it all. They said that Sharman's brother was in the 'broken-down' lorry. Maybe he was, or again maybe he wasn't. Even if he was, small blame to him. Suppose it was your brother! You might have wanted revenge too. But that was a long time ago — all of six months! An eternity it seemed. Things got nasty after that. Then it was the Auxies. They were different. Nobody minded to hurt them, even to kill them, if you could. That was why the boys were here at Coolnacahera. To kill. You hated the Auxies with a burning, blinding hate. You had good reason to. You came to fight them. To show them you weren't afraid of them. To keep the thing going somehow. For what? The humble soldier-without-uniform, in the so-called Irish Republican Army, checks his musing. He looks around expectantly for an answer to his question. He knows his limitations. He does not lay claim to any education worth mentioning, but he claims rightly to be able to understand when somebody lays the pros and cons, when the expert or the idealist makes his case. He expects an answer to his question (as he still does in 1994). Let those who know beware of subtlety and deceitful quibbling, unilateral declaration, to mystify with academic accomplishment and forked tongue the simplicity of his childlike mind, and his singleness of purpose in the pursuit of his own and his country's need.

*   *   *

The Macroom contingent, after the turmoil of the day, were

going home, and home for them lay generally in that direction where their battalion area extended to within three miles of them at Liscarrigane . . .

> We marched steadily in a north-westerly direction, climbing over a shoulder of mountain to reach Coomaguire glen and then again climbing to the crest overlooking Coomnaclohy . . . When we looked into the glen from our lofty position we had a grand stand view of an engagement between enemy forces and our advance party. This unit had apparently been seen descending to the glen by an enemy force hurrying from Killarney to the scene of the fight. They had switched to a by-road leading to the glen and had now halted their tenders and were advancing in extended order towards a number of houses which our men had occupied. Being alerted, fire had been opened on the advancing military as the Column prepared to retreat through a *cumar*, or depression, in the mountainside to the west. We had an elevated view of all this from our line of march and having joined forces with another section of our Column under Jack Culhane we immediately changed direction in order to get to the rear of the enemy forces. They saw us and must have sensed our intention because there was an immediate withdrawal to the lorries and the whole force left in a hurry the way it had come.
>
> (From *The Story Of The 7th*).

Unfortunately, Charlie Browne got it wrong, as will be seen in the next chapter. The Macroom men faced north-east. Skirting the brow of Ullanes mountain they drifted on into Liscarrigane and looked down on that peaceful valley made famous by Canon Peter O'Leary (*An tAthair Peadar*) in his many brilliant incursions into Gaelic Literature. Just beneath them was the home of the learned and kindly priest where he had spent his boyhood, all around it the streams and woods and fields through which he had wandered dreaming his boyish dreams of ancient Irish glory and musing on the wonderful tales and sagas of long ago which he would yet weave into a wonder of mellifluous native dialect fit to

grace the finest literature in the world – tales made so much
more wonderful to his impressionable young mind by contrast with the poverty and squalor of a decadent nation and
the downtrodden people living all about him. It was within
this little 'Sleepy Hollow' he had gleaned the material for
his greatest achievement, the fascinating story of the innocuous shoemaker, Séadhna (prn. 'Shay-anna'), the Irish
'Faust', who was believed to have lived just beyond at the
foot of the little cliff under Carrigvore where, until certain
troubles came his way, he had lived his life in happy con-
tentment with his *súgán* (hay-rope) chair and his pouch of
oatmeal for chewing, in his nice cosy little house that 'he
had built for himself alone at the foot of the shady side of
the hill' (Ir. *'a dhein sé féin dó féin ag bun cnoic ar thaobh
na fothana'*). It was a story of a peaceful, contented, homely
age when the great enemy was the devil – and now the devil
himself, for all that the people seemed to be concerned about
him, was on the run from the Tans! (*Note:* Canon P. A.
Sheehan, of Doneraile, became world famous as a writer of
Victorian-style novels. He was thirteen years junior to Canon
O'Leary, yet he was made a canon at the age of fifty-one
while 'An tAthair Peadar' was eighty-one when the honour
was conferred on him in 1920, just before his death, and
one year exactly before the battle of Coolnacahera. There
may not be anything sinister in this discrepancy, but I seem
to remember that the Bishop of Cloyne, Dr. Robert Browne,
was president of Maynooth when a dispute arose about the
viability of the Irish language in the context of the Christian ethos!). From the top of Liscarrigane the travellers had
an unimpaired view of their destination, the great bulk of
Mushera mountain away on the skyline. Not until they had
left the heights and dropped down into the lowlands, by the
banks of the Foherish river, did they move more cautiously.
Ignoring the little bridge they moved along by the fringes
of a wood and crossed the river lower down at the stone steps
below the village of Carriganimma. The dangerous Macroom

to Millstreet road was now so near that the one 'raid' carried them the whole way across and they were on the up grade once more. The worst was over. It was time to think pleasant thoughts of a bed and untroubled slumber, and so, in high hopes though weary of mind and body, they hustled on over the shoulder of Knockraheen (the 'hill of the little fort') towards the advancing night, through Meallnahorna and Cushloura, and stumbled into the friendly, downy lap of Musheramore; and when the day was well done and darkness had long since settled in around them, obliterating and enveloping, from out the vast bogland of Annaganihy, Commandant Dan Corkery and his little band finally and thankfully 'laid down their weary heads for to repose', as the song said. The long, long day for them had drawn to a wearisome close.

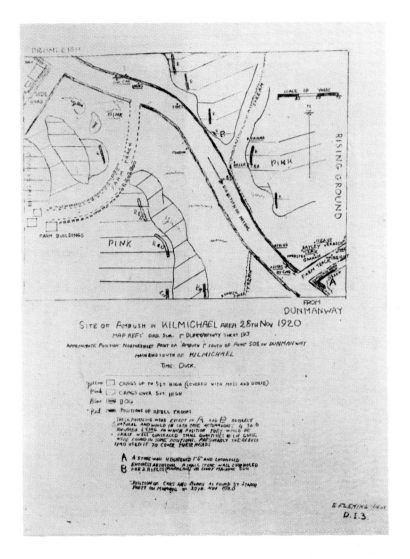

9. British Intelligence sketch-map of the Kilmichael Ambush, on the morning after, with bodies still in position.

10. Commandant Paddy O'Brien, Liscarroll, during the
Emergency, 1939-1945.

11a. Irish-speaking platoon from the Waterford *Gaeltacht* (Ring)
region, under Capt. Paddy Curran (seated left)
and Lieut. Jimmy Power.

11b. Fourth (North) Cork Brigade 'Flying Column' in training
near Newmarket, October, 1920.

12. Charcoal original of Michael Collins portrait, by
Sir John Lavery (signed by both).

13. Charcoal original of Arthur Griffith portrait, by
Sir John Lavery (signed by both).

14a. Lieut. Peter O'Farrell, of
Charleville, Republican
policeman, 1921-1922.

14b. D. M. P. sergeant,
Brunswick Street, Dublin,
circa 1914.

14c. Sergeant Mike O'Leary, V.C.

14d. General Denis Galvin, killed
in Mallow, 1922. He handled the
Hotchkiss machine-gun at
Clonbanin.

Composite picture of the twelve East Cork Brigade men who fell in the fight at Clonmult. Reading left to right:—(Back Row): Richard Hegarty (Garryvoe); Jeremiah Aherne (Midleton); Christopher Sullivan (Midleton); Joseph Morrissey (Athlone); Michael Hallahan (Midleton). (Second Row): James Glavin (Cobh); John Joe Joyce (Midleton); James Aherne (Cobh); Michael Desmond (Midleton). (Front Row): Donal Dennehy (Midleton); Liam Aherne (Midleton); David Desmond (Midleton).

15. (Courtesy of *Kerryman Publications*)

16. Brigade Major Montgomery (on right with pipe) and
Lieut. General Higginson interrogating prisoners
in Claedagh, 6 June 1921.

where adversity now held sway; every eye straining for the nearness of the tops of things and the high places, every ear earnestly sifting the noises of flight from the noises of pursuit, every heart intoning its *Gradual Canticle* to the rhythm of the quickly marching feet . . . 'I lift up my eyes to the mountains. Whence shall help come to me?'. The desire of the Eternal Hills could never have been stronger in the psalmist of old . . .

*   *   *

> *Cúm na Cloiche Gile,*
> *Agus Ladhar 'dir dá uisce,*
> *Nár bháidh riamh aon duine,*
> *Agus fiú nár chuir chuige;*
> *Cúm a' Ghadhair nár rith riamh,*
> *Is nár rug ar aon duine . . .*

> The Valley of the Bright Stone,
> And the Foreland between two waters,
> That never drowned anyone,
> Nor bothered to try;
> The Valley of the Dog that never ran,
> And did not seize anyone . . .

Thus chanted the professional chanters in the old-time funeral procession as it wended its way southwards through the pass of Béal a' Mháma, on the mountain road between Glendav and Mullaghanish, through the ensuing localities of Coomnaclohy, Lyre and Coomaguire as stated, paying its passing tribute in an aura of artificial mournfulness. It was the customary chant and, with suitable variations, was customarily chanted through all the districts on the established funeral routes. One may form a rough idea of its great age from the style of its metre which is syllabic rather than stressed, and the change over in Gaelic poetry had begun to take place as early as the beginning of the seventeenth century. The present piece would be regarded as a form of *Ógl. chas* i.e. loose verse or amateur versification of the *Dán*

Díreach i.e. straight verse, the ancient, regular, syllabic poetry of the still more ancient Bardic Schools, and it echoes the quality that may be regarded as the essential beauty and magic of Gaelic poetry of all ages, that close spiritual association with Nature and the varied features of the countryside.

*   *   *

> Away to the south-east I could see a white ribbon of road. I saw a speck appear on it, then another and another. They were coming, one behind the other.
> 'What do you think those are?', I asked the girl, indicating to her the road. With the teapot clasped between her hands, she regarded them.
> 'I think they are bicycles', she replied. Still watching them, she said again:
> 'No, they are lorries'.
> They were lorries, sure enough. We went outside, the better to investigate.
>
> (From *Where Mountainy Men Have Sown,* pp. 108-110).

My dear friend of long ago, the late Mr. Peter Cronin, of Slievereagh, Ballyvourney, told it to me somewhat differently in 1957. This is how he experienced an extraordinary event . . .

Four times in all Pete Cronin went out to climb the steps on to the landing by the barn-door. He was young, with the alertness and quick reflexes of youth, and he had the eagle eye of the mountainy man, the keen discernment of one used to the unbounded vastness of the hilltops and the scrutiny of objects far away. Inside, in the home of Dan Horgan, Mee-inglia, a section of the Brigade 'Flying Column' had just sat themselves down to tea. Pete had been helping at the ploughing there that day , but now, that more exciting things were happening, he was hanging around curious about these strange men whom he mostly did not know, and still more curious at the rifles and other trappings which they carried. The expected ambush to the east must have happened, although the sounds of it had not been borne so far. Rather grudgingly he went out to watch the approaches to the glen when they told him to do so. He scanned the roads careful-ly. They were all clear as far as he could see, which was to where the hedges began on the 'Top Road' above Bally-makeera village. Nobody could see through those hedges, and anyhow they were far enough away from him not to be very concerned about them. He began idly speculating on whether a lorry could hide behind them and be completely invisible. Suddenly he stared. Something had moved briefly at a gap in the hedge. As he watched it happened again, a peculiar fleeting movement 'like the little dooreen' (he told me) flitting briefly over the eye of a box camera. There it was again, and again — four times in all. He was puzzled and watchful. Suddenly the whole phenomenon repeated itself at another gap nearer to him. He was sure of it now. There was a row of things moving in regular formation at the back of that hedge and coming steadily in his direction. He waited until they had got clear and saw what appeared to be a string of four vehicles of some description. He went in to report. The reaction inside was not so sensational as he had expected for such a momentous discovery. They did not even seem to be interested, or were too tired to care, and he was just a 'gossoon'. They sent him out to have another look, and he could now report that they seemed to be soldiers' lorries and were coming right down the wide curve to the crossroads. It would be of primary interest to know whether they turned left or right. If it was right it could mean the hell of a pile of trouble. A third time he went out. The men inside waited, a little more strained and tense, a little less relaxed. Conversation quietened down. The teacups rattl-ed with less cheerful abandon. The watcher came in once more to make his report. Yes, they had turned right and were coming straight on and seeming to gather speed purposefully as they ascended the hill on to the level of the plain. There was still a chance. The 'mountain road' turned at right-angles northwards to skirt the foot of Mullaghanish and go through

Béal a' Mháma, wheeling round on to the Millstreet road between the sources of the Keel and Finnow rivers at Keim-carrige. This contingent might just happen to be the Millstreet contribution to the morning's work. They sometimes came through that way. Would they turn north? He was sent out to see, and now for the fourth time he was on his pedestal watching with bated breath as the four lorries of soldiers, already standing up in readiness, came right up to the junction, passed it unhesitatingly, roared on to the straight, and ground to a dusty standstill on the road beneath him. In the farmhouse kitchen the talk fizzled out and the teacups ceased to rattle. A woman stood with the teapot poised in mid-air, waiting. Eyes sought out and claimed ownership of guns reposing here and there against the whitewashed walls and in the corner by the 'dresser'. Hands that felt for holsters trembled a little, but a stark, burning glaze smouldered in every eye and the faces that had paled, becoming aged and drawn in those few palpitating moments, were set in a mask of grim determination and flaming resentment. So, they sat and waited, while the ticking of the clock on the wall grew abominably loud, every tick charged with the venom of a rifle's crack, and zero hour blazed like a comet through a boundless ether of intolerable suspense. Pete Cronin appeared and stood a moment in the doorway. 'They're here!', he gasped and vanished and simultaneously came the rattle of musketry from the valley below . . .

*   *   *

A little man guided a pair of horses and plough to turn a neat furrow in a field beside the Behill stream. He had no need or inclination to urge on the straining animals. The day was fine and the year still young for all the Spring work that had to be done. More important by far it was to get that sod of uniform depth and lay it neatly over with the finesse of the practised hand and the pride of the master. At the end of the double run he drew rein leisurely and

screwed up his bright, intelligent eyes to gaze critically back
along the mathematically perfect lines of the dark-brown
furrows. 'Sheer plod makes plough down sillion shine', indeed, but he had never heard of Hopkins, nor had anyone
until two years before. An approaching cataclysm of un-
precedented force would have been necessary to disturb
noticeably the composure that was second nature to this
ploughman. At the moment there was no indication that
anything of the kind might occur. Indeed, something rather
unusual had happened a short while back, but if Jerry Forde
(latterly Sacristan in Ballyvourney parish church) had noticed
the gangs of armed men who had suddenly invaded the quiet
valley of Coomnaclohy he gave no sign, but he could not
have helped noticing as they came streaming at him over the
hill, passed him by on the road to Dineen's and up through
the *leaca* (slope) to Dan Horgan's, Meeinglea, with scarcely
a glance. Ten of them had turned into Seán Lucey's house
beside him. He was sure it was ten, although if any of those
fellows had been asked they would have said that he had never
looked in their direction. Undoubtedly there was a reason
for their being there. Moreover he knew the reason. There
was also a reason for doing essential Spring work in the
Springtime. He knew the reason for that too. In some unaccountable manner the information had found its way to him
that 'a battle had been fought and some sort of round-up'
was in progress as a result of it. Once, when he thought he
heard a strange rumble in the distance, he wondered how
it would fare with those men if trouble happened the way.
They were badly placed to receive it, he thought, being
cooped up in a couple of houses on the floor of the narrow,
enclosed glen beneath the level of the road. Their only way
of escape would have to be straight up the sloping, open sides
of the hills. Evidently the men in Lucey's were thinking along
similar lines because they were leaving already. He saw them
go through the yard in a bunch, along by the little grove,
and head off across the 'ray' as if thinking to join their

comrades at Horgan's on the top. Then suddenly they changed direction, scattering out in a straggly line across the open,
and in the same instant he saw the lorries. He guided the
horses along to the end of the furrow and stopped. He could
see that the men were heading for the *glaise*, the deep cut
in the mountain side that brought the infant Behill down
from the heights. On a level with him on the road were four
lorries of soldiers newly arrived, and the manner of their
coming was surely breath-taking if not completely sensational. One moment there was nothing, the next, a rush of
noise and there they were. He looked again towards the men
on the 'ray'. They were being joined by a group of seven from
Dineen's, and the whole lot, still leisurely, he thought, for
such a stirring occasion, were drifting in towards the *glaise*
(prn. 'glosh-eh'). Then they began to run the last fifty yards.
The remainder of Dineen's party could be seen making the
best of their way to the top at various points and mostly
in a frantic hurry. By this time the road seemed full of
soldiers. The lorries were big ones, not the little Crossleys,
and could have accomodated, he figured, about twenty men
apiece. Strangely enough they did not take up firing positions while they had an unobstructed view of the men crossing the open. They may have feared that there were still more
at their back on the high ground north of the road. Perhaps
they saw Charlie Browne before he saw them. They advanced *en masse* across the little roadside field to the Behill. An
officer in the lead crossed the brook ahead of them. (*Note*:
I am remembering, with a certain degree of admiration, the
standard estimate of the position of an officer in the British
Army. He was the man who signed for everything, took unqualified responsibility for everything, and walked ahead to
be shot first).

In the meantime, from the looks of the situation that was
rapidly developing, Jerry Forde decided that it would be risky
to remain ploughing any longer. He loosed the horses from
the plough and, following the only course open to him, led

them down the pathway towards the house and the advancing soldiers. He might have been Rip Van Winkle strolling curiously out of another age to find the whole world gone mad. In the laneway he came face to face with the officer who looked sharply at him. 'Good day!', said Jerry politely, always, as I knew him, the *preux chevalier*. The answer was a mumble that he failed to catch. (I have always imagined it as 'G'awfternoon!'). The officer must have wondered at this chap who looked so out of place in the circumstances (like the 'Flanders Heifers' of the Great War), and spoke to him calmly and somewhat indulgently as if he were an eccentric foreign professor investigating the wild life of the locality. (*Note*: Jerry Forde's similar attitude towards a particular mad parish priest of a later era was equally hilarious!). The officer passed on and fired a single shot in the air from his rifle. It was a signal to his men. They fired a ragged volley and hurried on to take up positions behind the fence of the grove. Jerry led the horses into the yard at their back and took up his own position by the high 'landing' at the barn-door. There was somebody else there before him. A carpenter named Horgan, from Kerry, had been working in the yard. Somehow the soldiers took no notice of him. He coolly stationed himself in the lee of a rick of turf. 'Here, they can fire away now!', he said, as he settled down to watch. Further on and a little higher up Donncha (Denis) Dineen was also ploughing. As the world suddenly became unhinged about him he began to untackle the horses. Once released the startled animals started off at a wild gallop up the 'boreen' for home adding to the general confusion. The military ignored Lucey's roadside farmhouse and advanced into the fields at the back of it. They seemed anxious to come to close quarters. Most of the I.R.A. were by now within the comparative safety of the *glaise* that led away in a gradual curve to the high boglands above the valley. Some of them had already begun to return the fire from the shelter of it and slow up the pursuit. But the soldiers were pushing on towards the entrance. They took up new firing positions along a fence of the little meadow and established a salient in the vee-corner at the farthest end where they set up a machine-gun and opened fire.

Horgan, the carpenter looked out from his observation post and viewed the whole affair with a critical eye. He was enjoying himself. Bullets were whining like angry bees over the yard, knocking chips off the slates and showers of mortar off the barn wall. He seemed unworried about the vulnerability of a rick of turf and continued to survey the battlefield, sending out occasional bulletins on the progress of the fight. 'Begor, the lad in the *glaise*', he observed, 'is rising smoke fasht!'. Later — 'The "Sinn Féiner" is showing no slack !'. Then — 'But I'm afraid they'll come at him!'. A group of soldiers had just begun an encircling movement. They started off across the open 'ray', and obliquely up the incline, so as to get the advantage of the higher position and be able to see directly into the *glaise* which veered off in a curve and hid the retreating men. The soldiers raced up the incline for a few yards and then threw themselves flat on the ground. After a moment they jumped up to repeat the manoeuvre and on the third go came up against their first major surprise. The men above in Horgan's, unnoticed until now, came abruptly into the fight. They had resolutely lined the fence between the yard and the field below the house, and opened fire at the next rush. The soldiers dropped down on the spot. A herd of cattle grazing on the 'ray' gathered together in a bunch in terror, heads together and tails out. They were directly in the new line of fire and obstructed the view of the men above. The soldiers sensed an advantage and began to crawl forward under cover of the trembling animals towards the new menace. Cows or no cows, the men above blazed away again. A cow was hit. A bullet struck above her tail, scored all along the back and emerged again by the right shoulder. The khaki-clad figures flattened themselves once more into the ground. One of them started to rise. A bullet slapped into his chest, partly lifting him off the ground and throwing him heavily on his back. A couple of his comrades dragged him to shelter. In the process another soldier was hit and fell. They dragged him in also and dressed both of their wounds in the shelter of the fence. Thereafter they abandoned the idea of trying to carry that citadel by assault and concentrated on their crab-wise attack on the *glaise* under cover of their own fence. The little band above in Horgan'a yard decided it was time to withdraw. Their counter-attack had achieved the desired effect. They had delayed the enemy until their comrades in the Column had got through to the plateau above the Valley of the Bright Stone, where they lost themselves quickly among the turf banks. The watchers decided it was time to think of their own safety. Commandant Patrick O'Sullivan had been with them at the start but he had seen the trap the others were in and had gone down to help them out of it. It was well that he did. He had spotted the *glaise* as he sped past. Even then he had not realized how soon he would be needing it. He and some others fought a rearguard action while their ammunition lasted and then had to trust to fleetness of foot to outpace the pursuers. Two men failed to stand the pace. They hid in a hollow and hoped for the best. The soldiers ventured only a little way beyond the mouth of the *glaise*, and both would have escaped detection had not one of them, Paddy Casey, of Renaniree, raised himself up to see how things were going. He was spotted and ordered to come down. He obeyed the order and was taken prisoner. Had they gone up to collect him they would have found his companion hidden with two rifles and it would have been the end for both of them. Casey pleaded that he had been caught up in the general stampede. They probably believed him. Then the officer blew his whistle and the whole corps returned to their lorries carrying their solitary prisoner with them.

Jerry Forde came down from his watch-tower and returned to his horses and ploughing. He had to put up a reasonable show of industry before the lorries passed level with him. The military would probably appreciate the fact that a man putting his hand to the plough and not deigning to look back was essentially a man of peace and singleness of purpose. They did, in fact, take no notice. They seemed content to call it a day. They were humming or singing softly some popular tune of the time like a bunch of school children returning from a picnic or a romp in the woods. Evidently the battle had not fired them very much. One of them, at least, was in no mood for singing. He succumbed to his wounds on the following day in Tralee, and Paddy Casey was sent home having attended the funeral. (*Note*: This Paddy Casey was a cousin of young Jeremiah Casey, shot on the third of January by the Auxiliaries. His father was Jeremiah 'Tailor' Casey, well known in his professional capacity in mid-Cork. Paddy Casey was one of those who died young having succumbed to the rigours of life on the run, and as a fighting member of the Flying Column. His opposite number, the soldier from Tralee who was shot at Coomnaclohy and died later, is more of a puzzle. The Royal Munster Fusiliers occupied Ballymullen Barracks, in Tralee, until the disbandment of the regiment in 1922. It had been their Depot since 1881. It is still extant and is now used by the Civil Defence Forces, and the little military cemetery, on what used to be known as the 'Workhouse Road' and now simply as the 'Manor', is well preserved by a caretaker who is probably maintained there by the British Legion. There are only a few graves, seven or eight at most, and the last record of a military burial is for 1918. So, the dead soldier may not have been a member of the noted 'Munsters'. Tralee came within the ambit of the British Kerry Brigade, with headquarters at Buttevant, Co. Cork. Florrie Donoghue, in his book, *No Other Law*, gives a 'Weekly Intelligence Summary' for the Sixth Division, dated 17/5/21 in which is stated that Tralee had the '2nd Battalion, Royal Regiment'. Ballymullen Gaol, separated from the Barracks by a row of houses, was also a military establishment in which their prisoners were kept. It had a little graveyard at the back, now concreted over by the County Council who presently own the premises. It is probably there the soldier's body was interred. There is no other record. The Munster Fusiliers had a strong representation of itinerant and gypsy families from the south of Ireland, all noted fighters, who left their mark on the history of the Great War. I would like to think that the dead soldier belonged to some other breed. It is galling to contemplate the possibility that the Flying Column of the First Cork Brigade of the Irish Republican Army was chased about the hills of Ballyvourney by a bunch of tinkers!).

Beyond Meeinglia (Horgan's) hill the ground levels off for some distance and then dips into Commeen, a narrow, crescent glen that, like others of its kind, had been delved out by a glacier in prehistoric times. It is drained by the tiny Owengarve ('the little rough river') that flows out of Lough Carrignafararah, high up on the Derrynasagart ridge, just on the Kerry border. In fact the border goes through the centre of a chain of little lakes and impartially gives off a whole series of rivulets on both sides like ribs from a breastbone. Most of the men fleeing from the Coomnaclohy battle made their way over the border and took advantage of some of these gulches into Claedagh. A few crossed the main Killarney road making south and west for Inchamore and Coolea. They had just made the crossing and had barely time to throw themselves down in the heather when the four lorries returning to Tralee roared by on the road beneath them, laboured up the stiff pull of the *Cumar Duv* ('the black gulch') and came to a halt on the straight beyond the top. Only then did they notice some figures silhouetted against the skyline. A machine-gunner on one of the lorries loosed a blast at them from his weapon but the figures were gone. They were, in fact, the little band who had made the timely counter-attack at Meeinglia.

Leaving the front lawn by the farmhouse, where they had

made their stand, they retired along the bog road and headed westwards. As they slid over the highest point they came once again under fire. A volley from below knocked splinters and a cloud of acrid dust out of a rock on which Captain Patsy Lynch was standing. But nobody fell and they went on running across the open bog-land, over the barren brow of Slievereagh and down into Commeen. The main road was in full view only a quarter of a mile away. They dared not approach it at this point, so they turned away reluctantly and crossed the head of the valley making for the *cumar*, the dry, deep cut in the mountain side that led away to the top again and brought them out under the shadow of the clump of boulders known as Carrignafararah, the Rock of the Sentries. (*Note*: Tradition has it that this place was used as a watch-tower of sorts during the period of the Penal Laws in Ireland when the Mass was forbidden by law, when, in fact, an Irish Catholic was presumed not to exist in law, and 'red-coats' and other breeds of professional and voluntary priest-and-bounty-hunters were continually on the prowl for 'defaulters'). Carrignafararah had its stony eye on all the approaches, and there was Carrig-an-Aifrinn, the Mass-rock itself, over beyond the road high up in a declivity between the rocks, where the secret worshippers could 'make their souls' calm in the knowledge that they were being watched for and watched over. The 'red-coats' now wore a dusty khaki and the Mass-rock was only a wistful relic of a desolate and almost forgotten age; but the oppression was still there and while it remained the gallant young men of the resistance would pass and re-pass under the approving eye of the ghostly watcher on Carrignafararah. They were passing now, walking the border through open moorland. Presently they arrived on Cnoc-na-Lice (the 'hill of the flagstone'), high above the road whence they could look down on the spot where they hoped to make their attempt. On this hill, as noted in Literature, used to stand the now vanished cromlech known as *Leac a' Bhrannra* (the 'tripod stone'), but whether

Christian or pagan burial they paid scant attention. They
were watching the road. Everything seemed to be quiet. All
of County Kerry that was visible from where they were, seemed to be reposing in eternal sleep, from Mangerton mountain, brooding over the Killarney Lakes, to the Paps of
Danaan beyond the Claedagh valley to the north-west. The
east was their problem. The road disappeared under the hill
to their left, and all the trouble in the world might still be
lurking there ready to pounce. Patsy Lynch was sent back
to investigate. The day was fine, the sky was clear, and the
earth seemed to be 'void and empty'. Patsy duly made his
way back to Carrignafararah. Half-way there he sat down
to watch, but the peace and quietness and the effect of the
day's exertions got the better of him. He dozed. Presently
he awoke with a start. Paddy Donagh Owen and Danny Harrington were standing over him. 'Anything happening?', asked Paddy in an urgent whisper. Still bemused, Patsy's mind
reverted to the last impression it had received before obli-
vion, and he chanted,

> No stir in the air,
> No stir in the sea . . .

Paddy looked down towards the distant stretch of roadway.
'My God!', he shouted, 'look below on the road — four lorries of them!'. They waited for no more but slithered out
of sight and were already several yards on their way when
the bullets that were sent after them lost themselves harmlessly in volumes of all-absorbing bog-stuff. They threaded their
way through virtual catacombs of turf banks and bog holes,
expecting at every step to hear the clamour of pursuit. Then
they emerged onto a vast prairie of open moorland with
scarcely a mound or hollow. It sloped away gradually towards
the left, the Kerry side, dipped in a sweeping, shallow depression in the middle of which they could see the shimmering
waters of the Black Lake, levelled out again into the distance,

to be finally cut off sharp by the dark, forbidding gorge of Claedagh Valley as it swung away in a wide arc from Madam's Bridge, near the Killarney road, until it lost itself somewhere behind the back of Mullaghanish. Claedagh now spelled safety as no other place could. Without doubt, Nature was in a particularly rough mood when she set to the job of designing and endowing that rugged valley. However, the one thing that perhaps has done it most harm was not the whim of a wayward glacier, nor yet some prehistoric upheaval, but the satire of song-writer George Curtin, expatiating on the woes of 'the pup' that 'came home from Claedagh', and how glad he was that the said pup had finally got it into his emaciated head to do the same, and the wonder that his starving body had been able to stand up to the strain of belated homecoming. (*Note*: The famous ballad, 'The Pup Came Home From Claedagh', is a macaronic, a humorous twin-language song of a type popular in the last century). All this with due respect to the kind-hearted people who inhabit the place and somehow call it 'Home', because they were always ready with a welcome for the fighting men, and a bite and sup as long as it was there, and a place to lay their heads. And, if truth must be told, there were those in better land and in better circumstances who paced the yard uneasily while a weary republican soldier slept inside, and wondered how much the fine would be or if the house would be burned down in the event of any trace being found. The kind-heartedness of the Claedagh people transcended political cleavage and even racial animosity. In the 'Big Round-Up', which came a few months later, with Claedagh as its focal point, and the brilliant organizational ability of the future Field-Marshal Montgomery to lend it impetus, one salient fact stuck in an old woman's mind over the years. The 'Tommies' swept over Caharbarnagh mountain by bridle-paths or any paths they could find, or none at all, through the deep *cumar* between Knocknabro and Knocknagown — a cantankerous pair of twins — and swept on to the stony banks of the Claedagh river. It was anything but a morning's work-out on a barrack-square or field manoeuvres on Salisbury Plain. (*Note*: In 1954 I covered every step of the way with Patsy Lynch). The old woman said: 'The poor soldiers' feet were all red and sore!'. The old I.R.A. man, in bitter retrospect, whipped back: 'The feet of the fellows they were hunting were redder still!'. Just now we left a few of them getting in a bit of practice for that great day of cross-country racing. We left them gasping in dismay at the prospect of a vast expanse of open moorland. They set off at a steady pace keeping the Black Lake (where they say the trout are big and black and conveniently lazy) on their left, and wishing, not for the day, like St. Paul on a famous occasion, but for the night which was already sending previous notice with the lengthening shadows that it was on the way. By some miracle of endurance they made it to the valley rim. By some miracle of fate they got across without once hearing the vicious challenge of a rifle shot. They slid thankfully off the edge of the plain into the depths and the friendly dusk. Darkness seemed to come on quickly now as they made their way carefully downwards and the massive bulk of the Paps quenched out the last rays of the fading daylight. Presently they stumbled into Glashacurmick and they had arrived. The little glen is called after Cormac, not the kingly MacArt of ancient Tara, but a notable member of the Kelleher family whom, however, jolly Jeremiah (Thady Jerh) Kelleher in 1954 could not remember being ever alive, nor even the name to be in use among the Kelleher tribe, but could still give a reasonable assurance that he was a very notable character indeed. This blessed evening the lads honoured his notability — or was it notoriety? — by coming through his *glaise* on to the valley floor and the friendly homesteads. They left Glashacurmick close by Claedagh Lodge and its nearby coach-house which were kept in former times for the use of the 'gentry' when they drove out from Kenmare and Killarney on their shooting expeditions,

enduring monuments to the Ascendancy class and an abiding
affront to the subjugated peasantry. (*Note*: A very old lady,
the last remaining member of the class, still lived in the Lodge
until quite recently, in gracious decadence and an aroma of
lavender and old lace). Beside these buildings now, like thieves
in the night, footsore and weary, slunk some of the men who
were engineering in sweat and blood the end of 'Ascendancy' with all its implications and airs. They were looking for
their comrades of the First Brigade Flying Column. They
were located in the homes round about. Seán Hegarty, the
Brigadier, was there, calm, patriarchal and watchful; also
Commandant Patrick O'Sullivan whom it seemed years since
they had parted with at Coomnaclohy, although in reality
only a few hours; Dan 'Sandow' O'Donovan, gallant Column Commander; driver Jim Gray, irrepressible and spry,
singing his cheerful songs, cracking jokes when (as Patsy said)
there was no cause for laughter except maybe the relief of
reunion, putting the 'come-hither' on gullible and responsive old crones by the fireside, with a sly wink to the boys
. . . Jim, the play-actor, who had held up the retreat from
Coolnacahera for the purpose of upbraiding machine-gunner
Eugie O'Sullivan for his 'conspicuous cowardice in bringing the gun and leaving the bottle (of poteen whiskey)'. His
brother, Miah, had to be there too, for it was axiomatic that
'when Miah comes can Jim be far behind!'; and Corney
O'Sullivan, from Bantry, seconded to the First Brigade as
engineer, the man who, with 'Sandow', wrote 'Finis' to the
career of 'Bloody' Smyth, one other Englishman who suffered from the delusion, and forgot to his cost, that blood
is, after all, thicker than whiskey-and-soda. (*Note*: One-
armed Colonel Smyth, Divisional Police Commissioner for
Munster, gave his notorious 'shoot-to-kill' speech to the
Listowel, Co. Kerry, R.I.C. on June 17, 1920. The police immediately resigned in protest and Smyth was shot dead, a
month later, in the County Club, Grand Parade, Cork City,
his last impression being the famous address: 'Colonel

Smyth, you said "Shoot to kill! Well, here we are!"'. Still, Corney O'Sullivan, my father said, went to his grave a nervous wreck as a consequence).

*   *   *

Coolnacahera was Friday. Constable Cane, wounded in Pat Cronin's cottage, died on Saturday. Lieutenant C. L. Soady, having vainly withstood the traumatic effects of desperate facial injuries, decided the effort was not worth it and checked out on the Tuesday following. Somebody remembered that he had mentioned a wife. A telegram, signed by the Acting Commander in Macroom Castle, found her through the War Office. The message went (according to a staff member in Macroom Post Office): 'Regret to inform your husband died of wounds received in action Stop request wire instructions Stop'. Came the classic reply: 'Saw little of him in life Stop don't want to see him dead Stop bury him where he fell or in the nearest graveyard Stop'. She had her wish. In a little nook hidden away at the back of the Macroom Protestant church, a bowshot from the Castle battlements, under the crossed anchors of the Royal Naval Reserve cut on a headstone sadly listing to port (until the recent kindly efforts of the Macroom Historical Society), the mortal impress of the spirit of Cadet Clive Lindsay Soady has become part of the soil of Ireland. For him, as for so many others of his kind, Rupert Brooke had already pronounced:

> If I should die, think only this of me:
> That there's some corner of a foreign field
> That is forever England.
> There shall be
> In that rich earth a richer dust concealed.

15

HOME TO OUR MOUNTAINS

Early morning at Claedagh saw the men of the Column on their way again. They crossed the foot-bridge onto the rough road running through the valley, trudging on towards Madam's Bridge and the main Killarney road. Where the sides of the valley closed in to form a narrow gorge their local guide remarked on an historic association of the place, and those who had not known had the awful feeling one has on coming for the first time upon the location of a terrible tragedy, in this case the death of a community. It was the afternoon of the Fourth of August, 1831, in fine harvest weather, rather thundery, but giving no hint of the elemental visitation that was just about to wreak havoc and cause desolation in the homes of so many of the poor valley dwellers. No one bothered to notice the dark, ominous cloud gathering over Knocknabro until the air became hushed and abnormally oppressive. Suddenly the cloud burst open with a roar that could be heard for miles around, and the people in their homes and in the fields could hear the thunder of the deluge in among the hills. Those who lived beside the river banks wondered if the downpour would last long enough to cause the river to rise and reach out clammy fingers to pluck at the insecure walls of their mud cabins. Their fear soon gave way to terror as a new sound came to their ears, the rumbling of an approaching torrent. Through the *cumar* it raced, a veritable wall of water, carrying rocks, shrubs, small trees and practically all before it. The banks of the river disappeared in a boiling, foaming inferno and to the noise were soon added the shrieks of the people and the hysterical crying of children. The flood swept into the narrow gorge and the whole ground began to move in one mighty landslide of rocks, earth, trees, tumbling houses and churning water, and the demon-flood continued its mad career until its appetite for wanton destruction was finally quenched in the Killarney Lakes twelve miles away. Many people were drowned or killed, one family being completely wiped out . . . 'Lucey cried out that he should run to the assistance of his family . . . had gained his habitation but had only time to seize the jamb of the door when the torrent overwhelmed him and swept all before it; and he was found at a great distance with the piece of timber firm in his death grip'. (*Cork Constitution*, August 9, 1831).

The remnants of the Flying Column now moved through the place in silence, some surreptitiously making the Sign of the Cross as they noted places that marked the sites of cabins where children must have played, happy in their innocence but destined never to grow up, likewise young men and women who were destined never to grow old. So they passed, each occupied with the pensive, searing thought of 'sudden and unprovided death' the monstrous shadow of which hung over each and every one of them since they first took arms into their hands to strike a blow for freedom. Death to the young is always something unthinkable. The young die hard. It is comparatively easy to face and accept the end when the decay of age is on you and you are lying in bed racked with pain, waiting, wishing, praying for the end to come quickly and mercifully, 'half in love with easeful Death', yet bound to linger on a little longer. Death then is a friend. But when one is in full health and vigour with all one's faculties crying out for life and vindication, when every nerve and sinew reverberates to the undeniable urge to preserve continuity of existence, then death is an enemy that has to be hated, feared, spurned, kept at bay and thought out of reality into a realm of obscurity at the end of illimitable time. Death is then a point of perpetual future and life is one long scintillating moment of present. Life's subjective worth, therefore, is boundless, the value of its offering inestimable, and the manner of making the offering, whether it meant looking into the unwinking eyes of hungry guns by a blank wall at the corner of a barrack-square, or a short, sharp drop through a trap-door, or the long agony of hunger-strike, of no concern at all . . . no more than it was to Patrick Pearse facing the firing-squad, or Thomas Ashe wasting with hunger, or Kevin Barry, the hero-martyr, the paragon of republican youth, placing his boyish head in the noose in Mountjoy Gaol, one Monday morning . . . of no concern, except maybe for preference one would wish to meet the inevitable and go out beside the comrades who thought and felt as you did, making your stand and, if it so happened, falling beside them on your native heath or on the green sod of your own townland . . . of no concern when the spirit of the offering was as the spirit of Pearse and Ashe and Barry:

> Let me carry your Cross for Ireland, Lord,
> For the cause of Roseen Doo!

The long, long day had drawn to a close and a new one was dawning as they plodded down the main road to Poul Gorm (the 'Blue Pool') bridge and headed into the beautiful little valley of Freaghanagh (the 'whortle-berried'), where the River Loo flowed down against them to join the Claedagh river that from now on became the Flesk. This was their destination for the remainder of the night and morning. Over on their right, in vague outline, could barely be discerned the long, rough back of Fileadown (the 'cliff of the fort'), with the peak of Crohane brooding mightily over it, and the young Flesk hitting off its shin-bones before swinging away in a wide arc towards Killarney. The railway line crossed the road and ran close in by the foot of Freaghanagh mountain, by the wood with the almost unbelievable name of Rossacroonaloo. The effort of marching on the sleepers was 'the last straw' (said Patsy Lynch), too long for one step, too short for two. In the friendly households on the wooded slopes they slept just where they sat or rolled unconscious on to readily vacated beds. It was midday again before they awoke. They prepared to leave. Travelling by road was out of the question. They had to take to the heights once more, with three miles of sheer mountain before them. Their final destination was the quiet, sequestered valley of Knockaruddig that followed the Roughty river due southwards to its source in one big wedge of rising ground culminating in Bealick mountain that overlooked the source of the River Lee at Gougane Barra.

So, 'out again into the south wind and the sunshine', as William Bulfin had said (in *Rambles In Erin*). Fortified by a late breakfast they felt able to tackle the steep, boulder-strewn side of Freaghanagh mountain. Some locals call it 'Barna' mountain, from a noticeable gap at the top looking like a miniature 'Devil's Bit' against the sky. How 'Che Buono' (Bulfin) would have crowed and ruffled his feathers as he emerged triumphant through that gap on to the ceiling of the world, and gazed around him in rising pride and ecstasy. Much as he appreciated his beloved pampas of the 'Southern Cross', he appreciated so much the more, to the honest fellow's undying credit, his beloved Irish hills ranging tier upon tier until they melted into the sky at the hazy-blue horizon, *ag bagairt a gcinn thar druim a chéile*, nodding their heads over one another's shoulders, as the Gaelic poet, Brian Merriman, wrote in the eighteenth century. But in the present circumstances it is doubtful if even William

Bulfin would have delayed for long to dote on the scenery if he did happen to be here, instead of having spent most of his short life secure in his 'latitude 35 south', as he said, seven thousand miles away , while his friend, Arthur Griffith, was formulating the idea of 'Sinn Féin'. His current successors on the up-grade were now clinging to the western fringes of the Derrynasaggart range and travelling roughly parallel to the County Bounds which ran three miles to the east of them, quite in evidence where it lay dotted with a row of formidable peaks like a string of frontier posts. There was Knockbwee, Cummeenteige, Cummeenboy, and then Meelin, with, a little higher and a little nearer, Coomagearlahy. Their late H.Q. at Clountycarty would now be lying to the south-east and about ten miles away. At Knockaruddig they would have completed, like mountain hares in flight, a circle with a diameter of sixteen miles. They set off across the bog-land. A young lad was sent with them to show the way and direct them over the safe passages through the wet and marshy regions that would have been undecipherable except to one whose early lessons in walking had been complicated by having to pick a precarious way over isolated tufts in a morass or around a treacherous quagmire. And even at that, the guide's best efforts failed to keep them dry. Brigadier Seán Hegarty soon got into one of his testy moods. After a bout of floundering and 'bogging' he proceeded to rasp some skin off the lad's nose in his own cutting, characteristic manner that he freely exercised on anybody from a 'gossoon' to a Staff Officer from G.H.Q. But for once the noted sarcasm failed to produce an effect. It rattled harmlessly off the stolid, east-Kerry *sang-froid*. 'Be sure now, boy', said Hegarty, 'and take us through all the wet places!'. The answer was prompt and slighty stunning, like the kick of a starting-handle that was too late to prepare for when it had gone past. 'No need to tell me, Sir', he replied — 'Every place here is wet!'. They trudged on across the moorland by the Lakes of Doo, dipped into

Tooreen glen and climbed out over Meeing, getting their first glimpse of the valley of Glanlee. The Glanlee river is an insignificant little tributary of the Roughty, the fact being duly endorsed in the ballad, 'The Glanlee Exile'. If Patsy Cronin, the 'Bard of the Roughty', had really visited all those places mentioned so casually throughout the eighteen verses, from the mountains of Lebanon to the mines of San Francisco, he would surely have been the original rolling stone, the presence of the railway station reception committee at his home-coming apparently making the effort worthwhile as they . . .

> Raised a shout of welcome that shook with the vibration
> The surrounding elevation on the road to fair Glanlee.

The little band of Republicans left the 'surrounding elevation' of Glanlee without any serious regrets and sidled down the last incline to Coolnoohill on to the road by the banks of the Roughty, where a minor road led away into the obscure recesses of Knockaruddig. Following it they passed under the frowning portals of a seat of landlordism, Sillahertane Cottage, otherwise known as Lowe's Lodge. They had no occasion to feel any fear. It was deserted. A short time later the lovely residence was delivered to the general holocaust of such-like places and crumbled in all-consuming fire. Only the portals still stand. Lowe's Lodge presented no difficulty for the fugitives as a prelude to their final endeavour and the end of an odyssey.

*   *   *

Then, of course, there was the man who did not go far. He eased off the crest into the trough of the fleeing wave, let the eagerly pursuing wave roll over and away. (*Note:* Recently I was told of a fox who did that very thing a short distance from my backdoor. In Vincent O'Brien country, we are beset by 'the unspeakable in full pursuit of the uneatable'. On a day when the scent was poor for fox-hunting the wily Reynard joined the pack of hounds and hunted with them until he reached a convenient gap and said bye-bye!). Captain Tadhg Twohig, of Ballyvourney, my father's cousin, was that rare prodigy, the country fighter who became a city fighter and excelled in both elements, although his sister, Mrs. Mag Kingston, a bluff country woman, disdained his prowess, invariably referring to him as 'd'afficer'. Tadhg's concept of evasion was as elementary and elemental as that of the fox that crosses running water and returns on his own tracks, or even carries on as above. Returning on his tracks as darkness was setting in, his yen for investigation led him back into the recently occupied territory. The village of Ballymakeera he found apparently abandoned. There were no sentries in evidence, no clump of marching patrols, but the quietness itself felt ominous and deceptive. It might be just too quiet. So he waited, listened and watched. A few minutes later he froze as a light flared in O'Leary's bar, and subsided into a faint glow. Somebody held a match in there until it died. He heard the crack of the next one and watched as it moved along the bar. Two figures outlined in the meagre light were all too familiar, their present occupation all too obvious. They were mixing drinks from the remains of broken bottles. He wondered at their disregard for glass fragments and the irreparable damage they might do to the alimentary canal. Always the philosopher and good companion, he wondered at the resilience and virtual indestructibility of the human kind. A drinking man himself, he stopped wondering, went in and procured a candle. (*Note:* I wasn't at school but I met the scholars!) . . .

Well, the long day was over for all concerned, and as for the Auxiliaries concerned it really appeared that 'you could bate them with your cap', as they say in Ballyvourney. The British forces concerned were just as surprised as any, as shown in the reports, and the daily press opened its mouth wide in inane and voluble astonishment. The accounts were many and voluminous and special correspondents vied with one another in extolling the 'gallantry' (sic) of the Crown Forces in their efforts to police an unsettled countryside, and correspondingly deprecated the uncivic action of a supposedly enormous body of 'armed civilians' in their efforts to prevent them from doing so. An extra-special correspondent for the *Cork Examiner* really excelled himself. He paid an extra-special visit to the scene of the 'outrage' in the interest of truth in the news. Apart from the actual police and military reports, his predecessors seem to have built their graphic commentaries on certain unnamed and presumably unauthorized accounts from police sources. 'An inspector' was said to have made the statement that it was the biggest ambush so far in Ireland (Crossbarry was a month later). Engaged, he said, were from forty to seventy Auxiliaries (the breed seemed to defy exact or even approximate enumeration), some Police (they would be the Royal Irish and Black and Tans), and about four hostages (for security purposes or just plain cover). Of the I.R.A. engaged, several accounts placed them at about three hundred, some, more conservative, thinking that maybe they could be in the region of 200-250. All agreed that they had used bombs, machine-guns, rifles and small arms in unlimited quantities. They could have added field-guns and howitzers and nobody would have minded a bit. Beyond that the remainder of the reports could not be regarded as in any way flattering to the I.R.A. The police were reported to have said that a lot of blood was seen at the place of the ambush. Two of the attackers 'were seen to fall heavily against the rocks'. Finally, in their retreat, 'they suffered severely and many were seen to fall as they were under fire from several machine-guns'. The extra-special correspondent, as above, arrived on Saturday morning, a week later, to view the scene and draw his own conclusions. He gazed around on the rocks of Coolnacahera, and along the roadway, with a speculative and determinedly unbiased eye, and decided that there were no bombs. Definitely bombs were out. The I.R.A. had not used them. What had looked like bomb craters in the road were in reality pot-holes, he said. But one of them could not possibly be classified as such and could only have been made by a land-mine. So he concluded, and went his way feeling like Longfellow's 'youth, who bore, 'mid snow and ice, a banner with the strange device'. The truth in the news was going to be a bitter pill for the Crown Forces, so, to placate their sensitive natures, he increased the enormity of the 'armed civilians' to four hundred. That would be half-a-dozen or more Flying Columns. So, Tom Barry, Seán Moylan, John Joe Rice, Humphrey Murphy, Pax Whelan, Paddy O'Brien, Liam Lynch and other hard-grained guerrilla leaders throughout Limerick and Tipperary, had an opening to claim a part in the battle if they had a mind to do so. Nor was literary achievement wanting on the side of the 'armed civilians'. John P. Twomey, the afore-mentioned Secretary to the Republican, or 'Arbitration', Court in Ballyvourney, scratched his shaggy head, went into a huddle with his vengeful muse and came up with the following gem, which he called 'St. Gobnait's I.R.A.':

> Come on, come on, come on, brave boys, come on, I appeal to you,
> To prove your might in this righteous fight and join your comrades true;
> Show 'John Bull' that Erin's sons are united to a man
> To face the khaki, the R.I.C. and the savage Black-and-Tan.

Refrain:

> Hurrah! For St. Gobnait's I.R.A. were valiant, brave and true;
> They've shown the ruthless English 'Huns' what Irishmen can do.

> At Geata Bawn, that fateful day, it was in mid-July,
> When Captain Airey was shot dead and his men were forced to fly;
> With wounds galore their bodies sore, they'll ne'er forget the day

They met those gallant Irish lads, St. Gobnait's I.R.A.

At Knockanure brave Sharman too was made to bite the dust.
Then all at once his men gave in — and of course you know
   the rest:
They surrendered all, both gun and ball, and bicycles a score;
The boys made off with the bloomin' lot, determined for
   some more.

St. Gobnait's sons have met the 'Huns' in many a desperate
   fray,
And every time they won the fight — they drove the Tans
   away;
The last encounter that they had was beyond old Poulnabro,
When Major Grant and thirty Tans their bodies were laid low.

The poetic exaggeration of 'Major Grant and thirty Tans'
is paralleled, to my knowledge, only in Virgil's *Aeneid . . .
Multos Danaum demittimus Orco* ('We pitched a whole lot
of Greeks to hell!'). In a frivolous mood the Parish Priest,
Father Jeremiah Twomey (who later became distracted to the
extent of setting fire to his own house, and whom the Tans
had noted to the extent of remarking, as he walked along
reading his Breviary — 'Just look at the old devil praying
for more ambushes!'), subscribed a final verse to record the
last main event in the history of the local struggle:

On the fifth of June, in Twenty-One, as we'll remember long,
The Crown put up a big 'Round-up' of nigh ten thousand
   strong;
But our Patron was much stronger — her hive drove them
   away,
So give three cheers for those gallant boys, St. Gobnait's
   I.R.A.

*   *   *

A brass plaque on the wall of the Protestant church in
Macroom (at present removed to safety by Rev. John Fenn-
ing, of Aherla, while the building is being renovated) indicates that twenty-eight men, to wit, two majors, two

captains, thirteen first-lieutenants, three second-lieutenants, one sergeant (given as David Maunsell), and seven constables, from C and J Companies, Auxiliary Division, and the R.I.C., in the Macroom District, lost their lives during the period: September, 1920 — July, 1921. Some of them are still unaccounted for, unless one postulates the Coolnacahera ambush. In Cork the string of gun-carriages carrying coffins to the quays was not such an extremely rare sight that secrecy would be desirable. Rather, the British, inured to the expenditure of man-power in the furtherance of expansion campaigns and empire building, welcomed the opportunity of enforcing respect for their dead. As the files of soldiers went marching by they snatched the caps from the heads of men onlookers and flung them on the ground, while nobody really minded the cackling laughter of the shawled women from Cornmarket Street, the 'Coal Quay', as they screamed in that strangely whining and quite exasperating old city intonation (said to be akin to the Welsh, and aped so pathetically by their native comedians), as the sombre cortèges wended their way seawards: 'Don't forget to sen' back d'empties! We'll fill 'em again!'.

16

Court Martial

The one person who came dangerously near to paying for the Coolnacahera fracas was, strange to say, the Master of Coolavokig school. Though innocent of the whole affair, but too quick on the uptake, as always, he was drawn accidentally by design into the net and his experiences for the next couple of weeks, as a prisoner of the military authorities, were both trying and revealing; trying, in that he had to fight every step of the way for his life and succeeded only through the agency of a nimble brain and an honest-to-goodness attitude towards his fellow-man of whatever breed; and revealing, in that he profited thereby to the extent of a clear, firsthand insight into the affairs and 'lawful occasions' of the Auxies and Tans, that was food and drink to his inquiring mind and insatiable curiosity even in the shadow of the hangman's noose.

On the afternoon of the ambush his schoolhouse was surrounded. It re-echoed to the lonely hollowness of the tomb as only a schoolhouse devoid of children will do. Then his home, the farmhouse down in the valley by the Sullane river, was located and searched without result. His wife, Molly, ventured the information that he had gone about some school business to consult with his manager, the parish priest, in the village of Kilnamartyra. In response to the next question she pointed apprehensively to where a square stone church building stood, gaunt and commanding, away on the skyline to the south. Then they left, but not with the intention of putting him out of their minds. On the following Tuesday evening they struck with a suddenness that was deadly. They came in seven Crossley tenders led by an open tourer in which were the Acting Commander in Macroom Castle and two Intelligence Officers clad (rather incongruously, thought the Master, being currently at home to callers) in 'civvies' and light machine-guns. Evidently his arrest was being regarded as of special importance in military circles. Having raced the half-mile of by-road from the 'Half-Way House' ('half-way between Cork and Killarney, half-way between Cork and Bantry, half-way between Macroom and Ballyvourney, and half-way between any other two places that are equidistant from it' . . . Robert Gibbings in *Sweet Cork Of Thee*), they had the place surrounded at the double and in battle order before anyone could realize what was happening. He grabbed the baby and ran out the back way. Just short of the furze-brake, over the field behind the house, he was covered by twenty rifles. (*Note*: Being the baby in question, I have the distinction of having been arrested at gun-point by the British Army at the age of four months. These things rankle. Still on the baby theme, recently I had the unusual experience of meeting for the first time a sprightly and merry old lady who, at the age of twelve, had held me in her lap when I was only seven weeks old. It was just on Christmas, 1920, and she had been sent with a present of butter, eggs and cream to my mother as we were about to leave forever the old rented house at Capnahilla [Mick Sullivan's 'deserted farmhouse'], on the land of Timothy McCarthy, Candromey, destined to be burned down by the British after the Coolnacahera ambush. Young Katie Cronin was pleased to hold what she referred to only the other day as 'a most beautiful baby'. She later married Neilus 'Rahey'

Murphy, of Kilnamartyra, and now lives at Clohina with her son, Con, and his family. The 'Raheys' were nicknamed for their ability as runners. 'Rahey' is a corruption of *reatha*, meaning 'of running', and one of them, actually her father-in-law, had won a bet by running from Cork to Macroom, 24 miles, in bare feet and wearing only the standard flannel 'long-johns' of the time. Katie is still much more mobile than myself, as she showed when I tried to sit once more on that privileged knee!). Having taken the Master prisoner, the Tans made a fair bid at resolving the problem of what to do with him by taking him as a hostage, sitting in the cab of the leading lorry, on a tour of Coolnacahera where, according to a strong report, another party of the I.R.A. was waiting in ambush. And so to Macroom Castle. A day or two later he was interrogated by one of the Intelligence Officers, a man named Captain McConnell from Dublin. Despite the tension and uncertainty, he found an interest in the scene of the inquisition and fixed the details firmly in his mind while above his head the Sword of Damocles hung suspended by its single strand of silken hair. The place appeared to be a bedroom, either used as such by the former owners or having been converted by the present occupants. It was on the second floor up the main staircase of the Castle and opened off a large room which might have been either a dining-room or a drawing-room. Just inside the door was a four-poster mahogany bedstead complete with canopy. The names 'Hedges-White' were neatly carved on the headpiece, indicating (he thought) some kind of ceremonial nuptial couch, as the name 'Hedges' had drifted, through a marriage alliance, into the White family, the Earls of Bantry. Robert Hedges Eyre, whose family had bought the Castle from Judge Bernard, ancestor to the Earl of Bandon, had refurbished the Castle before his death in 1840. His only daughter married into the Bantry family, and her son, Richard White, became the third Earl of Bantry. The names Hedges and White appear in the famous song,

Cath Céim an Fhia, composed by the Ballingeary poetess, Máire Bhuí Ní Laoire, about the battle of Keimeneigh in 1822. The Master did not need to be the good historian he was, to be aware of all this. The bedroom had only one window. Beside it stood a little writing-desk and on the wall above hung the kismet of all defaulters, a huge file with the ominous words 'Black List' crudely hand-engraved on the cover. At the desk sat McConnell, the interrogator. The prisoner was made to sit at his left hand side, facing the window, where the full light of day might reveal any telling traces of hesitancy or fear, or any slightest deviation from the truth. So, let interrogation begin! For a while it followed the usual prosaic pattern. Name? Age? Occupation? Any marks on body? All for the record. Then . . .

Intelligence Officer: 'Do you belong to any organization?'
Master: 'No!'
I.O.:   'We've had another teacher prisoner here who stated that he belonged to an organization called the I.N.T.O. Do you belong to that?'
Master: 'Yes! That's a professional, non-political organization to which all members of my profession belong, and I didn't think it necessary to mention it'.
I.O.:   'Fair enough! How long have you been teaching in your school?'
Master: 'Eight years'.
I.O.:   'You should know the people of the district very well after eight years!'
Master: 'No, for I have not been actually living there. I have been there for only six weeks and have had very little to do with the people in that time'.

Now, sensing the line the questioning was liable to take, and having been given his opening, the Master began to elaborate on an idea that had been in his mind since the beginning. His original appointment (he informed the I.O.) had been opposed by many of the local people and for that reason he had continued to be *persona non grata* with several.

Getting an attentive ear, though covertly studied all the while, he proceeded to draw the long bow hoping to make an impression that might be the means of forestalling any further questioning on the theme. The effort involved a good deal of mental gymnastics, and an occasional reservation, and but for the argument he construed he would have found it very difficult to get out of their clutches, as subsequent events proved. The I.O. took up questioning him whether he knew a house here, a house there, on such a road, but designedly or otherwise he failed to locate any. Then he was asked did he know the Harringtons of Coolavokig. He said yes, the youngest daughter — quite a little girl at the time — who was attending his school. And he got his first real surprise when the I.O. shot back: 'I know! I have been speaking with her!'. Following quickly on this the next question simply stunned him, but primary instincts were strong and nerve and brain were equal to the shock. The question was direct, almost blunt, but the I.O. was casual as he spoke. It was textbook psychology. 'Have Harringtons got an outside farm?'. The Master knew quite well that Harringtons had an outside farm at Clountycarty and that a vacant house on the farm was being used as a camp by the Flying Column. The I.O. had asked a question and now waited, pencil poised, for the answer. There was no appreciable interval of time before he heard and duly recorded that the prisoner, being a virtual stranger to the place and having little or no social intercourse with the inhabitants, was not aware of the circumstances of anyone living there. Being an efficient I.O. he must have noted mentally that the voice which replied to his query betrayed no emotion and probably would not have done so if the prisoner had been informed that every householder in Coolavokig possessed an outside farm and a town residence as well. Then the reserve of the I.O. melted and he volunteered some information. 'Oh, yes', he said, 'they have got an outside farm with a house on it being used as a camp. I have been there and found some empty whiskey bottles with labels showing that they had been got at O'Leary's, Ballymakeera'. (*Note*: Whiskey was delivered in bulk in those days. It was bottled, labelled and even coloured by the publican himself). The Master said nothing because there was nothing to say, but he guessed that the house in question was one owned by the McCarthy family, Candromey, just off the road from Poulnabro to Kilnamartyra, right opposite the scene of the ambush, and which the British had burned down later that evening. The statement showed him also that the Auxies had some information but that they could not place it, which proved that members of the R.I.C. still on active service did not co-operate with them or only in a negligible fashion. At the time there were in Macroom policemen who had been evacuated from Ballyvourney and Inchigeela, any one of whom would have known Clountycarty quite well. Of two things the Master was certain. There were some whiskey bottles in the house in question. There were none at Clountycarty. To the first, it happened to have been his own house a few weeks before. To the second, no whiskey bottle or whiskey drinker would have survived for long the proximity of Brigadier Seán Hegarty at Clountycarty. So on . . .

I.O.: 'Do you know O'Leary?'
Master: 'Yes!'
I.O.: 'Are you a friend of his?'
Master: 'An acquaintance. I live too far away to know him intimately'.
I.O.: 'Well, I have been in O'Leary's bar of an evening, disguised, and the place was filled with I.R.A. Do you know anything about this or have you heard it?'
Master: 'Sorry! I don't frequent the place. I'm living too far away, and I have a wife and family to look after'.
I.O.: 'Well, I'm making you this offer. We are prepared to pay you a thousand pounds (about £40,000 by today's values), give you a job in England with full protection, if you help us to get any of those fellows. Are you prepared

to do this?'. (Then, without waiting for an answer, he added with bitterness . . .). 'They are too clever and seem to know everything, whereas we can't trust anybody, the R.I.C. or any of ourselves!'

It was a devastating admission from a Secret Service agent and made it appear that the arrogant, roughshod-riding of the military authorities was increasingly becoming an affectation. The Master was floored — the horns of a dilemma as never before! He could not accept the offer but his hand was in the dog's mouth. Meekly he said — 'I'll report to my manager and let him do what he thinks fit'. The masterful evasion cut no ice and the interview was over. (*Note*: The School Manager in question was Fr. P. J. Leahy, P.P., a native of Midleton. He lasted just another year. He died suddenly while distributing Holy Communion at the early morning First Friday Mass in February, 1922. My father, who was present, raced up and jumped the altar-rails to pick him up. The ciborium had fallen from the priest's hand scattering Sacred Hosts far and wide. Fr. Leahy was succeeded by Fr. Ned Shinnick, C.C., Coachford, who had got undue publicity for becoming involved in the affair of Mrs. Lindsay and the Dripsey ambush, but that is another story).

The Acting C.O. was in the adjoining room as they passed through from the interrogation. He reclined in an armchair in the company of two other officers. The man who had taken over in place of personable Major Seafield-Grant was noticeably pock-marked, disturbingly beady-eyed, with a long, semitic type nose and a tongue that savoured strongly of the guardroom — a not very prepossessing appearance for a not very lovable character. In fact, Mr. Pockface was an altogether depressing combination, much as a rat. Him the Master would never forget for reasons other than his looks and speech. From the arrest onwards he had shown himself an extremely interested party as if he bore a strong, personal grudge. At the moment Pockface was out of harness. He was dressed in a check suit of 'plus-fours'. When the I.O. appeared at the door he shouted

'Is he prepared to tell anything?', and when the Master's answer was duly repeated the look he got from Pockface boded no good for the future of primary education in Ireland. Luckily for the Master he was a military prisoner. Hence at no time during his imprisonment was he ill-treated in any way. (*Note*: His greatest discomfort was, not being used to spade and shovel, that he was obliged to move a large pile of rubble from the foot of the Castle keep to another position and back again almost without stop, while New Street ('Pound Lane') shopkeeper, Tom Gallagher, uncle of Patrick Gallagher, sometime journalist with R.T.E., recently deceased, strung his long, lazy frame over the Sullane bridge and laughed fit to split his perpetual raincoat). The Auxies were chary of falling foul of the Army. They had received orders from H.Q. to apprehend, interrogate and hold him in custody until the General Staff had decided what to do with him.

> The military was torn between those who thought it best to ride out the storm, letting politicians negotiate a settlement, and those who advocated sterner measures designed to stamp out the I.R.A. completely.
>
> (From — *Monty: The Making Of A General*).

The Master was an important prisoner, his importance being due largely to two things, a new order from General Higginson and a chance incident on the day of the ambush. While raiding a house in Rahoona, near Poulnabro, the I.O. had met a ten-year-old schoolgirl named Julia Bridget Lynch, and asked her why she was not in school. The child said that on the previous evening the Master had told her not to come to school at all that day, the day of the ambush. It was the childish foible sometimes called lying, and sure the mention of 'the Master's' name ought to be sufficient to fill the hearts even of 'the soljers' with dismay. In point of fact it had filled them with murderous intent and they had immediately switched their investigations to Coolavokig school . . .

*   *   *

There had been wild scenes in the Castle that night of the ambush. Crazed with drink from O'Leary's deserted bar in Ballymakeera, the Auxies had practically wrecked their quarters. A prisoner was beaten to death in the guardroom. An Auxie named Jackson, from Belfast, fired his revolver through the ceiling, narrowly missing the Acting C.O. in the room above. For this he was 'drummed out' on the following day. He was a very subdued and harmless ex-Auxie as he was being seen to the gate by, oddly enough, John Dineen, N.T., of Rathmore, the unwilling hostage who had led in the invasion to Coolnacahera (and who related this and other matters to my father). If the Master had been in the Castle that night even then he could have maintained his position of untouchability. Of course there were ways and means. 'Shot while trying to escape' could always be relied on and often was. An insanity plea in regard to an out-of-hand shooting was also known to work. The Master kept these things in mind. One night he thought his hour had come. It was late and the half-dozen or so prisoners were asleep in their cellar. The door creaked open. Always a light sleeper, he was instantly alert and listening. A torch light flickered over the sleeping forms, rested on him, and cautious footsteps approached his side. A revolver obtruded its vague, ominous bulk beyond the painful dazzle, and the quick 'Act of Contrition' was more instinct than deliberate intent. Then — 'Jus' coime t'ave a look. G'noight!'. It was the Sergeant of the Guard fearful for his responsibility after a late-night raiding party.

These officially known 'Temporary Cadets of the Auxiliary Division' had undeniable fighting qualities. They also had respect for their skins as well as for the fighting qualities of their opponents. This he discovered for himself. It was Saturday night, March the fifth. He had been a prisoner for a few days and was now well known to the garrison. Generally he was treated fairly and decently. Pockface bore him a grudge, as did Grundy from Northern Ireland. Grundy never looked at him, nor spoke directly, but managed to convey a feeling of hostility whenever he was near. A corrugated-iron 'Mess' hut had been erected on the Green on the side of the Castle facing the main gate. Two sections had their meals there. Grundy was a Section-Leader, which did not necessarily betoken a higher rank than that of the men under his charge. The Auxies were all ex-officers, Army, Navy or Air Force, unemployed from the Great War, who were venturing to function as 'policemen'. So there were lieutenants upstairs among the 'brass hats', majors and captains downstairs with the 'rank-and-file'. It was not a system that made for individual respect for authority except at the incentive of a pound sterling per day which, in those days, put a premium on affluence. On the Saturday an elderly attendant, an ex-soldier from Tipperary, named English, who, incidentally, had a magnificent tenor singing voice, asked the Master to help him wash up in the hut after tea. Apart from the Mess, the old fellow's duties were not clear. He was to be seen frequently walking to and from the town with a basket under his arm, presumably for shopping. That evening there was a certain air of excitement in the Mess hut. Grundy was parading up and down the centre with a rubber ground-sheet slung over his uniform as a cape. The Master went to the sink at the right-hand corner, near the entrance door, where there was a pile of dishes, some of them stacked high but mostly drawn together in grimy disorder. He kept on the alert. Grundy stopped his pacing and stood talking in a low voice to three or four others. From their furtive glances he knew it was something about himself. Corporal English continued indifferently washing up but in a moment he whispered — 'You'd better clear out, laddie, and get over to the kitchen. Those fellows are going out tonight on a stunt and they might attack you before they go, like that little shit of a New Zealander!'. The man from 'down under' had been drunk on Friday and had accosted him with — 'If you were free today would you be on parade with the

Sinn Féin army?', and other things to that effect. The Master could now plainly see Grundy's festering looks. He slipped out, went across to the kitchen and sat there. After a while Grundy marched in carrying a rifle, took not the slightest notice of him, spoke to the cook, a lean, hard, greying Scotsman. He simply said: 'Jock, you are my man (partner) tonight!', and then went out again.

The prisoners all now made themselves scarce in their cellar dump, going as quietly as they could. An air of expectancy hung over the Castle and a peculiar feeling of uncertainty seemed to be in everybody's heart. They put out the light and listened carefully, but they never heard a sound. The lorries that bore the warriors away to battle were pushed out on to Castle Street and let run down the steep hill to the bridge before starting up. Next morning the Master was told off again for duty at the Mess hut. He found a new President and Vice-President of the Mess as were customarily appointed on Sunday mornings. These were responsible for the following week's meals and began their duties *ad rem* by making out a provisional menu for each day of their term of office, and hanging it in a prominent place in the hut. The V-P, quite a callow young fellow (the Master himself was thirty, around average height, of square build and strong as a horse), spoke politely to him and said: 'If you are here for the week, and I hope you are not, I want you to take charge of the Mess tent and refuse to do anything for anybody else!'. So he laid the tables in due course and in the Auxies came, some in pyjamas with greatcoats over them, all bleary-eyed and 'simply gawsping' for tea. In the centre of the hut stood a stove and on it were several 'dixies' full of hot tea. They drank cup after cup. The Master was amazed as he had never seen anyone drink six or seven cups of tea with or without food. He reflected that as a tea drinking race the British must be in the world championship class. When things had quietened down the young V-P (gave his conscript dishwasher an idea of what had been on. An

ambush had occurred, he told him, at a place called Clonbanin and a brigadier-general had been killed. A call for help
had been sent out to Macroom Castle. 'If one of us gets
killed', the V-P said, 'it doesn't matter. But if one of those
fellows goes there will be something to pay!'. Everybody, it
seemed, had been out from the Castle that evening but they
had lost their way and were late for the show. As it happened the now historic battle, on the main road about midway
between Mallow and Killarney, must have been over long
before they left Macroom. It began around two o'clock on
the afternoon of Saturday, 5 March, 1921, and two and a
half hours later the din of battle had died away leaving only the cries of the wounded and dying amidst a shambles
of ditched Army vehicles and dead bodies, while the I.R.A.
columns from Cork and Kerry that had been engaged were
well away on their separate routes to safety and wholly intact. It had been a highly improbable position at Clonbanin
but had proved a highly successful one for the I.R.A. How
so? 'Well, Seán Moylan himself was there!', said veteran
Jamie Moynihan to me in 1956. Commandant (later General)
Moylan, with the agreement of Tom McEllistrim of Kerry,
had indeed been in charge of the operation (in conjunction
with Commandant Paddy O'Brien of Liscarroll), and
presumably that was a reasonable guarantee. The high-
ranking British officer who fell by the wayside, with his brains
shot out, was Brigadier-General (also referred to as Colonel-
Commandant) H. R. Cumming, D.S.O., in command of the
Kerry Brigade at Buttevant Military Barracks, mostly
members of the East Lancashire Regiment. A tall man,
General Cumming was seen to leap from the touring car in
the centre of the convoy. At the call to surrender he was heard
to shout: 'Surrender to hell! Give them the lead!', but was
shot down before reaching the cover of the fence. Two ladies,
of highly different background, come into the closing episode
of his life. (*Note:* General Cumming's name is often misplaced as Cummins, Cummings, etc., which is a small point,

but his rank also has an unusual feature of interest. Journalist Pat Lynch, in his admirable work, *With The I.R.A. In The Fight For Freedom*, and its accompanying series, shabbily and unworthily produced by *The Kerryman* newspaper, Tralee, and now unavailable, has this to say: 'About a month previously, the rank of Brigadier-General had been abolished in the British Army, and that of Colonel-Commandant substituted for it'. I have always understood, and was assured by late Colonel Barry O'Brien, military historian, Blackrock, Cork, that the rank of 'Commandant' existed only in the Irish and French armies. Inimitable novelist, Evelyn Waugh, introduced the rank of 'Colonel-Commandant' to the Halberdier Regiment in his wartime trilogy, *The Sword Of Honour*, but his biographer implies that both the regiment and the rank were fictional). For the record, Florrie Donoghue erroneously gives the date, Thursday, March 3, 1921, for the Clonbanin ambush. The official report gave thirteen Army personnel dead and fifteen wounded at Clonbanin. However, a local patriarch claims to have counted fourteen bodies laid out in a local shed at the historic crossroads, where they were left unattended for quite some time before transport was laid on to remove them. The 'Sword of Honour' can be an ungainly weapon!

*   *   *

There are no vultures in Clonbanin and never have been, so none could have been seen circling the field of battle, like the preternatural ravens of old Celtic literature, nor were there any hobgoblins or kites in evidence (*na bocánaigh agus na bonnánaigh* of the Fenian Cycle tales, if my memory serves me right), nor indeed had there been any trace of Morrigu, Badb or Macha, the crazed battle-harpies, screaming from the rims of the jarring shields, nor any other manifestation to mark the resting-places of the slain; but presently a wee slip of a girl might have been detected cycling along the roadway towards the spot, calmly dismounting, placing some of the brains of the dead British general in an envelope and calmly moving off again. Late that night, Nurse Singleton arrived at her destination, Ballyvourney, twenty miles to the south by road, and triumphantly produced her gruesome exhibit to the delight of some of the boys gathered in Cornelius ('Con the Shop') Lucey's shop in the village. There is an old saying in Irish: 'Do not trust the hind leg of a horse until you see it carried off on the shoulder of a dog!'. *A fortiori* (as we used to remark in Maynooth), do not trust the brain of a British general until you see it arriving in an envelope! The other lady (*supra*) was his wife. During the following cessation of hostilities (they would now refer to it as 'cessation of violence', depending on which side one favoured), from the Truce of July 11, 1921, she arrived at Clonbanin in a chauffeur-driven Rolls-Royce. There are some people still alive who, as children, saw the fur-coated lady step out of the unbelievable motor-car, gaze around for a moment, step in the car once again and drive away having remarked aloud: 'What a wretched place for that fine man to die!'.

*   *   *

During the Master's detention in the Castle they tried little ruses from time to time to discover if he knew anything, or so he thought. On one occasion 'Paddy Carroll', a supposed native of Westport, Co. Mayo, who posed as a particular friend of his and claimed to be a first cousin of Major John MacBride (a native of Westport, executed in 1916), which he may have been, asked the Master to help him pack his belongings. They went up the steps at the back of what had probably been the servants' quarters. Carroll asked about his arrest, told him the I.O.'s name was McConnell. He then produced a picture-postcard with a photograph on it of Sergeant Mike O'Leary, V.C. The Master had often seen the card before, a recruiting card for the British Army. It had been on sale in all stationers' shops during the War. Carroll asked him if he knew Mike. The Master said he did. They had actually been at school together. Then Carroll exclaimed: 'He was the chap in charge of the ambush!'. The Master replied that he could not venture an opinion, and after a few more remarks about O'Leary they finished up. As there were several Irishmen in J Company, 'Carroll' may have been the Mayo man he claimed to be. (*Note:* Just recently I came across sound evidence that Carroll was genuine, tried to help the prisoners anyway he could, and on one occasion saved the life of one of them). As well as Grundy, English, Jackson, McConnell, there were McCarthy from Dunmanway, Fothergill — an assumed name — from Kerry (can you imagine the accent!), an officer from Antrim, and the one, alas, who was said to have beaten the prisoner to death, answered to the name of Clancy.

On Monday, two weeks after his capture, the Master was court-martialled. On the previous evening twenty-one men had been surprised by the Auxies at Toames, south of the town towards Kilmichael. It was Sunday, March 6. According to Charlie Browne *(The Story Of The 7th)*, they were members of the Flying Column from the Macroom Battalion whom we left resting in Annaganihy after the Coolnacahera ambush. They had first moved to Laharn. While there Fr. Tim O'Mahony of Macroom, on leave from the U.S.A., arranged with Fr. Sheahan, P.P., of Aghinagh to give the Column members Mass and Holy Communion on the First Friday, March 4. They had breakfast afterwards in the parish priest's house, and moved on to Toames on Saturday for a new training programme. They were in the public house when the Auxies struck. At the time one simply ran. They ran. The Auxies opened fire, the usual routine. One Republican got hit. He was Cornelius Foley, quartermaster to the Toames (J) Company, and was known as 'Moses'. When the news came through to the Castle the Master's wife, Molly, happened to be in the guardroom visiting him, having walked alone the four miles from Coolavokig. An Auxie jumped clean through the open window and shouted that twenty-one 'Shinners' had been taken on the road to Inchigeela (which was incorrect). At the mention of Inchigeela — his native place — the Master told her to go away and he ran by the wall for the shelter of the kitchen on the far side of the yard. It was nearly dark and he just made it. Already he could see the men moving through the guardroom under heavy escort. If any one of them had given a sign of recognition he would assuredly have been called on to identify them. A bunch of Auxies came into the kitchen. They were, he thought, rather subdued. One or two blustered to him — why him, he didn't know! — about getting man for man. Somehow it fell flat. Grundy wandered in and held his hands over the fire in the stove. After a while he said to Jock, the cook: 'One of them's dying out in the hall. The priest is with him. I'm tired of seeing dead men!' (*Note:* Shortly afterwards he himself was fired on and wounded out near the Millstreet crossroads). Then another Auxie arrived and spoke of the dying man with something like awe in his voice — 'When we came up to him, lying wounded on the road, he said: "Keep your hands off me, you dirty English bastards! I don't want your help! Up the Republic!" '. It surprised and obviously disturbed them. They seemed to wonder at the mentality of it. Just then an officer came from upstairs, which was strange as they never appeared in the men's quarters. The Master's dodge had been spotted. The officer called him aside and asked him had he seen the prisoners and could he identify any. He lied stoutly, then parried some more and the officer went away. Poor 'Moses' was already dead.

On Monday morning the military arrived in several lorries from Ballincollig. The senior officer who came with them, and whose rank the Master could not ascertain, was an elderly man with steel-grey hair, dark complexioned, stern

and unbending. The Master was marched in under guard
and an armed soldier took up position on either side of him,
remaining throughout. The room was crowded with Auxiliaries and military personnel. There was evidently a good
deal of interest being taken in the trial, the first test case
under the new Martial Law regulations issued by Major
General Sir E. P. Strickland, commanding the British Sixth
Division, and military governor of Munster, with headquarters in Cork City. Part of the regulations had reference
to citizens living in the vicinity of an ambush. In this case
a citizen of some note was in the dock. The President of
the Court seated himself at the little desk presenting his back
to the room and all in it. ('From the back he looked like
a colonel', the Master said rather enigmatically). The 'Black
List' was not now in evidence. Those called upon to speak
had to address themselves to the back of his head. He
declared the Court open. The Master right away applied for
legal assistance. He was curtly informed that he was intelligent enough to defend himself. He had done so already,
he thought wryly. The trial opened and McConnell, the Intelligence Officer, was called. Under oath he affirmed that
he had passed by the schoolhouse at Coolavokig on the evening previous to the ambush at a stated time — something
like 'sixteen hundred hours', in Army parlance — and the
school was in session. He passed by on the following morning — it was closed. Finally he arrived in the afternoon and
found it just the same. He went to the teacher's house to
be informed that he had gone to visit the parish priest. He
was present at the arrest, which was ordered by Military H.Q.
(which meant Brigade Major Bernard Law Montgomery,
Divisional Adjutant, at Victoria Barracks, Cork City). In
subsequent statements, the I.O. declared, the prisoner had
denied any previous knowledge of the ambush at
Coolnacahera. The Master was then asked for his observations on the case that, it was alleged, had been built up
against him. He replied by repeating his demand for legal

assistance. This was again refused. Then he stated that he could not have known about the ambush as, firstly, it took place three miles away from his residence; secondly, it had occurred at 8.40 a.m. which was fifty minutes before the official time for opening school, 9.30 a.m.; and, thirdly, owing to his being a stranger in the place he could not have been privy to any local subversive activities. It was the best he could do by way of argument. To British ears, he knew, it must have sounded odd and supremely illogical but it made an impression of sorts on one man, the starchy President of the Court. He was ordered to be removed and he stood outside, under guard, for ten minutes while a discussion went on in the courtroom. Once he was recalled and asked what his official time was for opening school. He repeated — 9.30 a.m., and was taken outside again before being returned to hear judgement passed on him. Getting a signal that the prisoner was at his back, the President spoke to the wall. He had come to the conclusion, he announced, that the prisoner had known something beforehand of this ambush. It was his 'duty' to have reported it, and, for having failed to do so, he should be fined forty pounds or do six months hard labour. The Court rose, and it was lunchtime.

The Master was ordered to collect his few belongings and get on a lorry. It was assumed that the fine was prohibitive and that he had no choice but to go to gaol. He felt ill at ease at the prospect of a trip to Cork City in the company of disaffected British soldiers not to mention what twenty-four miles of open roadway might produce from a roving band of the I.R.A. (*Note:* Less than two weeks later, Tom Barry's Column, returning in formation after a stupendous victory over hundreds of British troops at Crossbarry, a few miles from the city, passed quite close to that road firing on everything in sight). When the President of the Court appeared outside — he looked still more like a colonel from the front and was undoubtedly Lieutenant-Colonel F. H. Dorling in charge at Ballincollig, or, possibly his subordinate,

Lieutenant-Colonel G. Evans, less flamboyant but more militarily motivated, who had so spectacularly and effectively handled the Dripsey ambush on January 28, previously (cf. *Lady Hostage,* by Tim Sheehan, for extensive details) — to inspect the bunch of Toames prisoners lined up some distance away, the Master called him over. Surprisingly he came. Pockface walked beside him. The Master asked to be given an opportunity of paying the fine. The officer seemed to sense a suspicious angle. He questioned the Master closely as to where he should get the money and why he wanted to pay. The Master explained about his job, and other circumstances, and how his wife was not well. (*Note:* She was an asthmatic and had almost died during the big 'flu of 1918-1919, which left her hearing permanently impaired). Pockface immediately interrupted and called him a liar saying that she had been in on the previous day and looked quite well. But the old man had a direct outlook and bore no ill-will. The Master was given permission to go and borrow the money. Tim O'Keeffe, draper, paid it for him right away. Then he received a lecture on his 'duties' and a warning that, if he came under their notice again, he would not get off so lightly. If it had been the notorious C Company of Auxiliaries, the crowd who had been withdrawn after their Waterloo at Kilmichael, he would have been lucky to have reached the court-martial alive. (*Note:* Does anybody in Dublin know anything of a Captain McConnell, the Intelligence Officer in the case? There are one hundred and two of the name listed in the phone-book for the metropolitan region. If I might just see his grave, and identify his full name, I could lay away forever the ghost of Coolnacahera . . . Author).

The Tans did not pass the Coolavokig schoolhouse again until a certain day in May, when they went out to Ballyvourney to dismantle a lorry, the property of Jeremiah Twohig of 'The Mills', or so the story went. From the rock 'forninst' the school door there was a clear view of the main road eastwards as far as O'Mahony's gate at Carrigaphooka. On a fine May morning Mary Jane O'Mahony stood gazing wistfully ('as was her custom', the Master said) at the distant gate and the sun-bathed fields of home. Suddenly she slithered off the rock and rushed into the Master's room screaming: 'The Tans are coming! The Tans are coming!'. It was indeed a terrifying sight the little girl had seen, though it had become rare nowadays. In a moment he was out and could see the clouds of dust quickly approaching along the straight. There were no tarred and rarely metalled roads in those days and, such as they were, the dust lay thick and heavy on them during that dry and warm weather. They came over the incline at Jerh 'Bwee' Kelleher's and dipped into the hollow beyond, finally coming to a halt at the 'Half-Way House'. A trench had been excavated at the bend below the school, so they could not pass. As Marshal Petain might have said, if he were present: *Ils ne passeront pas!*. After some negotiations among the scouts, in which the Master was an unwilling participant, they brought their transport up the 'Board of Works' road (part of the heritage of impossible and impassable cross-country passages initiated as relief works in the eighteen-eighties, which we knew as the 'Boar Works') that was no more than a rugged track through the fields, dramatically led by a local old fellow, named Moynihan, on a white farm nag, reminiscent, as the Master said, of 'Napoleon crossing the Alps'. So they rumbled and swayed and dogged, the little Crossley tenders and the big Lancia trucks with the steel-plated sides, over the hill and up the adjoining 'boreen' with its right-hand narrow bends, and heaved out sharp left onto the high road by the school gate while he watched in admiration, as fine a feat of driving, he said, as he ever expected to see. (*Note:* A poor driver himself to the end, he always admired good driving. A few years later, John ['Máire Connie'] Twomey, of Ballymakeera, delivered a lorry load of 'bags' to the farm gate at Coolavokig. The Master became agitated at the impossibility of the turning manoeuvre. His friend, John Twomey, put his mind at ease with the immemorial phrase — 'Watch my magic hand!'). Later in the afternoon the British contingent returned and all disembarked at the school. The lorries twisted and swayed their troubled way to the main road again, followed by the passengers on foot; and that was the last the Master saw of the 'Black and Tans' on the Ballyvourney road.

In fact nobody saw very much of them anymore until the colossal man-hunt by the British forces in June, that is ever since remembered as 'The Big Round-up', not even those who had specifically set themselves the task of seeking out and engaging the British in mortal combat. The Flying Column had made a real impression at Coolnacahera. A trooper fondly caressing the sleek sides of a Rolls-Royce 'Whippet' armoured car beside the gates of Victoria Barracks, Cork — now Collins' Barracks — was heard to murmur: 'Ah, you beauty, if I only had you at Ballyvourney!'. Coolnacahera had taught a lesson. The Column rested at Knockaruddig (as already noted) and, early in March, moved back to Coomiclovane, a secluded valley among the hills beyond Coolea. In the seclusion of the glen a daring project was conceived and put into operation. (cf. *Where Mountainy Men Have Sown*). The commandeered red BUICK open-tourer carried a party of six heavily armed men (Dan 'Sandow' O'Donovan, Drill Master Seán Murray, three O'Sullivans, viz. machine-gunner Eugie, Mick and Corney, with Jim Gray at the wheel) to keep a deadly tryst with the Divisional Commander, Major-General Sir Peter Strickland and a projected boating party on the River Lee, near Cork Harbour, forty miles away. (*Note:* Strickland had become restless and disconsolate, and disturbed by 'the damned efforts at peace'. He wanted out. In his diary [cf. *Monty: The Making Of A General*] for New Year's Day, 1921, he entered: 'Last year was bad enough, but nothing to this. We could move about, hunt, etc. and personally I can now do neither'). The group's daylight drive through the city, just after curfew had been lifted, with guns in evidence and ready for immediate action, must surely rate, for brazenness and audacity, with some of the most thrilling feats of the period. But the effort proved futile, as the general had changed his plans, and the return to base was fraught with even more danger, all enemy posts *en route* having somehow been alerted. Finding themselves once again within the homely peaceableness and palpable security of Coomiclovane, after a hazardous zig-zag night journey without headlights (cf. Introduction) brought forth from 'windy' but irrepressible Jim Gray the classic and passably devout observation: 'We're as safe here as if we were in God's pockets'.

(*Note:* About Jim Gray. He and his brother, Miah, were members of the Column and came from Cork City, where their father actually worked at Victoria Barracks. Jim was a noted singer and natural entertainer. He later married the lovely May McCarthy, of Candromey, a teacher in Cork. When she died of throat cancer, young and childless, he was inconsolable and put on her headstone in St. Finbarr's Cemetery, 'NOR LONG SHALL HER LOVE STAY BEHIND HER', from the song, 'She Is Far From The Land', Moore's eulogy on Sarah Curran. But he lived on and became quite a 'character', on one occasion, under the influence, chasing a Civic Guard with his lorry round and round a monument in the square of a West-Cork town. The revolver story, however, is far more historic. He and his brother ran a garage in the city and were well known to, and trusted by, the British authorities. They thought to get a licence for a revolver they had, 'for protection', and approached District-Inspector O.R. Swanzy. To those versed in the history of the times the irony will be immediately apparent. Swanzy had his office in King Street, later to be named MacCurtain Street. Their garage was in his district, opposite the gates of Victoria Barracks. Jim told the complete story to the *Sunday Press* in 1959. Swanzy gave them permits for two revolvers, with a handful of ammunition for each. Jim's gun was a shaky old Webley given him by Lord Mayor Tomás MacCurtain. Swanzy shook it and remarked wryly: 'I would rather be on the receiving end of that!'. He was. He was later identified as having been involved in the murder of the patriotic Lord Mayor on 19 March, 1920, and was transferred to Lisburn, Co. Antrim, where he was shot dead as he left church, on Sunday, August 22, by a detail from Cork City using Jim's revolver!).

In the same light as Jim Gray's observation, safe in God's Pockets, the Coolea region was regarded by the one person to whom the safety of the fighting men was to be of paramount importance until the end of the Civil War — General Liam Lynch, the newly appointed commander of the First Southern Division, who, late in April, was given the responsibility of organizing the resistance over the greater part of Munster. Liam arrived early in May to set up his Divisional H.Q. at Gortyrahilly, near Ballyvourney. His transport was a horse and side-car driven by Captain Patsy Lynch. Some security measures had been undertaken to ensure his safe arrival, but Liam never asked. Instead he showed a keen interest in the location and description of the 'Slippery Rock' ambush as they drove by. Security lay all around him, but history had been made, and would be his for the making until his devoted life should have ended tragically at the hands of his own countrymen. (*Note:* Everybody wants to know who shot Michael Collins. It has been dealt with exhaustively in *The Dark Secret Of Béalnabláth*, by the present writer. Nobody has ever asked who shot Liam Lynch, whose death is probably even more significant, if less sensational, than the death of Collins, as it effectively marked the end of the Civil War). Of a taciturn and retiring nature, he never spoke very much even in council. He listened, analysed and quickly decided, and any opposition sometimes brought a slight stammer into his voice. A stranger to the locality, he had been known by repute to all, personally only to a few, probably understood by none. 'He should have been a priest', the men used to say as their best way of expressing the intangible quality of him, the mystery that surrounded him, the occult power, as visualized, I may add, in those naïve and serious-minded days! Brigadier Seán Hegarty was probably a better leader of men, they thought (and I have in mind remembered debate and conversation snatches of half a century ago), but there was no denying that sense of personal commitment, that 'squareness' of character, that moral simplicity of purpose, that made Liam Lynch a dedicated man, a leader to be followed to the extremity, who would still be hankering after the old ideal when there was no one left to follow him; who would remain, if so it happened, not indeed as a crotchety Ossian after the Fianna of long ago, but as a noble and tragic Goll Mac Morna after the battle of Gowra, which saw the end of civic unity and the dissolution of the ancient national army of Fionn Mac Cumhail. He had best be gone . . .

*   *   *

The Master died twenty years ago, precisely on the anniversary of the Coolnacahera ambush, 25 February, 1974. Some additional notes, in his magnificent hand-writing, have recently come to light. Some of it is repetitive, but there are a few instances where further light has been thrown on the historical happenings of his time:

1.   After the release of the internees from Frongoch and other English prisons in 1917, Eamon de Valera, accompanied by J. J. Walsh (member of the new Executive of Sinn Féin, and later Postmaster General under the Free State Government), visited Macroom and addressed an enormous meeting from the balcony of the Town Hall. Previous to that there had been a review of Volunteers by Dev, in Coolcower, at which many officers of Volunteers appeared in uniform. The R.I.C. were there in force but to the best of my knowledge no military appeared on the scene.

2. Early morning raids by military, accompanied by a policeman, usually Constable Michael Dillon, a Kerryman, stationed in Macroom, were features of the time. O'Sullivan's, Kilnamartyra, was several times raided as it was known that 'strangers' often stayed there.

3. Kilnamartyra at the time was an object lesson in disunity. Largely owing to factionalism, family politics, parish politics even extending to the village pump about which a song had been composed, and business interests involving two public houses, as well as the nature of the terrain, the place was divided into two sections the members of which were known locally as 'Sinn Féiners' and 'Mé Féiners'. Each section had a drum, some few fifers, and in the long, calm Summer evenings the respective drummers beat it out in opposition, each in front of his selected pub. (cf. Bulfin in Belfast). The sound of the drums could be heard for miles. I myself have heard them at a distance of eight miles by road.

4. Miah's (O'Connell's pub) eldest son had joined the Air Force early in the War. He himself had presided at a recruiting meeting held in the village. He was a relative of the Goolds (who were involved in Home Rule type politics), and a follower of the Twomeys (as opposed to the republican Lynch faction), and, of course, a member of the A.O.H. (*Note*: The Ancient Order of Hibernians used Catholicism as a political big stick!), though, like all of that type, his politics were parochial and his outlook chiefly centred on having a good time (*Note*: His younger brother, William, became a missionary in the East Indies. He was known as Fr. Bill Miah. He was swept into the bag when the Japanese overran Malaya in World War Two. A huge, good-natured fellow, he had dropped from sixteen stone to seven stone when he returned home after the war. At one stage the Japs buried him up to his neck in sand. He shared a concentration camp with Bill Wall, a British policeman from Aghada in East Cork. The local curate, my classmate, now Canon Michael O'Brien, of Buttevant, said to Bill Wall: 'Tell me, Bill, how did ye survive?'. 'Well, I'll tell you, Father',said the ex-policemen. 'You might think it was religion, or prayers. No! It was just pure hatred!').

5. From 1916 onwards the Volunteers were being reorganized.
    Dick Mulcahy was in the district at the time of the Clare
    election between Dev and P. Lynch, K.C. I recollect Johnny
    Sullivan, Kilnamartyra, telling me a story of an incident in
    connection with this. Johnny was the Principal of the Boys'
    School and, like all elderly people at the time, did not believe
    in physical force. His eldest son, Patrick, afterwards Com-
    mandant of the Eighth Battalion, I.R.A., was at the time
    about twenty or so. He was more interested in politics than
    in studying. One Sunday after Mass Johnny spoke to Dick
    Mulcahy and asked him why he wasn't in Clare helping at
    the election. Mulcahy said, as his father was postmaster in
    Ennis he couldn't very well do so. Johnny immediately
    retaliated by saying to his son: 'Dick Mulcahy doesn't want
    to jeopardize his father's position by helping at the Clare
    Election, but it is no harm for you and him to jeopardize
    mine here in Kilnamartyra by acting as ye are!'.

6. Sinn Féin got control of Local Boards, got Justices of the
    Peace to resign their commission, set up Arbitration Courts
    and set about putting an end to the enforcement of English
    Law. The Justices of the Peace, or 'J.P.s' as they were called,
    were a curious body. They were magistrates of a sort, entitl-
    ed to sit on the bench and adjudicate in minor offences, like
    breaking the licensing laws, minor assault cases and so on.
    Usually a stipendary or Resident Magistrate sat also. He was
    a paid official, usually a retired army officer, and was sup-
    posed to have some knowledge of the Law. J.P.s were
    appointed on the recommendation of some politician and
    the honour was keenly sought after. Chairmen of Rural
    District Councils were also entitled to this honour, though
    Dan O'Leary never accepted it. I don't think there was a J.P.
    in Ballyvourney. Edmond Goold (Dr. Pat Goold's brother
    in the home farm in Kilnamartyra) was one, and there were
    two, as far as I'm aware, in Inchigeela. All resigned their
    commissions, though some say Edmond never did. In
    Macroom there were several J.P.s, all of whom gained an
    unenviable notoriety in 1915 for failing to turn up in court
    after having been requested to do so and adjudicate on
    the case brought by the Crown, in the person of Sergeant

Appleby, Ballingeary, against Claud Chevasse for refusing to give his name other than in Irish. Their refusal or neglect to sit on the bench and outvote the paid Crown magistrate in this case drew down on their heads the vituperation of the advanced National Press. 'The Leader' newspaper published a song, called 'The J.P.s of Macroom', which became rather popular. After this I don't think many J.P.s sat on the bench in Macroom, neither were their services needed, nor requested. (*Note*: Claud Chevasse, like Erskine Childers later on, was a strange phenomenon in the Celtic context both here and in Scotland, though he eventually favoured Ireland and lived out his life [1886-1971] in Connemara. His full name was Claud Albert. His father was an Oxford don and Claud was born there. The name was Sidney and he was a professor of Classical Languages. His antecedents were French, but Claud's mother was actually German. Claud affected a Celtic outfit, both kilt and tunic. Once he had discovered the Gaelic language, at a comparatively young age, he never looked back. In fact he became quite proficient and taught in Coláiste na Mumhan, in Ballingeary. He was referred to in a British newspaper as 'an Englishman masquerading as an Irishman'. He was committed to Conradh na Gaeilge and the Republican movement. Neither Sergeant Appleby nor the two constables, Butler and Bennett, had any Irish. To the sergeant he consistently gave his name as 'Clód de Siúsa' [written as 'Cluad de Ceabhasa'], which was technically against the law, though the irony is that his name was French, not English. He was said to have been a nephew of the Protestant bishop of Limerick. Appleby brought him to court in Macroom where he spent two days in gaol before arraignment. He was fined five pounds, with the option of a prison sentence. The case got wide publicity and was extensively reported in the Gaelic League magazine, *An Claidheamh Soluis,* 'the Sword of Light' [Ed. P. H. Pearse] in 1916. Claud had a daughter who was devoted to him and lived her life with him and his eccentricities. She may be still alive. When her birth was announced to him, he immediately named her for what he was doing at the time — fishing!).

7. An added impetus was given to the Volunteer Movement by the passing of the Conscription Act for Ireland on the 16th April, 1918. This set the country aflame. The Irish Party members were still attending the House of Commons. Their protests were received with derision. Even Lloyd George taunted them with the remark: 'You call yourselves a nation! Why, you haven't even got a language!'. He was on pretty sure ground here, and knew it, as he was a native speaker of Welsh himself and constantly used the language.

8. Up to this many 'respectable' people looked askance at Sinn Féin. I recollect being told by a young farmer: 'After all, you don't see many respectable people among the Sinn Féiners; they are all so-and-so!'. The word 'respectable' has many meanings when used in country districts in Ireland, but a meaning it certainly hasn't, and that's the orthodox one.

9. Ballingeary was different. This was the first place outside Dublin where a company of Volunteers had been formed either in the Summer of 1913, or early in 1914, by Piaras Beasley (Béaslaí). Owing to the influx of students to Coláiste na Mumhan, many of them Múinteoirí Taistil, or teachers of Irish under the Gaelic League, students from Dublin, Cork, Limerick (including Brian na Banban — i.e. Brian O'Higgins — Tomás McDonagh, Tomás MacCurtain, Peadar Macken), the majority of whom were Sinn Féiners, I.R.B. members, readers of *The Peasant*, many in that district had long known of Sinn Féin. Séan Hegarty had lived there for some time, when ordered by the British Government not to reside within forty miles of Cork City.

10. By that time many of the young priests had different ideas. I know from men who were students in Maynooth in 1918 that the majority of the students there then were rebels. But you must recollect that curates in Cloyne, that time, were men who had spent ten, twelve, and fourteen years on the Foreign Missions before returning to their native diocese. They had lost the enthusiasm and optimism of youth, had experienced the power and influence of British Rule, at first hand, where power and money were synonymous, so they could hardly be blamed if they considered physical force

futile. They had seen how miserable were the conditions in industrial districts in the North of England, and how unavailing seemed to be the struggles of the workers there against the forces of money and power, so it is probably no wonder that these men couldn't see how the new movement in Ireland could help. It should be no wonder, therefore, if they looked to an English Parliament to improve conditions, especially when a government ostensibly friendly to Ireland was in power. They had seen the revolution caused by the introduction of Old Age Pensions, National Health Insurance, so why shouldn't people wait and put their faith in those institutions which had conferred such immense advantages on the struggling masses of industrial England?

11. Carson and his Covenanters, the Curragh Mutiny, the Bachelor Walk shootings and, of course, the awful breach of faith in passing the Amending Act to Home Rule in 1914, served to turn the Irish people against Parliamentarianism. In Muskerry (i.e. mid-Cork) politics related to O'Brien v. Redmond policies. I don't think very many people realized the difference between the two. It suffices to say that the best off people followed Redmond, while the others followed O'Brien. In the Macroom area the Redmondites appeared to be winning. The Macroom Rural District Council and Board of Guardians had a majority of Redmondite followers. All were members of the A.O.H. and, as the Board of Guardians had many functions of the present day (i.e. 1955) Boards of Health and Boards of Assistance, such as the appointment of all officers connected with health, from Sub-Sanitary Officers to Dispensary Doctors, Veterinary Inspectors of Dairies and Cow-Sheds, Contractors for the repair and upkeep of roads and bridges in the rural areas, they were looked up to. The appointments made while these boards were in power were given to those who were either members of the A.O.H. or children of members. Home Rule, as visualized by country followers of Redmond at the time, meant more jobs. It is hard to blame them if they saw the prospects fading owing to actions of Sinn Féiners, human nature being what it is!.

12. One would think that the first thing to do in investigating the

affair (i.e. the Geata Bawn ambush) would be to cross-examine the children and teachers of the school (*Note*: At the time the Master had as assistant an aunt of the famous Gaelic poet, Séan Ó Ríordáin) about this, but, though military cars and lorries were constantly passing by, and though the school remained open until the following Friday, when it was closed for Summer holidays, this was not done. My explanation of the matter is that the survivors were unable to identify the place of attack and considered it to be around Poulnabro.

13. I was there (at Coolnacahera) buying some cattle. (*Note*: For a complete amateur, the Master had just invested rather heavily in a farm and farmhouse, and lived to regret it). I left about ten o'clock leaving business still going on. Some of the boys (i.e. the I.R.A.) at the scene of the ambush were quite visible to the people at the fair, who cared to look that way, even at that hour. The I.R.A. had great faith in the discretion and sympathy of those assembled at the fair to be so careless, if they wanted to ambush, that is, take by surprise, the Tans.

14. About noon (i.e. on the day of the Coolnacahera ambush) lorries of military came from the East and began firing indiscriminately when they reached Mons Cross (an alternate name for the Half-Way House), and along the road westwards. About one o'clock an aeroplane appeared overhead, cruising, proceeding along the river (Sullane) valley in perfect view. It was then I decided to inform my Manager, the Rev. P. J. Leahy, P.P., that I had not opened school that day. I proceeded to his house to find that he had closed the schools in Kilnamartyra that morning lest any harm might befall the teachers or those pupils who had turned up even though the place was miles farther away than Coolavokig School from the scene of the ambush. God rest his soul, the poor man was frightfully upset, and no wonder, as tales of the doings of the Tans were on everybody's lips at the time. From the top of the hill behind his house I had a perfect view of the scene of the ambush. There, lying down with one of the Connells, a British ex-soldier, brother of Neilus

Connell, member of the Kilnamartyra Company, I.R.A., I was able to see across the Sullane valley, with Connell's binoculars, the houses burning in Coolnacahera, the lorries on the road, and parties of military here and there . . . While in Kilnamartyra, two lorries of Tans passed through at great speed about two o'clock, coming down Cnocán na Móna ('the peat hillock') and going towards Renaniree. They didn't stop, search or make enquiries, but came and cleared out. Afterwards I made enquiries and learned (from Miss Lenihan, N.T., later Mrs. Jim Creedon) that they had come from Dunmanway, on to Dundareirke, and stopped there near the school. The children were at recreation and the Tans remained looking on for a while, taking refreshments on the side of the road, and apparently in no hurry at all to reach the scene of operations. Again, of course, from the hilltop here they could have a perfect view of the Sullane Valley to the North, from Codrum to Ballymakeera, with the main road now the scene of such military activity, and the scene of the ambush with its now blazing houses. Evidently the scene had no attractions for them — those mountains and crags were places to be avoided if possible. At any rate their route took them to Renaniree, and from there I couldn't discover where they went.

15. After my release from Macroom Castle I went back to school . . . I noticed one group of Tans taking the road back towards my own house from Mons (Cross), that is, the Renaniree road and another group going up the hill towards the right (Lacka-neen). I felt that those on the Renaniree road were again look-ing for me . . . so I went in to school to await eventualities. The night before the road had been cut at the turn of the school. A trench at least ten or twelve feet wide, extending from an overhanging rock at one side to a quay wall fifteen feet high on the other side, had been cut, thus rendering the road impassable. I surmised I should be held responsible again for this, as it was only a few yards from the school gate, and so I waited. I recollect well, I was calling the rolls loudly when I noticed two men in uniform walking on the wall behind the school, and then one appeared at the door and called me out. He, as it turned out, was C.O. (presumably

'Pockface'). A young man, tall, good looking and fair haired, in the uniform of the R.I.C., was standing on the road. He was an Irishman, with a Midland or Western accent, evidently a regular member of the R.I.C. The C.O. asked me about the trench, and I stated I couldn't account for it as it was cut only the night before. The policeman immediately came to my assistance with, 'Yes, we can see that it is quite freshly cut!'. The matter wasn't pursued further, but the C.O.'s preoccupation with me was to show him a way to get his transport up from Mons. Here, again, appearances were against me, as I knew of none. 'But' said he, 'a creamery cart went down here this morning, and we can go where he went'. John Kingston (nephew of Captain Tadhg Twohig) had taken Hegarty's milk from The Farmyard to Macroom creamery and, finding the road cut, had followed the old Board of Works road below the school, and had come out on the main road below. Poor John travelled back and forth all that Summer, from Ballyvourney to Macroom, and broken roads or lorries of Tans didn't upset him in the least. He took them all in his stride . . . I thought it was time somebody took notice of me, and so I said to the C.O., 'May I go in to my work, now?', and received as an answer, 'What work?', in such a contemptuous tone that I felt a miserable worm. However, I went in, and was not interfered with again. I was probably beneath contempt!. All the party assembled on the road outside the school. There were sixty or seventy of them, some of whom I recognized as being in the Castle in my time, and a woman searcher who had also been there. They waited opposite the school for a good while until they got the 'All-Clear' from the scouting parties who had been sent out to left and right at Mons.

16. The Intelligence Officer interrogating me (i.e. in Macroom Castle after the Coolnacahera ambush) had met a little girl aged about nine or so, and questioned her why she was not at school. Probably to people of his ilk, used to England where compulsory school attendance was in force, unlike Ireland where it wasn't enforced generally until 1926, it appeared strange to see a child like her absent from school. (*Note*: This Julia Bridget Lynch, already referred to, was,

in fact, just turned ten since January. She was a native of Clonkeen, in Kerry, and had come to live with her relations, Murrays of Coolnacahera, on the death of her mother. She had crossed the river to seek shelter from the ambush in Rahoona. Her youngest sister, Mrs. Katie Lucey, on whose birth the mother had died, still lives in Clonkeen, but poor Julia Bridget died in hospital in Cork City, at the age of sixteen, as a result of an operation to her nose, a little human mite, who, all unknown and unknowing, to a small extent affected the course of English and Irish History and almost earned for the present writer's father the firing squad or the hangman's noose!).

17

The Big Round-Up
Part One: Hue
and Cry

The man in the uniform of an officer of the British Army strolled into the village hall and took sombre stock of the bunch of 'other ranks' congregated there in various attitudes of resting. As they jumped to attention he took them all in with one possessive, sweeping glance through the smoke spirals ascending from the funnel of his crooked meerschaum pipe. They were his men and just now he felt friendly disposed towards them. He ordered them 'at ease', took his pipe in his hand, walked a few steps up and down, and addressed them magnanimously. 'Men', he said, 'I must congratulate you!'. He allowed time for that much to sink in. Then he continued: 'You have come through a long, arduous day, and you have come through it DAMN WELL!'. Discipline being what it was, and an officer being an officer, the oration was received in silence. He turned to survey the result of the day's commendable efforts. A solitary prisoner stood to one side looking completely unmoved by the performance and the occasion, though the look he received was not unkindly as if to betoken that he should feel honoured and show it. He failed to do so and the officer, having received no reaction from friend or enemy to his well-meaning overtures, made a parting gesture with his Sherlock pipe, hung it on his face

and strolled out again. It was, in fact, the aftermath of the
'Big Round-up', the misnamed and miscarried, the evening
of the day that witnessed one of the biggest manhunts in
the history of the British Army — and the biggest farce. It
began in the House of Commons, London, England, and
ended in the Claedagh Valley, in the County of Kerry, Ireland,
Monday, June 6, 1921. It was the brain-child of Brigade-
Major Bernard Law Montgomery, Adjutant to the Southern
Division of the British Army in Ireland. Monty had initiated
other large round-ups (or is it 'rounds-up'? Proper English
becomes more difficult all the time. Someone recently
classified it as Queen's English, American English, and
Sylvester Stallone. What's yours?). Monty to the last was
noted for overkill. He was prepared to meet and beat anybody
anywhere, given appreciably more men and equipment than
his opponent. The philosophy was far from new, likewise
its debunking. Subsequent to World War Two, the Americans,
with their built-in disregard for anybody else's military prowess, invented a drink named a 'Montgomery Cocktail'. The
ingredients, whatever they might be, were in the proportion
of fifteen-to-one. (Quoted by Hemingway in *Across The
River And Into the Trees*). Monty's two major round-ups,
beside the Claedagh one, were at Nadd and Kiskeam. In the
former Liam Lynch barely avoided capture, in the latter Seán
Moylan failed to do so. The Nadd round-up, on the wild
northern slopes of the Boggeragh mountains, where Lynch's
Second Brigade had recently established a 'barracks' and
training camp, would have been a major disaster for the
I.R.A. were it not for an intercepted communiqué at Buttevant post-office. It happened on March 10, 1921, in the early morning mist and rain. Montgomery's minute planning
almost worked but for the quick thinking and ingenuity of
Liam Lynch. The British were acting on 'good information',
according to Florrie Donoghue (*No Other Law*, p. 142 ff.).
The spy was a British ex-soldier from Kanturk who had joined
the column two months before. Some men of the Column

were killed and wounded, but most escaped. Protestant Ned Waters from Bweeng, a lieutenant in the Mallow Company, was one of the victims. John 'Congo' Moloney made a dash for liberty. He was wounded but escaped. His father dressed his wound in their home before he headed for the mountain. On the way he was intercepted by a British soldier, who said: 'Go as fast as you can — I won't shoot you!'. He was as good as his word. The next big round-up happened on Monday, May 16, 1921, in the Sliabh Luachra region around Kiskeam and Boherbue, apparently known as the 'Little Republic'. A detailed account appears in Fr. John O'Riordan's *Kiskeam Versus The Empire* . . . 'The "Little Republic" was invaded once more. The last time had been when Queen Elizabeth 1 had ordered the arrest of the Earl of Desmond about the year 1580 A.D.'. Brigadier (later General) Seán Moylan was captured. (*Note*: An account of his trial, and the valiant efforts on his behalf of young Mallow solicitor, Barry Sullivan, will be given later). After the 'Big Round-up' at Ballyvourney (centred in the Claedagh mountains to the west) Monty tried again for the big one with a major sweep around Millstreet and Kilcorney. Though dangerous for a while, it proved to be merely a gesture. A truce was in the offing . . .

Back to the 'Big Round-up'. For a week or so the troops had been on the move to and from the various military posts throughout south Munster. Everywhere there were new arrivals and early departures. Military vehicles were on the roads in unwonted numbers. Secrecy, for the first time, was not deemed necessary. There was an army waiting in the Kerry mountains. Horse soldiers made their appearance here and there and even mule trains were occasionally in evidence. Something big was afoot, and among the freedom fighters worried dispatches began to pass to and fro; but as yet nobody could venture an opinion as to what it was all about, except that the military were probably contemplating a large-scale manoeuvre and a mighty show of force. Tension grew in the South as the outer ring of forts began to deplete in strength and an inner ring became overnight packed to capacity. Dispatches were still somewhat vague, but a little more conclusive in their surmising as the week wore on. Midweek found the movement taking on a definite trend, or rather the trend now became more defined. It was south and west! Then the news came through that somebody had mentioned in the House of Commons (quoted in *The Morning Post*, 31 May, 1921) that there was a concentration of a thousand 'rebels' in the Kerry mountains — and the British lion was on the rampage! In fact the war of attrition had become a stalemate. The daily newspaper accounts, though carefully worded, were poignant testimony to the point and counterpoint of the struggle . . . a civilian shot here, an ambush there, a shooting of uniformed loiterers, an execution, an unfortunate non-combatant or a child caught by crossfire or by a misplaced, exploding hand-grenade in a city street, an imprisonment for 'seditious literature', a labelled spy found dead by a lonely roadside. So it went on, from day to day, and looked as if it might continue so indefinitely. Holders of predetermined points of view were becoming more insistent and clamorous. The Quakers were calling for peace. Newspaper editorials were pouring invective on the senseless carnage and demanding an end to hostilities that were disrupting the social and economic life of the country. (*Note*: Political killings are still very much a feature of life in our country, in the final decade of the millenium, and the media, who report them avidly and exhaustively and thereby promote the action, still inanely declare that certain notables of Church and State 'condemned the killings', as if the only alternative were to applaud them). The 'forces of law and order' were feeling the pressure of their side of opinion. Some drastic action had to be taken — either leave the field to the rebels or seek a showdown. The first was unthinkable, the second quite acceptable. But how? A showdown with a shadow army and a large bundle of speculations! Then, the story of the concentration of 'rebels' broke, and wishful thinking did the rest. But the shadow army had a habit of disintegrating at the point of contact and the elements coalesced immediately afterwards and elsewhere, like the reputed astral bodies of oriental fakirs. Could the globules of aeriform substance have finally solidified? Apparently, yes! So, it was Claedagh or bust! The 'Big Round-up' was under way from all points of the compass to the southern nerve-centre of Republicanism.

So, 'this way of an evening', as they say in story-telling, a strange sight startled the villagers of Ballymakeera. A colourful wave of khaki and tartan flowed down the hill into the village. It was the vanguard of the Queen's Own Cameron Highlanders, successors of the clansmen who had swept vengefully down from the misty Scottish hills, their claymores flashing, to the banner of Bonnie Prince Charlie, and then sold their birthright for a mess of British. (*Note*: The Camerons — in Scots Gaelic, 'Camshroinaich', the ' hook-nosed' — were an aboriginal clan, 'fiercer than fierceness itself', in the annals of Scotland. They were rather inordinately but lyrically promoted as fighting men the world over by the inimitable Scottish comedian and singer, Andy Stewart, who died on 11 October, 1993, in his personal song, 'The Scottish Soldier', with the puzzling alternative title, 'The Green Hills of Tyrol', but, whether there or on the brown hills of Claedagh, Hoots, mon!, they 'fought in many a fray and fought and won!'). Forward and downward they marched, big-boned, bare-kneed, kilts a-wagging, the red roughness of their faces accentuated by prominent cheekbones and noses, cruel looking and surly. They were here to take decisive action, and looked it, to achieve big things by the way. But not just yet, because evening time was camping time, a business of field-kitchens, latrines, bell-tents, bivouacs, yelling and hullabaloo, and the crack of dawn was 'zero hour'. By Monday evening the operation would be over and the tale would have been told. Apparently the tale was

not worth the telling. By Tuesday it still remained to be told.
Wednesday's lame, half-apologetic newspaper survey of the
operation was eloquent of failure and left for posterity and
country firesides other tellings that exulted in daring
achievements, cunning evasions, resignation to fate, and the
ineffectualness of brute force against a resurgent spirit . . .

Our intelligence staff at Macroom Post Office succeeded in
deciphering a code message from the enemy pertaining to
a large round-up in the Macroom-Ballyvourney area. Con-
firmation was soon received from Cadet O'Carroll at the
Castle and almost at once, on June 2nd, the first enemy reinforcements moved into Macroom.

> (Charlie Browne: *The Story Of The 7th*).

In a special order of the day General Strickland defined their
mission as that of 'seeking out the I.R.A. Columns, bringing them to action and annihilating them.

> (F. O'Donoghue: *No Other Law*).

All the following afternoon, and until late in the evening,
I lay stretched in the heather on top of one of the foothills
of Rahoona. It commanded an excellent view of the winding Ballyvourney road at Poulnabro and stretches here and
there as far east as Coolavokig. Equipped with a powerful
pair of field glasses, little could pass unknown to me. One
did not need glasses to see the enemy, however. About two
o'clock the procession started. The massed columns of infantry formed its principal feature. It was an imposing
display, calculated to overawe as well as to destroy. The infantry was made up of most of the regular troops from Cork
and Ballincollig barracks. Their motor transport, with tents,
field kitchens and other impedimenta, added to the display.
Besides these regulars and their gear, the Auxiliaries with
their Crossleys gave me the impression that, apart from the
cat, very few had been left to mind the house.

> (M. O'Sullivan: *Where Mountainy Men Have Sown*).

*   *   *

The following is an excerpt from the *Cork Constitution* newspaper for Wednesday, June 8, 1921:

EXTENSIVE ROUND-UP.
Military Makes Many Captures.
Three Civilians Shot.

Information has been received from an authoritative source that the military carried out very extensive movements in the mountain districts near 'The Paps'. A very large area was most thoroughly searched and there was gleaned a good deal of interesting information while the movement was in progress. The particular area covered had never before been visited by the military, and so their arrival and searches came as a surprise. It appears that the movements took a concentric form from Kilgarvan and Millstreet, and thus widely extended, with numerous ramifications, it was naturally to be expected that there would be exciting incidents and untoward happenings. And this proved to be the case. For instance, at Carrigaphooka bridge the military made an examination of the structure, and this occupied some time. The bridge, it may be remembered, was blown up some days ago by civilians, and presented a wrecked appearance. While the examination was being made there was a movement by a flanking party of the military, and this party came upon a young man who was at some distance and who was watching the troops. He was at once called upon several times to halt and come forward, but instead he set off at top speed. He was again called upon to halt but paid no attention. Whereupon the order was given to fire, and the young man, whose name was ascertained to be 'Riordan', and who, it seems, was 'on the run', was shot dead.

Old Man Wounded.

When the military were entering Ballymakeera, a body of young men was seen, and these at once made for the adjacent hills. These men were ordered to come to a halt, but they continued to run in the hope of quickly reaching the shelter of the hills and escaping detention. They were at a long distance when fire was opened on them. Whether any of them were wounded has not been ascertained, but the firing had an unfortunate and regrettable result. By some mischance an old man was hit by a ricochet bullet in one of the thighs and fell to the ground. The soldiers advanced and took him up and he immediately received the attention and care of a military medical officer. The old man was taken in a military car to Macroom, and it is stated that he is progressing favourably.

Numerous Arrests.

It is stated that the manoeuvres began at an early hour last Monday morning, and concluded the same day. In the course of the movements all young men, or practically all of military age, were taken into custody for identification, and when this had been completed, the majority of them were released.

Two Men Shot Dead.

When the military were carrying out a wide movement in the wild country between Millstreet and The Paps, they came upon two young men who were ordered to halt. This the men declined to do, and as a result of shots which were fired at them, they were shot dead. They are believed to have been members of the I.R.A.

Important Arrests.

It is also stated that several important arrests were made. In one instance five men were caught in a house and all of them admitted they belonged to a flying column. Men who tried to get away on bicycles, when they saw the military, were captured, and it is stated they are members of the I.R.A. Other arrests were made of I.R.A. officers and a certain amount of material fell into the hands of the military.

Cars Recovered.

Some military cars which had been seized by civilians were found, but the cars were in a damaged condition. Several bicycles were also found. There were no casualties to the military, who left the district on Monday night. An authoritative source states the military authority was very pleased at the way the troops carried out their marches in the very mountainous country in which they moved.

*   *   *

It was an authoritative account, sure enough, in the sense that it was the official one supplied by the competent authority for publication, carefully monitored in every line and turn of phrase, as befitted a journal of the time when most journals were under the thumb of the forces of occupation, and those that were not had had their equipment smashed. The reading public, no doubt, reserved its judgement and subscribed mentally to the old Irish proverb: *Ná tabhair breith ar an gcéad scéal go mbeirfidh an dara scéal ort!* — Do not pass judgement on the first story until the second story catches up with you! But, as far as the newspapers were concerned, the second telling was not forthcoming, nor, in the circumstances, even acceptable. Roughly it was this. Ten thousand troops (*Note*: Some said fifteen, others as many as thirty, although there were only nine thousand in Strickland's Sixth Southern Division), with mechanical and horse transport, with armour and air support, hemmed in a large section of countryside in a ring of steel, methodically sieved it foot by foot into the yawning chasm of a remote mountain valley, hoping to find an imaginary army of 'one thousand irregulars' (as stated), and a pitched battle to end a prolonged embarrassment. Relatively speaking they found nothing, or the soldier's 'sweet damn all'. More than that, it was not because there was nothing there after all, because part of a Divisional (First Southern) H.Q. Staff, a complete Flying Column (Third Brigade), and many active-service men besides, that came accidentally within their sphere of influence, almost literally slipped through their fingers and got away without leaving a whiff of suspicion behind them.

How was it done? How it was done is a narrative that would have delighted the noble heart, and likely stimulated the honey-gold pen of that true Scot, Robert Louis Stevenson, ever responsive to herculean effort, all 'good causes', and tales of human endurance in the face of adversity. Back to Saturday, June 4, 1921, and a little group of three or four men who sat on a knoll or turf-bank overlooking the main

Killarney road at the 'County Bounds'. A fine day it was indeed, extraordinarily fine, and so the days had been for some time past. It was getting late in the afternoon and they were discussing some recent ambushes and raids and, in particular, the impending round-up and its probable location. The Column had been temporarily disbanded the day before and the men were scattered far and wide. The fine weather, in so far as it concerned them, was more a source of worry as they leisurely discussed ways and means of evading the trap, if, and when, the need arose because obviously this kind of weather favoured the rapid movement of troops. But the preoccupation and the heat did not take from their watchfulness and the cyclist had barely swung into view, over a mile distant, when he became the object of careful scrutiny. Watchful eyes followed him as he toiled up the long, winding incline from the Kerry side. Cyclists were rare in those days and when they appeared it meant something more than healthful exercise. A cyclist was either a British soldier or an I.R.A. dispatch rider. He proved to be the latter. A cycle patrol of soldiers, he explained, had lately been making a habit of wheeling to Loo Bridge from a camp at Gortacuish. The Kerry men had a mind to knock spots off them. Would the Cork men help? The very extended order of the patrol, he explained, made a large number of men essential. This rare abdication of Kerry self-reliance and local pride passed unnoticed at the prospect of another fight. Vice-Commandant Paddy (Donagh Owen) O'Sullivan set out enthusiastically on the formidable task of trying to locate his superior officer, Commandant Patrick O'Sullivan. He had a notion that he might find Patrick, and Mick Murphy (from Cork City), the new Column Commander, at Kilnamartyra Cross. He did not care to walk, so he took a bicycle. He had no liking for a too direct route, so he went home to Danganasillagh for a change of clothes and a cup of tea, and then settled into a circuit that for straggliness and place-names encountered *en route* might have rivalled any missionry journey of St. Paul: Clondrohid, Gortnalicka Cross, Gortnapeiste, Lisacraesig, Half-way House, Kilnamartyra (where he discovered that they had left earlier), Renaniree, Gortnabinna, Bawnaneel. They had gone further west, he was informed. He went westward and finally located them at Neilus O'Leary's, Derrynaboorka, Ballingeary. They were in bed, which was natural as it was now 2 a.m. But they rose immediately and all three set out to traverse the mountains and valleys that lay between them and their objective near Glenflesk. Such names! Lovely names! Coomdorrihy to Lyrenageeha to the foot of Lackabawn. The top of Lackabawn was somewhere in the clouds but for the leaving it behind you enjoyed so much the more (Paddy Donagh Owen said) the sight of Knockanemoria in the dawning. An old man, with a white horse and sidecar, obliged by carrying them six miles in the early light to the foot of Tureen mountain. So they stepped over Tureen mountain (1221 ft.) and another step or so landed them on top of Freaghanagh (1183 ft.) where they rested awhile among the mountain gods. Far beneath them, in O'Connell's, it was breakfast time and they were made welcome; then on to Loo Bridge where a scout informed them that Jerry Kennedy, Vice-Commandant of the Fifth Battalion, Kerry No. 2 Brigade, and his men were waiting at Dan Lynch's, Clonkeen. So they continued walking until they reached there. Then, after a lengthy discussion on the intended ambush, the number of men required, the roads to be sealed off, the outposts, scouts and signallers, they travelled down the road to view the position. There was little danger of being surprised as men had already been posted at all vantage points in the vicinity. Arrived at the position they found that the fight had been visualized on a large scale and, although there were some obvious drawbacks, the place was probably the most suitable one on the line. They decided to take up positions on Tuesday morning, although they had been informed in the meantime that more military had poured into Killarney, and they seemed on the verge of a large-scale round-up. Undaunted the three visitors set off eastwards to mobilize the Flying Column, giving themselves over to the luxury of 'a tub-trap drawn by a magnificent chestnut cob with a flowing mane and tail', said Paddy, still fondly remembering thirty-odd years later; but every mile of the road brought more certainty that the British military were already closing in on every side, and the prospect of an ambush quickly faded away. Information was coming through at an alarming rate. A large detachment had arrived in Kilgarvan, only six miles to the south-west. Rathmore was occupied in the north. Killarney at their backs, as they were well aware, was full of troops. But no word yet from Ballyvourney, ahead of them, in the east beyond the County Bounds. Despondently they sent back their driver and walked on upwards to the top of the ridge once more, from where Paddy's journey had begun on the previous day. They were met by two local Volunteers. To their urgent question they were told that the village of Ballymakeera was in the hands of a large contingent of military, Black and Tans and Auxiliaries, who had taken over the community hall, the schoolrooms and several buildings, and were also camping in the surrounding fields. Coolea had been cut off by a detachment of Highlanders who had penetrated as far as the cross of Muirnebeg and established themselves there. Finally it was reported that the last remaining gap had been closed by the occupation of Ballingeary by troops from either Bantry or Bandon. So the trap had already been set and, from the information to hand, it was obvious to them that a major operation was due to begin at dawn the next morning, Monday. They had to try somehow to get all the wanted men out of the area as soon as possible. They quickly worked out a plan and a course of action and asked the two Volunteers to act as dispatch carriers and guides, which they willingly agreed to do. Their orders were to visit all houses where men of the Column were billeted, muster them and guide them along the rugged

Cork-Kerry border until they had crossed the Lackabawn road, and so on to the mountains over Gougane Barra where they were likely to be just outside the perimeter of the trap. They carried out their orders so successfully (*Note*: I regret that Paddy was unable to remember the names and location of the two gallant Volunteer guides) that they had all arrived at a spot five or six hundred yards to the west of Lackabawn by daybreak, and only just in time (as will be seen later) because already the British soldiers from Ballingeary had reached the crest of the hill and had fanned out in all directions.

Back on the Killarney road the three men debated their next move and finally decided that their only hope was to the west. It was getting late. Patrick and Mick were of a mind to return to O'Connell's, in the lee of Freaghanagh, but Paddy Donagh Owen argued — and wasn't he the great man to argue, God be good to him! — that all those mountains, from a line between Kilgarvan and Rathmore eastwards, were sure to be thoroughly combed. Subsequent events proved him right. He had in mind a little farmhouse he had noticed that morning as they rested on Freaghanagh, and some premonition must have etched an image on his subconscious mind. It nestled in an alcove away over against them, high up on the flank of Crohane. They searched around for transport and found three bicycles, more or less, which was the best they could do at short notice. Two of the machines had no air in the wheels and there was no hope of getting it in as the tubes were in shreds. The third was minus a driving chain, but that was of no concern as the journey was mostly downhill. There were no brakes worth mentioning, a drawback which was counterbalanced by the flatness of the wheels. Taking it all in all, the picture might have been a canvas depicting motion in the right direction, naturally downwards, by a rather frustrated artist. They got under way and eventually arrived towards morning at a house by Crohane wood, where they hoped to be directed to the house on the hill. Paddy was to do the talking as his accent was more akin to that of the locality, and at the time all strangers were looked on with suspicion by the settled population. He called to the people of the house and asked them for information, but in vain. They refused to answer. He shouted out who they were, what their business was in the district, names of cousins he had in the next townland, but still the inmates remained obdurate behind their shuttered windows. Good humoured Paddy remarked matter-of-factly, to Mick and Pat, that he wished there were more daylight because the last time he was in a similar predicament, in Renaniree, the woman of the house had eventually opened the door because, as she said, he 'was the ugliest man she had ever seen'. (*Note*: He frequently told the joke on himself, and laughed heartily, but he was in fact the nearest thing to a Red Indian I had ever seen!). He could just hear the voices inside and guessed that they were husband, wife and daughter. His two companions were getting uneasy and wanted to cross over to the far side of the road and so on to Freaghanagh, but he was adamant and would not give up. Once more he pleaded and when he mentioned the names of some of the local I.R.A. they seemed to become convinced that the three were what they represented themselves to be and told them how to get on the laneway to their objective. Their spirits rose and they lit their last cigarette. They did not have to return to the road but walked on westwards through the backyard and out onto the passage which led up to their destination. They trudged up the narrow, steep laneway little suspecting that the family they had just left behind were being ordered out of bed at gunpoint and the house was being thoroughly rummaged. The soldiers demanded to know who had been signalling. Apparently they had seen the flare of the match and the glowing cigarette end and rushed into the yard while the real culprits moved up the laneway blissfully oblivious of the hectic events taking place a hundred yards away. They had travelled about a quarter of a mile upwards when they arrived at the house, 'an ordinary, two-storey house facing north-east', Paddy remembered. They were glad to see it as they were completely worn out. They called and were readily admitted and, having explained their plight, the good man of the house — whose name was O'Leary — promised to watch out for lorries on the road below and any appearance of soldiers. They were shown to a bedroom and rolled into bed as the first faint streak of daylight was flickering tentatively into the room. They could have been asleep no more than half-an-hour when they were suddenly awakened by a rush of footsteps on the stairway and the urgent, half-suppressed shout of 'Soldiers!'. Their senses were so finely tuned that, at the first sound, they were out of bed and by the time O'Leary reached the bedroom door they were partly dressed and, with revolvers, boots and the remainder of their clothes in hand, they rushed out of the house and around by the gable-end to the back. They made their way upwards along a narrow gulch and on reaching a ledge of rock paused to look back. There at the bottom of the yard, less than forty feet from the front door, stood two soldiers with rifles at the ready. Their backs were partly towards them and they seemed to be looking down onto the road. Why the soldiers failed to see or hear them remains a mystery. They were certainly an advance party and their orders evidently were to keep the house under surveillance and to await the remainder of the platoon before beginning a search. Anxiety for reinforcements probably caused them to look back at the crucial moment. The three fugitives lost no time in wriggling further upwards along the drain, put on their boots and got fully dressed. By this time it was bright day. (*Note:* In high Summer in the South of Ireland there are only two hours of complete darkness). They turned to scrutinize the road that now lay far beneath them, and the mountains beyond. The road appeared to be choked up with military vehicles of every kind. The soldiers had dismounted and had begun to advance up the slopes in extended order. A section on the near side was approaching the narrow little Crohane wood. They halted and trained Lewis machine-guns on the clumps of trees, pouring pan after pan of bullets among them by way of softening up some imaginary resistance or flushing out some lurking foe. (*Note*: Unknown to the three fugitives Vice-Commandant Jerry Kennedy and a companion had taken refuge among the trees. I had the satisfaction of enlightening Paddy Donagh Owen on this point before his death . . . Author). The position was then carried at bayonet point but the storm-troops did not venture far beyond the edge of the wood. Now the sweep was opening up in real earnest. From Morley's Bridge in the south to the Paps mountains in the north stretched a continuous chain of khaki, with about a dozen feet between every two men. The watchers, eagerly taking in every facet of the scene, could distinctly see and hear the officers as they snapped out words of command. They moved to a higher position to get a better view and from a natural grandstand found that they could follow the whole operation for several miles in either direction, and so long as movement was away from them they began to regard the whole thing as a first-class show put on by the British Army specially for their entertainment. They were enjoying the feeling though, once in a while, they wondered uneasily about the fate of the Brigade and Divisional Staffs, whether all or any of them had succeeded in eluding the encircling forces. Had they known it, those others were at that very moment moving into Coomhola, that rugged glen to the west of Gougane Barra, and out of present danger. An aeroplane flew along the Loo Valley and swung around the mountains. It was followed by a second, and a third. They were spotters for the ground forces. Once again the Great War aces were going through their paces, but in a different and less honourable cause. Now they had the freedom of the skies, and their eyes were on the ground. Gone was the old fear that, at any moment, the 'Red Baron', Ferdinand von Richthofen's shining red biplane might come swooping out from behind a cloud bank as in the days of the 'Dawn Patrol'. The planes dived lower and ever lower, seeming barely to skim the mountain sides with their long, banking swoops at the end of a run, causing the tall, bleached 'finnawn' (wild mountain grass) to wave and flatten with the fury of their passing. The pilots shouted directions to the troops on the ground, when they could safely close the throttles sufficiently to make themselves heard, and sometimes got an answering yell in return. They dropped slips of paper, and an occasional long streamer, with written information for the officers. The three men hidden in the heather had to lie low several times as the planes swept over them. They could plainly see the pilots and felt that they could easily have carried on a conversation with them, if they had a mind to do so. But they were not on speaking terms just then, thought Paddy and Pat and Mick, as they lay back in the heather . . .

'Well, here's thank God for the race and the sod!',
Said Kelly and Burke and Shea.

18

The Big Round-Up
Part Two: Behind
the Lines

To Divisional-Adjutant Florence O'Donoghue the room seemed curiously empty without the noisy clatter of his typewriter. He was in the sitting room off the kitchen, in the home of Owen Cal McCarthy of Gortyrahilly. The 'parlour' they called it. Idly he glanced through the window towards the hill beyond. It was past dusk and gradually getting on for darkness, but in the silvery afterglow he could just make out the shape of the house, a mile away on the opposite slope, where Captain Jamie Moynihan was still standing by to receive any last-minute dispatches and pass them on to him at Divisional Headquarters. He thought and waited a moment or two longer, unperturbed by the fact that already beyond that hill British soldiers were 'as thick as Autumn leaves in Vallombrosa'. He had completed the final report for his absent chief. General Liam Lynch had gone away a few days before, the thirty-first of May, to be exact, on a tour of inspection to some of the outlying reaches of his Divisional area in Co. Waterford. With him had gone Joe O'Connor, Divisional Quarter-Master, and brother of Fr. Dominic, O.F.M. Cap., head chaplain to the First Cork Brigade. Staff-Captain Maurice (Mossy) Walshe, of Mitchelstown, aide-de-camp to General Lynch, still remained with the adjutant. (*Note:* The First Southern Division was in-augurated on 26 April 1921. It happened at the home of Dan Lynch, Kippagh, five miles to the west of Millstreet, high up on the western flank of Claragh Mountain. G.H.Q. in Dublin was represented by Ernie O'Malley, who presented the relevant document to the representatives of the southern brigades. The southern leaders were rather incensed that neither Michael Collins nor Richard Mulcahy bothered to appear on such an auspicious occasion. Liam Lynch was ap-pointed Divisional Commandant and Florrie O'Donoghue his Adjutant. In June Joe O'Connor, of Cork No. 1 Brigade became Divisional Quarter-Master and in July Liam Deasy, of Cork No. 3 Brigade, was appointed Vice O/C with Tom Barry as Training Officer. On the far side of Claragh stood Mount Leader, the southern headquarters of the Auxiliaries. Dan Lynch and his wife, Julia Sullivan, unfortunately left no family and the historic house has now passed into other hands, having sheltered and succoured so many important leaders of the Irish Resistance at the worst of times). So, General Lynch went to Waterford on inspection just before the Big Round-up, leaving his highly competent adjutant to mind the office. It was truly fortunate, thought Florrie, that Liam was away at this time. That fine man and fine soldier, *sans peur et sans reproche*, he would have wanted to be the last to leave, an extra worry at a critical time. 'Fearless and irreproachable' — that was Liam. In his book, *No Other Law*, Florrie quotes Owen McCarthy's Gaelic-speaking old mother, whom Liam greatly impressed. In translation it goes: 'I don't know what name was on him, nor anything about him or his business, but I know this much, whoever he was, or whoever his people were, he was a gentleman!'. So, Flor-rie was alone on this Sunday night in June, 1921. The others of his staff had left long ago. They had no business in stay-ing on. Jamie Moynihan had been back and forth all even-ing, reporting and checking, impatient to move and terminate his big responsibility. Earlier there had been the sound of rifle fire from two directions, first from Ballymakeera village, and a little later from Coolea. That sounded bad. Jamie was due any minute now and they would be packing up. He turned his attention to the page of neat, closely typed lines, scanning it briefly for errors. It was difficult to see now in the near darkness, but it seemed all right and he deposited it, with the rest of his correspondence, in a strong wooden box. He could hear Jamie trudge into the kitchen above and stamp about uneasily. He looked at his watch. Ten-thirty. It was time to go. He returned the typewriter carriage, locked it in place, boxed his machine and was ready to move when Jamie's urgent, 'Florrie! Ah, come on!', permeated through the closed door. They buried the typewriter in a little sand-pit to the west of the house, but the precious box of documents and sundry papers the adjutant brought along with him, to Jamie's chagrin and disapproval (so expressed thirty-five years later), to share in whatever fate or chance awaited them. (*Note:* Major Florence O'Donoghue showed unusual foresight. His vast accumulation of notes, known popularly as 'Florrie O'Donoghue's Papers', now reposes in the National Museum in Dublin. They had been deposited there at his death, with the instruction, 'Not to be released until 1990'. Even then a certain amount was still retained under embargo, 'for security reasons', I was informed in 1990, while researching *The Dark Secret of Béalnabláth*. The present volume was entered provisionally as an item, many years ago, while still very much in embryo. He was nothing if not thorough. Quite a good deal of his material appeared in an extensive series in the now defunct, *Cork Weekly Examiner*, in the Fifties, to eventually appear as his magnificent book, *No Other Law*, on the life and times of Liam Lynch. cf. Appendix One. As a final comment, the house in Gortyrahilly has now also passed into other hands. Only last year I was accosted by the mother of the present *bean a' tí* i.e. 'the woman of the house', with the words: 'You said the I.R.A. were in my daughter's house in Gortyrahilly!'. It was with reference to a previous publication and showed a curious misconception of the times that are and were). Carefully Jamie and Florrie planned their course as they moved along, aided by the latest information received as to the disposition of the enemy and the local man's expert knowledge of the extremely rough terrain.

> British forces had to bivouac during the short hours of darkness and, as they moved in a gradually constricting circle, it was not difficult for men who knew the country to slip through their lines. Good intelligence and prompt reports made it possible to keep all units informed of the progress of the raiding forces . . . to plan unhurriedly and deliberately their evasive or counter action . . . it was probably well within the capacity of either the Cork No. 1 or Cork No. 3 Brigade Columns to punch a hole in the ring . . .
>
> (From *No Other Law*. Florrie O'Donoghue, that superb historian of the period, was given to some categorical and sweeping statements).

Some of the reports referred to had been bewildering, some quite contradictory. Certain it was that a strong body of Highlanders had established themselves at Muirnebeg Cross, the other extremity of the horseshoe formed by the wide curve of the little road running beneath them. Those fellows would have to be given a wide berth. It wasn't for nothing that they were known and feared in the Great War as 'The Ladies from Hell', with their trim, colourful drindle-skirts they called 'kilts' ; and when they died in battle the chaplains had to move about the scene readjusting those kilts with their walking-sticks, like Lot's daughters, to hide the nakedness. At Coolea village machine-gunner Eugie O'Sullivan met the two travellers and went along for company. The war veteran was not unduly worried about the nearness of soldiers. He had fought with them in the trenches and knew their ways. It was common sense, he said. If you knew what a man was going to do, get before him. If not, remain behind. They faced the danger. All roads were closed, the dispatches had said, but the ring had not yet been welded in one piece. That would happen very soon — just before day. The problem was to find a convenient gap to slip through. They decided on Béal a' Mháma, the little mountain pass some distance to the north, under the wing of Mullaghanish. John C. Creedon had been on outpost duty there all day and evening. He might be there still, if he had not been dislodged. He would know a way through. He was, in fact, and did . . .

Like Cuchulainn, foremost champion of the men of Ulster, in the long ago, waiting impassively on the frontier with his face towards the advancing armies of Queen Maeve of Connaught on the cattle-raid of Cooley (*Táin Bó Cuailgne*), John C. Creedon maintained his stand at the pass facing towards the East and the long, straggly stretch of dusty by-road that wandered away from his feet through Glen Dav, the 'Valley of the Ox', towards Carriganimma village visible in the distance, towards Macroom invisible in outer space, and towards whatever lay beyond ready to materialize but still in the unproportioned realms of the imagination. Being somewhat of a realist (he was the first 'revisionist' historian I ever knew and the only countryman who had read and could debate, in his plaintive fashion, Darwin's *Origin of Species*), of an inquiring turn of mind and having a specific job to do, he decided, as the evening wore on, that a spot of investigation might be to the advantage of all concerned. It would be useful to know how far the expected enemy forces had advanced towards his 'frontier post' and, consequently, what chances any of the Column men or the Divisional Staff had of getting through to the vicinity of Carriganimma and points north and east that would be outside the perimeter of the military sweep. He began to walk eastwards. Some distance along he met a cyclist toiling up the incline but looking strangely untroubled by the heat of that sweltering afternoon. Tall, aquiline featured, dressed in the garb of a clergyman, following a route that was expected at any moment to carry a highly unclerical wave of military personnel, he might easily be an Intelligence Officer doing a preliminary survey. John C. engaged him in conversation, carefully maintaining a disinterested front, scrupulously avoiding any reference to current affairs, flogging trivialities of circumstance to death in the perambulating and tortuous quest for information so dear to the countryman and so characteristic of the West. Eventually he elicited the information that the traveller was Fr. Tim Kelleher, C.C., from Carriganimma, pursuing the legitimate business of paying a social call. No! He had not seen any soldiers on the road and, as far as he knew, there were none between Carriganimma and Macroom up to a short while ago. So they parted. Others he met as he travelled on seemed to be of the same opinion, and he returned to his post by nightfall satisfied that the danger from that point would not materialize. There still remained the 'Mountain Road' that wheeled around the foothills of Mullaghanish to join the Macroom-Millstreet road at Keimcarraige. The Millstreet garrison had been reinforced. Horse-soldiers were there too. They were almost certain to take this route to complete the encirclement. Had he known it, they had already arrived under cover of the hill, had established themselves, set up camp and tethered their horses in the 'inch' beside Droichidín na hÍnse ('the little bridge of the inch'), three miles away, completely oblivious to the lone watcher of the Pass at Béal a' Mháma. About midnight John C. made his way back down to his home, in Coomaguire, to make tea. He had scarcely arrived when the barking of the dog announced visitors and Jamie and Eugie came in to deliver their two charges into his hands. The Adjutant he knew by sight. The other was a stranger to him. He hung the big, black kettle on the 'crane', but they would not wait even for a cup. He reported that the route was probably still open but was not quite sure how far. The two local men went back and, on the Staff officers' accepting responsibility for the gamble, he led them through the

Pass. Arriving at the crossroads where the branch line led down into the valley of Gleann Daimh they paused a while. Safety probably lay that way but Florrie Donoghue, mindful of his records and documents, noted the more extensive cover that skirted the 'Mountain Road' (*Note:* The present extensive forestry in Gleann Daimh was non-existent then), and sent John C. forward almost two miles to the 'little bridge' to investigate. From there he could hear the unmistakable sounds of horses, and, although he knew the farmer on the spot generally kept two or three, the volume of sound, with the jingle of the trappings, could mean only one thing, that there were many more beneath him in the darkness and the way was closed. (*Note:* The little bridge, Droichidín na hÍnse, is still there with beside it the sloping fieldeen where the British cavalry tethered their long vanished horses). So they made their way down into Gleann Daimh and the two officers remained ensconced in Twohig's farmhouse until the danger had passed at daybreak. Much to his dismay, John C. was ordered back to watch out for more fugitives. (*Note:* Thirty-five years later he still bitterly resented Florrie's authoritarianism. The brilliant little adjutant of the First Southern Division already anticipated life after the Tans. He wrote — 'The general security practice of destroying documents has incidentally resulted in the almost complete disappearance of any written records of the Division'. Don't you believe it!). There were voices at the Pass before him, voices that he could not distinguish. The chance of friend or foe he considered not worth taking and crawled through a gully under the road to make sure. The accents now behind and above him were distinctly foreign. The trap had sprung on him. He was on the run. (*Note:* Every time I pass the spot, it gives me a peculiar thrill to re-examine the gully through which my old friend, John C. Creedon, crawled from Irish soil into British . . . Author).

In fact practically everybody was on the run, that midSummer night in 1921, every man and boy, that is. 'There were people out', said Eugie cynically, 'that were never out before or since!'. There were men out whose age alone should have entitled and obliged them to take to their beds in the usual way, and any military authority with any sense of proportion and defined objective would undoubtedly have left them so. Still they ran. Whither, nobody could tell. The general impression was that of a stampede, but the movement lacked direction and cohesion that are always associated with such a phenomenon. East ran west and west ran east, north ran south and south ran north, mostly blindly and unthinkingly. But thinkers ran thoughtfully — and philosophers walked. And the ogre of fear jigged along in step with one and all, an irresistible fear and a fear of the irresistible. It stalked, beckoned, goaded. It tripped and raised up again. It screamed for a place of safety, this fear of some relentless terror that followed, followed, searched out and kept coming. Fear of what, therefore? Of individuals, armed individuals? They had proved themselves insignificant on occasion, destructible even in a body. Fear of a power, maybe, a remote and primitive physical force whose will was unshakable, whose resources were unlimited, whose animosity was undying. The 'thin red line' turned khaki arose once again out of the ground to do its bidding. The infallible system never failed to get in motion, to subjugate, to kill. Seán Jerh Kelleher fell victim near Ballymakeera village — an old man driving his cow on Sunday evening. The 'authoritative source' had lied in its teeth, the newspaper likewise. No ricochet bullet, that! No immediate medical attention. No considerate trip to Macroom. No favourable progress. On the contrary, he died at home a couple of days later, and was content. His son, Jerh Kelleher ('Jerh Seán Jerh'), went to Macroom in a frenzy and hammered on the Castle gates which they had closed against him as if in fear of his anger, and no guns obtruded a nebulous warning in the face of this cosmic wrath. Riordan, too, of Carrigaphooka — the mentally deficient, the *amadán bocht* ('poor fool'), *duine le Dia*, the 'one with God', as they say, watching gape-mouthed the operation at the bridge, running like a frightened faun with schizophrenic ineptitude, cut down he knew not how. So they all ran from the fear of death and became liable to death for the running, though the eternal hills would once again do their hospitable best. They ran during the short hours of darkness and their running was greatly accelerated by the promiscuous firing of rifles at different encampments at their back, and the sudden, startling glare of the rockets from the 'Verey' pistols, harmless enough pastimes in themselves, that were meant presumably to keep the soldiers awake, or to terrify the inhabitants, or both . . .

> Trumpeter, what are you sounding now?
> I'm rousing them up, I'm rousing them up;
> The tents are astir in the valley.

The old mountain gods, also bestirring themselves as the Homeric 'rosy-fingered dawn' (Well, *rhododaktulos heōs*, if you insist!) came creeping silently over hill and vale and craggy buttress, must have blinked in amazement at the sight. The guns were temporarily silenced. The 'Verey' lights had burned themselves out. The childish game was finished but the serious game had begun, the age-old, sinister game of hunter and hunted, pursuer and pursued, that transposes the actions and reactions of men and animals on to a common plane. Thus, the dilated eyes and flaring nostrils of the antelope find their counterpart and nemesis in the deadly eyes and bared fangs of the leopard in hot pursuit. The satiated leopard awakes with dilated eyes and constricted nostrils to find himself gathered up in the trunk of a furious bull elephant. It is not a kind of life chain-reaction nor some sublime biological process, but the vulgar and elementary notion of the transposition of brute force, worthy and noble in animal life, perhaps, but unworthy of rational man, and just as inevitable in one as in the other, when resorted to.

So, ten thousand pairs of sinister and deadly eyes, human eyes, might follow closely the frantic scampering of other little humans over mountain country in Cork and Kerry and be quite unmoved by the grandeur and proximity of the scene, while a benign Providence looks down commiseratingly and visualizes the dilated eyes and sweat-flecked nostrils of two hundred and thirty-three thousand 'Sons of the Old Contemptibles', fleeing for dear life, who are quite moved by the grandeur and proximity of the sea at a Dunkirk of a later epoch. And so it goes!

19

Ͳhe Ꮞig Round Up
Part Ͳhree: Percival

Major Percival is dead! Lieutenant-General A. E. Percival, D.S.O., O.B.E., of Singapore, World War Two, notoriety, died, it is true, but for the purpose of any belated contribution, such as this, to the cause of political and civic freedom in my country, it is abundantly sufficient to credit 'the Major' with having accomplished the aforesaid. So, we may take it, on the word of the *Cork Examiner,* that Major Percival really, truly and finally 'shuffled off this mortal coil' on the thirty-first of January, 1966. Moreover, his epitaph has been solemnly spoken by a veteran of the War of Independence who was not precisely in a favourable position to write on the Major's slate, 'I love you, Joe!', when they 'were a coupla kids'. Patsy said: 'Late an' all as it is, he's great shtowing anyway!'. Apparently Percival was not a great favourite. He earned his O.B.E. for his work in Ireland, for which Montgomery got nothing.

> Nearly two hours had elapsed between the time of our cap-
> ture and Percival's arrival . . . I looked curiously at Percival
> as he approached. Dressed in tunic and shorts, he gripped
> a Colt revolver in his right hand. The cruelty of his set face
> was accentuated by the two buck-teeth, which showed like
> small fangs at either side of his bitter mouth. His hard eyes,

darting suspiciously from side to side, rested on me momentarily as he came up . . . halted a few paces in front of me, folded his arms and stared into my eyes as if he would read my mind . . . walked back and again stared at me before speaking the only words he uttered in my presence, 'Release him!'.

(Tom Barry: *Guerilla Days In Ireland*).

(*Note:* On the publication of Tom Barry's book, in 1949, Percival threatened a libel action against the publishers. Barry's reply was that if he came to Ireland to pursue his libel action he, Tom Barry, would see to it that he did not leave the country alive. Percival meekly responded — 'I'll keep away from Barry!'. Some years before his death he made a friendly overture. He asked to meet Barry who retorted that he would meet him only 'at the point of a gun' . . . Quoted from Mike Griffin in *The Irish Historical Review*. By strange coincidence the present writer lives on the ancient estate of the historic Percival family. Their great mansion, at Burton Park, stands a few hundred yards from my back door. As Earls of Egmont they owned a vast territory stretching from Buttevant to Kanturk, and, according to Jim McCarthy, a local historian, 'they held sway for almost three hundred years until their reign was terminated by the sale of their lands under the Ashbourne Act around 1895'. Though the family had 'come over' with William the Conqueror, they still retained their roots in the Low Countries, in the region of Egmont, where the Flemish nobleman, the Prince of Egmont, was beheaded by the Duke of Alva in 1567 for withstanding King Philip of Spain. The Percivals had their revenge when one of them managed to decode a secret document which was later responsible for the destruction of the Armada. Goethe's historical drama, *Egmont*, records in epic fashion the execution of the Prince of Egmont, while his friend and admirer, Beethoven, composed in 1810 the incidental music for its performance, known as the *Egmont Overture* in which a dramatic 'plonk' indicates the fall to the ground of the noble head. In my personal music room, where eager fingers ply their way to examination hopes, the tragic head is a frequent victim. In my writing room the Percival head is right now on a very shaky foundation!).

Major Percival was an early riser, or it may have been that he neglected to go to bed 'on the night of the Big Round-up', which was not, from any point of view, comparable with 'the night of the Big Wind' nor as disastrous in results, but judging from the tenor of country chronicles quite every bit as sensational and memorable. 'Percival's Crowd', as they were known, meaning Percival and his crowd (he had a jolly custom of riding in front on a white horse) were the much-hated, much-feared and much-despised Essex Regiment, mainly recruited from cockney East London and adjoining parts. Diminutive, volatile, out of element as any non-local human being or East Londoner could ever be, their tempers did not improve when they came to contemplate the mysteries of a bog hole or the difficulties involved in negotiating a 'turtogue' or such-like, on a work-out in the Derrynasagart Mountains, where rhyming slang and flashing sequins were at a discount. The little cockneys were easily riled and especially so on this occasion since the Major had decided to move under cover of darkness rather than wait for the appointed time at the crack of dawn. In this he showed unusual ingenuity. (*Note:* 'Strickland's order was in Liam's hands almost as soon as it reached his own brigade commanders'. . . Florrie O'Donoghue: *No Other Law*). From Kinsale and Bandon the ESSEX came, and on Sunday foot-slogged all the rough, cross-grained miles of stony by-road from Dunmanway, by Aultagh Wood, through Johnstown to Inchigeela and along by the shores of famed Lough Allua, on the River Lee, to Ballingeary. Passing by on the same way Padraic Colum, poet and dramatist of the Irish Literary Revival, was moved to song:

> On the road to Ballingeary there is many a pleasant glen,
> Where limpid waters glisten far from the haunts of men,
> And shy flowers bloom in beauty . . .

But the present wayfarers were not moved to dally longer than was necessary to occupy, in the name of his Majesty, the picturesquely situated little village before moving on up into the heights of Aharas. The Major divided his forces at Currahy Bridge. One section he sent on into Ballingeary village, the other he himself led across the sparse bog lands, through Teernaspideoige ('the land of the robin') to Aharas where he himself camped for the night within striking distance of his real objective in the region of Coolea beyond the mountain. On that scenic back road he passed by the home of Pat O'Riordan, of Derryvoleen, who, with Neilus O'Leary, of Derrinaboorka, comprise the last survivors of the Ballingeary Company. (See photograph from the Aharas 'Station' taken on 20 March, 1993). Percival pitched his tent for the night in the little sunken yard at the door of Jerry Connolly's cottage, on the left side of the Aharas by-road and within a short distance of the main Ballingeary-Renaniree road. He was poised for the kill, but he had just repeated history in a manner he could hardly be expected to understand. The great Dónal O'Sullivan Beare had tethered his horses just there on his tragic 'Retreat' from Glengarriff to Leitrim Castle, on 1 January, 1603. The name indicates as much. Aharas ('Each Ros') means the wood of the horses. In his epic Gaelic poem, 'The Retreat Of O'Sullivan Beare', Séamas Ó Céilleachair, eminent Ballyvourney poet, gives access to the episode and the tradition. A mere professional soldier would not spare a thought for the searing blood-let of Ireland's past:

> Let us move
> Step on step . . .
> Against the height,
> For the peace of night,
> On the bleak hill
> Of Aharas.
> Let's not light
> Any fire tonight;

> Our enemy's sword
> Is at the heel of us!
>
> (Translation from the Irish).

At 'three-hundred hours', on Monday, 6 June, 1921, Major Percival's plans for the invasion of Ballyvourney were laid on Jerry Connolly's kitchen table, at Aharas. Once again the forces were divided although this is a mere surmise. Neilus O'Leary said he passed their way and on to Lackabawn. Staff officers from Brigade H.Q., at Daniel McSweeney's, Gortnafunsion, Ballyvourney, said they had just made it beyond the heights of Lackabawn when his forces arrived at daybreak. It is doubtful if he himself went over the mountain. More likely some forgotten junior captain. Perhaps Colonel Hudson himself had come along. In that case the senior officer would have taken the shorter and easier route to the final assembly point at Ballyfinnane bridge, two miles to the west of Coolea while the other slogged the long way round by the 'Top of Coom'. (*Note:* I keep thinking of Percival in the role of Colonel Bogey in the context of Kenneth Alford's satirical 'Colonel Bogey On Parade', from 1914, when long retired officers in England lied about their age or even enlisted as privates with the patriotic idea of 'having a go at the Huns'. The piece may have been kindly meant at the time, though its many parodies would seem to imply otherwise, and none possibly as obscene as the one I heard as a kid in St. Colman's College, which began with, 'Where was the engine driver found when the boiler burst? They found his . . .', and so on!).

The ESSEX had not arrived unheralded in Ballingeary. Of all the various military contingents which converged on the region of mid and west Cork, on that lovely Sunday afternoon, Percival's ESSEX had the distinction (which they might or might not have appreciated) of being paged into his First Brigade area by no less a scout than the Brigadier himself. That he happened to be leaving the district on a lone walking tour of inspection of the various battalions scattered widely throughout his Brigade area (from Ballingeary to Youghal), on that particular day, was not a matter of convenience, as one might think, who did not know the man, but it was just a coincidence, and Seán Hegarty, O/C First Cork Brigade, was simply going ahead with a schedule which he had arranged some time before the word came through of an impending sweep. For Seán was like that. And it so happened that he had just surmounted the heights of Cleanrath, above Inchigeela village and the valley of the Lee, when his quick eye detected the sparkle and glitter of the Summer sun on burnished helmets and the wicked glint of bayonets, and his roving binoculars centred on the sizeable cavalcade approaching from the south. The man whose serious mien, unflinching purpose (according to Florrie O'Donoghue) and caustic wit had earned him (from some wry humorist) the nickname of 'The Joker', waited only long enough to make sure that the whole corps artlessly followed the road westwards by the lake. Then he quickly made off across country to bring his message of warning to his recently vacated H.Q. at Gortnafunsion. He found his staff already packing up in anticipation of an early departure, and the new information proved invaluable in planning their course. Then the Brigadier turned his thoughts to the job in hand and resumed his interrupted itinerary. For, again, Seán Hegarty was that way.

In the sphere of field tactics military skill might be regarded as a kind of Fourth Dimension over and above the three dimensions confining and governing the relations and juxtapositions of army, terrain and enemy. The skilful leader puts his acquired knowledge into effect to make these laws of nature turn to his advantage. His mind skips along outside and round about in a separate dimension of its own. But the real genius of the profession is the chap who can skip around the chap who skips around the regulation pawns in the game. In the sector of the circle which fell to Major

Percival to complete by daybreak, between Knockaruddig, on the Kerry side of the County Bounds, and Renaniree, just south of Ballymakeera, were several by-roads branching to all points from S.E. to S.W. A realistic military strategist would likely have sealed them off on his way in, and, without prejudice to the Major, he could quite reasonably have done so by dividing his forces at Inchigeela. But apparently he was already set on a little strategy of his own and, while showing good leadership, missed the touch of genius, overlooking the fact that until a circle is defined by a specific circumferance its potential radii may be protracted indefinitely to an infinite number of purely hypothetical rings. Consequently — if you follow — the prize birds had flown by diverse ways before the link-up was complete. The First Brigade Staff, and many others, filtered through to the south and east. Anticipating something of the kind, Major Percival had pushed on under cover of darkness and his men were already at their action-stations when they were supposed to be still in the vicinity of Ballingeary waiting for the daystar to wane. The surprise move proved almost disastrous for the Flying Column. A rare measure of luck brought them beyond the Lackabawn road unnoticed with only minutes to spare.

*   *   *

On a certain day, many years later, an old Ballyvourney man carefully reminisces on the Big Round-up. He is ailing and the curate is in attendance. Watching him, if you are of the countryside, you immediately know the type. If you are not, you may say — 'Nature's gentleman' or 'Nature's philosopher', but you would be wrong. His values are spiritual, being only partly bound to the rough soil where he had laboriously cut his groove, and is still thankful for hard work. Tall, stooped, his lined face is stamped with the stamp of eternal calm. His patience is infinite, but the peace in his grey eyes seems to be perpetually glossed with a mystic sorrow. You can see that it is an effort for him to construe his ideas because he never had more than a mild, semi-detached interest in the passing scene. He never raises his voice, but the soft, deep resonance carries easily across the room. 'Do you know', he said, 'what I made out of 'em, that you could meet worse than 'em — an' I was wit' 'em all day'. Moving his grizzled head knowingly from side to side he makes a brief concession to tradition — 'Of course they could be a lot worse if they'd like!'. (Pause for thought). Then — 'They was all colours, but moshtly the "kah-kee", an' they was a dale of 'em in the plain clothes like any wan'. I forget the old man's name, but I know where his tumbledown ruin of a house still reposes in cosmic quiet in a little fold of the hills by the Cumar Duv . . .

Well, anyway, the hunt was up. The big squeeze was in motion, and the overall mechanical efficiency of it proved a credit to the originators, although, the cogs in this particular machine being human, in fact and in effect it proved as unpredictable as any other human machine could be, and as capricious as a bomb blast.

*   *   *

EPILOGUE: It is hard to figure out why Major Percival had to conduct such an enormous route march. West Cork Military H.Q. was in Bandon but many of his troops had come from as far away as Kinsale where, as chief intelligence officer for West Cork, he usually resided at the ESSEX headquarters. The genial and courteous Colonel Hudson of Skibbereen, commanding the LIVERPOOLS, had a far easier access to Dunmanway and Inchigeela. Percival, however, had the sense to return home by Macroom and Toames where his men shot and killed a young scout named Dan Buckley. Percival himself had been wounded in a single-handed shoot-out with Captain Jack Ryan of the Ballinspittle company in the fields by Barrelle's Cross, four miles to the west of Kinsale, on 21st May. It is of interest to note that the gallant Jack Ryan emigrated to Australia due to ill health, became a prominent business man and eventually outlived Percival. Liam Deasy considered their encounter as one of the most outstanding incidents in the Trouble Times. Percival had actually taken a prominent part at Crossbarry, earlier in the year. He was nothing if not a soldier. Still, his presence at the Ballyvourney round-up is a puzzle. At Toames he once again caught up with Brigadier Seán O'Hegarty and almost captured him. Hegarty had been there for some days in conference with Commandant Dan Corkery and Adjutant Charlie Browne of Macroom, with Captain Billy Powell of Crookstown. Hegarty and Corkery escaped while the other two were captured. A couple of years later Percival had returned to the military Staff College, at Camberley, where he delivered a series of lectures on guerrilla warfare in Ireland, for which Montgomery sent him extensive notes. They differed in principle with regard to the Republican movement in Ireland. Monty regarded all Irish people as committed to Sinn Féin philosophy and Republican aspirations. Percival, in a curious restatement of Gospel, declared that one needed to distinguish 'the sheep from the wolves'. Monty had written: 'You probably won't agree with me!'. He didn't.

20

Ɔhe Biᵹ Rounᴅ-Up
Part Four: Officer
anᴅ Gentleman

'Death or Glory, I'll try and save them!'. Jerry Kennedy stood on Crohane Mountain and stared across at Barna. It put the heart across him to think that he had unwittingly sent several men to their doom — his friends, the lads who meant more to him than father or mother, brother or sister; his bedfellows, comrades-in-arms. The vexation and sorrow of it ate into his soul. Tough, hard-grained, and blunt as a bear with a grievance, his manner had always cloaked the fact that beneath was a heart of gold that beat to one steady rhythm, the rhythm of the cause he fought for — his first love — and the men who fought shoulder to shoulder with him. As he now looked and thought, the events of the past day or two kept careering painfully through his mind. It all began a week or so earlier, with Lloyd George's threat in that House of Commons in London. Apparently the so-and-so Prime Minister had begun to lose patience at the lack of initiative in the enforcing of the Defence of the Realm Act in the South of Ireland. That willowy damsel, DORA, seemed to be very much in distress. So Lloyd George raved, frisked his moustache and swore that he would not leave a mountain in East Kerry without having it fine-combed enough to bring the 'skirtawns' and turf bugs out of the bogs and heather. The *Morning Post* paper said so on the last day of May. Nobody cared to point out to the P.M. the ineptness of his metaphor, to wit, that a fine-combing can generally leave a man behind. The Kerrymen heard the story and smiled a slow, Kerry smile at the grief and chagrin of the feisty little Welshman in his Majesty's hot seat. Vice-Commandant Jerry Kennedy frisked his own moustache and mustered his men to blow a hole in the Prime Minister's encircling army wide enough to let every 'wanted' man inside the ring walk through with his hands in his pockets, whistling. And the bould Jerry never let any moss accumulate on his hobnailed boots. If he had one fault (Mike Donoghue, his local Intelligence Officer, told me. cf. *The Dark Secret Of Béalnabláth*), it was that he went into a fight or ambush at the double, while other battalion officers would be weighing up the last prudent detail. His code of action — 'Look! There they are! We'll attack 'em!'.

A miniature army of some hundreds of men moved out from Killarney by Muckross and camped in a field at Gortacuish, Glenflesk, under the very windows of Brewsterfield House. (*Note:* Ironically the landlord's old mansion came eventually into the possession of Jerry Kennedy himself who bought it from a family named Orpen. It is now demolished. Sir Francis, Lord Brewster, produced iron there in the early seventeen-hundreds . . . 'All that remain to remind us of this era of landlordism are the townlands of Brewsterfield and Iron Mills, the kilns where charcoal was produced and the mounds of *cac iarainn* [lit. 'iron excrement'], the waste that accrued from a thriving industry of more than two and a half centuries ago': Danny Doherty in *Knockanes National School*, 1887-1987). Another large contingent moved down from Castleisland through Scartaglin to Barraduff. These troops had been massing in the outlying towns for days, and it was still early in the week. For some reason they had moved into the area earlier than the forces detailed for the other fringes. The Gortacuish crowd were cautious. They were quite close to the location of the expected 'rebel army'. They began to reconnoitre. A cycle patrol went eastwards through Glenflesk a couple of times. It was enough. Jerry Kennedy decided to take it out of them for a start. Then the rumpus would bring reinforcements rushing down from Barraduff and the enemy's plan would be temporarily disrupted. So, once the cycle patrol ventured along the by-road under Fileadown, they were for it. Battalion H.Q. was down that way, high above the road in Michael O'Donoghue's home, beside the 'Robber's Den'. Mike himself was Director of Intelligence for the whole area. Jerry posted his scouts and waited. His plan of action was his very own — to grab what men he could get hold of when the signal came, rush down to the road side and take up firing positions; then, when about half of the patrol had passed, to open fire on them. (*Note:* It was a carbon copy of the 'Slippery Rock' ambush, Ballyvourney). At the same time the handful of men were to shout all together and the noted echo in the place would give the impression of a huge attacking force and shock the soldiers into surrender. It might, at that! When the signal did come eventually there were only seven or eight men available but, undaunted, Jerry put his plan into action, charging down to the attack. He had just cleared his throat for the vocal effort when the patrol halted, some distance short of his position, and went back again.

It was then he began to think of the Ballyvourney men. He had often thought of them before. Personally he had always wanted to join forces with their company and fight beside them. Real opportunities did not seem to come his way, and action was the acid test of a man's worth. It was an era when men were needed and it gave a lifetime's chance to any man to show his manliness and patriotism. Good men were the life's blood of Jerry Kennedy. He had a high regard for his own little company and the other companies of the battalion. 'They were gr-r-reat men!', he told me in 1957, and the rolling consonant dragged out to a growl of mighty approval. (*Note:* The very last of them, Pat O'Riordan, died only in the Spring of 1992. His story appears in *The Dark Secret*. The shooting of his brother-in-law, Mick O'Sullivan, by Lieutenant 'Tiny' Lyons, of the Free State army, was one Tragedy of Kerry). But the woeful fact remained that, apart from his own revolver, they had only shotguns; and beyond the County Bounds the Ballyvourney Company not only had rifles, machine-guns, and an assortment of small arms appropriated in various ways and on various stirring occasions, but they were, he opined, 'the besht men in Ireland'. He would have liked to join them. He used to cast a longing eye at the top with an ear cocked for the sweet song of rifles and the happy-careless purring of machine-guns. That would be the Ballyvourney boys in action again. It was fine music. Some day he would send for them to play their music west. Now the round-up was on and an opportunity for a combined action seemed to have presented itself. As usual he was at H.Q. at the 'Robber's Den'. (*Note:* The Black-and-Tans had come to know the name and had dubbed that part of the Flesk valley the 'Robbers' Glen'). He had with him about ten men on regular duty and others in the area were 'standing-to' awaiting orders. Scouts on all the high points kept continual track of the troop movements. His position was just on the outer rim of the round-up theatre and he calculated that when things got too hot they stood a good chance of bursting through the ring by attacking one of the advance columns. On Saturday evening, June 4, 1921, he sent a dispatch rider on a bicycle to contact Commandant Patrick O'Sullivan, O/C Eighth Battalion, Cork No. 1 Brigade. (*Note:* This part of the story is mainly taken from the official statement made by Jerry Kennedy to the Pensions' Board of the Thirties, or the Army Historical Society of the late Forties and early Fifties. Unfortunately nobody seemed to bother about exact dates in those times. Now nobody cares very much). Patrick arrived on the following day with Vice O/C Paddy O'Sullivan (Paddy Donagh Owen) and

Michael Murphy, Brigade Column Commander. (cf. Chapter 17). On examining the position Mick Murphy gave instructions to have Drumcarbin bridge, on the Barraduff road, demolished so as to prevent British reinforcements coming from that direction, and also Garries bridge on the main road, so as to drive them up along the by-road by the Robber's Den where the action would be placed. On this understanding Commandant Murphy agreed to bring over his thirty-five riflemen and two machine-gun crews into Kerry. In fact he would probably get some of them over that very night, and so Jerry Kennedy arranged to have them accomodated in O'Connell's, on the slopes of Freaghanagh, intending to meet them there himself on the following day. He then organized his two 'crowbar brigades' (as they were known since the land agitation days of the previous century), and sent them out to demolish the bridges. Garries bridge created no problem and was soon laid low. The second party went on to Drumcarbin, but just as they were attacking the superstructure some other battalion officers came along and stopped them, saying that the priest in his pony-trap would be unable to get through, in the morning, to say Mass at Barraduff. So, instead they cut a trench across the road a little further down.

In the meantime Jerry Kennedy had called in his remaining men and with two of them went to O'Donoghue's to sleep. A very short time it seemed, after they had turned in, when Mike Donoghue's sister, Hannah, roused them and said that the house was surrounded. British troops, she told them, had raided the house nearest to them and arrested the occupant, Humphrey Healy. When they had taken him out, his wife, knowing the others were near, slipped away by the back and stole along the bed of a stream to warn them. The urgent rush to get clear of the building was greatly aggravated by the darkness. Somebody foolishly struck a match but Mike Donoghue immediately knocked it out of his hand. (*Note:* The Intelligence Officer was a quick thinker. He similarly struck down the rifle at Béalnabláth, fifteen months later, when Dan O'Connor beside him fired at Michael Collins). After the sudden glare the ensuing blackness was a wall of stygian impenetrability. Out of the darkness came Jerry Kennedy's voice ordering them to grab what clothes they could lay hands on and make for the hill. Himself, he tried to get his pants on and failed. He swore at it and discovered that he had been trying to get his legs into the sleeves of a coat. So he put it on the orthodox way and ran with the others. On the hill, a few minutes later, he looked closely at it and thought that the 'witching hour of night' had cast a spell upon him. It was Hannah O'Donoghue's jacket. Worse still, his own coat was back in the house with his precious revolver and some incriminating documents in the pockets. Mike Donoghue, stolid and imperturbable, ran the gauntlet of the raiding party, went back and retrieved them. But they need not have worried. The British did not raid the house that night. Their programme was so set that they posted sentries twenty yards away and came no further . . .

Clothes don't make the man but, still and all, thought Jerry Kennedy, misconstruing Shakespeare, a man was at a distinct disadvantage without them even on a sultry Summer's night with hostile troops hot on one's heels. He got himself properly attired and, with a new feeling of self-confidence, he about-turned to the problem. His running away in the first place — 'with my hat in my fist', as he said — was due to a positional disadvantage, ignorance of the extent of the danger, and the need for a selective stand of his own choosing. With a gasp of dismay he thought of his men at the bridges. 'My God!', he cried aloud, 'they're caught and they'll all be killed!'. Then with a further pang he remembered the Flying Column from Cork. His heart sank. They would be surrounded by now at Freaghanagh. They wouldn't have a dog's chance only to fight it out to the last man. His own responsibility for inviting them over was settling on him like a pall. He moved along towards the brow of the hill, but still parallel with the road. Now there were voices beneath him in the darkness. It might be some of the men from the bridges who had escaped to the high ground. He began to work his way cautiously towards them. There was just a bare chance. It was getting light now and he could vaguely make out the shadowy figures. First the white armbands drew his attention. Then he knew they were men in uniform. One of them appeared to be using field-glasses. He could see the glint. He was about sixty yards away from them and in good cover. He retreated carefully keeping them under observation and having the compliment returned by the glass-eyed watcher. Then his cover gave out for a short distance and he was temporarily pinned down. He made a dash for it and was just across when a volley of bullets whistled by. He went on upwards over the back of Carrigawaddra ('the rock of the dog') and stood awhile on top considering the situation, trying to scrutinize, in the still feeble light, that vital farmhouse under Barna on the far side of the valley. Two miles was too far to detect, even in full daylight, and his thinking led him nowhere, except that he allowed that by now a sizeable chunk of the British Army held the intervening space. Then suddenly, with the iron-willed, dour determination of the man, he decided, and that, for Vice-Commandant Jerry Kennedy, was synonymous and usually simultaneous with action. He raced for O'Leary's farmhouse above Loo Bridge and beneath him. Somehow he would find a way across to the Column and lead them out or face it with them. But O'Leary's was strangely quiet. There was no sign of life at all. He banged, rattled and called, but in vain. In desperation he caught up a stone and was on the point of blowing in an upper window when he heard the unmistakable sound of someone running in the boreen at his back. They were reckless, fugitive, stumbling footsteps, and so he waited. A comrade of his came headlong into the yard, breathless and incoherent. When he recognized his Commanding Officer he tried to speak but the only sound that came was 'co-co-co-co . . . so-so-so-so'. Jerry decoded it to 'Come on! Soldiers!' and ran with him, full of regret at having accomplished nothing. But unwittingly he had done his good deed for the day and fulfilled his purpose indirectly. The Flying Column was already whistling the tune of the piper's son, over the hills and far away, in the seclusion of Coomhola glen. But the three officers, Paddy and Pat and Mick, who had returned, were at that very moment fast asleep in O'Leary's and in imminent danger. His banging had alerted the man of the house and the three got away with only seconds to spare. (*Note:* I learned this later and shall always regret that I never told Jerry before he died . . . Author). At the same time Jerry and his companion were making for the shelter of Crohane Wood. They were spotted as they ran, but they succeeded in getting in among the trees in safety and covered themselves in heather before the machine-guns already noted began to splutter their venom at the inoffensive vegetation. And there they stayed to bake and dehydrate in the shimmering, palpable heat until two o'clock in the afternoon. So the secret was out! 'Down in the forest something stirred', as the poem goes — but it was only the midges chewing the hide off Jerry Kennedy!

(His statement continues):

I heard the noise of running in a boreen nearby. A figure appeared and I recognized Timothy Donoghue, a Volunteer. He could hardly speak except to tell me that the British military were coming. (*Note:* My version is how he told it to me). I ran with him but we were spotted and fire was opened on us. We got into a wood and buried ourselves in heather, where we remained from 4 a.m. to 2 p.m. We were eaten by midges. Firing was going on all round and a plane was flying overhead. When things got quiet we crept out towards O'Leary's house and I saw the old man of the house nearby. I called him over and asked him how things were. He told me that the British had a cattle train at Loo Bridge station and were loading it with prisoners. The British had finished the round-up and were withdrawing. The party who had cut the road near Drumcarbin Bridge were captured coming from it with tools on their shoulders. During the round-up, Jimmy Donoghue and Florrie Con Rua were wounded. A civilian had been killed at Shrone. A large number of prisoners were taken out but the majority were not Volunteers. The British captured no arms or documents and after examination most of the prisoners were released. There was no one to identify the Volunteers. All our men were released, including officers who had been picked up. When I got to Loo Bridge I found that there was no doctor to attend to the wounded. I got two Volunteers and we went in a pony car to Kilgarvan. I saw Dr. Moore (who was hostile to us) and told him my mission. He refused to come saying that if we met the Tans we might be shot. I told him that if he did not come I wouldn't wait for the Tans to shoot him and ordered him out to the car. He came quietly.

People usually do after such a proposition!

21

The Big Round-up Part Five: A Pack of Cards

In classical times it was never a very far cry from the 'field of Mars' to the 'lap of Minerva', and vice versa, more especially and significantly so in modern times when mental acumen and technical achievement come in hot haste to the aid of the terrible warrior from outer space. Assessing the one, therefore, in terms of the other (i.e. War in terms of Wisdom) has its ancient precedents and current exemplars, abscinding, of course, for the immediate purpose, from logical ultimates which might easily squeeze the whole martial concept, the 'World at War', out of rational existence. In debate, let us say, a learned Scholastic hears his opponent's *Dissertatio* through to the end, looks up sagely and makes his pronouncement: *Quod nimis probat, Domne, nihil probat!* — that which proves too much, Sir, proves nothing; as much as to say: 'It sounds too facile, old boy, so there must be a catch in it somewhere. Let me see now!'. He consults his copious notes while an unspecified number of angels, dancing on the point of a convenient pin, cease and are still. Finally he locates the offending sweeping statement, adroitly swats it with a weighty tome of St. Thomas, *vel aliter*, and the august *disputatio* rolls on, while the angels resume their tripping the light fantastic within the confines of a *locus* that has neither length nor breadth. (*Note:* We were familiar with this boloney in the Maynooth of long ago. Still, it served its purpose, and the wonderful Latin language in which it was couched deserves far more consideration than at present. Strange to hear that a continental radio station has lately begun to use it for a news bulletin!).

So, a certain British military operation, identified in the present context as the 'Big Round-up', meant to be comprehensive, became simply sweeping and on that account accomplished nothing. It swept indiscriminately, or, rather, the magnitude of it engendered a fear which produced the same overall effect. Consequently, the stage became cluttered up with unwanted personnel, making segregation and identification wellnigh impossible, thus defeating the original purpose. Bernard Montgomery, at least, showed that he learned something from that lesson. That the round-up should, in the process, appear somewhat ludicrous and produce many paradoxical situations, goes without saying. When a section of roadway happened to coincide with the appointed boundary of the operation, every dwelling-place 'inside' came under close scrutiny (cf. previous chapter) while those on the far side were overlooked or ignored as if they did not exist. But the favoured houses were systematically knocked up and the inhabitants closely questioned. In most cases not a man of any description was found at home as they had already absconded. The frightened womenfolk could think of no other excuse for their absence than that they had 'gone to the bog'. It was at the height of an outstanding turf season, and the lie was feasible enough. So the local expression greeted the aggravated soldiers all the way. Once in exasperation a young lieutenant blurted out: 'You must have the hell of a large peat mine around here!'. Truth to tell it was a large peat mine when they came to investigate it, but yet not large enough to conceal the crowd of fugitives who had thought to take refuge amongst its banks and braes. Jerry Creedon and a handful of men from Coomaguire (cf. Chapter 14) were captured as they made their way into the eastern extremity of Claedagh valley. It was one of the earliest 'bags' and the soldiers were still in the mood to appreciate the fact. Nearby was the home of big Paddy McCarthy, that aberrant mountainy man, the Peter Pan of the hill country, owner of a thousand infertile acres (he came down from the hills to Ballyvourney to sow his annual half-acre of spuds), who in his sixties (1955) and onward still found it convenient and preferable to range his rolling moorlands on bare feet, his boots slung by their laces across his shoulder in case he took a notion to travel further on the main road to The Mills for the bus to Cork City. On this memorable occasion Paddy was at home to all comers. He was whisked into the bag along with the others and stood patiently waiting. Jerry Creedon was a shade slow in complying with an order and a young soldier, a sergeant, struck him with the butt of his rifle and sent him sprawling on the ground, but an officer who saw it immediately snapped at the sergeant: 'Conduct yourself!'. Then came the inevitable spell of indecision when both captors and captives wondered what would or should happen next. Some impression had to be made and Montgomery made an effort. He marched over towards the bunch of prisoners and barked: 'Line up! You are all going to be shot!'. Said Paddy McCarthy to him lugubriously: ''Tis too bad, Sir, but I s'pose it can't be helped now!'. As a speech from the dock it would have disconcerted any judge about to don the black and gone down as a most solemn instance of 'laughter in court'. Soon afterwards the prisoners were marched off westwards along the valley to a spot near Claedagh Lodge which appears to have been the focal point of the combined operation. In fact a sense of the bizarre had already begun to show itself in divergent incidents over that widely scattered area and steadily grew as the pursuing troops closed with the fugitives. Group after group of obviously unarmed civilians, haggard, partly dressed, raised their hands obediently in the air when confronted with a resolute line of

rifle-toting 'tommies'. And as the day wore on a further sense
of futility and surprise, as well as a growing sense of absur-
dity, took hold of the soldiers themselves. They had come
to grips only to find themselves at grips with nothing. A sense
of the bizarre seemed to be in the nature of things. And the
planes zoomed to and fro. A long streamer fluttered
downwards on the incandescent air, curled and writhed like
a live thing, and draped itself around a clump of heather.
Donagh Mike Lucey could not resist the impulse, reached
out and gathered it to him. It said: 'All running. No fight
on'. He had not needed to be told, nor those for whom it
was intended.

*   *   *

From Inchigeela, all the way,
I travelled into Kerry . . .

So sang 'Myles na gCopaleen' in Benedict's *Lily Of Killarney*
— and Mikey Tim Twomey, having picked up the trail, and
being well versed in the calling of Myles of the Little Horses,
recalled the lines as he strove to calm the frantic plunging
of the farm horse to which he had attached himself, as a
strict necessity of means, in Jerh Lucey's farmyard beyond
the 'County Bounds'. Two of his party, John Sheehan and
Jack Collins, had possessed themselves of a pair of 'shlawns'
(i.e. turf-cutting spades) and were going through the motions
of turf cutting on the edge of the laneway, because there was
no time to look for an authentic turf bank. The others, John
Harrington and the Hegarty brothers, Seán and Pat, were
endeavouring to get in the next farmhouse thinking to register
themselves on the back of the kitchen door on the orders
of General Strickland. And so the soldiers found them. A
fence being a convenient place to rest a rifle at any time,
Mikey Tim (as we knew him) was little surprised when he
noticed the array of menacing muzzles that suddenly
sprouted along the boundary of the yard and still less when
he was curtly ordered to raise his hands in the air. Being a

horseman, he continued to give his attention to the rearing animal until he was told to leave it and present himself for identification. A soldier immediately recognized him as being one of those who had been taken prisoner during the round-up following the 'Slippery Rock' ambush, in August of the previous year. The soldier had been friendly then. Now he was dour and suspicious. 'What the hell are you doing here?', he snapped. 'I'm here', said Mikey Tim, 'for the same reason that brought you over here from England — earning my living!'. The soldier let it pass with a bad grace. 'Look what a year in the army can do to a fella!', Mikey Tim commented drily to himself as they began their march across the boglands to Claedagh. Skirting the Black Lake, where a tiny tributary flows down to meet the Claedagh river, they dropped into the valley beside 'The Lodge'. They found the place in an uproar, full of alarums and excurions, hues and cries, and commotion. Quite near them were the captured motor cars, the much vaunted prize of the official reports. But they were either immobilized before capture or were considered not worth moving because right away some soldiers proceeded to set fire to them and when the fire failed to reduce them sufficiently they were smashed with axes and other implements into a pathetic looking tangle of junk. That same took a lot of doing. Veterans of the roads used to claim that the old cars were practically indestructible. 'I saw the old "Dodge"', said Mikey Tim (himself a pioneer wheelman in mid-Cork, with a magic hand), 'on the same engine to turn the two-hundred thousand and start again at WAN (one). And the EXHAUST! — you couldn't break it with a sledge! Wan night turning I struck Leary's house (Danny Arthur's) and the hole is still there in the wall. Leary's wife said afther that the house shook and the pitchers fell off the walls . . . You couldn't break the oul' cars!', he said. Well, in a manner of speaking!

*   *   *

The fallacy, frequently invoked, that because a man was big

and able-bodied he was sure to be a 'rebel', in one instance, at least, came near to being used as quasi-circumstantial evidence followed by summary execution. Pete Cronin (cf. Chapter 14) was big and able-bodied, and so was his brother, Denis. Hiding out in a bog-hole they 'made short work' (his expression) of the cake their mother had given them wrapped in her apron. Then some soldiers coming along 'the old Caharagh road' sent them, unwilling wayfarers, on their 'Oregan Trail' westwards. Entering Claedagh by the now well established route of Glashacurmick they found the hosting already in the making, while there was still the sound of heavy firing to the east and south. They had a mind to continue northwards along a *glaise* (cut) between the hills but came under heavy fire from a platoon lying prone on a field. So they returned to face the inevitable with the crowds on the valley floor. Already many of the troops had arrived at the southern rim of the valley and had sat down silhouetted against the sky and in full view of the fugitives. Pete and Denis, with two Rathmore men whom they had met on the mountain, moved away down the road to Healy's. A young lad was lamenting pitifully that his brother had been shot. Everywhere there was confusion, futile running to and fro like the frenetic scampering of little animals inside a cage, and all around, close in now, lynx-eyed custodians of the Realm, trigger-happy and peeved. In Healy's the big 'settle' was at the far side of the kitchen. They sat there in a bunch, despondently looking out of the big window, watching and waiting. The whole affair was fantastic, bothersome, like a bad dream. They might wake up eventually. Even the airman who flew his plane several times along the yard, between the row of trees and the house, and leaned over from the cockpit to peer at them through the window — he was fantastic too. They hoped he would go away, but he did not. Their nerves gave out and they went and sat on either side of the window where he could not see them. Then an officer arrived with a platoon of soldiers and placed them under

17. Ian Graeme Baun Mackenzie-Kennedy, 'a magnificent Scot' (Seán Ó Faoláin). Killed at Rochestown, Cork, August, 1922.

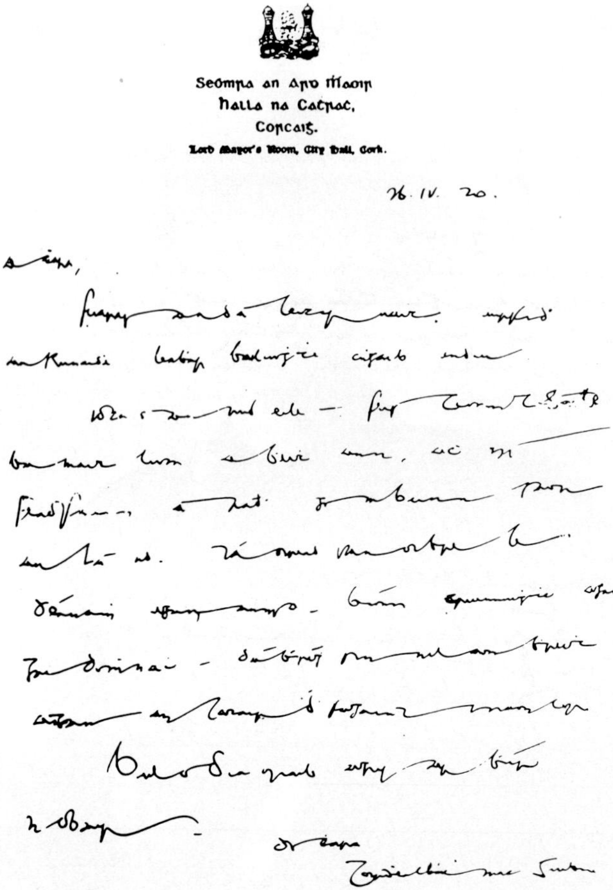

Seómra an Árd Mhaoir
Halla na Cathrach,
Corcaigh.
Lord Mayor's Room, City Hall, Cork.

26. IV. 20.

18. Letter of apology in Irish from Lord Mayor Terence MacSwiney, regretting his inability to attend a *Feis* in Coolea due to pressure of work.

Seómpa an Ápo Máoıp,
Halla na Cátpac,
Copcaıᵹ.
Lord Mayor's Room, City Hall, Cork. 19ᵗʰ April, 1920.

A capa,

I beg to bring under your notice the MacCurtain Memorial Fund, which has been inaugurated to provide for the widow of our late Lord Mayor, and for the education and future welfare of his children.

Though we have received generous support from outside Cork County, and gratefully welcome and acknowledge such support, we are confining the direct appeal to our own City and County, as we feel the obligation is specially ours, and that it lies on us primarily to discharge it. For this reason a united and very earnest effort on our part is needed to make the Memorial Fund a success.

The General Committee invite your cooperation and ask you to call a local meeting of representative men for the purpose of organising support for the Fund in your district.

Thanking you in anticipation for your kind services.

Mıse
le móṗ-meaṡ

Conseulḃaċ mac Suḃne
ápo máop

19. Copy of circular letter from Lord Mayor MacSwiney with regard to Memorial Fund for the late Lord Mayor Tomás MacCurtain's wife and family.

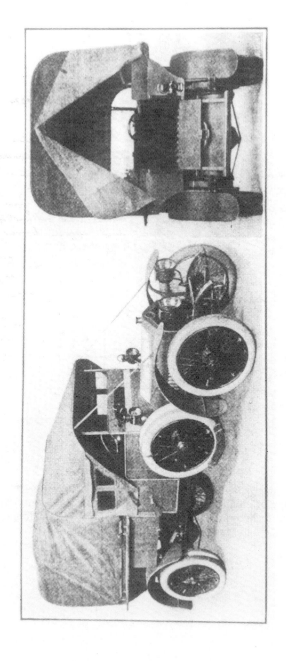

20. Two views of the famous 'Crossley Tender'. The Auxies disdained the weather hood and sat on a bench centre-ways facing outwards.

21a. Frontage and main entrance gate of Macroom Castle.

21b. Historic Béal a' Ghleanna, the 'Mouth of the Glen'.

22. Armoured Rolls-Royce No. 2, the famous SLIEVENAMON, as she is today in the Curragh of Kildare. Drivers were sometimes picked off through the open driving flap.

23a. Last of the Ballingeary Company, Neilus O'Leary (left) of Derrinaboorka, and Patrick O'Riordan of Derryvoleen. Picture taken at Aharas 'Station', 20 March 1993.

23b. The new 'Civic Guards' as founded by Michael Collins, in May, 1922. Car model unknown, probably a LANCIA.

24. NOTABLE GUNS OF THE PERIOD

From the top: 1. Vickers machine-gun; 2. Lewis-gun;
3. Hotchkiss; 4. Thompson sub-machine-gun ('tommy-gun');
5. Lee-Enfield rifle ('three-naught-three'); 6. (*left*) Mauser
automatic ('Peter the Painter'); 7. (*right*) Luger automatic;
8. Webley and Scott .455 revolver ('Long Webley'); 9. Smith
and Wesson ('New Century') revolver.

arrest. He was arrogant, told them they would be shot, had them stand against the outside wall with their hands elevated, told the man of the house to come out as he was going to burn the house, changed his mind on both scores and marched them down the road to join the other prisoners. (*Note:* I have often wondered if this were Monty once again. After Higginson he was the only officer who would have the authority to order a summary execution. His personal prestige was at stake in this operation, and he had written to his father to say that any civilian who obstructed a member of the armed forces in any way was 'shot at once'). As for the men themselves, they were a miserable looking lot, Pete Cronin said. Many were dressed in odd bits of clothes in an effort to make themselves look *suarach,* which means small, poor, pathetic, dejected and neglected — all of it. One man had managed to get into a boy's suit he had exchanged for his own. He looked totally ridiculous. Some of the others laughed at him in spite of their own plight. The four of them, Pete, Denis and the two Rathmore men, were singled out for special attention. They were placed on one side under a heavy guard. One of the soldiers made himself very objectionable, cursing violently and swearing that he would blow them up. He took a sadistic delight in their reaction when he pulled the pin out of a 'Mills bomb' and prepared as if to throw it at them. His comrades restrained him and when an officer came along, soon afterwards, he was reported. The officer immediately sent him headlong down the road 'with a few kicks in the ass'. The four prisoners were then marched off northwards through the 'Slogadal' the rough little glen between 'The Paps' and Knocknabro, so well known to May Day pilgrims to 'The City'. (*Note:* Nowadays a passable enough road for a tractor or 'Patrol' wagon goes along that way, but then it was only a crude, stony track though much frequented by visitors to the Penitential Station). Every now and again there was a *ciseach,* a rough lattice-work of rods over a gully to enable a donkey and cart to move in and out of the bog. The soldiers prodded each one of these with bayonets as they went by in case anyone might be lurking there. They came to Glannafreaghaun ('the valley of the crow') and the soldiers sat down to rest and drink some water. The prisoners were allowed to sit but not to drink. By now they needed it. Apart from the heat of the day, they had to carry in turn four haversacks and a Lewis-gun, with a tunic slung across the barrel for good measure, and even a detached rifle butt. Further on they hit the bog road into Shrone. It seemed to be an appointed station of some kind because there were a lot of soldiers and prisoners about the place. Over on their right a group of civilians stood clustered together. Beside them a man lay dead on the ground. They were told it was the brother of the lad who had been crying earlier in the day. Suddenly the lad himself passed like the wind through the midst of the military and all, on the back of a jennet. (*Note:* For some reason the odd little animal was known locally as *capaillín Spáinneach* i.e. the 'little Spanish horse'). The lad looked wild and distraught. He was going 'as fast as it was in the jennet's belly', said Pete Cronin, and his passing was something to behold. An officer had given him a permit to go for the priest. The four men, Pete, Denis and the two Rathmore men, were put on a turf bank apart, where they remained until late in the afternoon. Most of the others were allowed to go. At about five o'clock they were again told that they were going to be shot, but this time it was in earnest. A stronger guard came and escorted them down and across a little glen to a spot where a detail of riflemen was drawn up facing them. One of the Rathmore men took out his Rosary beads and prayed aloud as he went. In the meantime the priest had arrived. He stood on the knoll above talking to an officer. They looked awhile in the direction of the doomed men. Then the priest went down to the body of the dead man and had it removed out of sight. The officer came towards the group and surprisingly removed the firing-squad and all of the guard except two. After a while one of these went on one knee and remarked: 'There seems to be some change. Don't seem to be going to shoot you at all now'. And the face of Fortune wore a broad smile.

Presently the other guard sat down, opened his haversack and took out a can and four large biscuits. He dipped one in the can and began to nibble. At the sight of food the butterflies of fear reformed into caterpillars of hunger gnawing at their vitals. He must have guessed because he looked up with a tantalizing smile. He looked at Pete. 'Hungry, Paddy?', he said. It was more a statement than a question. The next dip was perpetrated with a care and the nibble with a relish that dog-biscuit and bully-beef had long since failed to inspire. He was facing them now. 'Hungry, Paddy?', he asked again. He reached for another biscuit but the slow deliberateness was belied by the twinkle in his eye and his intent would have communicated itself even to a watching dog. He held it out. 'Care to try one, Paddy?',he said. Pete took the biscuit and bit quickly. But incisors jarred on unyielding matter and eye-teeth tingled with the shock. Pete looked in consternation over the rim of the disc. The smile had expanded into an enormous grin. It was floodlighting the little drama with a kindly and sympathetic prescience. 'Hard, Paddy?', he said . . .

Once more the Auxiliary Division proved itself the *enfant terrible* of the forces of occupation. 'Cadets' they called themselves. They were apparently intractable, even to their own authority. To the Irish they were feared and hated most of all. They prided themselves in their reputation and created much trouble and many problems, not to mention embarrassment, for the regular army with its hidebound system, time-tested and passably honourable. On the road above (at Shrone village) were the lorries used to transport the troops who had come in at that side. In some of them the Auxiliaries had established themselves. According to Pete Cronin they appeared to be fighting among themselves, as evidenced by the garrulous cross-talk, yelling and rattling of rifles. In some unaccountable way they had managed to get drunk, probably 'poteen', he thought. Now they had got to know of the change of plan and a number of them were trying to come down and shoot the prisoners themselves. Acting on the advice of their guards Pete and his comrades lay down by a fence in case they might be fired at from above. Eventually the grizzled old army officer, who had made the arrest in the first place, asserted his authority and got them settled down.

*   *   *

Trumpeter, what are you sounding now? . . .
I'm calling them home. Come home! Come home!
Tread light o'er the dead in the valley! . . .

The 'Big Round-up' is over! After much ado about nothing, the monstrous machine is thrown into reverse gear through remote control by some invisible hand — puppets forever reacting to relayed impulses from the brain of the Comptroller General. The little martinet-puppets glance quizzically along the lines, stalk stiff-legged to the head of columns and platoons, stand erect and ready. The little soldier-puppets are brought into contact with a new thought process and automatically adjust themselves. The nondescript mass of prisoner-puppets unlimber and shuffle or march according to capability, within the limits defined by khaki-draped human fence posts. The toy airmen, in their screaming kites, fly away somewhere or perhaps are blown away with the flying insects and thistledown and *ceannbhán*, or bog-cotton, by the Summer evening breeze . . . and Claedagh Valley settles back into its cosmic sleep of heavenly peace: 'Who cares for you!', said Alice, in Wonderland — 'You're nothing but a pack of cards!'.

22

The Big Round-up
Part Six: Coming to
Terms

Mrs. Margaret Walshe stood by the fireside of her little house just to the east of the village of Ballymakeera. A brave little woman, though frail and ageing, she glared resentfully at the two soldiers facing her from the centre of the kitchen floor. The tabs on their tunic sleeves pronounced them ESSEX, their behaviour, as well as the odour which assailed her nostrils, pronounced them drunk. She moved across to the table for some support. One of the intruders held out a packet of tea. He wanted money for it and he wanted it badly. He looked as if he were prepared to go to extremes to get it. She did not need the tea and said so. His attitude became suddenly menacing. He staggered rather than stepped forward. At the same time a muted scream came from the region of the front gate and a glance through the window showed her a third soldier making unsteady overtures to a young girl who was apparently on her way in. She switched her eyes back to the two in the kitchen and said in a steady voice: *Johnny, rith amach agus glaoidh ar Sergeant Feeney!* (i.e. 'Johnny, run out and call Sergeant Feeney!'). The little boy disappeared through the back door. They did not seem to have noticed. The second man had begun to expostulate when there was a rush of boots across the stony yard and Sergeant Feeney burst into the kitchen followed closely by three of his MANCHESTERS with fixed bayonets. They almost lifted the drunken ESSEX through the doorway on the points of their weapons, raced them down through the village to their post at the western end, and that was that, so to speak . . .

About the sergeant. He was in charge of the outpost stationed on the rock at the back of the house. A friendly fellow, with a reasonable bias towards intimacy and homeliness, he liked to come and sit by the fireside and talk — mostly about his wife and two children back in Manchester. He had pictures of them. Talk was an outlet for his enforced repression. He wished this 'confounded trouble' were over and that he could go back to his family. He had a grievance against the I.R.A. for keeping him from them. Nothing more. He was a-wearying for his family. His kindly nature made a mockery of the word 'Enemy', which in effect he was, though in fact hardly. Only a trick of fate had implanted him on the wrong side of the fence because both his parents were Irish-born though he did not seem to have inherited any 'feeling' for their land of origin. He had confided, somewhat patronizingly, to Mrs. Walshe that this was 'definitely the last push and from now on, when those irregulars have been rounded up, you will be able to live in peace'. As he said it he indicated vaguely the mountains away to the North and West. His acquired and typically British outlook would prevent him from sensing the spirit of the Irregulars in the very kitchen where he sat. (*Note:* Young Johnny eventually was to become a teacher in Dublin, a spirited nationalist and friend and confidant to M. J. Molloy, the well known playwright. At the time I knew him in the Fifties he confided to me that M. J. was working on an exciting theme for a new play on Irish traditional faction-fighting, which he had extensively researched. It appeared that the whirling of the blackthorn sticks had been developed to an art form, much like sword fighting, and a good sticksman could remove a shirt button from an opponent's neck without touching the skin. I was bound to secrecy about all of this because of the cut-throat competition in theatre circles. I never found out if the play was finished or not. M.J. Molloy died recently).

The Queen's Own Cameron Highlanders had settled in the 'Gullane Field' by the river. It was the Second Battalion and there was a colonel in charge. When they marched in, on Sunday evening, his second-in-command, a major, stole the show by appearing in tartan plaid trousers (or 'trews') instead of kilts, with a low-slung gun-belt full of glistening shells, cowboy style. (*Note*: For a decade past, real-life U.S. Marshal, Tom Mix, as a silent film star, had been embuing even military circles with a sense of 'Cowboys and Indians', and society itself with the fantasy of 'good fellas and bad fellas', all unfortunately still very much in evidence, all false!). The First Battalion, the Manchester Regiment, had occupied the village itself. Every house was commandeered for the occasion. Major-General Strickland, General Officer commanding the Sixth Division in the South, had issued the order for the round-up but, like Moses, he was not to see the promised land. Brigadier-General Harold Higginson, one of his brigade commanders, took personal charge of the operation, arriving by car early on Monday morning and establishing his temporary H.Q. in O'Leary's Hibernian Hotel. (*Note*: It was Higginson, responsible for the Martial Law area, who had issued the order in the previous December with regard to the carrying of hostages in military vehicles, as well as the execution of prisoners found in possession of arms, an order sadly repeated by the Provisional Government in Dublin, less than two years later, after the death of Michael Collins at Béalnabláth. Strickland had become quite disgruntled with the state of affairs and wanted out. In his personal diary for 1 January, 1921, he had written: 'Last year was bad enough but nothing to this . . .I hope and trust I won't be here 1.1.22'. But he was!). Fronting the village houses now was a row of eight or ten large lorries stocked with supplies. They were a sort of mobile Quarter-Master Stores, part of the large Army Service Corps which provisioned the troops during the manoeuvres. Fronting the lorries again was a row of ten Lewis-guns on forked supports, facing directly across the road, ostensibly for the purpose of protecting the Army's supplies and the General's H.Q. (*Note*: The Lewis-gun became one of the 'personality' weapons of the Irish 'Troubles', that and the German Mauser automatic pistol known as a 'Peter the Painter' after Peter Piaktow, a Russian anarchist associated with the famous 'Siege of Sidney Street' in 1911. Made to rest on a bipod, the Lewis-gun was invented by a retired American Army officer of that name. It became the supreme achievement of an I.R.A.. man to be able to fire it from the shoulder. An authentic model appeared repeatedly in the extremely funny television series, DAD'S ARMY, and in one particular episode, itself and its supporting platoon of decrepit Home Guard, were put completely out of action because someone had mislaid the tiny but vital 'butterfly spring'. From our 'Troubles' I have in my possession a complete and detailed chart of the mechanism of the Lewis-gun). So, literally overnight, the village of Ballymakeera found itself an armed and provisioned fortress, the nerve-centre of a carefully planned military operation.

Still they did not appear to take it very seriously. Like overgrown boy-scouts they had had their outing. During the course of the day the British military screened their prisoners in an effort to pan out some vile residue of disaffection, failed and sent them home. The one prisoner of the hall, John Harrington (cf. Chapter 17), was escorted the three miles to Coolavokig. The pipe-toting officer walked beside him chatting affably about the sporting potential of the locality, elicited a promise that, when the trouble was over and he returned for a fishing and shooting holiday, John would act as his guide. (*Note*: He never returned. Another and sadder act of war, Civil War, intervened for his prisoner that neither

of them could have visualized). Leaning over the 'quay wall'
at Poulnabro they had a friendly dispute about a dark object in the water below which the officer claimed was a
salmon. It turned out to be a stone. John was already an
experienced 'poacher'. He was delivered to his mother with
the admonition that he was 'a good boy' only to keep him
at home in future. 'But that other son of yours' — Danny
— 'he's a damn scamp, you know!'. She let on to know.
(*Note*: Expert gunman and fisherman, die-hard patriot and
unrelenting sportsman, John Harrington told me the story
with great gusto in 1954 at his home in Ballingeary. He was
in a wheelchair. Danny's son, Father Michael, is presently
a parish priest in the diocese of Cloyne).

Major Percival alone seemed determined to prove
something about something. He marched his handful of
prisoners from Ballymakeera village all the way to Kinsale,
collected a few more and shot two men on the way, was trailed
first by Mick O'Sullivan (cf. *Where Mountainy Men Have
Sown*), and later by Tom Barry (cf. *Guerilla Days*), all eager
to get him on their sights as he sat his white horse at the
head of the column. In Kinsale six-foot five-inch John J.
Quill, of Coolea, dubbed 'Enormous Paddy', was gleefully
paraded through the streets by the diminutive ESSEX as he
bantered them slyly in return. 'Yerra, I could carry half-a-
dozen of ye', he told them, 'in the sate of my pants!'. It is
no wonder the caustic wit of the Irish dogged Percival to
the end. As late as World War Two, when he rather
outrageously surrendered Singapore to the Japanese (though
British historians claim he was just unfortunate and had no
other option), it was widely reported in this country that
the little Cockneys of the Orient had marched in singing 'The
Boys Of Kilmichael' in their notoriously Kerry accent! For
the record, General Percival surrendered Singapore's sixty
thousand troops to the Japanese on 16 February, 1942, not
ninety thousand in 1941, as Tom Barry claims in his *Guerilla
Days*. This Percival belonged to a cadet branch of the Earls

of Egmont on whose ground the present writer resides, with their main dwellings, Egmont House and Burton House, respectively to front and rear of me, and Egmont Castle just a grassy bump in a field across the way. In fairness to Percival, he was actually ordered to surrender the colony which was the most intensely fortified position in the region. In playing down the 'bump' on the Imperial floor, historians point to the fact that the guns, being naval, were all in fixed positions facing out to sea, while the cute little Japs simply walked in the back door. But the British had their revenge. After the war they executed the victor, General Yamashita, who to the last claimed that he was merely a soldier doing his duty.

Perhaps a final story about tough, irrepressible Tom Barry might be in context here. It was told to me just the other day by Mr. Wally Cronin, of the Cork Harbour Commissioners, whose family had supervised the export of cattle through Cork for several generations. Barry worked as yard supervisor for the Commissioners. The job was created for him and died with him. According to Wally, he was 'first class at the job', with complete efficiency and never a whiff of trouble or strike. Late in life he took to the drink and became a nuisance to his friends, who were usually blamed by his wife, Leslie, for 'leading him astray'. Sometime in 1957 Wally was walking in Oliver Plunkett Street with Denis Callanan, also of the Harbour Board, and brother of Eugene 'Nudge' Callanan, well known republican doctor of Clonakilty. They saw Barry in the distance. They ducked into a bar and out the back exit, but he had seen them and came raging in. He decided that they must have gone into the British Legion Club next door. He went in. There was no trace of them. He went up to the bar:

'Ball o' malt, please', said General Barry.

'Are you a member, Sir?', in an English accent from the attendant.

'I am as of now. Ball o' malt, please!'.

'You can see from the clock that it is two minutes to ten, Sir. We are just about to close. I'm afraid I can't serve you. Thank you!'.

Barry unlimbered a legally held pistol, plugged the clock on the wall twice, and said:

'Now, time is at a stand still! Ball o' malt, please!'.

He had two double whiskeys alone. The whole of the British Legion had taken to its heels.

Wally Cronin's own family provide an interesting footnote to History. His grand-uncle, Billy, climbed to the roof of the old Victoria Hotel, in Patrick's Street, and hurled a paving stone down on to the carriage of Queen Victoria when she visited Cork in 1900. He missed and was arrested. He was condemned to be deported as a felon, probably the last such para-legal phenomenon ever, and was sent to Tasmania ('Van Diemen's Land'). He never arrived there. They (i.e. the British guards) 'fed him to the sharks' on the way, or so the family say. Queen Victoria died the following year.

*   *   *

The kaleidoscope whirls on, the eager eye of the Watcher endeavouring to retain the stream-vision of symmetrical and exotic patterns while the incidence of a strange, indefinable mass begins to disturb the happy falling-into-place of colourful forms. Politics, with its intrigue and tricky reservations, insinuates itself in the hitherto finely rotating cell of 'the onward march of a nation', the vision of Charles Stewart Parnell, and fleeting, crazy images, chimeras of genetic fancy, give a premonition of things to come:- A 'Partition Act' imposed on a reluctant nation and repudiated in election by North and South alike as an enfranchised unit . . . 'Feelers' sent out to test Sinn Féin resolve with a view to determining future policy . . . Peace moves, diplomatic and otherwise . . . Letters, private and — when convenient — public . . . Self-appointed and quasi-official emissaries . . . Proposals and counter-proposals . . . Verbal disputes and hair-splitting . . .

Theorizing, sometimes logical, sometimes biased . . .
Arguments backed by the threat of intensified armed intervention . . . One nation, dichotomous treatment . . . One
nation, severed outlooks . . . One nation, dismemberment
and religious bigotry as instruments and catalysts for
catastrophic defeat not achievable honourably on the field
of battle. The burning of the Dublin Customs House on May
25, 1921, had opened many eyes both friendly and hostile.
A military operation involving hundreds of men, it had been
the death blow for British Civil Administration. It had proved a nation at war. That, and public opinion everywhere,
brought, on 11 July, 1921, a cessation of hostilities, a 'Truce'
so-called, as a prelude to future negotiations . . . And down
in Cork rebel leader, Liam Lynch, grinds his teeth in dismay
as the notification is handed to him at his mobile headquarters. The soldier's day is done . . .

> Liam was at Divisional Headquarters at Coolea when of-
> ficial notification of the Truce reached him on 10th July. He
> immediately issued the necessary order for the cessation of
> hostilities at 12 noon next day. This order averted what might
> have been one of the largest actions of his former Brigade
> — Cork No. 2.
>
> (Florrie Donoghue: *No Other Law*).

> We sat down to talk about the news in wonder. What did
> it mean?, and why had senior officers no other information
> than a bald message? Would the Truce last a week, or
> perhaps two weeks?.
>
> (Ernie O'Malley: *On Another Man's Wound*).

> At 11.45 a.m., on Monday, July 11th, I called the Column
> together and explained to them the conditions implied by
> the Truce. The column was dismissed at 12 noon, and at 12.15
> p.m., when the men were actually removing some of the
> mines from the road, a military party came on the scene from
> Newcastlewest. These, seeing our men on the road (*Note*: It
> was a massive mile-long position between Ardagh and

Templeglantine, and contained eight land-mines), first attempted to be hostile, but, when asked if they were prepared to observe the Truce, changed their manner and continued on their way to Abbeyfeale.

(Paddy O'Brien. O/C Cork No. 4 Brigade:
OFFICIAL STATEMENT).

Elsewhere rebel Commandant Seán Moylan is handed a form to fill and (as recalled by Jamie Moynihan who was with him at the time, though Ernie O'Malley gives an alternative version as usual) snarls: 'We started this war with sticks and, by cripes!, it seems we're going to finish it with fountain-pens!'. I recall, back in the Fifties, when General Seán Moylan, as an effective and down-to-earth Minister for Education, came to Coolea, in the Ballyvourney *Gaeltacht*, or Irish-speaking region, to officially open the new *Áras*, or Community Hall, dedicated to the memory of local republican, Ned McSweeney, who died young of ill health due to physical privations in the Trouble times. Moylan began his opening speech with the words: *'Siúinéir mise*! — I'm a carpenter!', (and he even put the accent on the second syllable, country style, and threw in a 'h' with the 't' in the same manner). And so he was. General Liam Lynch was a draper's clerk in Fermoy. General Seán MacEoin was noted as 'the blacksmith of Ballinalee'. General Michael Collins was a civil servant, a small farmer's son from West Cork. What was it Chesterton said? The shepherds had to turn themselves into rude warriors. At first they were utterly broken down in blood and shame. And then, after years of horror and humiliation, they gained a little and began to conquer, because they did not mind defeat! . . . But they still needed to gain a little more, always that little more!

23

Truce With Violation

It was one of those things that are made, like a china doll, to be broken. Nobody expects otherwise of it, neither the manufacturer nor the child-recipient. Each handles with care and hopes for the best in respect of heterogeneous points of view, and the best can be only the deferring or reducing the extent of eventual and inevitable fracture. The maker hands on the product with gentle misgiving, and goes sturdily in quest of his profit. The child accepts with gentle misgiving, wonders how long it will be before extraneous cause or intrinsic fault will shatter the bauble and, in a fit of senseless repression, throws it on the ground. Only to the child would it have been of real value if she had had sufficient confidence in the manufacture. Nobody really had . . .

But it was not even a china-doll Truce, just papier-mâché to be squeezed in the hand out of all recognition. The implications and even overt threats of further and more intensified war involved in the seemingly interminable negotiations, the gradual breakdown, had maintained the impression for many that hostilities had never ceased. Mr. Shakespeare was getting ready! For the fighting man, therefore, the war had virtually continued. The I.R.A., though thankful for the breather, had one firm conviction

— that it would be resumed actively in time, possibly in two to four weeks. So they followed the only course open to them — they prepared. Training camps, reviews, strict discipline, were the order of the day, with increasing violations of the Truce terms by both sides. For the record, there were the British themselves having violated an honourable truce with the Turks three years or so before. Bashibazooks or Irish Irregulars — what odds!

> The end came abruptly and indeed unexpectedly . . . Had I been asked my opinion beforehand, I should have opposed a cessation of hostilities at this time.
>
> (Liam Deasy, O/C Third Brigade in *Towards Ireland Free*).

> Early in June, 1921, I learned that a movement was on foot to effect a compromise with England. It did not surprise me then to hear that a Truce had been arranged as from July 11th, 1921.
>
> (Dan Breen in *My Fight For Irish Freedom*).

> No Divisional or Brigade officer of the I.R.A. knew anything about the negotiations of the Truce except through the reports appearing in the Daily Press.
>
> (Tom Barry in *Guerilla Days In Ireland*).

With regard to the above quotations, it is disturbing to reflect that they are at variance with corresponding ones as at the end of the previous chapter. To alleviate the confusion, seventy-three years later, one might take solace from Ernie O'Malley's last words in *On Another Man's Wound*: 'Put on the kettle, now, and make the tay, and if they weren't happy, that you may!'.

*   *   *

A Black and Tan was shot dead in Enniskerry, Co. Wicklow, one hour after the cessation of hostilities. One feels regret, even a twinge of remorse, at such an occurrence. A mother's son, I mean to say, and already a non-combatant, walking the street alone, savouring the new sensation of peace. What of the deliberate violation? How does one philosophize about such a deed, even at present, when civilian murder has become commonplace, and the 'Curse of Cain' seemingly ineffectual?

> The Brigade O/C decided, AS A LAST CHANCE, to stage an ambush in the town of Castleisland on the night of the 10th, on a nightly patrol of R.I.C. who were in the habit of parading on the main street each night, which was the only time they emerged from the barrack. They lost two men, but we lost two of our men killed also, and it might have been perhaps as well not to have bothered with it, seeing the Truce was on the following day!
>
> (Séamus O'Connor in *Tomorrow Was Another Day*).

By contrast, a touch of journalistic irony marked the demise of Constable George Duckham, of Millstreet R.I.C. barracks, who was killed at Carriganimma as he was returning from England 'on furlough' after his wedding, promiment in 'his new brown boots', as a senior citizen remembered, while his body was being removed for burial in a local bog. The story appeared in the Carriganimma School History. On Friday, July 8, 1921, a London newspaper ran the caption: *Hostilities in Ireland to Cease at Noon Next Monday.* In the same edition appeared: 'Mr. and Mrs. G. H. Duckham, of Beddington, Croydon, have received a packet of documents belonging to their son, George Duckham, with the intimation that he had been courtmartialled and executed. He belonged to the Royal Irish Contabulary and was on furlough (leave of service) some time ago. Since his return to Ireland, his parents have heard nothing from him, but learned from an indirect source that he had been kidnapped by Sinn Féiners. They still entertain hopes that he may be hidden'. The Carriganimma booklet gives lurid details of the affair, and the reason for and manner of his execution by the I.R.A. while Truce negotiations were already being made public, with the obvious comment that the affair 'became part of local lore afterwards'.

* * *

The acknowledgement by the British of the I.R.A. as the Army of the Republic was a proud occasion. 'Pride goeth before destruction, and a haughty spirit before a fall'. (PROVERBS, 16, 18). It proved a serious pitfall. It lured them into the open. Flashy new uniforms began to come into evidence. No more the trench coats and riding breeches with the slanted 'go-to-hell' pockets. Officers were being continually photographed by the Press at public events. No longer were they the reluctant heroes but swashbuckling socialites. British officers received them on an equal footing and with gentlemanly deference. It was a grave strategic error, though understandable, because British Intelligence decried an advantage while the negotiations were still at a critical stage. They could now estimate the potential of the 'shadow army' and identify some at least of the personnel. Later on this information was put to telling use against the I.R.A. But Cork First Brigade took a realistic view of the situation and Brigadier Seán Hegarty wisely forbade all uniforms, keeping his key men under cover and his brigade under active service conditions. So, British Intelligence turned its attention to the First Brigade. Four men (three officers and a driver) were sent on a secret mission into the heart of Republican territory. They were promptly executed . . .

The Republican policeman on duty in Macroom might never have taken note of the motor car standing before Williams' Hotel but for the fact that it was without a number plate. He put a question to the driver. The saucy reply in an English accent might be something in his line of duty. He reported to the Castle now occupied by Republican forces. Adjutant Charlie Browne, second-in-command during Commandant Dan Corkery's absence in Dublin, came down to investigate . At the bar he found three strangers. One of them he recognized as a 'hard man' from his own prison days in Cork City. (*Note:* in *The Story Of The 7th* Charlie Browne gives a detailed account of Percival's march back to Kinsale, the only one on record, during which he himself was captured, as well as an intimate account of the 'intelligence' methods in the 'Cage' at Victoria Barracks, all of which shows adequate justification for the justice meted out later to his prisoners in Macroom). The Adjutant immediately returned to the Castle and contacted Brigade H.Q. by telephone, and an order was sent out for their arrest. They were found making their way among the townspeople and were taken to the Castle for questioning. They claimed to be on a fishing trip but had no gear to show for it. Moreover they were in civilian clothes and carried concealed weapons. Another report to Cork City brought an immediate and unequivocal reply from the Brigade Council accompanied by a firing squad. These were dangerous men in dangerous times, and hopefully they died understanding. Victoria Barracks, however, refused to understand. They had been pipped and knew it. (*Note:* Brigade Major Montgomery, on his arrival at Victoria — now Collins — Barracks, in January, set out industriously to be 'the man who won the war').

> Perhaps Bernard believed, as did his C/O and Divisional Commander, that the I.R.A. could be defeated; at any rate he certainly set about organizing his 9000-strong brigade on the soundest possible military lines. A special 'Cork City Intelligence' unit was set up in the city, and a stream of orders issued from Bernard's desk to the brigade battalions.
>
> (From *Monty: The Making Of A General*).

A detachment of military arrived in Macroom within two days of the arrest. They had come to look for the men. (*Note:* This incident, noted as 'the final straw' of irritation by Monty's biographer, now enters a state of utter confusion in which this writer suspects Dan 'Sandow' O'Donovan as a sort of

agent provocateur with good intentions). A parley of officers
in the square, near the Castle gates, came to nothing. In the
next two weeks they came several times and each time their
attitude was more menacing. The last time but one they ran
two lorry loads of troops up on to Sleaveen hill overlooking the Castle. The gesture was taken note of, while the
I.R.A. still declined to furnish any information with regard
to the missing men. The next time had to be the last. The
British came in force. A long file of troops resumed position on the wall of the Park, machine-guns were set up in
the Square, and two armoured cars faced the Castle gates.
Above in the little turret the lone sentry, Neil O'Leary, effervescent young returned American, who, like the prisoner
of Chillon, held his ground,

> Until his very steps have left a trace
> Worn as if thy cold pavement were a sod,

pushed out his rifle and resolutely called on the British Army — 'Put your bloody hands up!'. This time the Adjutant
was in no parleying mood. He was prepared. On Sleaveen
Hill, behind the soldiers, was a strong detachment from the
Eighth Battalion. Elements from the Seventh and Sixth were
scattered at various vantage points about the town. The Castle itself was strongly garrisoned. On the roof Mick
O'Sullivan crouched behind his powerful Vickers machine-
gun. The Adjutant marched out. He was covered immediately
by several enemy guns. The Brigade Major advanced to meet
him. Neil O'Leary covered Montgomery. The impasse lasted
just long enough for the Adjutant to deliver his ultimatum.
'Unless your troops are withdrawn within five minutes', he
said, 'my men have orders to open fire !'. He turned on his
heel and not another word was spoken. Their bluff was called. On the roof the gunner had to be physically restrained
by the two Ballyvourney men, Patsy Lynch and Paddy
O'Sullivan, from opening up on them. They literally 'jumped

on him', Patsy said. In the open Square there would have been untold carnage. In the Park the ghostly and troubled shade of Boetius MacEgan, Titular Bishop of Ross, would be obliged once more to survey a bloody conflict such as had not occurred there for more than two and a half centuries, and World War Two would have to be written otherwise. But Ireland would have been spared her darkest hour. The obnoxious term, 'Civil War', would never have been heard, and that most glorious generation in the country's history would have continued to struggle on, side by side, as brothers and compatriots. *Miserabile dictu!*

Now, that was how the story was told to me by the Ballyvourney, Macroom and Kilnamartyra men who were present in the Castle at the time. And this is where the plot thickens — forty years later! Dan 'Sandow' O'Donovan, First Brigade Column Commander for three months after the A.S.U. had arrived in Ballyvourney at the beginning of 1921, never spoke about his exploits, not even to Ernie O'Malley in his note-taking visits to Ballybeg limestone quarry, Buttevant, where he was manager (cf. *The Dark Secret*), except to clarify the position of De Valera with regard to the death of Michael Collins at Béalnabláth. That was in 1960. Subsequent to that, the floodgates apparently opened. He spoke freely to another Corkman, Eoin Neeson (*The Civil War In Ireland*), and to others on record, and especially clarified his own position with regard to the shooting of Colonel Smyth, the R.I.C. Divisional Commissioner in Munster, at the County Club, Cork City. He and Corney O'Sullivan (a personal friend of the present writer's father) were deputed to do the deed. Corney went to his grave a nervous wreck for having killed Smyth. Sandow said that Corney lost his nerve at the very outset, firing wildly all over the place, or, as he put it, 'he couldn't have hit the parish he was born in standing at the chapel door'. Consequently he himself had to kill Smyth out of hand. No doubt he did. What he told his family later in life was that at the Brigade meeting called to deal with Smyth there was so much indecisiveness that Sandow said — 'I'll go myself! I'll do the job!'. He was always decisive. At the Club (*Note:* It still stands at the junction of the Grand Parade and the South Mall) he was able to spot Smyth right away because he wore khaki, was one-handed and had a patch over an eye. What he said was — 'Colonel Smyth, you said to shoot at sight. Now, you are in sight and you are going to be shot!'. Characteristically, what he said about the Macroom affair was — 'We sent out a firing-squad because the Macroom fellows had cold feet!'. Placing one incident against the other produces some conflicting notions. Corney O'Sullivan, seconded to Cork City from Bantry, where he was engineer to the Sixth (Beara) Battalion, had assembled and placed mines as required, in his time. Another report (Connie Neenan in *Survivors*) claimed that two men had gone with Sandow to the County Club, and still another version which I heard stated that Sandow was not present with Corney, but Michael Murphy of the Second Battalion, Cork City. At the same time the Macroom affair has been the most hushed up of any other incident in the Trouble times. Seeing that it was so immediate and deliberate one tends to look for cause. On the surface there seems to be none. This was April, 1922. Truce had long gone through an indeterminate Treaty, and though the country was being progressively evacuated by the British it was still teetering on the edge of renewed conflict, either war with Britain because of the Provisional Government's failure to implement the Treaty, or active measures by Michael Collins against the North, or, what did transpire, Civil War.

Dan 'Sandow' O'Donovan's account to Eoin Neeson, with regard to his dealings with Major Montgomery on the disappearance of his intelligence officers seems highly dramatized and exaggerated, if not simply imaginary. Nigel Hamilton takes it all for granted:

> For the British troops still in the South it was a tense period indeed and the final straw came when, on the eve of evacuation

by the remaining units of the 6th Division, three British officers and a private were kidnapped at Macroom, Co. Cork. One of them was a very popular Lieutenant from the Royal Warwickshire Regiment, H. D. Hendy, who was an Intelligence Officer at Bernard's H.Q. . . . The next day there was a conference between the Staffs of the British and Irish Brigades. Dan Donovan, the I.R.A. Commandant, who had been responsible for pirating the Upnor, and Major B. L. Montgomery were detailed to represent the two sides. Evacuation was temporarily suspended. Bernard wanted to search the area with British troops, but Donovan insisted this might only be done by the I.R.A. — who, according to him, 'knew nothing about the missing men'. Bernard replied: 'As far as I am aware, if a tramp left Ballincollig the news of his arrival in Macroom would be heralded!'. Days of fruitless meetings and I.R.A. searches finally drove Bernard to insist that he be allowed to take out a British Army search party, which he did on 30 April, 1922. By the time the convoy reached the outskirts of Macroom, it was stopped by the I.R.A.; and only last-minute intervention by the parish priest prevented bloodshed. Bernard was evidently in a savage mood, but there was little he could do, and the convoy had to return to Cork. He offered a reward, and on 2 May went out again with a detachment — although the I.R.A. officer refused to go with him this time, fearing a shoot-out . . . By 4 May there was still no news; but Donovan declared his opinion that 'it was done by some of the I.R.A. at Macroom who had temporarily seceded from control'. Nothing could be gained by waiting; and evacuation was recommenced. Some days later the I.R.A. announced that the bodies had been found in a bog, and Bernard went to recover them.

Want to know what I think? I think Sandow shanghaied Monty! *The Cork Examiner* waxed eloquent on the trials of a frail little old man, a Mr. Hendy, who made his way from England and stood leaning on his stick as his son's body was being removed from a bog hole in Clondrohid. Later he wrote a letter to the *London Times* declaring his view that the British Government's intransigence was

24

Treaty With Contention

Lord Longford (Frank Pakenham) writes (1990): 'With regard to your question, I really can't remember who "the famous bodyguard" was, as referred to in my book. It is all such a long time ago!'. This classic work on the Anglo-Irish Treaty of 6 December, 1921, brilliantly entitled *Trial By Ordeal*, was indeed written a long time ago (1935). During the Treaty negotiations, between October and December, the course of events threw up two outstanding characters who qualified for the honour of being Michael Collins' personal bodyguard in London. One was Emmet Dalton, the other Seán MacBride. They were both on hand in case of emergency, which meant that, if the negotiations broke down completely, Collins' life would be at risk. A small plane had been purchased in Canada (*Note:* For particulars see *Green Is My Sky* by Captain A. A. Quigley, and *The Dark Secret*), and kept in reserve, under pretext, at Croydon Airport, London, for the purpose of flying the great man to safety. The propellor is all that remains. So, Lord Longford regrets. It is, indeed, a long time ago. And so, for that matter, is all of History! Is it possible that everyone else is fast forgetting? Is the present writer to be the 'Minstrel Boy' whose 'one sword at least thy right shall guard, one faithful heart shall praise thee',

345

of whom Thomas Moore sang? Hopefully not so! Dalton and MacBride are indicative, and typical, of the 'Split' which followed on the signing of the Treaty, as not even Collins and De Valera were — the regular army man with a country to defend, a duty to perform, and the irregular and intensely idealistic republican. The 'famous bodyguard' phrase, therefore, reduces itself to transcendent and contrary philosophies from which our Civil War emerged.

The Treaty had been signed in December, 1921, and thenceforth the dispute at home had added to the confusion. For Republican thought it was an easy switch from disputing their set point of view with the British to disputing it with all comers, and the accepted form of compulsion was the gun. Moreover, national prestige had been re-established at the Truce. It had been sealed in blood, that ancient and effective sealing agent for castle walls. 'Who wins a wreath', asked Young Irelander James Fintan Lalor, 'that will be green forever!'. Who, indeed, wanted a Crown that would be Red, White and Blue forever! An Oath of Allegiance to an English monarch against twenty-six/thirty-seconds of national prestige as established by the Government of Ireland 'Border' Act of 1920, the land annuities to go out of the country, and pensions at home for the loyalist R.I.C. and the Black and Tans! Then the 'Staters' came. In Ballymakeera —

We bombed them out of Norrie's, and we bombed them out
    of Kate's,
And we gave them who-began-it with Battalion Number
    Eight.

But we had no heart in the fight, though, to quote our Vice-Commandant, Paddy Donagh Owen O'Sullivan, against our accusers, 'We didn't fight for fun!'; and we who had said our Rosary kneeling on kitchen flagstones facing towards the church, when it was too dangerous to go to Mass, were mindful of the moral issues as expressed by the bishops. So we laid down our arms. Among our mountains we had felt

secure, but we were sadly disillusioned. Only in the Eternal
Hills can there be ultimate security, in the Divine safekeep-
ing, in the pocket, so to speak, of the Almighty. Many of
us went into necessary, and often permanent, exile and wept
our tears by the rivers of Babylon, remembering Sion. Many
others, like Paddy Cronin, the Bard of the Roughty, had to
lead an outlaw's troubled life into more propitious times . . .

THE OUTLAW

(By Paddy Cronin).

The song of the skylark is blithesome and gay,
The cuckoo is calling to herald the May;
My heart it is bursting with passion and pride
As outlawed, undaunted, the moorland I ride.

The 'Shoneen' and 'Stater' are lords of the land,
The Church, as placator, has taken her stand;
My country partitioned, the Saxon o'erjoyed,
As outlawed, undaunted, the moorland I ride.

With strife and contention the island is fraught,
The prisons are bursting with men of my thought;
My comrades deserted, my gun now a-hide,
As outlawed, undaunted, the moorland I ride.

The Vale of the Roughty lies smiling below,
That sweet fairy-dell where the marigolds grow;
My love is repining to make her my bride,
As outlawed, undaunted, the moorland I ride.

And then the C.I.D. men came! And the Broy 'Harriers'! . . .

We are a logical people here in Múscraí Uí Fhloinn,
Muskerry of the O'Flynns, logical and consistent. For very
many years, many centuries in fact, we have been rising
logically and consistently against illogical and inconsistent
oppression. YOU CAME TO US. Under what guise we do not
ask. Nor even do we ask — Who sent you?, because it is
an unwritten law that anyone and everyone who comes to

us with hostile intent is an enemy to us and to our way of life. But now that you have been and gone, like the others, you may hear coming to you over the intervening distance and the years, whispering in the soft, mountainy accents of the South West, insistent and prevailing as the wind, more in sorrow than in anger, more in puzzlement than in censure, the question that never expects an answer because there never is any: 'Wisha, what brought you at all!'.

APPENDIX A.

Synoptics and Antithetics

1. Principles Of Freedom: (Terence MacSwiney . . . U.S.A., 1921).

This brilliant book comes within the ambit of the present work for the reason that it is a philosophical extension of 'Sinn Féin', but in a manner that Sinn Féin, its initiators, exponents and military strategists could never have expressed. Sinn Féin is never mentioned in the text, but as early as 1912 MacSwiney had coined the phrase, 'The War of Independence', while at the same time assuring his readers that 'Home Rule is likely to come' and disparaging the expediency of its acceptance. This is a medium-sized book of 50,000 words, in nineteen chapters, each divided into sections, written originally as a series of articles for *Irish Freedom* (Seán MacDermott's fortnightly review which took a line through Wolfe Tone in its stand for an Irish Republic) between 1911-1912. The book upholds the cause of Irish freedom in a manner never before expressed and never since equalled, all based on an idealism which seems too much for any living man except himself. In Brixton Prison in September, 1920, a month before his death from hunger-strike, he wrote a foreword for the American publication which appeared in January, 1921, the Irish edition coming during the Truce in July. In general Terence MacSwiney, a gentle, upright and saintly man, takes his philosophy from the world's greatest all-time philosophies superimposed on the Christian ethos. He saw a beautiful world of beautiful people (beware of the word 'Utopia!') in which everything was beautiful, except the 'Enemy' who could also be beautiful if he wanted to and real separation from whom would lead to a positive, counter-balanced unity, while the 'Empire' was a dreadful monster from outer space. * * * Not an easy book to read today when serious reading and study have become grossly diluted and the reaction of Seán Citizen, who might deign to take it up, would range from 'How do you do that!' to 'What the hell is he talking about?'. Reminiscent of latter-day Russian dissidents against Communism, his Impossible Dream is based on the theory that Patriotism is a virtue which does not destroy the better feelings but rather calls them forth and gives them wider play to the point where not all the armies of all the world, as he said, could curb the spirit of one true man; and Ireland's ultimate frontier was 'the secret power of the (Irish) language', far beyond 'the magic of her encircling seas'. Poor Terry!

2. *The Path To Freedom:* (Michael Collins . . . Talbot Press, 1922).

First published in the Autumn of 1922, shortly after the death of Collins, by Talbot Press of Dublin and reissued in 1968 by Mercier Press of Cork, this little book presents the thought of the 'Big Fellow' at the most critical and, indeed, the final period of his life — March to August, 1922. The introductory 'Notes by General Michael Collins, August, 1922', of 5,500 words, written in the first week of August, at a time when 'a new page of Irish history is beginning', gives his argument in favour of the Treaty, not only in its own context but in the overall context of Irish national endeavour over the centuries and, at the same time, condemns the intransigence of 'Mr.' de Valera. The words, probably intended as a Dáil speech, blazon a desperate appeal to the people of Ireland, 'the whole people, of every class, creed and outlook', to face realities and move forward towards 'our true goal — a Gaelic Ireland'. The introduction is followed by ten articles or essays, probably meant for publication in the Press (the *New York American,* according to Béaslaí. Also cf. Hayden Talbot, pp. 19, 154). a) 'Advance and Use Our Liberties': This is a plain statement on the signing of the Treaty, which he did not do 'under duress' but as a positive step in the fight for ultimate freedom which would only be achieved by uniting all Irishmen in the work of making Ireland a positive entity in the family of nations, and, in the context, he saw the Truce of July, 1921, as a missed opportunity in December, 1920. b) 'Alternative to the Treaty': De Valera's 'Document No. 2' was 'too loose' and its terms were merely a vague abstraction of the actual terms of the Treaty itself, and, consequently, counter-productive. c) 'The Proof of Success': The Fenian uprising of 1867 culminated in the fires of Easter Week, 1916, within which period Home Rule was 'the dangerous idea of seeking freedom by means of some form of political weapon', as against the long-standing English notion of what is today being termed 'ethnic cleansing'. d) 'Four Historic Years': The opportunity of a World War preoccupying the old enemy, a symbolic uprising in the centre, and a telling political upset at the end made 1914-1918 a very significant period in Irish History. e) 'Collapse of the Terror': The breakdown of British rule in Ireland was characterized, from 1918 to 1921, by our struggle to govern ourselves and 'the British determination to prevent us' from doing so. f) 'Partition Act's Failure': The Government of Ireland Act (1920), instead of solving the Irish problem, merely highlighted 'the unhappy fate of the North-East', which 'is neither English nor Irish'. g) 'Why Britain sought Irish Peace': He said — 'Peace had become necessary because it was essential for the British to put themselves right with the world', and, seeing that we had not the advantage of distance, as Canada had, the Treaty was our best effort, and 'it is now only fratricidal strife which can prevent us from making the Gaelic Ireland, which is our goal'. h) 'Distinctive Culture': The continuance of Ireland as a nation from before even Roman times in Britain was due to 'the democratic basis of its economic system and the aristocracy of its culture'. This the English almost succeeded in destroying. i) 'Building up Ireland': This essay is a work-scheme for the future and, while allowing that a country's greatest treasure is its people, nevertheless Collins puts forward an elaborate, foolproof plan for the working of all our natural resources. j) 'Freedom Within Grasp': Up to the time of Catholic Emancipation Ireland was still a distinctive Gaelic nation. From then on, through various movements to Home Rule, we were the 'beggars of the rich neighbours who had robbed us', and, despite the best efforts of Sinn Féin, the G.A.A. and the Gaelic League, 'are not even we, who are proudly calling ourselves Gaels, little more than imitation Englishmen?'   *   *   *   Thirty-three thousand words is a rather small book but it contains a lot of direct speech from Ireland's most outstanding patriot. Brilliant assessment or megalomania is the choice. In a recent review of my book, *The Dark Secret of Béalnabláth*, the journalist reviewer (T.P. O'Mahony in the *Cork Examiner*) accused me of side-tracking, for the sake of an inferior objective, 'the legacy of Michael Collins'. In fact Collins foresaw an Irish-speaking Ireland, the 'splendid people' (his phrase!), with all natural resources developed to the fullest extent by a people proud of their past history and the glories of a separate cultural development. In retrospect he was wrong. His legacy is nowhere in evidence today.

3. *Michael Collins' Own Story:* (Hayden Talbot . . . Hutchinson & Co., 1923).

The title is misleading. This is not a biography of Michael Collins, still less an autobiography. A brief sketch of his personal life appears in Chapter Two, irrelevant as may be, in a medium-sized book (22 chapters, 85,000 words) which deals essentially with the turbulent affairs of the country forever, and the turbulent views and contrary notions from the signing of the Anglo-Irish Treaty (6 December, 1921) to the death of Collins (22 August, 1922), in which an unbelievable amount of the great man's time (the last interview was in July, 1922) was given over to this pushy journalist-representative in London of the Hearst newspaper corporation of America. In regular journalistic style it contains many interviews with other people (Eoin MacNeill, Arthur Griffith, Mrs. Francis Sheehy-Skeffington, Erskine Childers, Seán McGarry, Desmond FitzGerald) and is, in fact, a compendium of articles written by Talbot himself, incidentally, and all too frequently, an extension of the material written by Collins himself apparently for publication (cf. previous book) in the public press. The largest chapter (Chapter Twenty-One) is merely an aggregate of replies from twenty-three important people to the question, 'Under the terms of the Treaty, what does the future hold in store for Ireland?'. And the final chapter, 'Addendum', is merely a newspaper row with regard to the authenticity of the script as it appeared in print, and from which Talbot exonerates himself very decisively.   * * *   Tim Pat Coogan (*Michael Collins: A Biography*) gives the publication year as 1932. Internal evidence (including an advertising blurb at the back) makes it 1923, correctly within its chronological context. The dates are historically significant. Talbot himself is chronologically chaotic, making for difficulty of grip in the reading, his unsolicited and contrary views on

Republican idealism strangely emotional, his interpretative spelling vile, and his timing of the death of Collins in error, but he does provide a thoughtful observation which should be helpful — 'They are a simple people, the Irish. They must have an object of devotion'!. To those who would question my Prologue to *The Dark Secret of Béalnabláth* ('He [Collins] did not just fight the Civil War — he invented it!'), I would say — Read Hayden Talbot!

4. My Fight For Irish Freedom: (Dan Breen . . . Talbot Press, 1924).

Tipperary stalwart, Dan Breen, began writing his memoirs in March, 1922, in the U.S.A. He completed the work after the cessation of hostilities in the Civil War. An introduction was penned by Joseph McGarrity, proprietor of the *Irish Press* in Philadelphia, founder member of 'Clan na Gael' and the 'Friends of Irish Freedom'. Talbot Press reprinted in 1946. Dan Nolan of Tralee (Anvil Books) produced an expanded and re-edited version in 1964, with a good deal of extraneous material (running to 22,000 words, an additional one-third of the original). This latter edition was translated into Gaelic in 1972 by Séamas Daltún, chief translator at Leinster House, and produced by Government Publications. It was called *Ag Troid Ar Son Na Saoirse*, but retained the author's name in English.   *   *   *   In my childhood there was only 'Dan Breen's Book'. We became familiar with what was in effect an alternative title to the above. In fact the brown board cover had embossed on it a sun-burst with the generally accepted title, *Dan Breen's Book*, holding pride of place in the centre, with the alternative title on the spine. (*Note:* There is only one known copy with the original cover still intact. It is held in trust by the present writer for Talbot Press). I have no idea how this book might rate in the modern eviscerated context of 'best-sellers' and 'world best-sellers', but it was unique and will remain so. During the World War Two years in Maynooth, a student friend of mine from Tipperary said — 'Dan Breen couldn't have written it because he is almost illiterate!'. In 1960 I found the book (the 1946 edition) being avidly read in Africa by a new generation of black rebels against the British Empire. To hold that the Anvil Press edition (1964) was still 'Dan Breen's Book' would be somewhat misleading.

Bowdlerizing is essentially a dirty business. To the extent that the original was bowdlerized is minimal, extending as it does only to the resetting of a few phrases and the expurgating of a few ideas, but the extra clutter, despite being further interviews with the man himself, the inclusion of text-book history by a 'ghost writer' and barely related documentation, destroys the unique freshness, the lyrical simplicity and rhythm, of the original. Further, the exclusion of Joe McGarrity's 'Introduction' of 1924 is a mystery. The famous Irish-American, who followed the Republican ideal when the 'Clan' split in America and the Irish split at home on the point of Eamon de Valera or Michael Collins, states the objective so succinctly that it seems a *sine qua non*. The only trace remaining of that prologue is the suggestion that the book ought to be translated into the native language, a project carried through half a century later, but one regrets the poignancy of such paragraphs as — 'Let us hope that some competent Gaelic scholar will translate the story into the language of Ireland's ancient champions whom she had gathered to her bosom centuries before this gallant son of Tipperary was ready to render to his beloved country the splendid services he has so willingly given'; and the immediacy of such phrases from the text itself as, 'By this time (1918) we had been getting a fair supply of arms and ammunition by channels which may not yet be disclosed'! *Esto perpetua*!

5. Michael Collins And The Making Of A New Ireland: (Piaras
   Béaslaí . . . Phoenix Publishing Co., 1926).
This massive work comprises 230,000 words in two volumes. Originally conceived as a politically neutral but definitive biography of Michael Collins, incorporating the great revolutionary's life story from birth to death, it emerges as an academic agglomeration of historical and quasi-historical minutiae with Collins himself as an intermittent and ever-recurring theme. General Béaslaí (or 'Beasley', according to Hayden Talbot and Lord Longford) departed politics and the army for the purpose of giving all his time to this work in an unbiased and factual manner, and in the process 'carried charity very far'. Less than 60% of the text (25 out of 41 chapters) has to do with the matter of the present work, the 'Black-and-Tan' period of Irish History. The introductory study, going deep

into the movements of the previous century, showed Collins as 'a great reaper where others had sown'.   *   *   *   We need to be grateful for Béaslaí's work and to realize that it was done at a difficult time. I read it first in 1940 and again in 1990. After half a century I was intrigued to find myself still toying with an alternative title, *Piaras Béaslaí And The Making Of A New Ireland*. He felt deeply for the sensibilities of ordinary English folk and wished them to understand that they really had no business in 'our country' and that 'all we demanded was to be left alone'. In his treatment of Eamon de Valera and Erskine Childers he failed to carry charity very far, leaning particularly on Arthur Griffith's 'damned Englishman' theme with regard to the latter. And Béaslaí himself was an Englishman until the age of twenty-three! *A propos:* 'A biography should be judged by its content, not by its size!'(Victor Frankl).

6. *Peace By Ordeal:*   (Frank Pakenham . . . 1935).

'Unfinished conquest', the title of Section 2, Part 1, is unsurpassed as the briefest of phrases to express the longest effort at domination, by one country of another, the world has known, the overpowering of Ireland by England. The culmination of that persistent historical phenomenon is almost equally pithy and decisive in Part 2, Section 1 ('The Way of Entreaty'), Section 2 ('The Way Of Violence'), Section 3 ('The Black-and-Tans'), and Section 4 ('Peace With Honour'). Part 3 (the major part) deals with the specific purpose of the book, the matter of the new Treaty between the two countries as the culmination of weighty negotiations in the Autumn and Winter of 1921. Part 4 covers the circumstances of the Anglo-Irish Treaty signing, on 6 December, 1921, and the chaotic and tragic subsequent events are summed up kindly and compassionately as follows, rather than by the reprehensible term, 'Civil War': 'Before, however, the later more heart-rending phases of the war were reached, three out of the four great figures of the revolution (Cathal Brugha, Arthur Griffith and Michael Collins) had fallen, and with them Erskine Childers, whose name, for twenty years a household word in England, the whole world seemed conspiring these days to defile'.   *   *   *   I like to think that his title (reminiscent of medieval 'trial by ordeal', when proof or persuasion failed and physical torture by fire ensued) implied that British political heresy with regard to this country had to have a final test in the furnace of a people's passion rather than the sacrificial and futile burning of the protagonists on all sides. In a letter to the present writer in 1990, Mr. Frank Pakenham (Lord Longford) wrote — 'I really can't remember . . . It is all such a long time ago!' This was in answer to the question as to whom he was referring, Seán MacBride or Emmet Dalton, as 'the famous bodyguard' of Michael Collins during the Treaty negotiations in London. Perhaps this is the best way to sum up the matter of his classic work — Such a long time ago!

7. Green Rushes: (Maurice Walsh . . . W. & R. Chambers, Edinburgh, 1935).

This is undoubtedly the prettiest piece of writing out of the Black-and-Tan War period, an' itself a novel no less, as the author might say. Part One, entitled 'Then Came The Captain's Daughter', takes up one-third of the book and the Troubles start and finish there. This is what concerns us, and a deeply touching account of a 'Flying Column', from the point where an ambush went wrong through others that went right up to the Truce with England in mid-July, 1921. There are, of course, recognizable features from the reality of the time, such as the capture while salmon fishing of Captain Archibald MacDonald, of the Seaforth Highlanders, and his imprisonment in the hills, reminiscent of Liam Lynch's capture of General Lucas near Fermoy. The redoubtable Column Commander, Hugh Forbes, is obviously based on Tom Barry. Séamas Robinson's famous bullet-holed bowler hat rests on the head of a character named Matt Tobin, 'Matt the Thresher', likewise from Tipperary, fighting with the Column in Kerry. And so on. The remainder of the book is taken up with the dramatic and romantic entanglements of protagonists and mutual enemies, where foe commendably becomes friend, in a 'happy ending' belied by, but surviving, the Civil War, the title of Part One being a line from a well-known romantic ballad of Ninety-Eight.   * * *   The present writer had the extraordinary experience of sitting in a ramshackle picture house in West Africa, amidst a sea of wondering black faces, and hearing Barry Fitzgerald 'hupping' his old horse with *Alley-vous, Napoleon!*. The film was, of course, *The Quiet Man* (in French) and the year was 1960. It may not be generally known that Ireland's most famous movie (1952) was based on Maurice Walsh's *Green Rushes*, with Part Three, entitled 'The Quiet Man', as the basic theme, and the other sections supplying various items of material. The local topography is teased out in the book. 'Castletown' is Castleisland, in the County Kerry. The world-renowned novelist and story-teller came from Ballydonoghue, northwards near Listowel. Having worked for the British Civil Service, and later for the Irish Free State, his *mens sana in corpore sano* approach, with the great outdoors as a revolving stage, even to the Tan War and subsequent events, has placed him deservedly on a par with John Buchan and Rider Haggard as one of the all-time greats of the *genre*. His feel for Ireland's 'Troubles' is patriotic but glossy, his inaccuracy — or carelessness — with regard to technical details relative to such things as tommy-guns and Crossley tenders no more than usual for the time. His die-hard Republican, Mickeen Oge Flynn, 'celibate by inclination, half priest by training', was based on John Stack, from Ballyconry, while 'Paddy Bawn Enright, ex-prize fighter, known as "The Quiet Man" . . .', was John McElligott of Listowel, while the famous fist-fight (expanded so outrageously in the John Ford film and at which the blacks of Bathurst laughed inordinately, though at nothing else) did indeed happen locally as recorded.

8. *On Another Man's Wound:* (Ernie O'Malley . . . Rich & Cowan, London, 1936).

O'Malley comes in sideways, as it were, to the Irish 'Troubles', and, while his intense and very personal form of complicity in 'the scrap' (his expression) is never clearly stated, he is positively the most die-hard of all die-hard Republicans as if the tragic political occurrences of the time were designed especially for his peculiar *persona*. 'This is not a history', he says, and that is the truth, the whole truth and nothing but. The unfolding of his young life and starry-eyed early existence, against the backdrop of a rapidly changing Ireland, set lyrically and sometimes tediously in the context of the flora, fauna, geography and social history, with his own life freely offered as the price of admission, places the red-headed, upper middle class, Ernie O'Malley, somewhere in the realm of Cúchulainn, Dermot O'Duibhne, Turlough , the grandson of Brian Boru and others of that ilk, through Robert Emmet to the self-immolating intellectuals of 1916. The book is divided into three large, larger and largest sections dramatically entitled FLAMBOYANT, GOTHIC, and ROMANESQUE, anachronistically but historically correct:

a) FLAMBOYANT: This part deals briefly with his youth, through an accidental and unpremeditated association with the Easter Insurrection, to his joining the Irish Volunteers a year or so later. The title of the section is justified in the Introduction with regard to his family's 'disturbance by certain flaring of outside events'.

b) GOTHIC: Sinister and eventually horrifying in the extreme, the history of Ireland, from the Spring of 1918 to the Autumn of 1920, is viewed as the unfolding of age-long hatred between two neighbouring countries, one intent on prolonged conquest for no clear reason, the other equally intent on resisting now or never for the sake of an ancient and proud heritage the denial of which would be death in any form.

c) ROMANESQUE: Glorious and triumphant, the final six months of the struggle, through the Winter of 1920 to the Truce of 1921, shows a nation at war with no great sense of direction but playing heart-brokenly with a bare chance of ultimate success where others before them had failed so miserably.   * * *   This book could not be re-entitled as 'Ernie O'Malley and the Making of a New Ireland', but could quite conceivably be seen (in Griffith's phrase for Collins) as 'Ernie O'Malley, the Man Who Won The War'. Trouble-shooter for G.H.Q., Captain O'Malley roamed the countryside apparently at will, reckless, lonely, disconsolate, firing at will, inciting to fight where the spirit was willing and the flesh weak, to G.H.Q. a useful nuisance, to the fighting Corkmen (as I remember in Ballyvourney) 'a bit of a shit who talked too much', a member of every group while belonging to none, exulting in the fray, trying laughter and literature equally for the sake of sound, the quintessential Irishman, personification of the civil war to come which he indirectly predicts by showing the essential distinction between the pundits in Dublin, playing at paper-weights and politics, and the hard-grained countrymen of the South and

West who were gradually forming themselves into a national army of resistance and who, given sufficient weaponry, were firmly convinced that 'we could bate them into the sea'.

A book with a plan, but lacking a chronology, this is probably the most successful literary effort of the period denoted in Irish History as the 'War of Independence'. Undoubtedly it gave Ernest Hemingway the idea for his classic novel on the Spanish Civil War, *For Whom The Bell Tolls*, and the similarities run much further and deeper than the titles. 'The sardonic old Irish proverb, "Is furasta codhladh ar chneá duine eile", means "It is easy to sleep on another man's wound". Hemingway's title was also a proverb: "Ask not for whom the bell tolls — it tolls for thee!" ' (From *The Dark Secret*). A literary comparison, even in style, would be a delightful exercise for one who had the time. 'A bloody nuisance of a red-headed bastard' is how O'Malley self-indulgently told himself that the boys probably regarded him as, which is how Hemingway saw himself to the point of self-destruction. Two Ernies with but a single theme, only O'Malley came first.

O'Malley's book is extremely quotable and certain references need some attention . . . 'Mulcahy never said anything stronger than bloody; he did not smoke or drink. Cathal Brugha neither cursed, smoked nor drank. Collins was an adept at all three' . . . 'The hills stretching towards West Cork were naked as fear and the desolate stretch of them as wide as hunger' . . . ' "What the hell was I doing this for?", I often asked myself' . . . 'Always for me there was the relish of a phrase' . . . 'County Cork had no great love for G.H.Q. officers' . . . 'I resented their (Mulcahy and Collins) jokes at the expense of the Long Fellow' . . . 'G.H.Q. issued general instructions, but our operations were our own'. Without the benefit of a first edition any nit-picking of print errors may be necessary or not. It is hard to say. 'Dunboyne', in place of Dunboy, is historically misleading. 'Erewonian', for Samuel Butler's 'Erewhonian', is mere erudition today. Misquoting of episodes garnished in transit (which the present writer got from the original authors, as Seán Moylan's 'land-mine' and Patsy Burrick's 'hill tribes') is part and parcel of the general writer's agony. However, 'the soldier's word', accompanied by a dash, needs to be laid away forever seeing that it has become, through familiarity with American television, the common cant of respectable people, clergy, children, and one nun from Galway. On all military 'bumph' emanating from imperial activities in India and South Africa, around the end of the last century, when British soldiers were forbidden to 'fraternize' with native women, army personnel put on such a charge were always referred to by the duty officer as 'F.U.C.K' — 'Found Under Carnal Knowledge'. My condolences, Mr. O'Malley!

9. The Irish Republic: (Dorothy Macardle . . . Gollancz Ltd., London, 1937).

If 'massive work' suits Béaslaí perhaps 'colossal' would be the apt term for Miss Macardle's 350,000 words. Under the title the lady speaks for herself. After such a labour of love she deserves to. What she says is: 'A documented chronicle of the Anglo-Irish conflict and the partitioning of Ireland, with a detailed account of the period 1916-1923'. There is, however, a large introductory historical pastiche which endeavours to show that the republic idea may have existed in this country, as a sort of dream sequence, from the days of Norman King William Rufus (in the Chestertonian sense of 'they were republicans, like all simple and primitive people'), expressed in real terms by Wolfe Tone during the French Revolution, and put into positive action at the founding of the Irish Volunteers in 1913.   *   *   *   Unfortunately the dream sequence is what has endured, and the historical pastiche is, in fact, a vast fallacious syllogism without a logical conclusion. Macardle's so obvious response to Béaslaí could have been entitled: *De Valera And The Making Of A New Ireland*. The catch comes in 'PART XIV' (comprising four chapters), under the general heading of 'The Republic Defeated', as a presumptive conclusion to the Civil War in May, 1923, while the concluding 'PART XV' would appear to be an indeterminate, though historic and necessary, mish-mash of material not clearly related to the title of the book and to the original theme. As in Béaslaí's work, trivial details abound with more emotive content than is proper in any history so called. In 1924 Dorothy Macardle had published *Tragedies Of Kerry*. Two introductory pages in this Irish Freedom Press pamphlet-sized publication are designed to show that the Free State Army in Kerry were 'worse than the Black and Tans'. The rest is, indeed, composed of tragedies of Kerry during the Civil War, the first noted being just five days after the death of Michael Collins. For a restricted clientele, and latterly a reprehensible point of view, the booklet is still in publication, being now in its fourteenth edition. Protestant daughter of a knighted beer-baron, Dorothy Macardle seems an unlikely candidate for die-hard republicanism, but such was the case, which she proved by bravely enduring her own share during the 'Troubles'. It is a pity that she did not trouble to balance one patent 'Terror' against the other, in context, because the Kingdom of Kerry, even still, seems to know all about the 'Tragedies' but relatively little about the 'Tans'!

10. The Big Fellow: (Frank O'Connor . . . U.S.A., 1937).
Parts One and Two only are relevant to the present work, Part Three dealing with the course of events from the opening of the Treaty negotiations in London to the death of Michael Collins. 'A labour of love' O'Connor called the book in his preface to the revised 1965 edition by Clonmore and Reynolds Ltd. The Poolbeg edition (1979) has on its cover the ill-advised logotype of a 'tommy-gun' wrapped in the Irish tricolour. The famous American Thompson sub-machine-gun has, through mis-directed propaganda, become associated with the Irish 'Troubles', particularly the I.R.A., just as it was symptomatic of American hoodlumism during the years of 'Prohibition' in the early 'Twenties', despite the fact that the first model to bear the name of the inventor (American Col. J. T. Thompson) appeared only in 1921. Because of its failure in popularity over there, a few of the models found their way into this country in the early stages of the Civil War in 1922. A further interesting fact is the manner in which 'FRANK O'CONNOR' tops even 'THE BIG FELLOW' himself in Poolbeg's final cover in 1986. At 75,000 words this is just a medium-sized book, and, as it follows the course of the War of Independence, rather maximizes the role of Collins in Dublin to the detriment of all others, particularly the great-hearted men of the south-country regions. In the process he freely paraphrases Béaslaí (including the irritating affectation of dashes and blank capital letters in place of the names of some people involved on both sides, which may have had reason in 1925 but not in 1936), borrows from Macardle despite his

political *volte-face*, and includes some anecdotes of his own which must have been vicariously gleaned from other participants, as O'Connor (then known as Michael O'Donovan of Cork City) was only eighteen when he first appeared on the Republican side at the start of the Civil War.   * * *   In reviewing a writer of the stature of Frank O'Connor I find myself in the uneasy role of *Arbiter Elegentiarum*. The late Dr. Leon Ó Broin, himself an historian of note, in the *Irish Press* review of the 1979 edition, wrote that O'Connor's was 'far and away the best biography of Collins so far written'. Extremely doubtful, I should think. Robert Kee had said approximately the same thing, three years previously, about Margery Forester's Pygmalion-wise worship of an ivory statue! Contrariwise, my preference would be Leon Ó Broin's own job of work for *Gill's Irish Lives*, already on the stocks in 1979. However one might regard O'Connor, as Janus-faced turncoat ('Tadhg a' Dá Thaobh', in the Irish), or merely neophyte Republican belatedly worshipping at the shrine, his contribution to the cause of Irish History is rather negligible. He declares that he originally meant to write a novel on the theme. Unwittingly he seems to have done so, as did Desmond Ryan and Francis Carty a few years before and in the process (cf. *The Dark Secret*, Appendix A) contributed much to the prevailing confusion with regard to the death of Michael Collins at Béalnabláth:

> Some grief shows much of love,
> But much of grief shows still some want of wit.
> (Lady Capulet).

11. Guerilla Days In Ireland: (Commandant-General Tom Barry . . . Irish Press Ltd., Dublin, 1949).
'This policy (guerilla tactics) had prevented British authority from functioning in Ireland, laid its administration in ruins, driven out or under cover the British minions, necessitated a large and costly army of occupation, humiliated British military power, caused the name of Britain to stink in the nostrils of all decent peoples, and inflicted sufficient casualties on their soldiers, Auxiliaries and Black and Tans to seriously disturb a Government finding it difficult to supply reinforcements'. That's the world-famous Tom Barry's war

in a nutshell, deposited on the second to last page of a ninety-thousand word book. If O'Malley's is the most literary effort, Barry's is the most military. From first to last it is redolent of struggle and strife, his own personal contribution being enough 'to seriously disturb a Government', even the British, and his field of influence, broadly referred to as 'Macroom', was specifically excluded from the preliminary Truce negotiations in 1921. His battles read like Napoleon's in his heyday. His book became a military textbook throughout the world. His fame stands with the great guerrilla (my spelling, not his!) leaders of history. If Collins may be arbitrarily referred to as 'The Man Who Won The War' (cf. Professor T. Ryle Dwyer's sub-title), then it is likely that there would have been no War to win if Barry hadn't happened along at the right moment. A textbook ambush, like Kilmichael, and a textbook battle (not an ambush!), like Crossbarry, textbook errors, as he freely admitted he made, textbook planning, at which he was adept, novel-like interpretations of fear, love, hate and human suffering, all make for a book of peculiar fascination that must be personally read to be believed. This reviewer is left with mere criticism as an incentive to study.   * * *   I saw Tom Barry only once. I walked down 'Pana' (Corkonian for Patrick Street). He walked up. I caught his eye ten paces away. His appearance was quite familiar from photographs. The crowd scene was average. He was neat and smart, average height, hat and raincoat (I would like to say, 'snap-brim hat and grubby trench-coat', but I couldn't lie), hands in pockets, waiting — hoping, possibly — to be recognized. He acknowledged my recognition with a flash of the protruding eyes. He was grateful for it. 'Hello, Tom!' . . . 'Father!'. We were passing Danny Hobbs' 'Man's Shop'. He lived over beyond in a flat system above Woodford Bourne's, with his wife, Leslie, and had just stepped into the street, by far the most important man there, completely unnoticed; but I had achieved an ambition of sorts — I had suddenly become an honorary member of the most famous 'Flying Column' of all time!

About his book. Like O'Malley, he deliberately stated that he would not be retrospective and fall into the trap of anticipating the Civil War. Like O'Malley, he failed. And he did worse. He jumped the gun by trying to explain away ('kill the canard', he said) the death of Michael Collins, and gaffed outrageously (cf.

The Dark Secret of Béalnabláth). His megalomania is equally outrageous, as witness his plan for the conquest of Ireland in a sort of geometric progression through Bandon, Cork and the country at large, to Dublin, with the incidental accumulation of arms as the obvious necessity of means. 'A distinct possibility', he said, and one is almost convinced; but he landed in a Cork hospital bed while the city burned and the bishop fulminated, the pathos of the situation being offset by the thought that 'Curfew of the Irish people by a gang of foreign hooligans was to us a humiliating reality'. He details futile operations and plans that did not work, while he moralizes about the necessity for the execution of spies, all to the extent that one wonders if he really was the man for the job — but he was! His shrewd estimate of men and women runs the whole gamut right up to the Big Fellow himself, and his heavily implied indictment of G.H.Q. in Dublin, just like O'Malley, gives one an eerie premonition of civil war to come. When it did come he showed that he had not forgotten his plan for the reconquest of Ireland. He led an armed column a long way towards the gates of the metropolis, before being stopped, just like the equally flamboyant General Jeb Stuart and his cavalry in the American Civil War. Barry, like Stuart, has brought more than a touch of romance to the eternal monotony and tragedy of historical warfare. Unlike so many others of his time and avocation (e.g. Ernie O'Malley, P. S. O'Hegarty, Seán O'Faoláin, Mick O'Sullivan, Michael Collins, Frank Busteed and many others) General Tom Barry favoured the Church in the worst of circumstances, and retained his sense of the fitness of things to the end.

12. The Four Glorious Years: (David Hogan . . . Irish Press, Dublin, 1953).

'It was a remarkable time, one that is experienced but seldom by a nation . . .'. Thus the publishers, and they probably never spoke a truer word. However, 'It is no more than one man's story . . .', seems to underrate the power of this book in laying bare the soul of Ireland during those four glorious years and before and after. There are sixty-seven chapters, which seems exhorbitant, but when one sees them as originally serialized in a national newspaper, all becomes clear. In fact, each appears as a separate episode in the country's history, all carefully correlated and orchestrated, and so expertly written that one gets the impression of a collection of short stories, one of which (Chapter 22, entitled 'Match-Making') would have made a prize-winning entry in any literary competition. At the same time this book is probably one of the most comprehensive, and certainly the most genuine and credible, histories of that vital period, 1917-1921. Finally, 'the extraordinarily moving Epilogue', with its Fourth-Gospel-type peroration, could have been better done without, but this is essentially hindsight, even for a committed Republican.   * * *   And the antithetic to end all antithetics, David Hogan was not David Hogan. He was, indeed, Frank Gallagher, Cork-born compiler, with Erskine Childers, of *The Irish Republican Bulletin*, propagandist newspaper of Sinn Féin, Dáil Éireann and the Irish Republican Army until the 'Split' in the Spring of 1922 (Macardle, p. 391, says December, 1921). As a young lad he had joined the staff of the *Cork Free Press* in 1913, under its proprietor, William O'Brien, M.P., and five years later was given the onerous task, while still only twenty, of travelling to London to inform the old man, at his rooms in the headquarters of the 'All For Ireland League', that it was the considered opinion of his staff in Cork that the old days had gone forever and that Sinn Féin was now and for the future the all-for-Ireland league. Indicative of the confused and still debatable issues of the time is his attitude towards the clergy. He saw them in the main as patriotic and long-suffering, in continual danger of death from the forces of occupation, always supportive of the movement even at great risk, losing their lives on occasion. This attitude is totally at variance with the bitter anti-clericalism of Ernie O'Malley and Séamas Ó Maoileoin, and to a lesser extent of Todd Andrews, while all of these great men, in about equal parts, subscribed to the dictum of the Duke of Wellington: 'Men who are nice about religion have no business to be soldiers!'. Frank Gallagher became the first editor of the *Irish Press* when it was founded by De Valera in 1931. Why, you ask, did a man so well known use a pseudonym on the publication of his book in 1953? And, you reply, because it was his 'alias' during the Troubles. No, in fact. During the Troubles he was 'Henry O'Neill'. It probably was for legal reasons. Where Piaras Béaslaí (followed by Frank O'Connor and others) used irritating blanks and even more irritating initials, thus causing

problems for future students, David Hogan goes blithely onwards
telling every tale, quoting every name. Which brings up the question of journalism and history, more specifically, when is a journalist a historian, or vice versa. An outstanding journalist like
Gallagher, who fought on the streets of Dublin against trained
soldiers of the king, then dashed back to his office and staff to
rush out the next issue of the 'Bulletin', is entitled to claim as he
pleases, even when he believes that his publication, with its clever
counter-propaganda, was a major contributor to ultimate victory.
Mere journalists, on the other hand, have a problem of credibili-
ty. The 'penny-a-liner' process has the inclination to stretch beyond
due and decent limits, to quote authoritatively from other like
sources, leaving one with the puzzle of trying to find the hook on
the wall with which to anchor the chain. An outstanding example
to my mind (because I was personally involved) in recent times
is Coogan (*De Valera*) quoting Coogan (*Michael Collins*) quoting
a couple of women writers of the somewhat recent and more remote
past who concocted erroneous material and drew illogical conclusions on a vital issue of the Civil War, to wit, the circumstances
surrounding the demolition by Republican forces of the great
Mallow railway bridge (cf. Chapters Ten and Eleven, *The Dark
Secret of Béalnabláth*), to the detriment of two outstanding patriots
of the time, Erskine Childers and Eamon de Valera. Frank
Gallagher's attitude towards Childers is particularly interesting.
That much maligned man, who gave his life for his ideals and was
better known to Gallagher than to anyone else, he regards as a
gentleman and a scholar, calm and innocuous but unrelenting, the
only one of his era who dealt in absolute truth. And that is the
truth!

Chapters 26-35 of *The Four Glorious Years* produce a major
analysis of the problem of hunger-strike in all its physical, moral
and political implications. It is interesting to note that the great
hunger-strike in Mountjoy Gaol, in the Spring of 1920, and in
which Gallagher participated (he had already published a book
on the matter, called *Days Of Fear*, in 1928) he considers one of
the prime reasons for the failure of the British terror campaign
in this country, while Todd Andrews, who took part in it at the
same time, pooh-poohs it as of little consequence. Andrews says
he was just hungry for a while, got his release, and wondered what

all the fuss was about. What do you think?

13. No Other Law: (Florence O'Donoghue . . . The Irish
    Press, 1954).

Purporting to be a biography of General Liam Lynch, this volume
gave Major Florrie Donoghue full and ample scope for expatiating
on the theme of Ireland's final resurgence from imperial despotism.
An expert writer, he does this with consummate skill. Liam Lynch's
activities, from early beginnings in the Volunteers to being appointed Commandant of the First Southern Division of the I.R.A.
in 1921, flavour the narrative only like cherries in a fruit cake, but
are adroitly manipulated to indicate that the microcosm of such
activities was the inspiration of the national macrocosm, and the
history of the time would have been still more glorious if the country as a whole followed the lead to the letter. An ongoing lack of
liason, rather of complete understanding, between what he likes
to refer to as 'the Army' and 'the Government', with particular
reference to G.H.Q. in Dublin, gives a foreboding to the
knowledgable reader of trouble to come, with slight but ominous
shadows of Civil War. *No Other Law* was serialized in a weekly
newspaper in the early Fifties, practically back to back with Mick
Sullivan's *Where Mountainy Men Have Sown*. The present writer,
forty years younger, found one of them quite easy to read, the other
quite difficult. Take your pick!   * * *   I met Florrie
Donoghue only once. That was in the mid-Fifties. He sat in his
rate-collector's office in Cook Street in Cork City. I was doing
some preliminary work on the present volume under the original
title of *In God's Pockets* (cf. Introduction). An insignificant little
man I thought him but the aura of recent history made me give
the man his due. Little did I know! Thirty-five years later, long
after his death, when the famous 'Florrie Donoghue's Papers' were
released to the public (minus a certain section 'for security reasons')
by the National Library, I found, in a transcript of his work for
posterity, a reference to a certain non-existent *In God's Pockets*
by Patrick J. Twohig! He was the intelligence man *par excellence*.
Moreover, a short time later (it was 1990, the centenary of the birth
of Michael Collins) I was given, as a secret, by his sister-in-law,
the noted Mrs. Nancy McCarthy-Allitt, the family confidential

story of his significant meeting with the Big Fellow in Macroom on the morning of Béalnabláth (cf. *The Dark Secret*, pp. 132-3, 294-5). The second half of *No Other Law* is dedicated to the Civil War, its presumed causes and general effects, with the political philosophy and military outlook of Liam Lynch (to live under no other law than that of an all-Irish Republic) running steadfastly through the whole era. Despite being made Lynch's adjutant in the new First Southern Division, Florrie Donoghue did not participate in the Civil War, staying neutral but partisan. Like so many of his comrades he returned to the colours in the Emergency period of World War Two, as a major involved in Army Intelligence. In fact his whole milieu was intelligence, and if a central theme in his writing can be justly isolated it is that our intelligence, eventually superior to that of the British, was what defeated the Black and Tans, as some people, following the well-known phrase of Arthur Griffith, claim for Michael Collins that he was 'the man who won the war'. (I am reminded of that Great War tableau in Madame Tussaud's waxworks in London, where a lot of be-medalled generals stand about, but the caption, 'The Man Who Won The War' subscribes Tommy Atkins in a dug-out!). Beyond that, Florrie Donoghue's attitude, in a notable work of history, tends to make one think of a director of M.I.5, writing in the context and atmosphere of the second Great War, with particular reference to the Second Front, and holding rather a Churchill than an Eisenhower in the hot seat of ultimate responsibility.

14. B'fhiú An Braon Fola: (Séamas Ó Maoileoin . . . Sáirséal & Dill, 1958).

An Irish language account of the War of Independence should have at least some sentimental value for a cut-and-dried posterity. This book has that and more. To the linguist it is fluent and well written. To the historian it is one of the best books on the period, if not the best i.e. quality-wise. It is rarely heard of because of the language barrier. That is not a pity — it is a privilege. At fifty thousand words it is quite long as Irish books go, and is quite readable but for the amazing array of Gaelic names for otherwise familiar places throughout the country. (*Note:* His daughter, Bríd, eventually married Seán O'Hegarty, son of P. S. O'Hegarty. They were, in fact, 'Sáirséal Agus Dill'. His daughter, Úna, began a translation but gave it up. The book is well worth translating. Perhaps I shall do it some day).   * * *   Séamas Ó Maoileoin (James Malone), of Tyrellspass, Co. Westmeath, had a still more notable brother, Tomás, alias 'Seán Forde', one of 'The Three Toms' of Michael Collins' peace efforts in the early days of the Civil War. 'Seán Forde' was one of the most wanted men in the Black and Tan times. His elder brother, Séamas, was less so, but, as an intelligence operative, òr 'spy', as he himself says, was more highly regarded by Collins as Director of Intelligence. Both brothers spent the final six months of the fight with the East Limerick Flying Column, the first to be set up in the country and arguably the most effective despite desperate fighting conditions in flat (i.e unprotected) country. Séamas Malone, a teacher when 'off duty', writes in a manner that is reflected in the writing of another off-duty teacher, Kerryman Séamas O'Connor (in *Tomorrow Was Another Day*), but is far more effective, comprehensive and enlightening, and he sedulously avoids the Civil War in which both brothers participated on the Republican side. The humour, in the midst of tragedy and despair, is delightful, the irony is unique. Much of it is reflected in his brother Tom's account related in Uinseann Mac Eoin's *Survivors* (Argenta Publications, 1980). A couple of references may be in order . . . 'I could write a book about what Brigid Walshe did and suffered for the country'. (*Note:* She was his wife, likewise a teacher, whom he had met in Tipperary after his release from Frongoch in January, 1917) . . . 'That first night, when we had been acquainted for only an hour, Brigid and I decided to get married. Neither of us had a red cent but we didn't give a damn'. His treatment of Richard Mulcahy (Free State Army Chief of Staff after the death of Collins, and the man who signed the notorious execution order), is excruciatingly funny . . . ' ''Freedom will never come'', said he (Mulcahy in a speech at Frongoch prison), ''without revolution, and I greatly fear that the Irish people are too soft for revolution. For a revolution to be successful we need bloody, ferocious men, who don't care a hoot for death or the spilling of blood. Revolution is not child's play. In the process of revolution, any man, woman or child who is not for you is against you. Shoot them and be damned to them!''. My heart went out to him right away. In my view Mulcahy was a champion who would lead us to freedom'. (*Note:* The book title means 'The drop of blood was worth it', a reference to the oft-quoted declaration of Daniel O'Connell that the freedom of Ireland was not worth the shedding of one drop of blood. I thought, therefore, to entitle the proposed translation: *Blood On The Flag*). Richard Mulcahy, who was Minister for Education until 1957, and Fine Gael Party leader until 1959, actually attended the launching of the book in 1958, but took the opportunity to snarl at the author — 'As long as I have any influence you will never publish anything again!' It has been a source of amazement to me how General Mulcahy, as everybody knew him, escaped when decent men like Seán Hales and Kevin O'Higgins managed to get themselves murdered early in the game. Magic, I suppose.

15. *Vive Moi!:* (Seán O'Faoláin . . . Rupert Hart-Davis, London, 1965).

'A warm, cheerful autobiography', from the *New York Times*, hardly states the case for what is in effect a literary reprise of many of the greatest writers and much of the greatest writing of a century, from the middle of the previous to the middle of the present one. O'Faoláin's friend and fellow Corkonian (and, indeed, fellow Republican), Frank O'Connor, may have been a great story-teller, but O'Faoláin was a truly professional littérateur and academic. His contribution to the history of the Irish 'Troubles' is merely one chapter (Chapter Ten), but in some inevitable manner peculiar to his tormented state of mind, that one section of thirty-odd pages (including the Civil War), emerges as a pivot for the whole from childhood to disaffected old age, while his retroactive disgust for himself and all concerned in the Fight for Independence — and their opponents — is reserved as a judgement on the politicians in Dublin and the political go-getters of that historic period, but not on the Cause and the young men and women of the countryside, the people generally, who suffered and died for it. His warlike role was merely as bomb-maker for the Republic in the Tan War and as director of publicity for the same Republic in the Civil War. He partook in only one battle when he, with eight other companions, lined a fence on a hill outside Ballymakeera village and fired down on a double rank of green-clad Free State soldiers who were advancing on Ballyvourney, the ultimate Republic. * * * Vive Moi!, Up Me, was what the man said, but To Hell With You is probably what he meant. I had one slight brush with him. I wrote politely and obsequiously in 1990 to ask some question about his association with Erskine Childers and Frank O'Connor in West Cork (for *The Dark Secret*). He declined to answer, but later his daughter, Julia, phoned and told me politely but stiffly that he was not interested and that anyway he was too old (he was just the age of the century) to bother. There was a conviction abroad that he had never recovered his (Catholic) Faith since those old bothersome times and I thought that maybe I could do something, however slight, like Florrie Donoghue gruesomely pouring a bottle of Holy Water on the grave of P. S. O'Hegarty, in Glasnevin Cemetery, the day after the funeral. It was not to be. As another old soldier had told me, many years ago, he was not in need of ministrations!

Seán O'Faoláin's father was an R.I.C. constable, as was the case with so many of the disaffected young men of the time (as well, indeed, as so many of the students in Maynooth in my time. My father said that policemen's children were 'the ones who got on'). His father's agony, a simple countryman who worshipped the faraway and glorious Empire, at the son's republican activities is finely drawn and his mother's tears at their angry disagreements are hot and copious. He does supply one historical fact in context, which I had seen nowhere — his father's constable's pay was one pound sterling per week, equal to an Auxie's and twice a Black and Tan's, the difference being that they were 'all found' while he was 'ate yourself' in a condition of grinding poverty. In England likewise 'a policeman's lot was not a happy one', somewhat better and somewhat worse . . . 'On the outbreak of war (1914) a constable's weekly wage was 30s to 42s, depending on his length of service. During the next four years there was no increase in police pay although the cost of living had more than doubled . . . Consequently by 1918 many policemen and their families were living in poverty and some . . . were actually undernourished'. (From *London's Armed Police*, 1986).

As a student at U.C.C. Seán O'Faoláin was, from first to last, a member of the university section of republican fighters. Many students of the time left college for the purpose. There is an echo of Todd Andrews in 'during the "Troubles", as we were ironically to call those not so dangerous and very happy years'. His gun was 'a lovely long-nosed Webley', with which he claimed to have been 'a good shot'. Actually the long Webley and Scott was quite an ugly, ungainly and inaccurate weapon, standard for British officers of the 'Great War' and later, and notable only for its 'stopping power'. But, then, O'Faoláin saw his life of the time, and much of his later experience, as an 'encounter with the absurd' but 'if ever a revolution was run on faith, hope and charity ours was'. By then he had met some fine men and women of the West, a new experience for an impoverished Cork City youth, who deeply and lastingly impressed his neophyte mind. And he had met 'Scottie' at Dick Twomey's of Tureenduv, Ballingeary. 'I slept there (in a haybarn) many a night beside a magnificent tall, kilted Scot, named Ian Bawn McKenzie Kennedy, who had come over to Ireland to fight for the Republic'. Seán was eighteen, and his girlfriend (later his wife), Eileen Gould of Sunday's Well, Cork, effervescent and righteous and red-headed, had introduced him to the Irish language at a Gaelic League class in the city and then proceeded to show him the Irish-speaking people of the Southwest. It was an unspeakable revelation. On an August morning in 1918, in company with Eileen, 'I got off my bicycle on the hillock outside Inchigeela, always afterwards to be my mark of arrival in the true West'. (*Note:* If it matters, and it does to me, the hill was Rossmore, and my father and mother, respectively from the cottage on the hill and a nearby farm, had just settled down to married life!). By evening Eileen and himself had arrived in Tureenduv, and the late John Whelan had become the future, famous Seán O'Faoláin. From then onwards he was to be a committed Republican, for better or worse, the only Ireland he knew and loved being the Gaelic-speaking West, and, as he said, he had nothing to guide him but those flickering lights before the golden icons of the past. Beautiful writer! Beautiful cause!

16. Where Mountainy Men Have Sown: (Mícheál Ó Súilleabháin . . . Anvil Books, Tralee, 1965).
The blurb says: 'Through mountain passes and along the beds of creeks Mícheál Ó Súilleabháin takes us to attack an armed police

patrol here or to plan a large-scale engagement there against the élite of Britain's specially recruited fighting forces in Ireland — the famous Auxiliaries, all ex-commissioned officers and, to a man, much decorated veterans of World War One. The rank smell of cordite and the smoke and dust of battle on rock-bordered roads are in this book. But in it, too, is heard the beating of the hearts of the mountainy men. Through it rings the gay laughter of its comely young women and the warm affection of parents, sons and daughters in the mountain homes of Muskerry'. That about sums it up, except for the title, which is from Patrick Pearse's poem, 'The Wayfarer', and a foreword by Daniel Corkery. The erudite littérateur and professor, author of *The Hidden Ireland* and many other works of quality, takes the book apart in a way that must have surprised the author, but he puts it together once again in a pleasant and incisive manner which shows the outpouring as for real where someone who did not personally know the writer might be inclined to think the work as too personal and bombastic, too stylistically contrived.   * * *   Mick Sullivan has always been, to my mind, one of the toughest fighting men of the period. I knew him since childhood. A personal friend of my father's, when he passed by with his inevitable fowling-piece my old man said — 'Pádraig, watch!', picked up a stone, threw it in the air while the friendly, perpetually smiling man smashed it to pieces or blew it out of sight. It was inevitable that he won the cup at the Kilnamartyra clay-pigeon shoot but his 'lap of honour' was what numbed my nine-year-old brain, as he lay on his back on a barrel and demolished every clay in turn out of the trap. Stiff-necked I thought him, and it was many years later when I learned that he had six splinters from a Civil War revolver bullet permanently embedded around his cervical vertebrae. However, the fowling-piece rarely if ever shot a bird and had the reputation that it might indeed destroy a man who would dare to injure a living creature. Mick was resident engineer in Coláiste Íosagáin in my time. There was a story that he somehow slipped a cog in his final exam in U.C.C., and when he appeared before the responsible professor produced a Smith and Wesson revolver from inside his jacket, showed it to the man and said — 'Take a look at that! I shot better men than you with it!'. Hasty? Perhaps, but reasonably true. Undoubtedly true was his reaction to the news of the attack on

Brookeborough Barracks in the 'Six Counties', in December, 1956. (cf. Chapter Two). A great-hearted fighter for freedom to the last! By strange coincidence he and I crossed swords about the writing of this book. I arrived from England in 1948 and began collecting material, with the help of the remnants of the local company, about their Tan War efforts. Mick attended only one or two meetings and in a state of evident tension. A couple of years later, when the work was barely moving, we learned why. He had been privately working on the same lines himself for quite some time and his efforts suddenly began to appear in serial form in the *Kerryman* weekly newspaper in the Spring of 1956. A perturbed Patsy Burrick (Captain Patrick Lynch) put the question to him. His answer is a classic, for then or now. He said — 'Anybody can write a book!'. Today, when everybody does, Literature has been mauled beyond recognition.

Mr. Dan Nolan, proprietor of *The Kerryman* newspaper (publishing as Anvil Books), took almost a decade to produce the book. He had married a Spanish countess, ran into marital difficulties, became a very disgruntled man, and moved to Dublin. For the publication in 1965 Mick revised his material, rather disconcertingly making it retrospective of forty years rather than thirty, and dropped some relevant items from the original. Anvil Books went further. They excluded all of those fine photographs taken by the author (his daughter, Máire, is now a top-class artist working from home), and produced a cheap, once-off edition unworthy of the man and his subject. Because of the serialization *Mountainy Men* tends to be episodic by chapter. My favourite number is fifteen, 'Knocksaharing', in a book which is lovely in its own way and keenly reminiscent of the emotions and feelings and sorrows of our people in an age that is long past and almost forgotten. His wife, Máire, lives on, a gentle and delightful old lady, member of a noted Coolea republican family, the McSweeneys. Too young to be an authorized member of Cumann na mBan (the women's associative republican organization), she nevertheless did trojan work as a youthful courier for the Cause, and is eminently proud of same. In a sweet and touching interpolation he slips his future wife into the action . . . 'We needed another companion since we had left the river, and the road to Coom (above Coolea) was dreary enough. Soon we had him.

Someone [was it himself!], thinking of the river, sang John Keegan Casey's song, "Máire My Girl" '! (*Note:* John Keegan Casey, 'Leo' of *The Nation* newspaper, 1842, belonged to an earlier revolution and yet another age).

17. The Story Of The 7th: (Charlie Browne . . . Macroom Printing Works, 1971).

It purports to be 'a concise history of the 7th Battalion, Cork No. 1 Brigade, Irish Republican Army, from 1915 to 1921'. Eighty-eight pages of centre-pin, in a 'jotter' cover, simply states the case of the ordinary Irish fighting man, the man who wanted freedom for his people from foreign oppression, and states it in terms of the common human emotions of joy, fear, love, hate, anger, hope, pride, gratitude and personal satisfaction. He had nothing to lose but his life and, in the historic and changing circumstances of his time, he was glad to do so for posterity, for his people. That he was not called to do so, as so many others of his comrades, was just the fortunes of war, extremely thin and precarious on numerous occasions. Still, the highlight of Adjutant Charlie Browne's little book comes in 1925, when even the Civil War was being forgotten by the people if not by the politicians. Republican Dan Lynch, of Ballyvourney, went to Australia to look for work, as there was none available in the country he had fought for. A year later he was followed by Ned McSweeney, of Coolea, who was in ill health due to the privations of the struggle. Even in the fine climate Ned continued to decline and Dan relinquished his job to bring his friend home to die. Then he returned to the Antipodes. Charlie, who had fought beside them, concludes his volume with: 'I have never come across a finer example of true comradeship and I am glad to be able to pay this deserving tribute!'. * * * Charlie Browne may not have made a major contribution to History but he has brought to light a notion which may be generally headlined as 'Attitudes'. His almost obsequious appreciation of the Irish people for allowing himself and a few other fellows of his kith and kin to fight for the people's freedom does set a problem of projecting one's mind into the real spirit of the time. By contrast Mick Sullivan has a rollicking good time cheered on by a grateful and totally dependent community. Ernie O'Malley sees himself as the lone gunman moving fast about the country at the rising of the moon or otherwise, the mythical Paul Revere of neo-resurgence. Florrie Donoghue is the brilliant organizational brain destined to co-ordinate and revitalize the dormant soul of Celtic self-determination. Dan Breen sees himself symbolically standing up to the traditional enemy of the Irish people, to kill or be killed. Tom Barry is the champion of champions who has been there already and knows it all. Liam Lynch is the hero of Nordic saga destined to die a thousand deaths for personal honour . . . The Theme is endless in its ramifications. One thinks of the steel-clad warriors of the past who went about in excruciating garb (I suffer from nervous itch!), and for no quite certain reason, to hack away at one another with sword or battle-axe until legs, arms or heads gave way with the pressure. One thinks of, let us say, a spot in World War Two, when the British and Germans fought for possession of the Mediterranean island of Crete, when a British column was relieved by a group of New Zealanders and, to quote a British officer on the spot, were 'perfectly good chaps. Very polite. They just drifted in and said — "Please, may we join in your battle?" '. It brings one down to one's own attitude from a safe distance — Why doesn't everybody just go home and be quiet! Our already sufficiently tormented planet would be so much the better for it!

18. *Towards Ireland Free:*   (Liam Deasy . . . The Mercier Press, Cork, 1973).

Mick Sullivan said — 'Anybody can write a book!'. The question is — Did Liam Deasy do so? The publication says — by Liam Deasy, edited by John E. Chisholm, University College, Dublin. Rev. Dr. Chisholm, of the Holy Ghost Order, who now lives in retirement with his mother, has assured the present writer that he did the job but was underrated by Mercier, and will not admit to being merely a ghost writer, not even a holy one. In the 'Editor's Note' Dr. Chisholm says — 'In an endeavour to fill some lacunae in the accounts put at my disposal, I undertook a work of research in the West Cork area (his native place) among surviving participants in the war, and was fortunate etc.'. In the 'Preface' Liam Deasy says — 'I am particularly grateful to the Rev. Dr. John

Chisholm . . . who . . . kindly consented to edit the work'. Tom Barry extensively refuted Deasy's full and comprehensive account in a booklet published by Anvil Press and entitled 'The Reality of the Anglo-Irish War, 1920/21, in West-Cork', and, finally, a letter was sent to all Irish newspapers in 1974 (Appendix J in the second edition of Deasy, 1977), signed by some of the most famous men in West Cork during the Trouble times, refuting Barry. How's that as a fight for Irish History! In Barry's favour it can be said that he did his work just a quarter of a century after the fact, while Deasy waited for half a century, On the other hand, Barry's experience of the campaign was only a matter of ten months (September, 1920 to July, 1921), while Deasy's extended back into the dim beginnings of uprising. Likewise Deasy's book is an in-depth and extensive work, with rather uncharacteristic academic overtones, while Barry's is popular, racy and readable. I may say — take your pick of two of the most notable fighters for Irish freedom against the Black and Tans, who fought for their lives while treading on each other's toes. * * * There have been times when I have regarded General Liam Deasy as 'the noblest Roman of them all'. There is a reassuring consistency and logic about his daring work for the Republic right from the start until the end of the Civil War. All he needed was to have emulated Brutus by falling at Philippi and he might have shared the same pan-national pedestal with Liam Lynch and Michael Collins. They are all pleasant companions in my historical dreamboat!

19. *Soldier Of The Rearguard:* Bill Hammond . . . Éigse
    Publications, Fermoy, 1977).
This is the active-service record of Matt Flood, of Fermoy. It is a relatively small book of twenty-two thousand words. It portrays, above all else, a peculiarly detailed memory after half a century, and a peculiarly technical memory of a tall, gentle and kindly machine-gunner, of all things. (*Note:* I try to picture Hemingway's character, the white hunter of Nairobi . . . 'Wilson looked at Macomber with his flat, blue, machine-gunner's eyes . . .'. I fail to get the picture). Having eliminated a lot of Germans in the Battle of the Somme, at the age of sixteen, he was invalided home. This was only a preliminary to joining the Irish Volunteers and

eventually becoming a permanent member of the Second (North Cork) Brigade 'Flying Column', with responsibility for training in, and actual use of, any machine-guns to hand. His committment lasted to the end of the Civil War.   * * *   'I can still picture him in that long sort of rain-coat he wore and his keen eyes peering through the glasses down the road looking for the approaching lorries'. To whom was he referring? Who, of course, but General Liam Lynch! 'Where else would you get a General going out at night guarding his troops while they slept! That was Lynch!'. Also Stonewall Jackson in the American Civil War. Great men, lost causes! In a favourable estimate of the above, in a British newspaper, the reviewer said — 'War is about chaps!'. Not really. War is about weaponry, and in the Irish Troubles the gradual balance of power depended on the shifting of weapons from one side to the other. Mallow military barracks, which housed the 17th Lancers, was captured by Lynch and the North Cork A.S.U., on 28 September, 1920. Among the weapons taken were two Hotchkiss light machine-guns. Now, Hotchkiss was *terra incognita* to the 'boys', likewise to the 'chaps'. In fact, though an excellent machine-gun, it was a kind of joke in military circles world-wide, and ended up with the cavalry who were ending up themselves, and travelled about rattling ignominiously on the back of a pack horse, but, for the chosen few who could handle it, it had more fire-power and adaptability than the Lewis-gun. The Battle of Coolnacahera (cf. Chapter Twelve) is a case in point. (*Note:* Though named after an Austrian, the Hotchkiss was a French invention, but was adapted by the British in 1914. Also, I do wish that people would realize that being knowledgeable about guns doesn't make one a 'Terrorist' in the accepted sense. Some time after the publication of my 'Béalnabláth book' my phone was tapped for a month by the relevant authorities, a presence at the 'Battle of the Bogside' being cited). Matt Flood knew the Hotchkiss. 'The lancers in Mallow said we could never use the Hotchkiss . . . A funny thing was that when I was in France I was in a town called Etaps on a special course when some Lancers arrived . . . These fellows were training on stripping and assembling a Hotchkiss gun . . . Well, I took the lesson . . . Little did I think that I would have to instruct the lads on using the only two Hotchkiss guns in the Brigade!'. Matt Flood did more. He used a Hotchkiss at Ballydrochane ambush (between Kanturk and Newmarket) a few days later (6 October, 1920), putting a truck load of British soldiers out of action by killing the driver, 'the first time', he said, 'the I.R.A. had used machineguns in action'. (*Note:* A Hotchkiss was used even to greater effect at Clonbanin, 3 March, 1921, by Denis Galvin, later General Galvin of the Free State Army). Matt tells of an incident when the North Cork flying column was stationed at Glounicomane, near Freemount, in the Autumn of 1920. It was in a farmhouse owned then by a family named Murphy, two brothers and a sister. One of the boys was in the column. Matt had the Hotchkiss all set for training when Ernie O'Malley blew in. Matt continues: 'When I said the gun was loaded, he replied, "That's alright, I'll be careful" . . . Anyway he sat down and whatever way he tipped the trigger four or five shots went off and a woman (Ellen Murphy, the sister) milking a cow outside in the yard, believe you me, the bullets went between her legs and riddled the bucket. There was milk flying out of four or five holes. I kept looking at the woman waiting for her to fall over. I was sure she was hit for she was directly in the line of fire. But O'Malley said, cool-like, "It's alright!" '. O'Malley tells it somewhat differently. 'A hail of bullets one day announced to the scattered members of the A.S.U. that I had learned to work a Hotchkiss gun by experimenting with it'. It's the way they tell 'em!

Matt Flood also demonstrated the 'tommy-gun' when a number of them were brought over from America, during the Truce, by Colonel Prout, later General Prout of the Free State Army, the man who rolled back the Waterford-Limerick Republican front during the Civil War, albeit a Yank! So, War is not only about 'Chaps' and 'Weaponry', but it is also about bitter irony, more especially in retrospect. 'It was Christmas Eve', the man said, 'but it was all over . . .!'.

Finally, with regard to the title of the book, Robert Kee (in *Ourselves Alone*) has this to say: 'In his last message to the "Soldiers of the Republic, Legion of the Rearguard", De Valera had assured them that their sacrifices and the deaths of their comrades had not been in vain, and that in a little time the civilian population, who were now weary and needed a rest, would recover and rally again to the standard. "When they are ready", he wrote, "you will be, and your place will be again, as of old, with the vanguard".' Then, someone wrote a ballad called 'Legion of the Rearguard', as a consequence , which was to become a rallying cry for Fianna Fáil through the political turmoil of the early Thirties. Dev could be quite dangerous without knowing it!

20. *Memoirs Of Irish Volunteer Activity, 1917-1924:* (Peter O'Farrell . . . New York, 1978).

'January, February and March, 1921, were busy months. The British military were pushing hard with round-ups in every area. Our company was in the unhappy position of being between two very active columns, the East Limerick and the North Cork columns. The columns had to keep on the move all the time, which meant that the local companies had to supply guards and scouts, day and night. We had East Limerick coming into Tobernea, Brickfield and Ballymack, and our own North Cork Column coming in at all times and places . . .' This effort of the flamboyant Peter O'Farrell, from Thomastown, Kilmallock, is little more than a pamphlet and moves in its peculiar sketchy manner through the whole era with particular weight given to the Civil War rather than the Tan War. It is valuable in its own way but frequently quite incoherent, with the simplicity of the countryman's view of things in general, combining with the later American experience to produce a document that is quite hilarious if rather historically restricted. The above paragraph, with its localized estimates, is probably the best in the book. O'Farrell appears more in the role of a Republican policeman and did, in fact, become such at the Truce and continued so through the Civil War. There is some information relevant to the last days of Michael Collins which is significant and has already been used by the present writer in *The Dark Secret.* (*Note:* Incidentally, one statement I made in that book is incorrect. I wrote: 'O'Farrell rather needlessly gives his name'. It is with reference to the shooting of a local Republican by a Free State soldier in the battle for Kilmallock, July, 1922. The soldier was also a local and his name, regrettably, became known later causing him to emigrate to San Francisco). Still the author remains as a being apart. His style would now be termed 'individual', a euphemism to end all euphemisms. His little war as a company commander, astride the Charleville-Kilmallock road, approaches the

unbelievable. His ambush plan was to string a steel cable between two trees and sweep everybody, including the driver, off the top of a military lorry. He and a comrade held up a British Army meat cart and gave out its contents to all the locals as the spoils of war. And so on. You would need to read it to believe it.   *   *   *
'In the middle of September (1921) we had a battalion review at Milltown. All companies were in competition and were supposed to turn out in full strength. Our company turned out with sixty-four men, all armed with shotguns and equipment. We had close order and extended formation exercises and cross-country simulated enemy action. Ballyhea only paraded thirty-two men, and Liscarroll only paraded thirty-two picked men. This resulted in Liscarroll (P. O'Brien, Brigade Commanding Officer) getting first place, Ballyhea (N. Ryan, Battalion Training Commanding Officer), second place, and Garrienderk (his own company), third place. The thing was rigged as usual and was very much responsible for the dissension in the company that resulted in regard to Beggar's Bush (Free State Military H.Q. in Dublin) later on'! Try that on your 'Tim Pat Coogan' as a main contributory factor in Ireland's tragic Civil War! O'Farrell is full of 'Firsts' and 'Onlys' in his fight for Irish freedom, but he certainly had one unique experience. He was sent with a detail to help a landlord's agent in the collection of rents from 'dangerous' tenants. The landlord was Major Eyre Ivers of Mount Ivers, Six-Mile-Bridge, Co. Clare, and the tenants, who were apparently taking advantage of the disturbed times, had refused to pay up. The agent was a Protestant farmer named John Winter . . . 'My first contact with John Winter, Granard, Liscarroll, was when I was called in to Brigade Headquarters by Commandant Brislane and Commandant O'Brien, Brigade Commanding Officers, towards the end of January, 1921. John Winter had requested protection to help him collect his rents from the tenants around the Meelin and Rockchapel areas (beyond Newmarket). He had been threatened by the tenants there, as he had had them all served with summonses to appear at the Sinn Féin Court the following week. So, early the following Monday, Pat Sullivan and I were driven in our high back-to-back trap (which, in fact, belonged to Winter) to Meelin Courthouse. Quite frankly we were rather squeamish about what to expect from the Meelin boys, not knowing how the land lay or what it was all about.

However, everything went off fine. When they saw who the escort was everyone started to pay up and there were no incidents. We arrived back at the Winters' house at about 6 p.m. and were treated to a sumptuous dinner and enjoyable evening. Pat Sullivan was a fabulous violin player, and Louise Winter, the youngest daughter, played the piano.

This continued for several weeks until all the rents were paid. I started doing a line with the youngest daughter ('He only thought it', says delightful old Louise Winter, Mrs. George Gardiner, who still lives hale and hearty in the home place at the age of eighty-eight), and Sullivan with the other. Every Sunday (we now switch to the Civil War period) the family drove into Buttevant, to the Protestant church, which was across from the Police Barracks (where O'Farrell was in charge, cf. *The Dark Secret)*, and after their services came over and spent about an hour visiting us in the barracks. We had open invitations to their house and often sneaked out there on evenings when they ran parties for us. (*Note:* The Protestant involvement in the Republican movement in the South of Ireland is dealt with in *The Dark Secret.* It indicates a further complication in our country's curious history. Billy Winter, of Aghaburn, near Churchtown, was Adjutant at Buttevant military barracks during the vital Civil War battle for Kilmallock, Co. Limerick. A convert to Catholicism, he it was who arranged the burning of the great ex-British military barracks before the advancing Free State troops. The present writer holds a docket signed by him requisitioning bread from a local baker for his amateur soldiers. It is unfortunate that, in a recently published article, an *Irish Times* journalist, named Kevin Myers, accused the I.R.A. of the time of the slaughter of innocent Protestants, under the pretext of their being informers. The article is bitter and divisive, historically inaccurate, and very untimely in that it comes at a point when everybody seems to be genuinely concerned in healing wounds across the denominational barrier, North and South). 'Apparently (O'Farrell continues) I had made a real impression on old man Winter. He had written to the chief of London Police (actually just an inspector named Paddy Brosnan from Liscarroll) and asked him if he would take care of me if I decided to go to London and join up. Winter got a reply immediately — send him over now. Winter was a personal friend of the Police Chief. In 1971 I finally decided to call on the Winter family. I did and we went over the whole story again. Mr. Winter was dead and I visited Louise who told me that Ned Riordan (an obstreperous Free State officer who had been a teacher in Milford) had been killed and that he was no loss. The morning of the raid on Winter's house, in 1922, Riordan had taken all of Mr. Winter's papers, pertaining to his business as land agent, to the Military Barracks and afterwards denied taking them. Winter had to take him to the high court and court martial. Louise also brought up the opportunity I had missed in not accepting the offer to join the London Police Force. She often wondered why I had not taken the opportunity. I didn't tell her that the offer never really meant that much to me'. Pipe dreams — but how lovely!

21. Dublin Made Me: (C. S. Andrews . . . Mercier Press, Dublin, 1979).

This is a genuine autobiography and as a statement of living conditions in Ireland, particularly in the environs of Dublin City, during the first half of the century, may be regarded as a valuable document. The War of Independence, which is referred to as the 'Movement', comprises one third of its three hundred pages, and the Civil War, more lucid and coherent, another third. Dr. Andrews, known to his family and intimates as 'Christy' but to the world at large as 'Todd', became a power in the public life of the country and made his contribution to its welfare as a civilian which he had set out to do, but failed to do, as a young man behind a gun.   *   *   *   Todd Andrews writes smoothly and entertainingly like the good and erudite talker he was. Genuinely deprecating any academic qualities in his make-up he, nevertheless, displays a real grasp of the implication of things, which was rare among his peers, a view of the inner meaning of life and society worldwide that could cause him to say of President Woodrow Wilson, 'You'd think he'd have more sense!', or of the British Government, 'Will they never have any sense!'. As Eliza Doolittle might say — 'Anybody would think you was my father!'. His political philosophy, when he bothers to state it, is somewhat reflected, though in a much less personal manner, in Dorothy Macardle's *The Irish Republic.* Like anyone of surprising bent of mind and the 'mental pabulum' (his expression) of wide reading, his observations on familiar themes are unexpected, even startling. Dan Breen's (and modern Tipperary's) high-minded claims with regard to the Soloheadbeg ambush he tends to discountenance with the phrase: 'I think it was an operation that just went wrong!'. New to me was 'Guerilla tactics were never mentioned'. His lads had not even heard of Seán O'Casey, still less of his claim to have been the proponent of such activity. The G.A.A., and their ban on foreign games and dances, did indeed keep rural Ireland from becoming 'just as anglicised as was Dublin' but their claims, even the reflected glory of 'Bloody Sunday', to have been an integral part of national resurgence, was just so much eye-wash. His idea that the G.A.A. was being promoted by the clergy for religious purposes is significant but extreme. In Dublin you either came from a tough revolutionary breed and fought hard against authority, or from an Anglophile family whose members naturally joined the British Army. Both species loved soccer. So did Todd Andrews.

In this book the process and principle of hunger-strike is stated in a new light — they were just hungry and thirsty for ten days and later wondered what all the fuss was about. (*Note:* Frank Gallagher, as already stated, took an entirely different view of the situation). His incarceration with young Cecil Salkeld, later to become famous as a writer, poet, critic and artist, produced an illuminating character study ('Salkeld's interminable talk began to weary me!'), but he seems to have missed the fact that Salkeld's daughter, Beatrice, was to become the wife ('My first wife!') of another famous Dublin rebel and littérateur, name of Brendan Behan. Todd Andrews' story of the 'Sacred Heart' is priceless (no offence!). This was a man with a northern accent who was a hunger-strike leader and got ill in the process. With his magnificent red hair and well-trimmed beard 'he could have been a model for the statue'. Fawned on by priests, nuns, medical staff and just about everybody in the Mater Hospital (including one visiting bishop), where he and Andrews landed in adjacent beds, 'his large brown liquid eyes expressed fortitude, compassion and sadness', but, in the course of the night, 'my Christ-like companion of the ambulance . . . had succeeded against, it must be said, mere token resistance in pulling one of the nurses onto his bed!'.

Todd Andrews was proud of the fact that he was writing from

memory in his seventies though 'aware of the fallibility of memory',
but the present writer thinks that the Mercier editorial staff might
have been more careful with such things as that Kevin Barry 'was
captured shortly after this incident' which was a brush with the
Black and Tans in December, 1920, and that Terence MacSwiney
died after seventy-three days' hunger-strike in Wormwood Scrubbs
instead of seventy-four in Brixton. The song, 'I'm Forever Blowing Bubbles', seems to have been almost a British military anthem
of the time. A lorry load of them were singing it as they were attacked by the boys in Rathgar Avenue in January, 1921. Todd's
companion, Larry Kane, shouted as they opened fire — 'We'll give
you f---ing bubbles!'. By coincidence Ernie O'Malley had a Tan
singing the song at the Modreeney ambush (North Tipperary, May,
1921) but (in good old O'Malley style) 'a frothy blood closed his
mouth before he finished the chorus!'. At the end, before the Truce,
internment in the Curragh of Kildare was an irritation because of
absence from the fight. Conditions were good. Desmond Fitzgerald, Garrett's father, the camp leader, was a poseur and a pain
in the neck. To all the internees 'the Rosary was much more than
a prayer. It came to be a secular slogan interwoven into the fabric
of the Movement', while 'The Soldier's Song' (the abomination
of abominations to the present writer) 'had no special significance
and never rated as a National Anthem'. The question of continuing internment in the Curragh after the Truce (July, 1921) is an
historical dilemma, except that the place was still within the
authority of the British Army, and the need for a successful escape
by means of a tunnel, in September, when the Treaty negotiations
were aleady beginning, is a real puzzle, while Seán MacEoin and
Seán Moylan had been released at the Truce though under sentence
of death. Todd Andrews does not help to clarify the puzzles. Surprisingly, the bourgeoisie and ascendancy types had continued with
their fun and games, and race meetings, regardless of the passing
scene. 'I began to wonder did it really matter to the man in the
street whether the British stayed or got out!'.

22. *The Hope And The Sadness:* (Siobhán Lankford . . .
    Tower Books, 1980).
This fine book, with the intriguing title, is more than just 'personal

recollections of troubled times in Ireland', as the dust-cover says. It is the actual autobiography of Siobhán Creedon (Mrs. Séamus Lankford), of Mourne Abbey, Mallow, one of the most highly regarded of intelligence agents, frequently mentioned in Republican dispatches, regarded by both Liam Lynch and Florrie Donoghue as one of the greatest, whose work for the Cause was so often a matter of life or death for the freedom fighters of the time. It is a complex but beautifully written book, a reprise of Irish country life from the final decade of the nineteenth century right through to the Civil War and after, involving thereby some of the most historical events of the early twentieth century, correlating them as through the evolving moods and forms of classical musical composition. The Civil War is dealt with briefly but poignantly as 'The War Of Brothers', the dénouement as 'Farewell To The Brave', while the *Coda* is a pastiche of her late husband, Séamus Lankford, who did trojan work for the poor of Cork city and county during the Black and Tan times, and whose final report on the revitalization of the work-house system was to become a model for Union control by Poor Law commissioners both in Dublin and London, and was the cause of a bizarre murder attempt on his life by a high-ranking member of the new Free State Government in 1923.   * * *   Anybody can write a book, Mick Sullivan said, and in middle life he proceeded to prove his point, and reasonably well at that, in the context of the Tan War. On the other hand Mrs. Lankford, at the age of eighty-six, produced a superb book in the alternating context of the Land War, the Boer War, the Great War, the Tan War and the Civil War, while retaining the freshness and exhilaration of the web of 'the spider on a dewy morning'. Moreover, her best material is still the record of childhood, youth and adolescence, unique even today when such records are a dime a dozen and in the context of a much later and far less historic and productive age, while her effort exemplifies the essential distinction between true Literature and the modern mere stringing together of commonplace words and superficial notions. 'Siobhán Lankford's story is an absorbing piece of personal reminiscence, a valuable insight into a lost rural culture and a fresh perspective at local level of the revolutionary period, 1916-23'. Just so! 'The author's account of her childhood on a small farm in North Cork at the turn of the century re-creates in vivid, authentic

and anecdotal detail a way of life long since vanished'. Indeed!
'She weaves the tapestry of small-town Ireland, at a slightly later
date, as she recounts her experiences in Mallow'. Right! 'And finally, she adds informative and valuable detail to our knowledge of
events after 1916, when she participated in the National Struggle
as an intelligence officer'. Oh, yes! Now . . . can anybody write
a book? I wonder!

23. *Raids And Rallies:* (Ernie O'Malley . . . Anvil Books,
1982).
'Most of all I would have liked to talk about the rank and file where
I found solace . . .'. In *On Another Man's Wound* O'Malley talks
mainly about himself. In the quiet of a prison cell, during the Civil
War, while under sentence of death, he had thought of others with
kindness and appreciation. This book, based on smuggled out
notes at the time, is a massive afterthought and does full credit
to the man's writing as well as fighting ability. There is extensive
coverage of three attacks in which he participated, where previously
(On Another Man's Wound) there had been only brief reporting
in the course of a hectic existence. They were: Hollyford Barracks,
Co. Tipperary, May, 1920; Drangan Barracks, Co. Kilkenny, June,
1920; and Rearcross Barracks, Co. Tipperary, July, 1920. Other
battles, in which he did not actually participate, are dealt with in
detail, accompanied by intense map reconstruction, exactly as I
have seen with regard to the American Civil War. O'Malley had
the advantage of knowing these places, and the men involved, during his period of nation-wide rambling as an instructor-organizer
on behalf of G.H.Q. in Dublin, with sole responsibility to Michael
Collins. There was Rineen, Co. Clare, in September, 1920;
Scramogue, Co. Roscommon, in March, 1921; Tourmakeady, Kil-
meena and Carrowkennedy, Co. Mayo, and Modreeny, Co. Tipperary, May-June, 1921. Finally, there is a ten-page insert entitled
'The British Enforce Martial Law' (Chapter Five), a survey of the
Winter of 1920-1921, which mainly displays his die-hard
republicanism and anticlericalism, the intellectual rather than the
historian thinking and speaking for the mainly uneducated men
of the resistance, but fascinating in its clarity and bias just the
same.   * * *   Was O'Malley mad?, you might well ask.

388   APPENDIX A

Matt Flood describes him in action, lying prone on top of a barricade instead of behind it with the men, pumping away with a
Winchester repeater (something I find difficult to visualize considering the peculiar bolt-action of said gun, but he did carry a
Winchester about and tells about using it, while the only thing he
learned to dread, in his warring around Erin, was the country
'bacon and cabbage'!). You might also ask — Was Collins mad?,
or Cathal Brugha?, or even De Valera? It was a mad time. With
Pearse a terrible madness was born. I don't know if anyone has
ever won two Victoria Crosses — Ernie could have had ten!

O'Malley returned to Ireland from New York in 1935, having
separated from his wife, a rich American lady and a sculptress and
definitely of 'The Four Hundred' of New York high society. He
spent the next twenty-two years until his death working on his
memoirs, not always well received by old comrades in his many
note-taking visits, as to Dan 'Sandow' O'Donovan at Ballybeg
quarries near Buttevant (cf. *The Dark Secret*). He deposited his
three children with the *Fear Mór* (Séamus Ó hEocha), president
of Rinn Irish College in Co. Waterford, with instructions to guard
them well. His wife arrived and took them to tea in neighbouring
Dungarvan, hired a taxi to Dublin and had them on a plane for
New York before they were even missed. O'Malley was furious and
quite abusive but, as Mícheál Ó Domhnaill (author of the history
of Rinn College) reasonably told me: 'We weren't their legal guardians!'. He liked Ó Domhnaill and frequently had a drink with
him in the local pub, but on one occasion at least curtly dismissed
an old comrade who wished to have a word with him. But then
he had taken more bullets for his beliefs than anyone else, except
maybe Cathal Brugha, and was on borrowed time since his recovery
from paralysis and certain death while under sentence of death
in Mountjoy prison hospital at the end of the Civil War. Like Collins, Dev and Cathal Brugha, there are some men who should remain forever untouched by adverse criticism and disdain. (*Note:*
I have never seen a picture of Ernie O'Malley in any publication,
only one of his head which his wife sculpted in better times, but
even that looks as if she had done so for the purpose of severing
it with a sword!). On her return to New York Mrs. O'Malley sent
a large cheque to the *Fear Mór* for his Irish college, but he politely returned it. Incidentally, the *Fear Mór* (the 'Big Man'), famous

in his own right, was the only Irishman I have known of who could literally look down on Eamon de Valera. General Michael Collins would have liked that but not Commandant-General Ernest O'Malley!

24. The Man With The Long Hair: (Maud Mitchell . . .
    Glenwood Publications, 1993).

And here is where *Synoptics* and *Antithetics* become one and the same thing — in the shadow of a gunman. This is the book that should have been written but never was, the negative that was never developed, the shadow without the substance, the gunman without the gun. It is the 'Woman's Story'. The man, her husband, refused to write it. She was, and her family had to be, content with a meagre diary, which is impressionistic to the extent that both historically and socially it needs a 'Key' as *Finnegans Wake* needs a 'Key'. She was Margaret Maud Mitchell (*née* Mulvihill) of Coosan, Athlone, and was arguably more beautiful even than the other Maud who stole the heart of Yeats — Maud Gonne Mac-Bride. Her man was Herbert James (alias 'Seán') Mitchell from 'the heart of the Midlands'. She was 'young, talented, she lived, married, raised a family, sparked off a revolution. She suffered the vicissitudes of war, tragedy and death. Yet through it all she maintained an almost mystical innocence, hope and courage'. Her book is one side of a coin that when tossed in the air comes down on one side or the other. With both sides fully complementing each other it would have been of great value, probably unique in the history of the times. For he was a Protestant convert to Catholicism, a die-hard Republican, a wool merchant from Athlone who came to live in Cork City to pursue his republican wool-gathering right through the Tan and Civil Wars, through the in-decisive and disturbed Twenties, until Dev came into power final-ly in 1932. The enigmatic title of the book refers to an ageing Fenian of her childhood, a cattle drover, who wore his hair in a long plait, a quiet man who in his time had been imprisoned and excom-municated after the uprising of 1867. His name was Keegan, and he represented for her the life-long spirit of Irish freedom. The protagonist in the story is a Black and Tan sergeant, with the rather incredible name of 'Charlie Chance', who terrorized the western side of Cork City from Washington Street to the outskirts.

Maud Mitchell's posthumous book is both fascinating and tantalizing. One needs to be well versed in the 'Troubles' period to follow the half of it. One regrets the lack of capable editing, the lack of clarification, the aribitrary omissions which could have helped our knowledge of the time. There are errors which could have been avoided. But there are innumerable touches that tease out the picture in a way that a fighting man's words could never have done . . . 'Two of his (i.e. her elder brother, a teacher in Athlone) most famous pupils became Count John McCormack and Bishop Curley' . . . 'Fr. Brophy, who was Parish Priest of Portarlington (1907), had organised a meeting and parade through the town in support of Bishop Mannix who, at the time, was opposing the teaching of Irish in Maynooth'. (*Note:* The present writer finds this strange, as a branch of the Gaelic League was established in Maynooth in 1898 and continued active down to my own time) . . . 'Why not organise men Scouts?' (Maud Mulvihill suggested this at a rally of 'Fianna Éireann' boys in Athlone in 1912, Liam Mellowes duly took note, and as a result the Irish Volunteers were instituted in 1913 and Pearse wrote — 'Is it a dream? Or do I hear the sound of marching men?'). . . . 'He was on a train that was ambushed by Dan Breen at Knocklong' (and as a direct result of the famous incident her husband got away safely with a bag of thirteen guns), and 'A British soldier in uniform was shouting, "Up the Republic!"' . . . 'The interment (of Terence MacSwiney, 31 October, 1920) was over. The field opposite St. Finbarr's (cemetery) was full of Tans and there was a piano in a Crossley tender which they played' . . . 'When in bed I could hear the Tans spitting and moving in their noiseless footwear' . . . 'When the raid was over and the Tans had mounted the Crossley they spat out on the people' . . . 'The place became so bright (i.e. the burning of Cork City) that I could see the remains of the swallows' nests in the high buildings across the yard. I prayed the Rosary all night'. Wasn't it always so!

APPENDIX B.

Curmoil to Cruce:
A Chronology

1916

April 24: INSURRECTION. Easter Monday morning. The Irish Republic Proclamation read from the steps of the General Post Office, Sackville (later O'Connell) Street, Dublin, by Patrick Henry Pearse (Pádraic Mac Piarais), Commander-in-Chief of the Republican (Volunteer) Forces and President of the Provisional Government of Ireland. By noon the Volunteers had occupied various strong points around the city. The British authorities poured in reinforcements and the fight was on. It was to continue for five days. (*Note:* At 1 p.m. on Monday a squadron of Lancers from Marlborough Barracks galloped from the Rotunda end of O'Connell Street as far as Nelson's Pillar. They were fired on from the G.P.O. and several were killed. They retired in disorder. Technically it was a 'charge', the last ever to be laid on by the British Army, but historians claim that the last cavalry charge was, in fact, at Omdurman, in the Sudan, in 1898, in which Winston Churchill first came to fame).

April 29: SURRENDER. Saturday afternoon. At 3.30 p.m. Elizabeth O'Farrell carried a white flag towards the British lines and Pearse, having issued a surrender communiqué to all units, surrendered his sword to Brigadier General Lowe. The historic G.P.O. was a burnt-out shell.

May 3: The execution of the leaders began. By May 12 fifteen had been shot, including the seven signatories of the Proclamation, P. H. Pearse, James Connolly, Thomas Clarke, Seán MacDermott, Thomas MacDonagh, Eamonn Ceannt and Joseph Plunkett.

(*Note:* Today, 5 June, 1994, even as I write, it is announced that the European Commission on Human Rights declared that a British S.A.S. unit did not use unnecessary force in shooting out of hand three unarmed Irish people, one of them a woman, for a presumed I.R.A. mission against doubtfully held British territory, to wit, the Rock of Gibralter. In an age when political murder has reached enormous proportions, it would seen that British world-wide *charisma* is still capable of transcending even normal distributive justice!).

August 3:   Sir Roger Casement was hanged in Pentonville Prison, London, for indirect complicity in the Rising. Dublin-born son of Northern Ireland Protestants, he was an ex-member of the British Colonial Service and was executed under the obsolete Norman-French statute: 'High Treason without the Realm of England'. His memory is enshrined by Yeats in:

> *The Ghost of Roger Casement*
> *Is beating on the door.*

December 6:   Prime Minister H.H. Asquith was replaced by David Lloyd George, and just on Christmas the first of the two thousand or so Irish men and women deportees began to return home, having furthered their knowledge of rebellion in such 'universities' as Frongoch in Wales. (cf. *Frongoch, University of Revolution*, by Seán O'Mahony, 1987).

1917

January 22:   President Woodrow Wilson, speaking to the American Congress, reiterated the 'Monroe Doctrine' in modern terms of War and Peace, and the essential equality of rights among nations. Of necessity Lloyd George echoed the sentiments two weeks later: 'We are struggling in this war for the principle that the rights of nations, however small, are as sacred as the rights of the biggest empires'. One great man was a saint, the other a lecher. Small nations had to wait their turn. Ireland advanced alone.

February 3:   George Noble, Count Plunkett, father of Joseph Plunkett, won the North Roscommon by-election on behalf of 'Sinn Féin'. The die was cast. Dublin Castle responded by arresting twenty-six national and social leaders.

March 7: Lloyd George proposed partition as the only solution to the 'Irish Problem' . . . 'Ireland today', he said, 'is no more reconciled to British rule than she was in the days of Cromwell!'. (*Note:* It is a strange thing that Montgomery had a somewhat similar notion five years later. In a letter to Percival, he wrote: 'My own view is that to win a war of that sort you must be ruthless; Oliver Cromwell, or the Germans, would have settled it in a very short time!').

April 6: The United States declared war on Germany. The American Ambassador in London declared: 'There is only one obstacle left . . . Ireland!'.

April 19: Count Plunkett presided over a national convention in Dublin to determine future progress. It was characterized by the gulf between Arthur Griffith's reserved Sinn Féin position and the extreme republicanism of Rory O'Connor. They compromised with a responsible National Council, and the country proceeded with a first anniversary celebration of 'Easter Week'. The 'terrible beauty' (Yeats) was one year old and was already showing distinctive features.

May 9: In the South Longford by-election Joseph McGuinness, a prisoner in Lewes Gaol, was put forward by the National Council on behalf of Sinn Féin. McGuinness defeated the old Parliamentarian candidate by a narrow margin. Under De Valera's direction the prisoners still in Lewes Gaol began a system of civil, and sometimes violent, disobedience to authority.

June 10: A huge prisoners' protest meeting was held in Beresford Place, Dublin, and was addressed by Count Plunkett and Cathal Brugha. The police used batons and the onlookers used hurley-sticks. Police Inspector Mills was killed by a blow on the head, the first casualty since Easter, 1916.

June 16: The remainder of the prisoners were released, and, under the leadership of De Valera and the Countess Markievicz, received a tumultuous welcome in Dublin. Dr. Patrick McCartan was dispatched to America to remind President Wilson and Congress of their acknowledged commitments.

July 10:   De Valera had a 'sweeping victory' in the East Clare by-election on the platform of 'frank Republicanism'. A month later William T. Cosgrave, who had fought in 1916 and had been interned in Frongoch, was elected Sinn Féin Member of Parliament for Kilkenny City.

September 25:   Thomas Ashe, a Kerry schoolteacher, who had fought in the battle of Ashbourne during Easter week 1916, died in Mountjoy Gaol as a result of hunger-strike and forcible feeding. He and some others had been arrested for 'speeches calculated to cause disaffection'.

October 25:   Sinn Féin Convention (*Ard-Fheis*) held in the Mansion House, Dublin. A draft New Constitution was proposed and accepted unanimously. Eamon de Valera was elected its new President in place of Arthur Griffith. Dev called on all to be united under the flag of the Irish Republic.

November 19:   Third Convention of the Irish Volunteers Organization held in Croke Park, Dublin. De Valera was elected President of the Volunteers and was now in full command of both wings of the new movement. Lloyd George's proposed all-party Convention of Irishmen, to clarify the future government of Ireland, set up in the Spring, thus came to nothing.

December 5:   Lord Midleton, a leading southern loyalist, wrote that if he and his people in the South had realized the separatist intentions of the North's Unionists they would not have participated in Lloyd George's plan.

1918

January 14:   F.E. ('Galloper') Smith, later Lord Birkenhead, Attorney General, was reported in the *Boston Post* to have said that Lloyd George 'hired his Convention to keep talking' as an American smoke-screen.

January 15:   John Redmond, leader of the Irish Parliamentary Party in Westminster, retired from the Convention in despair, and died shortly.

February 23: Sir Bryan Mahon, British Commander-in-Chief in Ireland, issued strict disciplinary orders with regard to the possession and carrying of arms throughout the country.

February 25: Ballaghaderreen (Co. Mayo) Sinn Féin Club issued instructions with regard to the re-allotment of large holdings for the purpose of tillage. Lloyd George called off his Convention of Irishmen.

February 27: Co. Clare was proclaimed a Military Area, the British Army took over control, and the suppression of newspapers began.

March 7: Editors of Irish newspapers were warned by the Press Censor to 'exercise the greatest care' with regard to what they published.

March 17: A minute after midnight, in Belfast, the R.U.C. charged the speaker's platform as De Valera was saying: 'The spirit that has outlived centuries of oppression will not be stamped out by the Cromwells of today'.

March 28: The British Cabinet decided to apply the Military Service Act (Conscription) to Ireland.

April 1: President Wilson warned Lloyd George not to impose Conscription on Ireland because, he said, it would cause trouble in the United States.

April 16: The new 'Man-Power Bill' (Conscription for Ireland) was passed in the British House of Commons. The fat was in the fire.

April 18: A convention of all parties met in the Mansion House, Dublin, and set up a 'National Cabinet'. Its manifesto was 'to resist Conscription by the most effective means at our disposal'. The Bishops' Manifesto from Maynooth changed that to 'every means that are consonant with the Law of God'. The British and their allies had to hold the trenches until the Yanks stepped in. One feels for their misery and chagrin, but the war was not of our doing. Still they had a right to feel grieved later.

April 25:   The Defence of the Realm Act ('D.O.R.A.') was extended to people of Irish birth. They were referred to as 'persons of hostile origin'.

May 17:   Seventy-three arrests of Volunteer and Sinn Féin leaders, including Eamon de Valera, Arthur Griffith and Countess Markievicz. They were deported to England. Field Marshal Lord French, the new Governor General, blamed them for involvement in an imaginary 'German Plot'.

June 15:   Two cities (Cork and Limerick) and thirteen counties (Cork, Limerick, Clare, Galway, Kerry, Leix, Offaly, Longford, Mayo, Sligo, Tyrone, Tipperary and Westmeath) were made 'proclaimed districts'.

June 18:   Certain districts were proclaimed as 'Special Military Areas'.

June 21:   Griffith, in gaol, won the East Cavan by-election for Sinn Féin.

July 4:   Sinn Féin, the Volunteers, Cumann na mBan and the Gaelic League were proscribed by law as 'dangerous associations', to be followed by the prohibition of all meetings, including sport and cultural. Nevertheless, the succeeding month saw literally thousands of such proscribed activities taking place. Who was it said: If you persist in going outside the gates too much, you may find yourself locked out? — or some such!

July 7:   The first ambush of armed police in Ireland took place at Béal a' Ghleanna (the 'Mouth of the Glen'), near Ballingeary, Co. Cork. The doubtful honour is still claimed for Soloheadbeg, Co. Tipperary, where Dan Breen and Seán Treacy shot dead two armed policemen in January, 1919. One way or the other, the 'cleansing of the Augean stables' had begun.

August 4:   Sunday. Despite the Prohibition, fifteen hundred hurling matches were played throughout the country. (*Note:* The soccer — British association football — deluge of the present time would have made a 'nice point' of Law in those faraway, simpleminded days!).

August 15:   Hundreds of illegal public gatherings, sporting and cultural, occurred at various venues. The Coolea *aeridheacht* (*aeríocht*) had been a test case on July 7, just two days after the military order of the day from the Commander-in-Chief, Major-General Sir Frederick Shaw.

October 10:   The LEINSTER, a mail-boat plying between Kingstown (Dunleary) and Holyhead, was sunk by a German submarine with the loss of almost five hundred people, including Máire Comerford's uncle, T. L. Esmonde. (*Note:* The present writer's aunt, Julia Twohig, a young nurse returning to England, had a dramatic escape. An hysterical group of seamen, getting off in a life raft, prevented her getting on board. A stranger, standing at the rail, covered them with a revolver, and they took her on. She turned to thank him but he just smiled and waved them on with his gun, saying to her enigmatically: 'We'll have a drink together in Macroom sometime!'. She never saw him again and had no idea who he was or how he knew her, or what became of him. Perhaps Michael Collins would have known).

November 4:   Donagh McNelis, a Sligo man living in Cork, shot and killed a police superintendent while resisting arrest. (cf. Chapter Six).

November 11:   The 'Great War' came to an end with a carefully timed Armistice. Fifty thousand native-born Irishmen had died in the war. Suitably orientated they could have driven the British Army out of Ireland forever . . . 'He fell in October, 1918, on a day that was so quiet and still on the whole front that the army report confined itself to the single sentence: "All Quiet On The Western Front" . . . His face had an expression of calm, as though almost glad the end had come'.

November 25:   Dissolution of the British Parliament with a view to a General Election, and the Nationalist Party at Westminster prepared to fight Sinn Féin to the last. John Dillon had succeeded Redmond as leader.

December 14:   Polling Day. Tentatively 'free' Ireland crossed the Rubicon for better or worse.

December 28:   Election results. One hundred and five candidates were returned for Ireland: seventy-three for Sinn Féin, twenty-six for the Union, and six for the Parliamentary Party who, uncharacteristically, died with a whimper. Everybody expected blood, and blood it was to be!

1919

January 21:   The first 'Dáil Éireann' (Irish Parliament) assembled in the Mansion House, Dublin. Only Republican deputies attended, thirty-six of whom were in gaol, including Eamon de Valera. Cathal Brugha (Charles Burgess) presided. A provisional Constitution of the Dáil was passed, a Declaration of Independence was read and a Democratic Programme, based on the Easter Week Proclamation, was unanimously adopted. By coincidence the Soloheadbeg ambush happened on that very day.

February 3:   De Valera escaped from Lincoln Prison with the help of Harry Boland and Michael Collins, but was compelled to remain in hiding.

February 8:   Seán T. O'Kelly, Republican Envoy to Paris, explained by letter to President Wilson his mission to get Ireland a seat on the Versailles Peace Conference, but was rebuffed. The new victors were apparently intent on being oppressors in their turn, and World War Two was already in the making.

March 6:   The British Government decided to release all Irish internees and convicted prisoners.

April 1:   De Valera appeared before the Dáil and was elected President of the Republic. His Ministers in Cabinet were Arthur Griffith, Count Plunkett, Cathal Brugha, Constance Markievicz, Eoin MacNeill, William Cosgrave and Michael Collins. Richard Mulcahy became Army Chief-of-Staff.

April 11:   At a discussion on the League of Nations, De Valera raised the controversial question of the essential relationship between the Dáil and the Volunteers. Raids for arms and other hostile activities were causing deaths on both sides of the Law. The problem went through to the Civil War.

April 18:   The National Executive of the Irish Labour Party and the Trades Union Congress in Dublin approved the strike of Limerick workers due to restriction of their movements by the British military.

May 3:   An American-Irish delegation arrived to investigate conditions in the country. Snubbed by Woodrow Wilson, but accomodated by Lloyd George, they sent an adverse report to the Peace Conference in Paris.

May 13:   Seán Hogan, arrested for the Solohead ambush, was rescued from the R.I.C. at Knocklong railway station by Dan Breen, Seán Treacy and Séamus Robinson.

May 17:   Ireland wrote once again to Republican Prime Minister of France, Georges Clemenceau, but 'the Tiger' proved unresponsive. His love for England and hatred of Germany coloured his presidency of the Peace Conference.

May 26:   The official statement of 'Ireland's Case For Independence' was sent by the Irish presumptive Government to the Peace Conference.

June 6:   The United States Senate reiterated the resolution of Congress, of March 4, that Ireland should have representation at the Conference.

June 11:   President Wilson finally admitted that there was nothing he could do. His hands obviously were tied by forces beyond his control. 'It is', he said sheepishly, 'the great metaphysical tragedy of today!'.

June 17:   Arthur Griffith, Acting President, announced to the Dáil that the President had gone 'on a mission abroad'. He had landed in America and made a triumphal tour of the United States. At home the Dáil set up National Arbitration Courts and floated a National Loan. Michael Collins, as Director of Intelligence, came to prominence with his deadly game of counter-espionage. Needs must, he said, when the devil drives!

June 24:   An hierarchical directive from Maynooth stated that the recurring acts of Republican violence stemmed from one cause only — 'the rule of the sword, utterly unsuited to a civilized nation', meaning Britain.

June 25:   On a more pedestrian note, the Churchtown hunter, 'Loch Lomond', won the Grand National at Aintree. Mrs. Crofts, of Churchtown House, the usually parsimonious owner of the horse, placed four tierces of porter on the village street, one from each of the pubs, for the celebration. A convoy of British soldiers from Buttevant arrived to investigate the huge confluence of excited fans, dispersed the crowd and demolished the porter.

July 21:   On a characteristically dramatic but despairing note Lloyd George complained of the difficulty of ever getting Irishmen to agree among themselves. Frankly it had a grain of truth. Dev was finding the same difficulty in the United States with the 'Friends of Irish Freedom'.

August 19:   Arthur Griffith reported to the Dáil on progress with the setting up of parish and district courts, urgent now because of increase in a new form of land agitation. British administration began to disintegrate, while attacks on R.I.C. barracks became commonplace throughout.

August 20:   Cathal Brugha proposed that every member of the Volunteers 'must swear allegiance (both) to the Irish Republic and to the Dáil'. It was an unpopular proposal with the Army Executive and the I.R.B., especially Michael Collins. It was carried and the Army became subject to the Dáil.

August 23:   The American Commission on Irish Independence opened headquarters despite De Valera's difficulties with the Bond Drive ('Dáil Éireann External Loan'), and disunity among the Friends of Irish Freedom.

September 7:   Serious hostilities, and the germ of guerrilla warfare, came with the attack by Liam Lynch, Commandant of the Second Cork Brigade, on a church parade of soldiers in Fermoy, with a view to capturing arms.

September 10:   The British Government, labouring the obvious as always, suppressed Dáil Éireann, declaring it to be 'a dangerous association'.

September 21:   A Commission of Inquiry into the country's industrial resources held its inaugural meeting. With secretary

Darrell Figgis it consisted of people from many walks of life. It was not interfered with.

October 16: Despite the official suppression of Dáil Éireann, its *Ard-Fheis* (Convention) met, but in secret session.

November 10: British soldiers looted and burned Patrick Street, Cork City.

November 11: First issue of the *Irish Republican Bulletin*, a counter-propaganda and publicity sheet. Enormously successful, even abroad (all other newspapers had now been suppressed), it was written mostly by Frank Gallagher and Erskine Childers and continued until the Spring of 1922.

November 16: Vice-Comdt. Moss Donegan and Captain Ralph Keyes raided the naval sloop, *M.L.171*, in Bantry Bay and removed some weapons and ammunition.

December 13: 'The prospect of dying for Ireland haunts the dreams of thousands of youths today'. (Special Correspondent in *The Times*).

December 18: Winston Churchill, Secretary of State for War, reported to the House of Commons that 'the number of troops at present employed in Ireland is 43,000, and their monthly cost . . . is £860,000'. According to Tom Barry twelve thousand six hundred of them occupied County Cork and were opposed by three hundred and ten riflemen, and Barry might have added — if he had thought of it — that 'never in the field of human conflict was so much owed by so many to so few!'.

December 19: Field-Marshal Lord French, Lord Lieutenant and Governor of Ireland, was ambushed at Ashtown, Co. Dublin. He escaped injury but a young Volunteer, named Martin Savage, was killed in the attack.

December 22: In the House of Commons the Prime Minister introduced his 'Better Government of Ireland Bill' proposing partition, with separate parliaments North and South to satisfy the aspirations of all the people.

1920

January 15:   Polling day for triennial Local Government elections to Urban and Municipal Councils. The vote was overwhelmingly for Sinn Féin in towns and cities North and South. This was the real Ireland, but for our ever spiteful neighbours; not Utopia, indeed, but a consistency of social life for the good of all concerned. It was not to be. Terror loomed.

January 20:   The town of Thurles was shot up and bombed by police and military. Newly elected councilmen were arrested and deported.

February 15:   The Irish bishops, in their Lenten Pastorals, protested against the new Reign of Terror, reminiscent of the worst excesses of the French Revolution. The British Government, said Dr. Robert Browne, bishop of Cloyne, were out to 'exasperate the people and drive them to acts of desperation'.

March 1:   In the search for Republican funds bank managers were ordered to appear before a commission in Dublin Castle to account for transactions.

March 20:   Tomás MacCurtain, Lord Mayor of Cork, was murdered by masked R.I.C. in his home and in the presence of his wife and family. He was replaced by his deputy, Terence MacSwiney. The jury returned a verdict of 'wilful murder' against the R.I.C. and the British Government . . . 'Important information on the killing of Cork Lord Mayor, Tomás MacCurtain, is still being hidden by the British Government 72 years later'. (*Cork Examiner*, quoting the London based *Independent* on Sunday, 24 May, 1992).

March 25:   The 'Black and Tans' began to arrive in Ireland just as General Sir Nevil Macready was seconded from the London Metropolitan Police to be Commander-in-Chief in this country. Macready, whom historians like to refer to, rather smugly, as 'son of the famous actor', maintained quite a friendly association with Sir Henry Wilson, Chief of the Imperial General Staff ('C.I.G.S.', in Army parlance), a 'rogue' Irishman from Co. Cavan, especially with regard to their mutual objective of 'stamping out rebellion with a strong hand'. Wilson paid with his life while Macready was cheered to the echo, as they say, on the arrival of the Truce. Still, we beat them both to their knees. For what it is worth, Macready was an only child who never knew his father, corresponding to Michael Collins in the old father: young mother situation.

April 4: Many Revenue Offices and vacated police barracks throughout the country were burned down by the Republican Army.

April 5: The great hunger-strike began among Republican prisoners in Mountjoy Gaol. It was to last ten days and end with release of prisoners.

April 12: A General Strike was called by the Irish Labour Party and Trades Union Congress in support of the protesting prisoners in Mountjoy.

April 14: 'General Macready relinquished his appointment as (Police) Commissioner in order to take command of the British troops in Ireland'. (From *London's Armed Police*). Six weeks before this he had reported: 'The present course of instruction is, in my opinion, quite useless, and should be increased to ensure that the men who are trusted with pistols are able to make effective use of them without danger to the general public . . . It would be inadvisable to make pistol practice too public, as we might lay ourselves open to the accusation of training the police to shoot down their fellow creatures in case of labour troubles'. Considerate?

April 21: Sinn Féin prisoners in Wormwood Scrubs, London, went on hunger-strike for political status. They were released. Evidently there would be a dramatic sequel to this form of legal blackmail (though it had due and recognized form within the ancient 'Brehon Laws'). It happened in the Fall of the year . . . 'For young Irish men and women it was a life of hardship, strain and danger, and of glorious activity, faith and hope. They never doubted they would set Ireland free'. (Macardle — and she herself was one of them!). One wonders why Britain, in the face of world opinion and even shock, should proceed with such terror methods. One thing, though — despite much opportunity and rampant drunkenness among the soldiery, there never was any rape, a usual concomitant of oppression in other climes.

May 13:   'The UNION is broken. England can never govern Ireland again' . . . (From the London-based *Globe* Newspaper). But England still persists!

May 17:   In Ballinrobe, Co. Mayo, the first public Law Court was held under the Arbitration Courts decree of June, 1919. Established legal representatives attended. Growing land trouble became the main issue. It had been always so in the impoverished West regardless of the passing scene (cf. Fr. Jarlath Waldron's *The Maamtrasna Murders*).

June 5:   Saturday spectacular at 'The Mile Bush', Midleton, Co. Cork. Twelve Cameron Highlanders, newly arrived that day, were disarmed without bloodshed by Commandant Diarmuid Hurley (later shot by the Black and Tans) and eight local men. The angry Camerons later shot up the town, and the R.I.C., in their barracks, returned the fire by mistake.

June 12:   The results of the elections for County Councils, Rural District Councils and Boards of Guardians were made public. Once again a sweeping victory for Sinn Féin, north and south. The 'Hidden Ireland' was now a curious matter of a nation going its own way while imbued with a surrealist sense of aliens in our midst from outer space, and lethal to boot.

June 15:   District Inspector Lea Wilson was shot in Gorey, Co. Wexford, on the orders of Michael Collins. The job was done by four men in a motor car, two of them personal aides to Collins, namely Liam Tobin and Frank Thornton. When the news was relayed to Collins he ejaculated gleefully to another aide, Joe Sweeney: 'We got the bugger!'. Who was he? What made him so important? Despite his apparent relevance to the Irish cause, he has been misplaced by some historians, mis-spelled by others, including journalists, and ignored competely by many. Local historian in Gorey, Mr. Michael Fitzpatrick, told me that Lea Wilson was a broken man at the time of his death, expected hourly to be killed, and awaited the end by practising alcoholism in a local hotel, and walked alone to meet his death without even his regular bodyguard who had been sent on a mission elsewhere. He was shot at 9.45 on the morning of Tuesday, the fifteenth of June, 1920. When they found him he was lying on his left side on the sidewalk of Ballycannew Road, two hundred and fifty yards from the rented house in which he lived with his wife, a young beauty from Charleville, Co. Cork. Michael Geary, of Charleville, Adjutant to Commandant Paddy O'Brien, still going strong at ninety-four, knew Lea Wilson. 'He was slightly built', Mick said, 'of average height, somewhat abrupt in manner, noted for party gaiety, and loved a horse which he kept in the yard of the police barracks', and the old man hastened to add, 'but there was no trouble then — it was before the War!'. He was then D.I., First Class, having been promoted from elsewhere. He came from Galway to Charleville, where, in a short time, in January, 1914, he married Marie Ryan, daughter of a local solicitor. It was a 'mixed marriage', he being a Protestant. Then he went to war, as did many of the R.I.C. Percival Lea Wilson was a native of Kent, had come to Ireland to join the police force for some unaccountable reason, became a captain in the Royal Irish Regiment, stationed in Buttevant, and returned from the war in 1916, just in time for the Insurrection in Dublin, and apparently a changed man. His abuse of the surrendered men, at week's end, particularly Tom Clarke, has been widely publicized in recent times. His mistake was that he did so in the presence of the unknown Michael Collins. After his death his childless widow went to Scotland, qualified as a children's doctor, and came face to face with the now world famous *Caravaggio* (for which see any one of a countless number of publications in 1993). She bought it for a song in an auction in Edinburgh, and later, when she returned to practise in Dublin, presented it to the Jesuit Order. I particularly like the following: 'The sensitive pained face of Christ in Caravaggio's painting, the grubby hand on his shoulder and the shriek of horror from the fleeing disciple, whose cloak is securely in the clutches of the soldier, must have attracted the grieving woman trying hard not to forgive or forget'. All this, and much more, from Anne Cahill in the *Sunday Independent*, November 28, 1993, very sweet, very womanly, quite blasphemous and false.

June 19:   In Listowel, Co. Kerry, a complete unit of the R.I.C.

rebelled against General Tudor, Head of Police, and Colonel Smyth, Commissioner for Munster, and resigned in a body because of orders to shoot to kill.

June 22:   The British Attorney-General for Ireland complained in the House of Commons that the 'forty-five thousand executives' (Churchill's phrase) in Ireland had been instructed to proceed on a warlike footing.

June 23:   A patrol of seven British soldiers was disarmed under cover of the crush at the annual horse fair at Spencill Hill, Ennis, Co. Clare.

June 28:   Lloyd George in despair before the House. He said that the Irish were impossible. They had to have imposed on them a split-level 'Home Rule' for their own good. One sees his point of view. Elsewhere, Fermoy was sacked for a second time in a year because of the capture of Brigadier-General Lucas, and the Connaught Rangers mutinied at Jullundur, India.

June 29:   Arthur Griffith, Acting President, reported to the Dáil on the progress of the various departments of Government, with particular reference to the Internal Loan, which was over subscribed and would close soon. He also drew attention to De Valera's success in the States despite bitter opposition from Judge Cohalan of the 'Friends of Irish Freedom'.The judge was a cousin of Dr. Daniel Cohalan, bishop of Cork, known to his intimates from Maynooth days as 'Old Blocks', and who initiated the idea of excommunication for Republican freedom fighters who, in fact, paid his salary.

July 12:   Sir Henry Wilson suggested the elimination of a select list of leading Republicans rather than the less expeditious method of haphazard reprisals. Troops were needed in India which was following Ireland's lead towards self-determination. Republican prisoners were being tortured.

July 17:   Ambush at Geata Bawn in which Captain Airey was killed, resulting in a further sack of the town of Fermoy, and D.C. Gerald Smyth was shot dead in the County Club, South Mall, Cork, for his Listowel speech. He was shot in the Smoking Room, beside the fifth window down on adjoining Smith Street. He had belonged to the King's Own Scottish Borderers.

July 19:   The Belfast pogroms began. Incited by Sir Edward Carson (Dublin-born leader of the Ulster Unionists, and the man who legally crucified Oscar Wilde), Protestant mobs attacked and murdered Catholics and destroyed their homes and property in an effort to drive them from the province.

July 29:   Countess Markievicz, Minister for Labour, ordered all Sinn Féin clubs to give all necessary assistance to resigned members of the R.I.C. Resignations were now continuous, as also among magistrates and J.P.s. Those who stayed in the Force were clamouring to be disarmed for their own safety, which had already happened to the Dublin Metropolitan Police.

August 8:   Archbishop Daniel Mannix, of Melbourne, a native of Charleville, on his official *ad limina* visit to Rome was taken off the liner BALTIC, which had been intercepted by a British destroyer, and was landed at Penzance, Cornwall. He was sent on his way without being allowed to visit his native place. An outspoken upholder of the Irish cause, he had helped Eamon de Valera in the United States while on his way to Ireland.

August 9:   The 'Restoration of Order in Ireland Act' ('R.O.I.') became law and gave unlimited powers to the British military and police. DORA now was King (French pun!), and for the Irish it was death at a blink!

August 12:   Terence MacSwiney was arrested at Cork's City Hall and taken to Brixton Prison, in London. He went on hunger-strike immediately and was to die without food ten and a half weeks later. His self-immolation for the Right, in accordance with Brehon Law, did much harm to British prestige.

August 17:   The 'Slippery Rock' ambush, Ballyvourney, in which a large cycle patrol of British troops, under Lieutenant F. C. Sharman, came to grief. (*Note:* His name was 'Sharman', not 'Sherman' as in Pádraic O'Farrell's *Who's Who in the Irish War of Independence*, Mercier, 1980, in which, unfortunately, occur quite a few errors of a similar nature).

August 22:   District Inspector Swanzy was shot dead in Lisburn,

Co. Antrim. He had directed the murder of Tomás MacCurtain, Lord Mayor of Cork. Two other policemen were shot for the same atrocity, one in Tipperary and the other in Kildorrery, Co. Cork. They had been recognized at the scene, despite wearing masks, and were transferred immediately afterwards. Reprisals followed in the North, but serious ambushes proliferated elsewhere. The essential nature of the distinction is still with us to disturb the peace of the country — the Republican element fights British authority, while the Protestant 'Unionist' persuasion fights Catholics as such.

September 3:   Coroners' inquests were abolished and were replaced by secret military tribunals committed to cover up their own atrocities and report accordingly. As Juvenal, ancient Roman poet and satirist, might have remarked (if he were still around) — *Quis custodiet ipsos custodes*? (Who shall guard the guards themselves!). Juvenal was an early arrival in Britain. He had seen military service there in the first century. In Belfast an anti-Catholic pogrom, aided by the police, left thirty-one dead, some of them Protestants by mistaken identity. It still happens.

September 20:   The terrible sack of Balbriggan took place. A small town in south Co. Dublin, it got nation-wide and world-wide attention despite the fact that this type of localized offensiveness had become commonplace. The sack of Balbriggan has taken its place in History alongside the sack of Baltimore, Co. Cork, by Barbary pirates in the early seventeenth century.

September 28:   In a lightning swoop Mallow military barracks was invaded and cleared of arms and ammunition by a couple of platoons of the I.R.A. under Brigadier Liam Lynch, Commandant Paddy O'Brien and Captain Ernie O'Malley. As a result the complex Hotchkiss gun became a feature of Irish warfare.

October 9:   Lloyd George declared in his native Wales: 'We have murder by the throat!'. He was himself proud of being a Celt. It is curious to note further that some of the very worst atrocities in Ireland were committed by Scottish regiments. No wonder the native English, if there are such, always had the last laugh on us Celts! (*Note:* I said to my friend — 'Do you think Lloyd George is in Hell?'. She considered a moment. Then she said — 'I think so!'. I said — 'Thanks! I needed that!'. Irish History is hard on the system, as Tim Pat Coogan could tell you. That is why so many people tend to overlook it nowadays. They call themselves 'Revisionist', but that is really showing off, like saying one is an Agnostic, which is Greek and translates into Latin as 'Ignoramus').

October 17: Commandant Michael Fitzgerald, of Fermoy, died on hunger-strike at Cork Gaol. He had been arrested with Terence MacSwiney.

October 25: Terence MacSwiney died on hunger-strike in Brixton Prison. The Dáil ordered a day of national mourning for his funeral in Cork on October 31. The world, it seemed, went into mourning, even ordinary English people along the funeral route in London. Permission was refused for his funeral cortège to pass through Dublin. That, at least, made sense.

October 31: District Inspector Phil Kelleher, a native of Macroom, was shot dead at the bar of the Greville Arms hotel in Granard, Co. Longford. Philip St. John Howlett (his mother was a Howlett from Millstreet) Kelleher was a young man of twenty-three, of fine physique, international class rugby player, quite popular, son of well known Dr. Pat Kelleher, had been 'unguarded' in his remarks about the I.R.A. in the wrong place, General Seán MacEoin's home ground. His death lie was the home of Kitty Kiernan, already the *paramour* of Michael Collins. His execution had been ordered by G.H.Q. in Dublin, but was contingent on the death of Terence MacSwiney or the execution of Kevin Barry. Kelleher lived in the Greville Arms, and went across to the police station at nine every night. The plan was to shoot him on the way. On the night in question he was still inside at 9.30 p.m. The two men assigned to the job went inside to look for him. They saw him at the bar having a drink and from a stance in the doorway shot him in the back. Sam McCoy, of the American Committee for Relief in Ireland, investigated the matter and added: 'Kelleher put down his half-finished glass limply, and fell dead before the spilled liquid could drip to the floor'. A piano tinkled upstairs in the drawing room, a regular party venue. According to Mr. Pádraig Greene, ex-N.T. and the age of the century, who knew Kelleher, it was said that Collins himself was upstairs, which is hardly likely as he would have been in Dublin waiting for Kevin Barry's execution and hoping for a last-minute chance of reprieve or rescue. Collins was a frequent visitor. He was also a frequent visitor to the North Offaly village of Horseleap where his brother Johnny's sister-in-law, a Mrs. O'Mahony, lived. Phil Kelleher's youngest sister, Mrs. Patricia Glancy, widow of a police superintendent of Tralee, who died only last year, informed the present writer that the Last Rites were given to her brother on the spot. Fr. Hugh Lynch the senior curate in Granard, later told the family that Phil had been to Mass and Holy Communion that morning. He had been a captain in the British Army during the Great War and had earned himself the M.C. His life and death are a maelstrom of the confused activities of the time. A few days later the Greville Arms was burned down as a reprisal, but received full compensation and was rebuilt in 1922. Michael Collins called Seán MacEoin to Dublin to answer for the bungled assassination. 'A District Inspector named Daniel O'Keeffe, who was a native of Dungarvan, had issued car permits to some I.R.A. officers . . . O'Keeffe was dismissed from the force as a result, and was replaced by a young ex-army officer who was given orders to take action against the I.R.A. and clean up the area. The new District Inspector was fatally wounded in the Greville Arms Hotel in Longford (error for Granard) on the night of October 31st, 1920. The I.R.A., under Vice-Commandant Seán Murphy, occupied positions in the street the same night and an engagement took place during which the police were forced to retreat to their barrack'. (Seán MacEoin in *With The I.R.A. In The Fight For Freedom*, editor Pat Lynch for *The Kerryman*). The following is an interesting account of the matter penned for this publication by Pádraig Greene, ex-N.T., of Ballinalee:

The Shooting of Inspector Kelleher.

This is the story as told to me (i.e. Mr. Greene) by Thomas Kiernan (76) of Barrack St., Granard, on June 29th, 1994. (*Note:* Tommie Kiernan was a distant relation, and his wife a close relation, of Kitty Kiernan. The Kiernans first arrived in Granard in 1620).

The week before Kevin Barry was due to be hanged the Granard company of the I.R.A. held a meeting in Cosgrave's barn outside the town. The group was told that there was a job to be done, and they would pull straws to see who would do it. They were not, at this point, told what the job was. The straws were pulled and Bernard Kilbride and Tom Heany had the short straws. They were then told that the job was to shoot Inspector Kelleher as a reprisal for the death sentence on Kevin Barry. At this point Joe Lynch spoke up and said he would take Heany's place as Heany was not reliable. This was agreed.

On Sunday night — it was Hallow Eve — the two picked men were given loaded revolvers. They proceeded to Ledwith's pub and drank milk. (*Note:* They probably went into the kitchen, for Kilbride was courting a Ledwith girl whom he afterwards married. Kilbride was a Civil Engineer on the staff of Longford Co. Council). Now follows the story which Tom Kiernan heard many times from Barney Macken, now long dead. (*Note:* Barney Macken was grandfather of Eddie Macken, world-renowned show jumper — Author). Barney was in the bar of the Greville Arms hotel that night chatting to Inspector Kelleher, and complaining to Larry Kiernan that his sister Kitty, who was serving in the bar, had given him a bad 'half-one', hoping that Larry would give him a good one. Kitty went upstairs and the piano started playing. Kelleher was drinking sherry and was telling Barney about the fine cheap wine to be got in France. At this point two men came to the door and shot Kelleher in the back. He fell on the floor in a pool of blood. V. Rev. Canon Maguire, P.P., V.F., administered the last rites.

Police armed with carbines came on the street immediately. Two of them, Doherty and Healy, fired at the presbytery shouting: 'Come out, Lynch, you Fenian bastard!'. Fr. Hugh Lynch was the senior curate, and was supposed to be in sympathy with the Volunteers. *Críoch.*

(Mr. Greene added some additional notes to the above).

1. Tom Kiernan says that there was no Volunteer presence in the street that night.

2. Barney Macken's story of Kitty Kiernan serving in the bar, that night, and that her brother, Larry, was also there, cancels the yarn of music and song upstairs. If any of her boyfriends were there, i.e. Harry Boland or Michael Collins, she would not have been in the bar.

3. Tom Kiernan did not know the name of the captain of the Granard unit. It could have been Kilbride. He was on the run during The Trouble, in the Ballinalee area. Two young Protestants, Elliot and Chartres, were shot by the I.R.A., accused of telling the Auxiliaries of his whereabouts. He was never caught.

November 1:   Eighteen-year-old Kevin Barry, a medical student, was hanged in Dublin for having taken part in a street ambush in which a British soldier was killed. A ballad about the event was popularized in the Thirties by the famous black American bass singer, Paul Robeson, himself an activist for Civil Rights. The opening lines went:

> In Mountjoy Gaol, one Monday morning,
> High upon a gallows tree,
> Kevin Barry gave his young life
> For the cause of Liberty . . .

(*Note:* Kevin Barry's college girl-friend, 'Baby May' Corbett, came from my neighbouring village, Liscarroll, and died a Carmelite nun only a few years ago. Her twin brother, Fr. James Corbett, still lives on, hale and hearty, at the age of ninety-four. He taught me the Classics in college).

November 2 - 9:   The astonishing defence of Ballinalee, and points east and west, by Seán MacEoin, Vice-Commandant of the Longford Brigade and Commander of the Flying Column, exemplifies the extraordinary natural generalship of the noted 'Blacksmith of Ballinalee'. Unfortunately his true grasp of battle under correct war conditions was to be used to greater advantage against former comrades in the Civil War to follow.

November 2:   'On the morning of (Private) James Daly's execution the effect of the death-dealing volley was a mental trauma. Men had the pallor of shock on their faces. Their gait became listless and food lost its appeal. On that morning the spirit of the Connaught Rangers died'. (T. P. Kilfeather: *The Connaught Rangers*).

November 11:   The British Labour Party proposed in the House of Commons the withdrawal of the Army of Occupation from Ireland and the setting up of an Irish Constituent Assembly to run the country. Deaf adder response.

November 16:   The American Association for the Recognition of the Irish Republic was inaugurated in New York.

November 21:   'Bloody Sunday'. On the orders of Michael Collins fourteen spies and British secret agents in Dublin were shot by his private squad, a committed and floating number of active service men, known rather humorously — and irreverently — as 'The Twelve Apostles'. The last of them to die was Commandant Vinnie Byrne, only last year. (*Note:* When interviewed for television, some years before, Vinnie was asked what he expected from his country for his special services. His answer: 'Plenty of porther!'). His particular victim on that day was Lieutenant Peter Ashley Aimes, from Titusville, Pennsylvania, U.S.A., a soldier of fortune. As a consequence the Tans attacked a crowd assembled for a football game in Croke Park, Dublin. Several of the onlookers were killed or injured. That night two notable Dublin Volunteer officers, Dick McKee and Peadar Clancy, were murdered in Dublin Castle while in custody. (*Note:* The best account of Bloody Sunday appears in Joseph Brady's *The Big Sycamore*).

November 26:   Arthur Griffith was arrested and imprisoned and Michael Collins became Acting President of Dáil Éireann and the Republic. (*Note:* As a matter of social, if not historic, interest, the portraits of these two great Irishmen were painted by Sir John Lavery, R.H.A., during the Treaty negotiations in London. The charcoal originals for same were discovered in Vaughan's Hotel, 29 Parnell [originally Rutland] Square, Dublin, in 1932, with the great artist's signature and stamp attached. Any writing on Collins has to introduce Vaughan's Hotel, one of his chief ports of call during bad times. T. Ryle Dwyer refers to it as 'Joint No. 1' and Margery Forester as 'Joint No. 3' in Collins 'lingo'. No one seems ever to have asked — Who was Vaughan? Well, Vaughan was Mrs. Maguire in the time of Collins. She sold out to a Miss Sheila O'Brien, from Kerry, in 1932. Sheila had gone to Dublin to work in hotels, did quite well, and bought Vaughan's. During preliminary restoration work, she found the charcoal sketches from which the portraits were done. They are now in the possession of her niece, Mrs. Breda Coghlan, Kilfinane, Co. Limerick, and are probably priceless).

November 28:   Seventeen Auxiliaries were said to have been killed in ambush at Kilmichael, south of Macroom. But . . . 'Barry states that the only survivor never recovered consciousness, but he can be seen sitting up in bed with a bandage round his head in the *Freeman's Journal*, 17 January, 1921'. (Robert Kee: *Ourselves*

Alone). He was, indeed, the elusive Cadet Ford whose body position is shown in the officer's sketch map of the following morning (cf. Chapter Ten). He had been shot through the head and was thought to be dead at the Castle. An orderly noticed some movement and he was rushed to Cork and to England. A few years ago an English newspaper published an account of the Kilmichael ambush, saying that all had been killed. They received a letter from a Mr. Ford who stated — 'I was there and I'm alive!'. He had been in a wheelchair all those years. So, in a way Barry was right and wrong. Seventeen were killed, including Guthrie, but the error historians have been making is that there were eighteen rather than seventeen i.e. nine in each of two Crossley tenders. How's that? The Auxies had begun to arrive in Ireland in September and were placed, with other police bodies, under Major-General Hugh Tudor, at headquarters at Inistioge, Co. Kilkenny. The attacks by Flying Columns of the I.R.A. now became a vital instrument and so until the end. The same night as Kilmichael a major campaign of destruction of property was started in Liverpool, but did not persevere.

December 1:   Archbishop Clune, of Perth, Australia, visited Lloyd George in London with a view to negotiating a truce. He then visited Collins and Griffith in Dublin and returned, full of hope, to London to find the P.M. in a different mood. The idea had come to him that the I.R.A. were now on the run and would not last much longer. Hope springs eternal!

December 10:   Lord French placed four southern counties under Martial Law.

December 11:   The centre of Cork City was destroyed by the Black and Tans.

December 15:   Canon Magnier, parish priest of Dunmanway, was shot dead on the roadside by a man named Harte, an Auxiliary from Macroom Castle.

December 18:   Brigadier General Higginson decreed the carrying of hostages in military transport for the future.

December 23:   The Government of Ireland Act (i.e. Partition of Ulster — the Unionists opted for only six counties out of nine) became Law with effectiveness from May, 1921. Ireland prepared for all-out War.

December 25:   Christmas Day. President Eamon de Valera arrived back secretly from his campaigning in the United States of America.

December 27:   New regulations concerning the death penalty came into force.

1921

January 3:   The remaining four southern counties were placed under Martial Law. Major-General Strickland, Military Governor of Cork, decreed that no citizen could be regarded as neutral or be allowed to default by not reporting any information which they might be presumed to have with regard to Volunteer activity. So, whoever would be responsible for the application of the principle of the Hague Conventions (1899, 1907) would become squiggle-eyed at the prospect of reprisals under state-of-war and non-state-of-war simultaneously. Killing to extinction, or 'ethnic cleansing' in the cynical metaphor of our time, was now the last resort for victory.

January 28:   Dripsey ambush. The failed ambush, near Coachford, Co. Cork, and its tragic aftermath, the execution of several republican prisoners, deserves record mainly for the associated *cause célèbre*, the execution of the only woman shot by the I.R.A. during the War of Independence. She was Mrs. Georgina Lindsay, of Leemount House, Coachford. Her crime was that she revealed to the British authorities the fact that an ambush had been laid in waiting for them in a certain position near her dwelling. Two books have been written on the subject, Seán O'Callaghan's *Execution* (1974) and Tim Sheehan's *Lady Hostage* (1990). A cursory glance through both volumes would seem to indicate that the central theme was a mere catalyst for a spot-check history of the whole period, salted with a good deal of rather incredibly long conversation pieces from those far distant times. I feel that the particular lurid incident in question could have been best left to obscurity and fireside chatting.

February 9:   General Crozier began suspension of Auxiliaries for proven atrocities, but was himself forced to resign as head of the Auxiliary Corps.

February 11:   Attack on troop train at Drishanebeg, near Millstreet, proved an unqualified success for the I.R.A., but a copy-cat attack at Upton, near Bandon, four days later, proved a tragic disaster. (*Note:* During the 'Battle of the Bogside', Derry, 1969, I was surprised to hear the ballad, 'The men who died at Upton for Sinn Féin', being used as a rallying song).

February 12:   Constable Patrick Walsh shot in Churchtown village. He had been to Buttevant for medicine for the sergeant's child, who was ill. Aged nineteen, he was a native of Connemara. His mother was transported from Buttevant station by Denny 'Booney' O'Sullivan, the local jarvey. She was a 'native speaker' and had not a word of English.

February 15:   De Valera had letters delivered to all British M.P.s, holding them severally responsible for the war being waged against the Irish people by their men-at-arms.

February 20:   Massacre at Clonmult, East Cork, of unarmed Volunteers who surrendered after resisting surprise attack on their hide-out. (See composite photograph of those killed).

February 25:   Large-scale Ballyvourney (Coolnacahera) ambush in which

> Major Grant and thirty Tans
> Their bodies were laid low.

(*Note:* Macardle is in error in saying 'a Republican hostage was killed').

March 5:   Colonel-Commandant H. R. Cumming killed at Clonbanin, near Kanturk.

March 6:   In Limerick Lord Mayor George Clancy and ex-Lord Mayor Michael O'Callaghan were murdered in their homes in the presence of their wives. British General Hubert Gough, K.C.B., said that in Ireland now, instead of law and order, there was 'a bloody and brutal anarchy'. In England itself a new Republican campaign of arson begins in various towns.

March 19:   Massive battle at Crossbarry, Co. Cork, in which the Third Cork Brigade Flying Column, under Tom Barry, defeated several hundred British soldiers.

March 21:   Formation of First and Second Southern Divisions under Liam Lynch and Ernie O'Malley respectively. The I.R.A. were now respectable.

March 23:   Ambush at Scramogue, Co. Roscommon, in which the I.R.A. capture a valuable Hotchkiss from the Lancers and cause further cleavage between the regular army and the Auxies who failed to assist them.

March 30:   President de Valera told the international news media: 'From the Irish Volunteers we formed the Irish Republican Army to be the military arm of the Government . . . It is the national army of defence . . . If they use their tanks and steel-armoured cars, why should we hesitate to use the cover of stone walls and ditches?'. Good point!

April 3:   Catholic and Protestant prelates in England equally protested to Lloyd George with regard to the known activities of the Auxiliaries in Ireland. On the previous day Michael Collins had told a representative of an American newspaper that it was only a matter of time before all Crown Forces would be cleared out of the country. But time stands still!

April 15:   The tall, burly, handsome, fearless and murderous Major McKinnon, the scourge of Tralee, was shot dead by Connie Healy, of Boherbee, ex-soldier and noted marksman, at 3 p.m. at the third green of Tralee golf course. The story still persists locally that the major was wearing not only a bullet-proof vest but some kind of helmet with a visor. He raised the visor to wipe his brow and Connie got him dead centre at a hundred and fifty yards:

> The rebels of 'The Kingdom' swore
> Our dear old land to free,
> And shot the tyrant Major on
> The Golf Links at Tralee.

April 16:   'Woodfield', the home of Michael Collins' family, was burned down by the Essex regiment. The place was restored, and presented to the State, as a memorial site, on the centenary of Collins' birth, 14 October 1990. On that occasion the present writer had the honour of presenting exact replicas of the Collins car rug, which he had with him at Béalnabláth, to President Patrick Hillery, Mr. Alan Dukes, Mr. Peter Sutherland, and historian, Mr. Tim Pat Coogan, whose definitive life of Collins had just been published. The rugs were made in Foxford, Co. Mayo.

April 19:   Lloyd George replied to the English bishops: 'So long as Sinn Féin demands a Republic the present evils must go on!'. Were it not for the fact that they are still going on in 1994, one might wonder if his obstinacy were some kind of complex due to the fact that Wales (and also Scotland) had failed pathetically with regard to self-determination in the past. The Basques in Spain and the Bretons of France, who are likewise Celt in some measure, are still dreaming of ancient tribal identity.

April 21:   Lord Derby, in an unofficial visit to De Valera, hinted that the British Government might be prepared to offer something better than Partition, after due consideration. Dev offered to meet the Prime Minister.

April 25:   Lieutenant Francis Fielding, from Buttevant Military Barracks, was executed in Freemount, for alleged spying. He, and some others from Buttevant, had taken to making long walks through the countryside. They called to shops on the way, and two of them, who came round by Charleville, and mailed cards at each Post Office on the way, marking their route, were shot at Dromina and buried in a nearby bog.

April 26:   First Southern Division inaugurated at Kippagh, Millstreet.

April 27:   Pope Benedict the Fifteenth sent £5,000 to the 'White Cross', an American based society for aiding the impoverished and hungry in Ireland. He sent his Apostolic Blessing to the suffering people, at the same time elevating some Irish saints to the Liturgical Calendar. The British Ambassador to the Vatican had tried in vain to get the Pontiff to issue a general condemnation of Sinn Féin.

April 28:   Major Compton Smith and District Inspector Potter were executed in return for the multiple hangings of Republican prisoners.

May 3:   The optimistic 'Better Government of Ireland Act' came into force.

May 4:   Captain Manus Moynihan carried out a successful ambush at the Bog Road, Rathmore, using as decoy the body of executed 'Old Tom' Sullivan, the singing beggarman, who allegedly sang, both really and metaphorically, for the Black and Tans of Rathmore and Killarney. He was seventy-five.

May 5:   Sir James Craig had a secret meeting with De Valera in Dublin. After a long conversation they discovered that they had both been tricked.

May 13:   Nomination day for a new General Election, North and South. It was to become known as the 'Partition Election'.

May 14:   Attempted rescue of Seán MacEoin from Mountjoy Gaol, by Emmet Dalton and members of the Dublin 'Squad', using a captured armoured car.

May 16:   Seán Moylan taken prisoner at Kiskeam. He was sentenced to death but his sentence was commuted to fifteen years through the tremendous efforts of young Mallow solicitor, Barry Sullivan, and Albert Wood, K.C. On the day of his capture the last official execution in the South took place at Cork Gaol — Dan O'Brien, brother of Commandant Paddy O'Brien, Liscarroll, and first cousin of Tom Barry. (*Note:* An excellent account of Barry Sullivan's work may be seen in Mrs. Lankford's *The Hope And The Sadness*). A huge dossier of the trial of Seán Moylan is available.

May 19:   Election Day in the South. All Republican candidates returned. James Talbot, Lord Fitzalan, appointed first Catholic Viceroy to Ireland.

May 24:   Election Day in the North. Sinn Féin campaigners assaulted and injured. Unionists got majority of seats. Partition a *fait accompli* (Winston Churchill).

May 25:   The Dublin Customs House, with tax files, Local Government Board records and much else of administrative importance, was destroyed by the I.R.A. 'The destruction was an unavoidable military necessity' (The *Irish Bulletin*). British administration was now in abeyance. Significantly enough the first 'tommy-gun' to arrive from America was demonstrated in Dublin by Tom Barry himself in the presence of Collins and Mulcahy. It has ever since been associated with American gangsters and Irish Republicans.

June 1:   Cycle patrol of Tans, including a District Inspector and two sergeants, annihilated at Castlemaine, Co. Kerry.

June 8:   New anti-Catholic pogrom began in North and lasted a week.

June 14:   Commandant Seán MacEoin charged with murder, by court martial, and condemned to death. De Valera wrote to Art O'Brien, President of the Irish Self-Determination League in England, indicating that he was aware of peace moves through General Jan Smuts of South Africa.

June 16:   The House of Lords heard an appeal against execution of Irish prisoners, and found that both Courts Martial and executions were 'illegal'. The same day saw a major engagement at Rathcoole, between Banteer and Millstreet. Newly arrived Auxiliaries at Mount Leader were actually blown up by a series of mines laid in the surface of the dusty roadway.

June 21:   The House of Lords debated the unhappy and desperate state of affairs in Ireland, and De Valera visited the Irish hierarchy meeting in Maynooth College, as a result of which they declared the Partition Act to be 'a sham settlement', leaving the Irish free to decide their future.

June 22:   King George the Fifth was in Belfast to formally open the new northern parliament. He said he looked forward to the day when the Irish people would be at peace and, whether with one parliament or two, would work together for their mutual benefit. (*Note:* Seventy-three years later we are still being subjected to old moronic catch-phrases like 'Unionist sell-out' and 'Tory backlash'). On the same day President de Valera was arrested in Dublin but was unaccountably released within twenty-four hours.

June 25:   President Eamon de Valera received a letter from Prime Minister David Lloyd George proposing a Peace Conference.

June 27:   Constable Thomas Shanley, R.I.C., was shot in the village of Kildorrery, North Cork, for his implication in the murder of Lord Mayor Tomás MacCurtain. Two known Ballindangan men waited in the porch of the church, during Mass on Sunday, and followed him home. He was shot in front of the Castle Gate Bar owned at the time by a Mr. Collins (to whose son, P.J. Collins I am indebted for this account). The sergeant, who was with him, was wounded but escaped. Young Jerry O'Donovan (still living) was hit in the back of the knee as he ran home from Mass. Shanley was a bachelor and was said to have got on well with the people, even helping to save the hay on occasion. He was said to have helped financially with his brother's education to the priesthood. Years later his brother and another priest came and knelt to pray on the spot where he fell. Still, he had been identified, to the satisfaction of the Brigade Council, as having been present at the killing of MacCurtain. In a struggle with him Mrs. MacCurtain pulled a button off his tunic and kept it in her hand. At the assizes in Cork, on the following day, he was seen without the button. Another policeman named Cody was shot in south Tipperary and Swanzy was shot in Lisburn. It was said that Michael Collins had ordered the shootings. The best information is that it was a Brigade decision . . .

> 'Inspector Swanzy and his associates put Lord Mayor MacCurtain away, so I got Swanzy and all his associates wiped out, one by one, in all parts of Ireland to which they had been secretly dispersed', Collins explained afterwards. 'I found out that these fellows we put on the spot were going to put a lot of us on the spot, so I got in first'.
>
> (T. Ryle Dwyer: *Michael Collins: The Man Who Won the War*).

In my view this is extremely doubtful. Anyway, Collins never talked like that. Nobody talks like that!

June 28:   Dev replied to Lloyd George that he had gone into consultation with representatives North and South. It was the day on which the 'Southern Parliament' was due to meet. It failed to do so.

July 4:   American Independence Day. Leaders of Protestant and

Unionist sectors, north and south, met Dev by invitation at the Mansion House, Dublin, all except Sir James Craig of Ulster. They discussed terms for a reply to Lloyd George. Dev insisted on an agreed Truce before Conference.

July 8:   Dev sent a message to Lloyd George saying that he was ready to meet him in London on July 14. The P.M. said — 'Come on and bring your friends!', or some such. General Macready visited the Mansion House to discuss terms of a Truce. It was set for Noon, July 11, 1921.

July 11:   TRUCE. At 11.45 a.m. Commandant Paddy O'Brien, Fourth Cork Brigade, began to dismantle a massive ambush at Templeglantine, Co. Limerick. A huge convoy of British troops passed at a quarter past twelve, and went on their way, while Republican soldiers were still on the roadway. In fifteen minutes, a morsel of time, a great vacuum had spread between the fighting men of our two countries. It was only a symptomatic yawn.

*   *   *

L'envoi:

Blows the wind today, and the sun and the rain are flying,
Blows the wind on the moors today and now,
Where above the graves of the martyrs the whaups are crying,
My heart remembers how!

(R. L. Stevenson).

Finis.